D1570792

Affording Defense

Affording Defense

Jacques S. Gansler

The MIT Press
Cambridge, Massachusetts
London, England

This book was set in Times Roman by DEKR Corporation and printed and bound by Halliday Lithograph in the United States of America.

Library of Congress Cataloging-in-Publication Data

Gansler, Jacques S.
  Affording defense / Jacques S. Gansler.

    p.   cm.
  Bibliography: p.
  Includes index.
  ISBN 0-262-07117-7
  1. United States—Armed Forces—Appropriations and expenditures.
2. United States—Armed Forces—Procurement. 3. United States—
Armed Forces—Management. I. Title.
UA23.G36   1989
355′.335073—dc19   88-32653
                                                                        CIP

To Leah for her extensive help with the book, her encouragement, and, especially, her love.

And to Christine, Douglas, and Gillian; may their generation and their children's live in a world of peace.

Contents

Acknowledgments

Thanks are due to the many friends and acquaintances in the so-called military-industrial complex from whom I have learned so very much. Special thanks go to Professor J. Ronald Fox and Brigadier General Lee Denson (U.S.A.F., ret.), who reviewed portions of the manuscript; to Mary Schaefer, who greatly assisted with the notes; and to Mary Shover, who helped with the final manuscript. I am particularly indebted to Paula Meredith and Laura Rusiecki for their extensive extra efforts in preparing the numerous early drafts. Also, I want to thank Dr. Arthur Gelb and Harry Silverman for their long-term support, understanding, and friendship. Finally, I want to acknowledge the truly outstanding job of my manuscript editor at The MIT Press.

Affording Defense

1 The Dilemma

We live in an age of great insecurity. At the lower levels of conflict, the sources of this insecurity range from terrorism and insurgency through national radicalism and religious fanaticism; at the upper levels, they include the poised armies of NATO and the Warsaw Pact in Europe and the nuclear weapons ready to be launched in an instant from silos, submarines, and bombers around the world. For the overwhelming majority of the world's people, peace is clearly the desired objective. Yet violence, war, and even nuclear holocaust are constantly present threats. In this environment, most people feel that a nation must use both diplomacy and military strength to ensure the security of its population.

Military strength is expensive. At the end of the 1970s, the United States was spending approximately $150 billion a year on its defense establishment. The public felt that this did not provide a "strong America," and gave Ronald Reagan a mandate for significant increases in the defense budget. Within six years the defense budget had almost doubled and an extra trillion dollars had been spent on increasing America's military power. Yet by the end of the Reagan presidency the defense establishment was decrying the "defense budget crisis." It was noted that just to pay for programs already approved, the budget would have to rise to over $400 billion a year[1] (an additional 30 percent increase). And because of continuing Soviet advances in weaponry, many new programs that were already on the drawing boards—such as a strategic-defense system, a whole new generation of "stealth" aircraft, and a new generation of armored vehicles—could not be put off. Furthermore, agreements to control nuclear arms brought demands for increased quantities of expensive conventional weapons to counter the Soviet Union's overwhelming numerical superiority in that category. Finally, there was a recognized need for the United States to develop and produce the specialized equipment that are required for regional conflicts around the world—the most likely future military scenarios, and the ones for which the nation was least prepared.

These equipment needs were mirrored by requirements for increased personnel dollars to pay for higher quality and numbers of people in the all-volunteer forces, and for the modernization of facilities and equipment to house, train, transport, and support them on a worldwide basis.

The traditional solution to all these problems has been to increase the defense budget. However, there are other demands on the nation's resources—among them the huge national deficit; the valid calls for a refurbishing of the nation's highways, bridges, and harbors; the trade imbalance and the consequent need to revitalize the nation's industrial competitiveness; and the nation's growing needs for health care, education, Social Security, child care, and other social measures. Thus, an increasing number of people are questioning the affordability of America's security posture.

Extreme solutions have been offered from both ends of the political spectrum, from isolationism to unilateral disarmament. However, the overwhelming majority of Americans simply express extreme frustration over their country's inability to grapple with the dilemma. There are no easy answers, and the extremes are unacceptable. Yet, as the data will clearly show, something must be done to address the rising costs of national security and the continuing sense of insecurity.

This book is an attempt to offer steps that will lead, over time, to a solution to this dilemma. In places, the presentation may appear overcritical; however, the underlying hypothesis is that the system can and should be improved.

The Challenge

The current national-security posture of the United States is based on a structure of forces, equipment, alliances, and military strategy that, in large part, dates from the 1950s, when the United States enjoyed strategic nuclear preponderance, superiority in tactical forces, world economic and political dominance, and a strong and growing domestic economy. These conditions have disappeared. The old paradigm has broken down, but there is no new one. There is a large gap between America's *actual* national-security capability and the *posture* statements and assertions of American policymakers. For example, in 1979 President Carter threatened to send the "rapid deployment forces" to the Persian Gulf—but no such forces existed, and if they had existed they could not have been rapidly transported. In Europe, NATO cannot sustain a conventional war for more than a few days, and it would be outgunned at the nuclear level; thus, U.S. policy in regard to Central Europe lacks credibility. In fact, our European allies often resist initiatives to strengthen their conventional forces, and the various national forces are not well integrated; yet the viability of our defense posture rests on joint NATO operations. At the strategic level, we are pouring billions into new systems, but their incremental value to the nation's security is continually questioned. For example, we spent $20 billion for the fixed-site MX missile, which was to be installed in our Minuteman silos; but we had previously acknowledged that those silos were vulnerable to Soviet attack. The list goes on and on.

The incongruity between our posture statements and the reality of our capability has become widely recognized, here and in the Soviet Union. Yet it has not been accepted by most of those in the executive and legislative branches of the U.S. government who develop and approve defense programs and budgets. Worse, this strategy breakdown is perceived as being matched by a lack of resource control. Even with the increased defense budgets, we get less defense equipment each year, because of the high and growing cost of each new system. Therefore, without very significant changes in the balance of deployed forces or in the stated national-security objectives, the gap between posture assertions and actual capabilities will widen. Just continuing to spend hundreds of billions of dollars on defense each year will not reverse the perceived decline in the nation's security.

As a result of the significant growth of the defense budget during the 1980s, national security has, in the public eye, become an increasingly important and controversial issue. On the domestic level, there is the growing "guns vs. butter" debate. On the international level, there is rising concern about nuclear war, about America's declining economic and military strength, and about the absence of a coherent and affordable U.S. national-security posture (across the spectrum—from nuclear deterrence to a wide range of potential, conventional-warfare crises, especially in the Third World). Historically, during peacetime, U.S. national-security policy has been largely left to the "experts"; however, the above-mentioned trends have caused this to change dramatically. Today national security is near the top of the list of issues about which the public is concerned, and the involvement of citizens (with diverse perspectives and interests) is growing rapidly. Part of this is due to the sheer size of the defense budget (the Reagan buildup being the largest peacetime increase in America's history); however, part of it is due to the growing concern over whether, as the budget grew, we got a proportionate increase in our nation's security. In fact, since the mid-1980s there has been an increasing perception of mismanagement, waste, and

even fraud and abuse in defense budgeting and procurement. Headlines
have pointed to the Defense Department's paying $5,000 for an ordinary
hammer and $2,000 for a plastic cap for the leg of a stool. At the other
end of the equipment spectrum, many opinion leaders have questioned
the wisdom of spending billions on building extra strategic missiles just
to offer them as bargaining chips in our arms-control negotiations with
the Soviets. The questions of where defense dollars go, and why they
go there, do not lend themselves to simple answers.

   Problems of defense management should be put into perspective. The
Department of Defense is bound to get lots of public scrutiny, and
bound to make some mistakes. It implements over 15 million contracts
each year[2] (52,000 contracts each day), and it spends around $300 billion
a year. Even if it were 99.99 percent perfect in its procurement actions,
it would still commit over 1,500 errors (or "abuses") each year.[3] The
overwhelming majority of these millions of contract actions involve
inexpensive items (in the jargon, "socks, shoes, and underwear") rather
than weapon systems. Indeed, in the case of big-dollar weapon systems,
all comparisons of defense management with other federal, state, and
private agencies (including those done by the General Accounting
Office[4] and those done by the House Committee on Government
Operations[5]) have shown that the Department of Defense is one of the
best-managed federal agencies. As figure 1.1 shows, the average cost
overrun on a weapon system has been around 40 percent. In comparison, many public construction projects (such as the Hart Senate Office
Building, the Rayburn House Office Building, and Dulles Airport) have
had overruns of around 75 percent, and the overrun on the New Orleans
Superdome was more than 200 percent. The overruns on projects more
comparable in technical difficulty to large weapon systems, such as the
Concorde and the Trans Alaskan Pipeline, have approached 600 percent. Thus, one can argue—as Secretary of Defense Caspar Weinberger
did during most of the Reagan years—that "The system ain't broke, so
why try to fix it?" However, the data clearly substantiate that there is
still ample room for improvement. For example, at the beginning of the
Reagan administration, the Department of Defense planned to buy
approximately 4,000 M1 tanks, for approximately $6 billion. Five years
later, the planned 4,000 tanks had in fact been bought, but at an actual
cost (with the effects of inflation removed) of $9 billion. Thus, over five
years the cost of the tanks had grown by 50 percent.[6] Clearly, such data

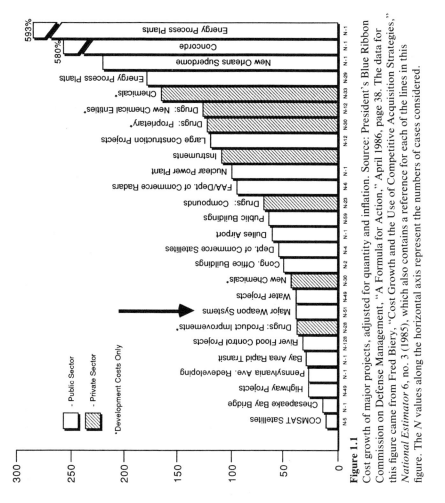

Figure 1.1
Cost growth of major projects, adjusted for quantity and inflation. Source: President's Blue Ribbon Commission on Defense Management, "A Formula for Action," April 1986, page 38. The data for this figure came from Fred Biery, "Cost Growth and the Use of Competitive Acquisition Strategies," *National Estimator* 6, no. 3 (1985), which also contains a reference for each of the lines in this figure. The N values along the horizontal axis represent the numbers of cases considered.

indicate the need for improvements; however, the favorable comparative data of figure 1.1—and numerous other examples, which will be presented below—show that it would be equally wrong to say "The system is so bad that it should simply be thrown out, and we should start over" (a frequent cry of "reformers"). There is a real danger that, if we are not extremely careful in the way changes to defense management are implemented, the result could be a system that is far worse than the original. This observation must be constantly kept in mind.

Broadly, the major problems are these:

- deficiencies in military strategy, weapon selection, and budgeting
- shortcomings in the process of acquiring weapons (i.e., weapons cost too much and take too long)
- growing problems in the defense industrial base, in terms of both the efficiency and the effectiveness of the development and the production of weapons
- growing personnel and facilities costs (e.g., due to excessive overseas deployments and the expanding military retirement fund).

Each of these problems will be examined in detail; first, however, some of the issues need to be highlighted.

Deficiencies in Strategy, Weapon Selection, and Budgeting
The basic issue here is whether or not the existing institutional structure provides for the most effective development of military strategy and force structure, and then for the selection and budgeting of the most cost-effective weapons. Although the various armed services would go to war together and would be expected to fight as an integrated system, each service compiles a separate budget. In addition, the requirements for the weapon systems to be bought by the various services are established separately. Thus, the decisions about which weapons to buy, and how many of them, are made by the independent services—almost as if they were going to fight separate wars. A commonly quoted example of the problem occurred when American forces were sent to Grenada. The Navy was controlling the operation from offshore, but the Army soldiers onshore could not communicate with their commander because each service had a different kind of radio. Another example is the annual debate over the allocation of billions of dollars of defense funds—for example, whether a 600-ship Navy, more tanks for the

Army, or more fighter planes for the Air Force should have the highest priority. Far too often, the selection and budgeting of weapon systems determines the military strategy, rather than vice versa. These questions of strategy and weapon selection are then further compounded by interservice rivalry for resources. Is it any wonder, then, that it is hard to develop a strong link between strategy and resources?

The matter is complicated further by the opportunities for revolutionary shifts in the composition of the military forces and in military strategy that are offered by technological advances. These shifts are capable of multiplying the relevant military capabilities enormously if the new technologies can be "absorbed" by the military institutions. However, it is often "culturally" difficult for the armed services to accept such technology-motivated shifts. For example, in some parts of the world, perhaps the Navy could carry out its mission of denying use of the surface of the seas to an enemy by using reconnaissance satellites and land-based missiles rather than ships; but such concepts are so foreign to traditional notions of naval operations that they receive little attention.[7] We continue to concentrate on building improved versions of traditional platforms (ships, planes, and tanks) at significantly increased costs. Thus, as the former Army Chief of Staff General Edward C. Meyer stated in 1984, "Either we are going to spend ourselves into extinction, or we have to come up with alternative strategies and new ways to allocate resources."[8]

Shortcomings in the Process of Acquiring Weapons
The United States has clearly kept its military equipment at the technological forefront, but the cost of this has been an increase of around 5–7 percent per year in the unit cost of each new generation of equipment (even after adjustment for inflation and for the higher unit prices associated with the reduced quantities typically purchased today).[9] An aircraft carrier now costs about $3.4 billion,[10] a B-1B bomber well over $200 million,[11] an F-15 fighter plane around $38 million,[12] and an M1 tank around $2.4 million.[13] Therefore, it is not surprising that, as costs have been rising, we have been buying fewer and fewer weapon systems. For example, in 1955 the Department of Defense spent approximately $7 billion (adjusted to 1982 dollars) to procure approximately 1,400 military aircraft. By 1982 it was spending $14 billion a year for approximately 200 aircraft.[14] As Norman Augustine has pointed out,[15]

a continuation of this trend would result in the building of one fighter plane per year in the year 2054. Even with outstanding performance by individual weapons, there is still a minimum quantity of weapon systems that is absolutely critical for the successful completion of a military mission. This becomes even more important as the Soviet Union steadily improves the quality of its weapons while maintaining relatively high equipment stocks and production rates.

The impact of the rising costs of weapon systems due to increasing performance has been compounded by the differences between initial estimates for programs and the programs' final price tags.[16] Recognizing the difficulty of buying enough weapons with the dollars available, the armed forces have historically been optimistic in estimating the likely cost of weapon systems—especially when first requesting funds for their development. The hope has been either that costs will turn out to be unexpectedly low or that more money will become available. More cynically, some suggest that unrealistically low cost estimates reflect a bureaucratic tactic intended to get a development program started and to leave the matter of how to pay for it to those who will be in office in later years.

Thus, although the United States has been buying extremely capable weapon systems, it has been buying them in smaller quantities each year. Additionally—and again because of the high costs associated with the development and the production of weapon systems—the United States is forced to stretch out the overall acquisition cycle dramatically. Part of this stretching is due to the increasing complexity of modern weapon systems; however, there are two other important causes: stretch-outs of the acquisition cycle resulting from an increasingly burdensome and indecisive managerial and budgeting process (in both the executive and the legislative branch) and stretch-outs resulting from program cost growths and program budget reductions. The overall effect is that, whereas it once took 5–7 years to acquire a weapon system, a new systems now can take 12–15 years to move from exploratory development to initial deployment in the field.[17] Then, even after development is complete, the high cost of each weapon system means that only a few production units can be purchased each year, so the fielding of any significant number is delayed still further. It becomes a vicious cycle—the equipment is very expensive because of its design; then, the small quantity that can be afforded results in a further reduction in the efficiency of production, and thus in still greater unit costs and still lower quantities. The lengthening acquisition cycle has a compound military effect. First, it results in a decline in America's technological advantage over the Soviets, since most of the systems deployed in the field are of older designs; second, the longer cycle itself raises costs and thus further reduces the quantities in the field.

Growing Problems in the Defense Industrial Base
With the long-term decline in rates of production, one would expect to see the industrial base "drying up." In fact, during the dramatic shrinkage in defense procurements in the post-Vietnam era,[18] the weapon-system prime contractors remained in business by building equipment at very low rates (one airplane per month, in some extreme cases), while many parts suppliers and subcontractors were allowed to go out of business and were later replaced (during the Reagan years) by foreign companies.[19] A series of reports issued in late 1980 indicated significant problems in the U.S. defense industrial base.[20] These studies identified areas of substantial inefficiency for normal operations in peacetime, as well as critical bottlenecks (e.g., in selected critical parts and production equipment) amounting to an almost total lack of industrial capability to respond rapidly to an emergency. For example, it was reported that it would take over three years for an existing aircraft production line to increase its output significantly.[21]

The national-security strategy was partially at fault for this declining industrial responsiveness. After World War II, the United States shifted to a strategy and a force posture that relied heavily on nuclear superiority to deter war. The ability to mass-produce huge quantities of weapons rapidly (as had been done during World War II) was no longer considered an element of national security. Beginning in the 1960s, however, as the Soviet Union began to acquire strategic nuclear parity, the threat of an American nuclear response to a conventional attack became less credible as a deterrent to war. Thus, the United States shifted to a strategy of "flexible response," according to which it would respond to conventional aggression with conventional weapons while maintaining nuclear weapons as a deterrent to nuclear attacks and for "first use" if conventional defenses failed. To keep the United States from being forced to employ the nuclear option, however, the conventional-warfare portion of this strategy has to count heavily on increased numbers of existing non-nuclear forces and on a greater U.S. industrial responsiveness capable of augmenting, in a crisis,[22] the still relatively small capability for tactical warfare. But improving industrial responsiveness also requires money, which compounds the squeeze on available acquisition funds; thus, for the last three decades, successive U.S. administrations have been reluctant to take significant steps in this area. The result is a national-security goal that is not matched by a corresponding military or industrial capability.

The problems of the U.S. defense industry reflected the broad problems of U.S. industry that were "discovered" during the early 1980s. American weapon systems paralleled American automobiles, electronics, and steel in terms of high cost and low quality. Short-term objectives were outweighing the long-term pursuit of higher quality and lower costs throughout the U.S. industrial economy. The results in the defense industry were, in many cases, even worse than the results in other sectors. The difference was that the defense industry had a customer who had to buy what it produced (at least at the level of weapon systems), whereas the other U.S. industries were losing out to foreign competition at a rapidly increasing rate. This leads to the idea that, while we go about improving the defense industry, it would be highly desirable to improve the competitive posture of American industry in general—if that is possible.

Rising Costs of Defense Personnel

In spite of the sophisticated weapons being added each year, the military forces of the United States are still extremely labor-intensive. Since the shift (in 1973) from a military draft to the "all-volunteer services," the costs of recruiting and retaining the skilled personnel needed to operate and maintain today's equipment have increased greatly. The shrinking population of 18–21-year-olds and the complexity of advanced weapon systems make this problem more acute.

Improving the quality and morale of military personnel was one of the most important steps taken by the Reagan administration. However, the price tag was significant. Personnel expenditures increased at an annual rate of over 3 percent (from 1981 to 1985), even with the effects of inflation and the costs of deferred benefits excluded.

In the future—with, at most, level defense budgets projected—increased wages and benefits will not be an affordable solution to the problem of recruiting and retaining sufficient numbers of qualified defense personnel. Costs will have to be reduced, and the choices will be difficult, both politically and strategically. The short-term options include closing obsolete military bases, reducing personnel (starting with support functions), using women in combat operations, significantly reducing the assignment "rotation rate" (which affects efficiency and the costs of training and moving), and restructuring military retirement pay (which grew from approximately $4 billion in 1972 to approximately $24 billion in 1989, and is the second most expensive federal entitlement program—after Medicaid—to be financed exclusively from general revenues).

These reductions still will not be sufficient to reverse the continuing cost increases. In the long run, one or both of two major changes will be required: a shift to far greater dependence on the use of ready reserve forces and/or a shift to a draft or some form of universal service.

There are both economic and social arguments for conscription; however, the likelihood of this change—at least without some major crisis to cause a shift in public perceptions—is relatively small. A continuation of the current trend toward more and more emphasis on the ready reserves is more likely. This means a dramatic restructuring of strategy and force structure, as well as changes in the training and equipping of the reserve forces and the provision of equipment for their rapid deployment—all steps that Congress and the Department of Defense have been reluctant to take.

Directions for Solutions

These four broad problems of defense management are of such complexity and magnitude that they do not lend themselves to quick or simple solutions. Unfortunately—partly out of frustration and partly in reaction to the clamor of the public and the press for "corrective action"—both Congress and the Department of Defense have pursued quick fixes, such as adding more auditors and detailed regulations.[23]

Instead, to reverse the significant and undesirable trends in the Department of Defense's management practices, four broad sets of changes are required.

The first priority is to improve *long-term* strategy and resource planning, and to improve the selection of weapon systems correspondingly. Once this has been accomplished, more stability in the programs and budgets must be achieved. (How can anyone manage efficiently if the programs, and the dollars for them, are always changing?)

Second, a shift must be made from the *regulation* of quality and costs in the procurement of weapons to the creation of natural *incentives* for higher quality and lower costs. (It is harder to get people to do things by directive than if they really want to do them.)

Third, there must be a greater emphasis on the importance of the health and responsiveness of the defense industrial base. Its role as a vital part of our national-security posture must be recognized.

Fourth, ways must be developed to improve efficiency and effectiveness in the personnel and facilities areas—which represent half of the defense budget.

These four broad areas of corrective action might be categorized as follows:

• reform of military strategy, weapons requirements, and the budgeting process
• reform of the weapons-acquisition process
• revitalization of the defense industry
• reform of the defense personnel system.

In order to develop an affordable and credible national-security posture, it is essential that the improvements suggested in all four of these areas be made. If implemented over a five-year period, they could result in annual savings, based on an overall defense budget of $300 billion, of around $50 billion[25] (about 17 percent).

In spite of the potential for savings in some areas, it will be impossible to develop a balanced and credible defense posture without increasing expenditures in certain other areas (for example, for special-purpose equipment that could be used in likely future regional conflicts, and for increased quantites of conventional-warfare equipment for Central Europe). The proposed improvements will allow a shifting of defense resources, so as to achieve a stronger overall posture for the same amount of money.

One reason for some degree of optimism that the needed changes can be achieved is that the problems and solutions described herein have not gone unnoticed. In fact, many initial steps have already been taken to address them.

For example, in early 1985 the findings of an independent, bipartisan,

18-month study on defense organization were released.[26] This report—
which emphasized the need for broad structural changes—was done by
a senior panel, including representatives from the Congress (including
the chairmen of the Senate and House Armed Services Committees)
and many former Defense Department officials and former military
leaders (including a former chairman of the Joint Chiefs of Staff and
some former service Chiefs of Staff). Additionally, the recommendations of this study were endorsed by six former Secretaries of Defense,
who, in their introduction to the report, stated that "there are serious
deficiencies in the organization and managerial procedures of the U.S.
defense establishment." This study was followed by the release of a
similarly detailed investigation by the Senate Armed Services Committee,[27] also recommending broad institutional changes and again supported by a bipartisan coalition (led by Senators Barry Goldwater and
Sam Nunn). At the same time, on the House side, Congressman Les
Aspin (chairman of the Armed Services Committee) initiated a set of
far-reaching hearings on defense procurement and management.

In February 1986, the President's Blue Ribbon Commission on Defense Management (chaired by industrialist and former Deputy Secretary of Defense David Packard) released its set of preliminary
recommendations on defense reorganization and procedural changes.
These recommendations centered on the need for a new system of
planning and budgeting, for significant reorganization of both the Office
of the Secretary of Defense and the Joint Chiefs of Staff, for major
changes in the acquisition process, and for changes in specific weapons-
management and weapons-buying practices. The Packard Commission's findings received wide support from the executive and legislative
branches. President Reagan immediately directed the Department of
Defense (both in writing and on a national radio program) to "implement
the Packard Commission's recommendations, even if they go against
the system." This was followed by Congress' passage of the Goldwater-
Nichols Bill,[28] which required a very similar set of broad structural
changes.

As the cynic will point out, such calls for broad changes in the way
the Department of Defense conducts its business are nothing new. In
1958, President Eisenhower attempted to develop a more unified military structure, but the institutional resistance of the various services
prevented many of the proposed changes from taking place. Similarly,

in the Kennedy administration, Defense Secretary Robert McNamara (with his famous "Planning, Programming, and Budgeting System") attempted to get control over the allocation of resources; again the system continued to resist long-range, integrated efforts and instead favored the shorter-term, more parochial view that can be expressed as "Let's get a program started this year, and we'll worry about next year when it comes." In the 1970s and the 1980s, Congress—attempting to control the overall allocation of dollars—moved to an annual budget process with four cycles: Budget Committees, Authorization Committees, Appropriation Committees, and the sequestration process introduced by the Gramm-Rudman legislation. Even most members of Congress will (unofficially) acknowledge that this system is overburdened and could use significant improvements.

Thus, although there is clear recognition of the problems and of the directions in which corrective actions should be pursued, and although some initial steps have been taken, there is almost universal agreement that the changes made so far are inadequate, and that without additional efforts the great resistance to such broad changes is likely to prevent their happening. However, there is clearly cause for hope: Historically, the United States has—when it has "set its mind to it"—been able to achieve significant changes. What is required is a recognition of the need for action.

2 Potential Conflicts

Can the United States afford the required level of national security? This question must be addressed in three very interrelated parts:

- How much do we need to spend for defense, on the basis of current security objectives, perceived threats, and the costs of equipment?
- How much can we afford to spend? That is, how does defense spending affect the economy?
- Can we reduce the cost of defense by changing the way we do things (e.g., by adopting different defense strategies, new and lower-cost technologies, and better methods of managing defense resources)?

The economic and management questions will be dealt with in considerable detail in subsequent chapters; first must come the issue of "military need."

Around 500 B.C. the military analyst Sun Tzu emphasized that armed strife is not a transitory aberration but a recurrent, conscious act, and that it is therefore susceptible to rational analysis.[1] More recently—in the nuclear era—the military historian Lendell Hart wrote, "If you want peace, understand war."[2] The message is clear. Thousands of years of history have shown that war is likely and that to avoid it we must work at preventing it.

Historically, as Barbara Tuchman has pointed out, "Americans have shown their dislike for organized war by a desperate attachment to three principles: unpreparedness until the eleventh hour; the quickest feasible strategy for victory regardless of political aims; and instant demobilization, no matter how inadvisable, the moment the hostilities are over."[3] But today we live in a world in which these principles must take a back seat. Since the Korean War, the United States has been forced to maintain a relatively high level of military readiness. With thousands of nuclear warheads aimed at our cities, millions of troops and tanks lined up along our allies' borders, great instability in critical portions of the Third World, and growing worldwide terrorism, we have had little choice but to arm. Yet historical practices still influence our military planning. For example, we have tended to rely on nuclear weapons rather than conventional forces for our military strategy, as a quick and less expensive solution.

Today, warfare threatens to bring not only defeat but extinction. Thus, we must use all of our power—military and (especially) political—to prevent the initiation of conflict or to constrain it to the lowest possible level, to prevent the use of even a single nuclear weapon (by a terrorist or by a superpower), and to terminate any conflict as rapidly as possible. Therefore, deterrence and crisis management are the themes of modern warfare. Military victory—"winning"—has lost much of its traditional meaning. In fact, whereas military action was once seen as an alternative to bargaining, it is now a part of the bargaining process.[4]

With intercontinental nuclear weapons, the traditional military objective of defeating an enemy has given way to preventing him from attacking in the first place. The word *deterrence* (from a French root meaning "to frighten from") appeared as early as 1820 in the Oxford English Dictionary,[5] but not until the 1950s (when Bernard Brody popularized it[6]) did it come to signify the essence of defense strategy. Even then, however, deterrence was seldom presented as more than an interim strategy with which to buy time until a more permanent and viable solution to the problems of security could be worked out.[7] Today, it is still the accepted posture of the nuclear powers of the world; but it is not a "comfortable" one for anyone—civilians or military.

This book focuses on the issue of an affordable defense, so the details of various potential military strategies and policies can be omitted. However, the critical relationship between which weapons are bought and which conflicts are likely cannot be passed over.

A massive nuclear surprise attack by a superpower on a superpower is unlikely. It is much more plausible that a U.S.-Soviet conflict would evolve out of a situation elsewhere—for example, a superpower intervention in the Persian Gulf, another Arab-Israeli war, a U.S. military intervention in Central America that comes to involve Cuba, a Soviet imperial policing in Eastern Europe that spills over into a NATO country, or a Sino-Soviet war.[8] None of these scenarios begins with a U.S.-Soviet confrontation, but all have the potential, unless controlled, to develop into that, with escalation to the use of nuclear weapons likely. Thus, the second of the major changes of the nuclear era comes into play: Where force is actually used, not merely threatened, it must be deliberately held down and controlled. All-out war is far too costly and risky; the resolution of conflict must take place first through threat and then through crisis management[9] (including the use of force—limited in size, extent, and duration).

It is essential that military strategists consider in great detail what they would do if deterrence were to fail, first if it were to fail at the conventional level and then if there were to be escalation to the nuclear level. Many will argue that such planning reduces the effectiveness of deterrence—i.e., that if there are no military choices except mutual annihilation then there will be no nuclear war. However, this argument fails to recognize the possibility that the Soviet Union has made plans and the United States hasn't. It is our fault, not theirs, if we have not made plans; and the purposes of these plans should be to limit escalation and then, through a variety of techniques, to de-escalate and terminate the conflict as quickly as possible. Military action may well be a part of this bargaining process, but it must again be emphasized that the objectives have changed. At the strategic level we are not trying to win, but to avoid defeat; in conventional warfare, we are trying to deter our opponents from going to higher levels (by having them perceive that the cost would outweigh any potential gain). Simultaneously, we are attempting to terminate the conflict as quickly as possible while still achieving our political objectives. Depending on the stakes, our ability to terminate a conflict—regardless of who started it—may well be more important than our ability to fight.

With today's weapons, it is hard to see any issue over which any nation would genuinely prefer to go to nuclear war rather than negotiate. However, it is not hard to see how nuclear war could come about from a crisis getting out of hand. Thomas Schelling notes: "There may be very few points at which such a war could be stopped. Thus, it would be important to identify them ahead of time."[10] In addition to this planning, the weapons themselves must be designed to *not* put a premium on haste in a crisis (in particular, they must not be designed so that they must be used before the adversary "goes nuclear").

Furthermore, neither side must feel that it is under pressure to initiate a nuclear exchange in a crisis. Here too, planning is essential if one is to take full advantage of the tools that are available for crisis management. Among the most valuable of these tools are the instruments used to gather intelligence, including satellites and ground-based systems. Not only must our intelligence-gathering systems be designed to operate *before* a potential crisis (so as to prevent it by decreasing the uncertainty); they must also be designed to operate *through* a crisis (even a limited nuclear battle), so as to be of help in controlling and terminating the crisis.[11] In addition, it is critically important that the opponents maintain a continuous dialogue during the crisis. Again planning is required to ensure this, and practice is highly desirable. The creation and improvement of the "hotline" between the White House and the Kremlin (which has alternate paths for the communication links, so that they can operate during conflicts) is an example of the sort of planning that is extremely desirable for such crisis management.

A crucial matter regarding a nation's security posture is that of who decides on military strategy and on the selection of weapons (political leaders? military officers?), and at what level in the hierarchy. A related question concerns the extent to which these decisions can be decentralized.

In the Soviet Union, decisions about military doctrine are made by two closely connected groups, one political and the other military-technical; the political leaders are dominant.[12] In the United States, there is a far greater split. We acknowledge that national security is primarily a political concept rather than a military one; and yet most of our military strategy is actually based on the weapon systems proposed by the military services to the Secretary of Defense, the President, and the Congress.

American institutions make it difficult to develop a coherent national-security policy, and any breakdown of policy consensus (such as exists today) exacerbates the difficulties created by a system of divided powers.[13] As Henry Kissinger states, "We have a weakness for considering problems as 'primarily' economic or 'primarily' military rather than as total situations in which political, economic and military considerations merge, which is the way the Soviet leadership regards policy."[14] Yet the issue is clearly one of national goals—linking foreign and domestic policies—and these are political decisions, which are the preserve of the civilian leaders. (Specifically, the Congress is responsible for structural issues and the executive branch for programmatic ones.[15])

National "intentions"—our own and those of our potential adversaries—should be driving our military strategy and thus our equipment selections. However, this has not often been the case. In Clausewitz's mind there was no question as to who should make the decisions about military strategy: "It is an irrational proceeding to consult professional soldiers on the plan of war, that they may give a purely military opinion upon what the cabinet ought to do—the leading outlines of a war are always determined by the cabinet—that is, by a political, not a military, organ."[16] Thus, the dilemma for the United States is that institutional memory and expertise on military matters rests with the military, while political appointees and elected officials, who come and go, are in the positions requiring stable and experienced judgment about military strategy. This problem must be recognized, and civilians versed in military strategy must be appointed to key national-security policy positions.

Another lesson we should learn from Clausewitz is that "war is a remarkable trinity, in which the directing policy of the government, the professional qualities of the Army, and the attitude of the population all play an equally significant part."[17] Thus, the social unity and political resolve (the "will") of the public to deploy and support forces—particularly in peacetime in the nuclear era—is crucial. To have a credible deterrent to the Soviets, the United States must be perceived by them as willing to initiate a retaliatory nuclear strike (or even a first strike, if that is required in order to defend Europe). Additionally, actions we take can significantly influence the Soviet perception. For example, some point out that the absence of a program to protect the population ("civil defense") is a sign that the United States is not serious about its nuclear deterrence.

Perhaps the dilemma of American national-security policy has its roots in Americans' love of simplicity and in their belief that problems are solvable (both of which were observed by Alexis de Tocqueville).[18] However, a valid, integrated military, economic, and political strategy in the current era will not be simple, nor will it fully "solve" the problems of the great powers or even those of the Third World. As Stanley Hoffman states, "What is needed is a vision of inevitable, but limitable, conflict; of unavoidable, but manageable, contradictions; of solutions leading to new problems; and of no exit from competition with Moscow, from torment and regional disputes and in world economic issues, from potentially anti-American revolutions. Excessively high expectations lead to too many domestic vendettas and sudden reversals of course."[19]

With this rather pessimistic warning, let us consider the three major categories of potential conflict for which we must be prepared and must select appropriate equipment: strategic nuclear warfare, conflicts with the Warsaw Pact (a category that would include a Soviet attack on Japan), and regional conflicts (including sustained warfare in the Third World and terrorism). Clearly, the first of these is the most dangerous to both America and the world—and the least likely to occur, if détente works. Regional conflicts will (if properly controlled) have the least impact on the United States, but are the most likely to occur. Equipment for one of these three categories will not necessarily be suitable for conflicts of lower intensity. This has been a major problem for the United States. Because our resources are limited, we have tended to first make sure that our strategic needs are covered (perhaps even to excess), and then to do our best to "match" the Soviet bloc in Central Europe—and this leaves few resources for dealing with regional conflicts. The hope has been that the equipment specifically intended for use in Central Europe could be also used in jungles, deserts, and mountains elsewhere. Unfortunately, since this has not been the case, the military conflicts that are most likely are the ones for which the United States is least prepared. The danger here, of course, is not that we would "lose" some Third World encounter, but that something of vital interest to us or to our allies (e.g., oil) would be involved and that this would force the United States to escalate the conflict in order to "win." To understand this dilemma it is necessary to look at each of the three broad categories of potential conflict in terms of current U.S. strategy, and then to turn to the question of how that strategy influences the choice of weapons.

Strategic Nuclear War

Many believe that the presence of nuclear weapons has kept the United States and the Soviet Union at peace since 1945,[20] while others argue that this could be accomplished with dramatically fewer weapons on both sides. Clearly, the concept of deterrence with nuclear weapons is that the weapons are really aimed at people's minds rather than at physical targets. The strategic credibility of the United States is based partially on a refusal to deny the "first use" of nuclear weapons as a basic strategy, and on the fact that we have already used atomic weapons; the Soviets' credibility is based on their extensive writings on nuclear war, on their history of suffering very large numbers of casualties (as at Stalingrad in World War II), and on their extensive efforts to protect their leaders and their military industry from nuclear attack. It is the fact that such threats are believable that makes the world so insecure, and as more and more weapons are added we face the essential conundrum of the nuclear arms race: "steadily increasing military power and steadily decreasing national security."[21] As Reinhold Niebuhr decreed, "atomic weapons are our immediate security, but our ultimate insecurity."[22] Two ways out of this dilemma have been proposed: systems to defend against ballistic missiles (the technical solution) and arms control (the political solution). Perhaps the real answer is a combination of the two. In any case, to see how these solutions might work we must look into the various plans for how nuclear weapons might be used.

Essentially, there are three alternative uses: all-out attacks against populations and industries (known as "countervalue"); all-out attacks against weapons ("counterforce"); and limited exchanges, in either a countervalue or a counterforce mode, in a "controlled" nuclear war.

The first of the three plans is best known under the acronym MAD (mutual assured destruction). The concept is essentially one of mutual hostages. The key to MAD is the ability to retaliate after a strike. James Schlesinger has rather clinically defined "assured destruction" as the ability to absorb a first strike and yet retaliate and destroy at least 70 percent of the industries that a nation would need to recover from a nuclear war.[23] The MAD concept leads each superpower to feel that its nuclear forces must combine "survivability" and very large numbers. A MAD variant, namely to "launch on warning" after signals are received from satellites or from over-the-horizon radars that the Soviets have launched an attack, has been largely rejected by the United States because of the danger of a false alarm. (Many false alarms have actually occurred.[24] Because of a specific instance of a false alarm early in his tenure as Secretary of Defense, Robert McNamara specifically rejected the concept of launch on warning,[25] even though it has obvious advantages in terms of reduced requirements on either survivability or numbers.)

Since the 1950s, when the Soviets developed the capability of striking U.S. cities, the concept of U.S. nuclear preemption (i.e., launching first in the crisis and killing many of their missiles) has had obvious appeal—particularly among the military. In the late 1970s and the early 1980s the United States shifted to the development of high-accuracy missile systems, like the MX, the Trident D-5, and the Pershing II, which had sufficient accuracy to attack even hardened military targets such as missile silos and military command centers. With this shift, the United

States moved from full dependence on MAD to a counterforce capability (essentially a "nuclear war fighting" posture). During the Carter administration, National Security Advisor Zbigniew Brzezinski convinced the president that it was possible to fight and win a nuclear war.[26] Naturally, such a belief justified the further development of counterforce weapons. Nice words were even developed for it, such as "preemptive defense." The rationale was that we had to be sure of the credibility of our deterrent and that, if deterrent failed, we could still "win."

As the Unites States' capabilities expanded, so did the targeting plan (known as the Strategic Integrated Operational Plan, or SIOP). President Eisenhower felt that perhaps our ability to hit 80 targets in the Soviet Union would represent a sufficient deterrent. (At one point, he exploded in exasperation as the Air Force continued to increase the numbers, stating, "Why don't we go completely crazy and plan on a force of 10,000?"[27]) By 1974 the number of targets in the Soviet Union marked for possible action in the event of war had risen to 25,000.[28] President Carter (in Presidential Decision Memo 59) raised the number of "potential" Soviet targets to 40,000.[29] Today, the United States has approximately 12,000 nuclear warheads in its long-range strategic arsenal[30]; thus, the military could conceivably justify still further increases in the numbers of warheads.

However, the real issue is that of military "need." An analysis of the options leads many to the conclusion that Stanley Hoffman reached: "Neither massive retaliation nor counterforce (if the enemy can maintain any significant retaliatory capability) makes any sense."[31] As Robert McNamara stated, "We clearly need nuclear weapons but 'the only purpose of them is to prevent their use.'"[32] Others will not go nearly that far; they raise the question "What if deterrence fails?" However, there clearly is a question of numbers. If several hundred nuclear weapons are adequate to destroy a modern society, why build thousands, especially if the global damage and loss of life resulting from their use would be so significant? Secretary of State John Foster Dulles and many others argued that if we could get far enough ahead of the Soviets, they'd quit. Another claim (heard frequently during the Reagan administration) was that we could get the Soviets to run their economy into the ground trying to keep up with us.[33] Others say that we should have a lot of warheads for the sake of international "prestige." Still another argument is that having large numbers of warheads has a very long "political shadow," especially in periods of crisis.[34]

The two real questions are these: How many warheads do we need, and do we need more than the USSR? With regard to the first, Retired Admiral Noel Gayler has stated that "a difference of a thousand weapons or so makes very little difference in terms of potential for destruction."[35] On the issue of nuclear superiority, Henry Kissinger has asked "What in the name of God is strategic superiority? What is the significance of it, politically, militarily, operationally, at these levels of numbers? What do you do with it?"[36]

The issue of how many warheads are needed comes down to what you are going to do with them. Clearly, you need some weapons—if the other person has some—in order to present a credible deterrent. However, this deterrent is credible only if your systems can survive his attack and allow you to retaliate. Your adversary must know that even attacking you by surprise would bring his destruction.[37]

The United States has long held that the way to ensure survivability is to have a "triad" of airborne, ground-based, and sea-based nuclear weapons, which would be extremely difficult for the Soviets to attack simultaneously. The "triad" concept has become so ingrained in our thinking that even when Secretary of Defense Casper Weinberger stated that "there isn't a ground-based system that is survivable,"[38] we still went ahead with an expenditure of over $20 billion for 100 MX missiles. There is nothing sacred about having *three* different approaches, or about having weapons based on *land,* in the *sea,* and in the *air;* rather, there is simply a need for one form or another of survivability[39]—and probably for multiple approaches to guard against technological surprises.

But even if we have a survivable force, it is only a necessary—not a sufficient—condition for strategy. As President Nixon stated, "The President of the United States shouldn't be left with only the option to kill millions, and know that millions of U.S. citizens will be killed in retaliation."[40] For this reason, Defense Secretary Schlesinger developed the "limited nuclear options" concept,[41] which essentially gives the president the option of initiating a "controlled" nuclear war (the third way in which nuclear weapons might be used). The theory is to have the ability for "proportional retaliation," and the objective is not only to bring the violence to a rapid conclusion but also to create a precedent that will prevent a recurrence. Critical to the success of this policy is continuous intelligence gathering and communication between the countries involved (a capability that requires extensive planning and financial expenditures if it is to even have a chance to be effective). The valid concern is that one of the two sides will break out of the controlled environment when it perceives a significant advantage from being the first to escalate. As Thomas Schelling argues, the logical progression would be "he thinks we think he'll attack; so he thinks we shall; so he will; so we must."[42] Notice that, in this case, to attack is a desperate decision, based on a need to strike first in a time of crisis. Also, notice that this strike would be aimed at weapons, not at cities; the objective would be to take out the adversary's missiles before they took out yours. This constitutes a valid argument for having an anti-missile system around your own missiles, as a way of increasing deterrence by discouraging a first strike. It also argues for a civil defense program, which would be far more effective at protecting the population from the effects of an attack on your missiles than it would be at protecting them from an attack on your cities.

Where does all this lead us? The data and the logic seem to imply that each superpower should have only a few hundred, highly survivable nuclear weapons, for the purpose of strategic deterrence. However, this argument assumes rational behavior on both sides; and today many believe that it is too risky for either superpower to assume the other's rationality. Thus, the actual state of affairs is that the United States and the Soviet Union are apparently planning for a first strike on each other[43]—and a relatively large one.[44] However, each of the superpowers has a stated *policy* of "absorbing" a first strike and then retaliating. Part of the problem is that the military on both sides see it as a completely unmilitary notion that a country would let itself be destroyed and would then retaliate simply for the sake of getting even—a concept that bothers most civilians, as well. Besides, as George Orwell wrote, "traditions are not killed by facts." There is enough narrow logic behind the existing first-strike plans that, as long as weapons suitable for a first strike are available, they are not likely to be abandoned.[45]

If the U.S. military believed more strongly in the possibility of a failure of deterrence and in a U.S. second strike, they would pay far more attention to the vulnerability of their command, control, communications, and intelligence systems. Similarly, if the American public believed that their country should be postured only for a second strike (or only for retaliation), they would support some civil defense measures. (Edward Teller has estimated that with such measures, casualties could be held to 5 percent of the population.[46]) But, in Herman Kahn's words, the basic position seems to be that no one really wants to think about the unthinkable.[47] Clearly, the issue is extremely complex; however, the fate of the world rests on it, and, as Robert McNamara stated, "it is absolutely essential that the leaders with control over nuclear weapons understand their responsibility from the outset."[48] By that, he meant that U.S. presidents should take part in simulations ("war games") and fully understand the dangers and the means available to them to control and terminate—before it builds up—any nuclear conflict. Unfortunately, thinking out the U.S. strategic posture and taking part in strategy "war games" has not been a high priority for American presidents.

Europe

Since 1948, Europe has been the only continent not to experience a war between nations.[49] It is generally believed that an all-out war in Europe would probably bring about a nuclear exchange between the superpowers and an end to society as we know it today. Thus, Europe continues to submit to the conditions (many call them unnatural) that were established at the end of World War II: a divided Germany and a subjugated Eastern Europe. The United States spends about 50 percent of its defense dollars in an attempt to deter and defend against war in Europe, while the Soviet Union spends about 60 percent of its total defense dollars countering NATO. Together, NATO and the Warsaw Pact nations spend about $250 billion annually on ground and air forces in Central Europe.[50] Two million military personnel, from NATO and the Warsaw Pact nations, "glare at each other across the border that divides the two Germanys."[51] Both sides know that NATO will not attack first; and both know that if the Soviet Union tries to do so it will have to break through the barrier of troops and airmen from six countries. Yet, even though the numbers of troops on the two sides are approximately equal (NATO forces—including the French—number about 990,000, Warsaw Pact forces number about 1,180,000,[52] and each side has more than 4 million reservists[53]), it is clear that today there is a gross mismatch in the amounts of *equipment*. As will be discussed in chapter 3, the Warsaw Pact outnumbers NATO dramatically in tanks, artillery, helicopters, fighter aircraft, and other categories. Thus, former Army Chief of Staff and Chairman of the Joint Chiefs of Staff Maxwell Taylor wrote, in 1982, "A sustained conventional defense is not possible by the NATO forces currently available or likely to be available."[54] Worse still, the 27 NATO divisions in Europe would—according to General Bernard Rogers, who served as Supreme Commander of these forces— run out of munitions within ten days of a Soviet attack.[55] Thus, without considerable additional expenditures (or other options discussed below), the United States will have to make a nuclear response in order to halt, or push back, a Soviet attack in Europe. As the balance now exists, the troops of NATO must be viewed as expendable elements for enhancing the credibility of nuclear responses—a large "trip wire," or, at best, a way to slow down the escalation response. An example of the effectiveness of even a small trip wire is the fact that only 12,000 NATO troops (of whom 7,000 are Americans) are garrisoned in West Berlin— an island in the middle of East Germany—where their purpose is, as Thomas Schelling stated rather bluntly, "to die heroically, dramatically, and in a manner that guarantees that the action cannot stop there."[56] Thus, these few troops have apparently held the entire Red Army at bay, through the obvious threat of escalation by the NATO forces.

As with strategic nuclear war, the likely military threat to Europe is not a "bolt out of the blue" Soviet attack but the buildup of a crisis that gets out of control, beginning with a conflict in the Third World or some unrest in Eastern Europe, then building to a conventional conflict across the East-West border in Europe, and then—through U.S. reaction to the threat of the Soviets taking over in Europe—escalating to nuclear exchanges of one form or another. How did we get into this situation, and what can be done about it?

During the Eisenhower presidency, the United States made a critical decision (referred to then as the "New Look" in national-security posture) to view the use of nuclear weapons as a low-cost reaction to a conventional attack in Europe.[57] Indeed, to use conventional forces for this mission would be far more costly. Various estimates have been made, but they tend to conclude that for each dollar spent on nuclear weapons, five dollars would be required to achieve the same effectiveness with conventional forces.[58]

Thus, the concept—later known as "extended deterrence"—was to threaten "first use" of nuclear weapons by the United States or by NATO in response to a Soviet conventional attack on Europe. Some (for example, General de Gaulle of France) questioned whether the United States would, in fact, escalate to nuclear weapons in Europe— would the United States "sacrifice New York to save Paris"? The U.S. hope was that, somehow, the nuclear war could be constrained to the European arena and quickly terminated. Many Europeans still question the United States' resolve to defend them, on the grounds that 116,000 Americans but 10 million Europeans died in World War I and that it took the United States 26 months to get into World War II.[59] Clearly, "extended deterrence" raises concerns among Europeans (the nuclear exchange would take place in their territory)—yet they do believe that the U.S. "nuclear umbrella," combined with the U.S. troops stationed in Europe and the reluctance of the Soviet Union to risk a U.S.-Soviet nuclear exchange, has sufficient credibility to deter a Soviet conventional attack.

Once Eisenhower made this commitment to the nuclear defense of Europe, many argued—as many still do[60]—that the United States could greatly reduce its conventional forces in Europe. However, others— concerned that the nuclear threshold was already too low—argued that just the opposite direction should be pursued—i.e., that the United States should greatly build up its conventional forces, so that it would not be *required* to "go nuclear"—in the early stages of a European conflict, anyway. The result was an ambivalence in U.S. and NATO posture that still exists today. The compromise has been to maintain both a large conventional capability and a large nuclear force in Europe (although neither is equal to its Soviet counterpart). There are around 5,000 American tactical nuclear weapons in Europe, and the effect of the intermediate-range nuclear force (INF) arms-control agreement of 1988 was simply to cause a reduction of a few hundred (although obviously critical ones, from the Soviet perspective, since they were the ones—the Pershing II and some Cruise missiles—that could reach the Soviet homeland from Europe).[61]

What then are the choices? Clearly, there is a need to achieve some balance of conventional forces in Europe in order to increase the likelihood of deterrence and, simultaneously, to avoid the use of nuclear weapons. This could be done by a unilateral Soviet force reduction (a highly unlikely occurrence, given the Soviet Union's history), by a significant buildup of NATO conventional forces (an extremely expensive option), by a U.S. technological breakthrough in conventional weapons such that Soviet numerical superiority could be overcome with advanced low-cost technology, or by bilateral agreements on the (asymmetrical) reduction of conventional arms. All four options must be seriously considered, but the last would appear to be the one with the most near-term promise. In any case, it is definitely time to rethink the United States' dependence on a nuclear response in Europe. Particularly with the INF agreement,[62] there seems little choice but to pursue, simultaneously, both the buildup of NATO's conventional forces and conventional arms-control agreements—with the hope that the latter can be accomplished quickly, so as to save a great deal of the cost of the former.

The most significant concern about a potential conflict in Europe is not a Soviet takeover of Europe, but the fact that the U.S. nuclear threat would not be considered credible (because of the vulnerability of the American homeland) and that—with its superior conventional capability—the USSR could significantly weaken the unity of the West. Thus, the United States must focus its political and military strategy in the direction of a conventional "balance."

Achieving significant agreements to control conventional arms will be very difficult, and any buildup of NATO's conventional forces will be very expensive. The problem is that there has been an incredible enhancement of conventional firepower, on both sides, over the years. For example, a modern platoon of 30 men has over three times the effective firepower of its 1945 counterpart.[63] Thus, according to one estimate, building up the NATO forces sufficiently to balance the Soviet deployments facing west would require, essentially, a doubling of the NATO countries' arms budgets.[64] Another estimate was that it would take real defense-budget increases of 4 or 4.5 percent per year for a period of 10 years to give NATO the needed conventional capability.[65] These are, obviously, very big numbers—particularly in a period when, in order to balance their budgets while satisfying their other social requirements, the United States and the European countries are trying to cut back on their defense budgets. Any such military buildup would require far more public support for NATO's conventional forces than now exists.

Finally, it must be emphasized that any "beefing up" of NATO's equipment should be not only quantitative but also qualitative. There are many significant yet relatively inexpensive "force multipliers" that should receive high priority—for example, improved infrastructure items (such as shelters for European-based aircraft, better communications and identification systems, and real-time intelligence systems) and "deep attack" capability to take out the Soviet Union's airfields and key logistical choke points.[66] Nonetheless, many institutional barriers will have to be overcome before such items will receive adequate funding. For example, airfields and logistics points are fixed targets, and thus they are ideal targets for conventionally armed missiles. But such missiles would be resisted by the Air Forces of the United States and the other NATO countries, since they would be considered not a complement to aircraft but rather a lower-cost, unmanned replacement. Similarly, to develop an effective NATO fighting force would mean far more cooperation and less emphasis on industrial and military self-sufficiency in each of the separate NATO countries—again, something that will be difficult to achieve.

Thus, the United States and its European allies must face the fact that, as it currently exists, the NATO defense posture lacks a great deal of credibility. NATO is not capable of stopping a Soviet conventional attack; and escalation to nuclear war is neither credible nor attractive from a military viewpoint (and, far worse, is likely to lead to the destruction of Western civilization).

"Regional" Conflicts

The United States has military obligations to some 60 foreign governments, and in the Reagan years it also pledged support for anticommunist insurgents in the Third World.[67] Thus, the probability of our getting involved in a conflict—either directly or indirectly (through our allies)—is high. The possibilities include a conflict between Third World countries, a situation in which a weak power exploits the weaknesses of a powerful adversary (particularly a superpower) through guerrilla warfare or terrorism, a situation in which either of the superpowers chooses to take on a very weak adversary, and a case in which special-interest groups exploit nationalism (either in the Third World or in a superpower).

The regional conflicts in Afghanistan, Iran, Angola, Ethiopia, Nica-ragua, Lebanon, Grenada, and the Falklands have not threatened the superpowers' national survival, but they certainly cannot be ignored. Every regional conflict must be kept from spreading to Europe and from going nuclear. In general, both superpowers have acted, in these cases, with considerable restraint.[68] Essentially, both superpowers appear to want to build military and economic "barriers" (like Eastern Europe), and each seems to want to prevent its adversary from advancing into areas it considers critical.[69] Similarly, each of the superpowers avoids taking any action against a Third World country that could have the effect of bringing it into alignment with the other superpower. In many cases, this creates strange bedfellows. The United States must learn to tolerate and coexist with a variety of social and economic systems. To date, the United States has a relatively poor record in this regard, with a long history of siding with repressive and reactionary totalitarian regimes and of having equated regional stability with maintaining the status quo in a country.[70] What the United States badly needs to rec-ognize is that regional balances depend on underlying political and economic factors far more than on military factors.[71] Domestic political factors also are critical. In recent years there has been ample U.S. public support for actions in the Third World that are speedy, that achieve a "big win," and that minimize American casualties. (Consider Grenada, the *Achille Lauro* incident, and the bombing attack on Libya in contrast to the war in Vietnam or the bombing of the Marine barracks in Lebanon.) It is also clearly important to avoid having U.S. citizens taken as prisoners. To quote the Chairman of the Joint Chiefs of Staff, Admiral William Crowe, "The threat of picturing captured pilots parad-ing through the streets of Tehran on American television forced the U.S. to use Navy power in the Persian Gulf in 1987 rather than air power."[72]

Perhaps because it is a way of exploiting the mass media, there has been a steady increase in terrorism (from 125 incidents in 1968[73] to 812 in 1985[74]). In the decade from 1975 to 1985, there were 4,172 people killed and an additional 8,834 wounded from terrorists' attacks.[75] Be-hind these acts of terrorism are a wide variety of organizations, ranging from nations using terrorism as a technique to achieve their broader objectives (e.g., Iran and Libya) to smaller organizations that harbor political grievances for one reason or another (from the followers of

King Leka of Albania to opposition parties in Zimbabwe—and some of the causes date back to the twelfth century).[76]

So far the terrorist movements have used relatively primitive weapons; however, it is likely that in the years ahead they will acquire precision-guided munitions, chemical and biological weapons, and even nuclear weapons. In some cases the resources will come from national governments; in others (as in the case of chemical and biological weapons) they will develop them on their own. In either case, these weapons represent an enormous danger, not only in the Third World but also to the United States.

The effect that chemical or biological agents could have if placed in the air-conditioning system of a New York skyscraper is obvious. However, we must also consider other "conventional" terrorist actions, such as the sabotage, at various choke points, of the electric power system of the United States (which is believed to be quite vulnerable, as was demonstrated by the northeastern blackout of 1965). If some of these critical choke points (e.g., large transformers, switches, and computers) were to be hit in a coordinated fashion, it could result in extended outages of electric power—estimates range from eighteen months to three years. Similarly, taking out certain gas pipelines at key points could affect major metropolitan areas. The U.S. air traffic control system is also vulnerable, especially to a coordinated attack. And there have been a number of articles about the vulnerability of the U.S. banking system—for example, tampering with the choke points for international financial transfers could dramatically affect the overall U.S. economy for an extended period of time. Naturally, there has been much discussion and considerable awareness of these issues, but to date there has been very little action. The private sector is not particularly motivated to address such expensive and national-level issues, and the federal government has taken a view of terrorist operations in the United States somewhat similar to its view of nuclear war: "It can't happen here."

It would not be at all surprising to see terrorist acts linked to Third World conflicts begin to take place in the United States. For example, in 1987, when the United States was virtually at war with Iran in the Persian Gulf, it would not have been at all inconsistent for Iran to encourage terrorist acts within the continental United States—with or without attribution. Alternatively, terrorist actions could be used as precursors to conflicts elsewhere, as a way of both introducing confusion and affecting the outcome of the conflict. (For example, logistics resupply choke points might be attacked prior to any large-scale conflict.)

The "linkage" between actions in the Third World (including terrorism) and U.S. commitments is of critical concern. For example, in his 1980 State of the Union address, President Carter stated that "an attempt by any outside force to gain control of the Persian Gulf region will be regarded as an assault on the vital interests of the United States of America, and such an assault will be repelled by any means necessary, including military force." Thus, a Third World conflict could, in fact, represent a very real threat to world peace. Yet, traditionally, U.S. defense decisionmakers have placed regional conflicts extremely low on their lists of priorities and have not allocated nearly enough resources to address such issues. Again, the focus has been first on nuclear war and second on Europe. In 1950, General Omar Bradley declared that "we will refuse absolutely to allow local wars to divert us unduly from our central task. They must not be allowed to consume so much of our manpower as to destroy our strength and imperil our victory in a world war."[77] During the Vietnam war, comments such as "It's the wrong war; our equipment was designed for use in Europe" were heard continually. There is no question that the equipment and the planning required for regional conflicts differ from what is required in Central Europe.[78] Yet—even though these are the most likely conflicts to occur—resources have been withheld for "higher priority" areas. A classic example of the effect of the maldistribution of U.S. defense resources occurred during 1987: With the Navy escorting ships in the Persian Gulf, it was realized that Iran was mining the Gulf and that the United States had for many years neglected to build minesweepers.

Even the military objectives in such conflicts may well be different. It has frequently been suggested that the best tactic in a Third World conflict is simply to defeat the enemy's leadership rather than its army (another very untraditional approach).

The United States needs to rethink its whole approach to regional conflicts, with particular emphasis on intelligence, influence, and power. Particular attention must be paid to what will work, since raw military power is often ineffective.[79] Intelligence gathering is obviously essential, and we need not only the traditional sort of information about forces but also information about the vulnerability of leaders and about local political and social forces.[80] Additionally, one of the most effective things that the United States must learn to do in regional conflicts is to get its allies much more involved. Collective efforts of military forces involving both European and Asian allies tend to be less susceptible to superpower escalation (and more acceptable to world opinion) than those of the United States alone. Additionally, we must learn to stress mutually beneficial political and economic links with stable, cooperative, and democratic local power groups. Finally, we are going to have to face the fact that regional conflicts will become much more dangerous in the future, with the likely use of chemical, biological,[81] and even nuclear[82] weapons, delivered by precision-guided and long-range ballistic missiles.[83] The United States would do well to plan for these eventualities far in advance, both by developing and deploying equipment appropriate for such conflicts and (equally important) by deciding how to respond. The need for specialized equipment and specialized training will entail a significant change in the Defense Department's resource priorities.

Summary

This chapter has defined a very wide range of potential military conflicts, from nuclear war through European conflicts to Third World and terrorist actions. The difficulty is that, on the basis of the United States' current force structure and national-security posture, one canot—with equal clarity—see the relationship between the weapons historically selected and the military strategy for each of these potential conflicts. There is a mismatch between means and objectives, and it is likely to get worse. Thus, the next step is to look at this link between strategy and weapons choices in order to examine what affordable options should be pursued in the coming years.

3 Selecting Weapons

Strategy and Weapon Choices

The challenge facing the military planner is to convert the demands of a wide range of potential conflicts into decisions about which weapons should be developed and how many of each should be bought. The selection of an appropriate military strategy for each of these potential conflicts dramatically affects the answer to the question of the appropriate weapon.

Consider the example of nuclear weapons. In an oversimplified view, the various potential U.S. nuclear postures can be categorized into four broad options: (1) that the world should be rid of nuclear weapons, (2) that nuclear weapons have value for deterrence only, (3) that nuclear weapons can be used for both deterrence and war fighting, and (4) that the only safe solution is not to be vulnerable to being threatened. These four positions lead to dramatically different force structures and weapon systems.

The first of the above options—ridding the world of nuclear weapons—is the natural position of the public, which is appalled by the potential for nuclear holocaust. Presidents Carter and Reagan, early in their administrations, took this position and spoke out strongly about the desirability of eliminating all nuclear weapons. Thus, this position is not simply one taken by the "peace groups." The principal focus of this option is on arms-control agreements. Such a focus is required, since unilateral nuclear disarmament by the West would not prompt the Soviet leadership to disarm. Rather, it would place the West at the mercy of the Soviet Union; and history offers abundant proof that mercy has not been a salient characteristic of any Communist regime.[1]

The difficulty with this option is the difficulty of getting there and staying there. A violation of an arms-control treaty when there are only a few nuclear weapons on each side (for example, the doubling of a small number of weapons) would make a very significant difference, whereas the same numerical increase would have very little impact if there were large numbers of weapons on each side. Many opponents of drastic cuts have pointed out that, as the number of weapons gets smaller, the situation becomes increasingly unstable, and that a country with only a few nuclear weapons has an extremely strong position relative to a country that has gone to zero. However, advocates of total nuclear disarmament argue that they are willing to take that risk, and that nations would then work to reduce the instability in other ways.

From a weapons-selection perspective, the first requirement implied by complete nuclear disarmament is a dramatic increase in intelligence gathering, in order to achieve the stability required for this option; the second is a significant increase in NATO's conventional arms. Many of the advocates of this option will argue equally strongly that the quantities of conventional arms should be reduced, that weapons should be removed from close to the borders, and that the equipment should be changed to "confine the role of conventional military forces to defensive use only, in order to move safely toward a world in which conventional forces are limited to short-range, defensive armaments."[2] This also leads to a concept of "defense of the homeland": "If all countries maintained military forces solely for the purpose of defending their national territory, only conventional, short-range forces that provide air, coastal and border defense would be needed."[3] This position obviously has significant implications for the United States' military role in the world: We would have to depend solely on political actions for that achievement, and we would have to count on all other nations— large and small—to take similar positions. (For this reason, this aspect of the policy might be questioned on historical grounds.) One very interesting aspect of this position is that, while its advocates argue strongly for a "defense only" posture, they are vigorously opposed to any defense against ballistic missiles. They see such a defense as the basis for the other extreme position (the fourth option), and they fear that such a defense would actually encourage nuclear war fighting. (In contrast, President Reagan, in arguing for the Strategic Defense Initiative, has stated that it could eliminate nuclear weapons, because it would make them no longer useful.)

Contrary to the above "desire," it is important to recognize that, in the absence of dramatic reductions in conventional arms, the elimination of nuclear weapons would require significant increases in the conventional capability of the United States—if we were to maintain our commitments around the world and, particularly, in Europe. Additionally, this option would place very heavy dependence on mobilizing industry (to rapidly produce weapon systems, should there be a crisis) and on the use of the manpower reserves (to rapidly build up forces, should they be required). The implication of this option for weapon selection is that we would pick weapons that would be very simple and easily produced (but would not have to last for twenty years, and would not have many of the characteristics of current weapon systems). There would have to be a very considerable investment made in industrial mobilization potential, in order to make any form of military capability at all credible under these conditions. In the absence of such planning, the United States would be in the position that it has historically always been in: unprepared for war, should it come, and unable to get equipment rapidly enough even if it could mobilize its manpower reserves. The fact that the weapons we are talking about here would be designed to be produced rapidly would be another reason why a great deal of attention would have to be given to intelligence gathering, which we would have to rely upon to provide the warning time necessary to make any defense posture credible.

The second strategic option—that nuclear weapons have value for deterrence only—has been held by leading thinkers in the defense area since the beginning of the atomic age. For example, Bernard Brody wrote in 1946 that: "The first and most vital step in any American security program for the age of atomic bombs is to take measures to guarantee to ourselves, in case of attack, a possibility of retaliation in kind. . . . Thus far the chief purpose of our military establishment has been to win wars. From now on its chief purpose must be to avert them. It can have almost no other useful purpose."[4] In 1983, Robert McNamara wrote: "I do not believe we can avoid serious and unacceptable risk of nuclear war until we recognize—and until we base all our military plans, defense budgets, weapon deployments, and arms negotiations on the recognition—that nuclear weapons serve no military purpose whatsoever. They are totally useless—except only to deter one's opponent from using them."[5] This view is also held by many military leaders. For example, Admiral Noel Gayler, former Commander in Chief of U.S. forces in the Pacific, testified in 1981: "There is no sensible military use of any of our nuclear forces. Their only reasonable use is to deter our opponent from using his nuclear forces."[6]

The credibility of deterring threats is—given a large number of weapons—relatively insensitive to variations in the size of the strategic forces. Therefore, from an arms-control perspective, it is considered a relatively "stable" condition. However, in order for your deterrence to have credibility, your potential adversary must be convinced that you would, in fact, launch your nuclear weapons if attacked. Therefore, to convince your adversary of your resolve, you must act "strong," even in minor crises, since "even if it has no great intrinsic significance, [your] losing [any] test would encourage [your] adversary to test [you] again."[7] This point—made by Henry Kissinger—raises the obvious paradox of the credibility of deterrence: The less the occasion, the greater the response must be for deterrence to have credibility. The other requirement for the credibility of your deterrence is that of "survivability." The assumption is that you are using your weapons only for deterrence, and that if deterrence fails you will avenge the attack by wiping out the attacker's society. Therefore, you design your weapons to be invulnerable to the enemy's weapons. This leads to greater reliance on mobile missiles (launched from trucks, from the sea, from the air, from space, or from rail vehicles). It also requires that the command and control system for these weapons (as well as the leaders who would "push the button") be able to survive a nuclear attack. Again, it is not that a nation necessarily will avenge itself; it is, rather, that a nation must have a credible deterrent capability. This requirement for a "second-strike" capability makes the weapon systems far more expensive, since they must be survivable. It also suggests specific weapons—for example, a mobile "Midgetman" rather than a fixed-site MX missile. Furthermore, it eases the targeting requirements for these missiles—they need not have the high accuracy required to strike an opponent's missiles; they need only be capable of hitting industrial areas and population centers.

This second nuclear option also has obvious implications for conventional weapons. If one is going to use nuclear weapons only in a reaction mode (i.e., "no first use"), then one must be prepared to fight conventional wars at any level of intensity. This places requirements on both the size and the capabilities of one's conventional forces.[8] Many argue that it is the fact that the Soviets do not plan to be the first to use nuclear weapons that causes them to have such an extremely large conventional capability.[9]

The high cost of conventional forces, and the fact that nuclear weapons are much cheaper for the same mission capability, lead President Eisenhower to move toward option 3: the use of nuclear weapons not only for deterrence but also for "war fighting." By the early 1970s, many U.S. officials recognized that "assured destruction"—aside from the moral issues—was no longer a credible doctrine for deterring the Soviets from an attack with conventional forces in Europe. Thus, during the Johnson and Nixon administrations the United States developed a position of "flexible response," which it has maintained—in various forms—since then. Some argue that the ability to respond at varying levels—on up through nuclear war fighting—makes deterrence even more credible. While they do not necessarily believe that the United States can "win" a nuclear war, they believe that this ability on the part of the United States keeps the Soviets from thinking that they could.[10] This posture clearly includes "extended deterrence," a policy that allows the United States to use its nuclear forces to deter Soviet use of conventional forces (for example, in Europe).

From an equipment viewpoint, this option allows "first use" of nuclear weapons, and therefore does not require that they all be hardened. However, it does require that all of one's command, control, communications, and intelligence-gathering systems be able to survive an extended nuclear exchange. The Soviets have been spending vast sums of money building hardened and redundant command, control, and communications systems to survive nuclear attack. Additionally, they have an extensive civil defense system that can protect a significant percentage of their civilian population and that keeps key officials in hardened and redundant locations.[11] This option also requires that missile systems be designed for very high accuracy, as they will be used "first" to attack the enemy's hardened military forces. This option also places great emphasis on maintaining communication links with the enemy, for the purpose of clearly communicating the intent of the limited nuclear use and initiating bargaining for a termination of the conflict before it has the opportunity to escalate out of hand.

Without mutual strategic-arms limitations ("arms control"), this option has the potential to stimulate a strategic-arms race in which each side will try to get more and more "war fighting" capability. It is the fact that both the United States and the Soviet Union are following this strategy that had led to the deployment of more than 50,000 warheads around the world. Nonetheless, this option is considerably cheaper than "deterrence only" (option 2), which requires a much greater conventional capability (in the absence of extensive agreements to limit conventional arms). One of the major arguments against this alternative is that, with each country able to attack its opponent's missiles and thereby thinking that with a "first kill" it would have a strategic advantage, this is a highly destabilizing environment. The more weapons that are put on any single vulnerable missile (through the use of multiple independently targeted reentry vehicles—MIRVs), the more unstable the concept becomes, since each of these missiles is an extremely desirable "target" to try to take out before it is used.

Because options 1, 2, and 3 all represent varying degrees of instability and insecurity, many people have moved to the fourth option—the only one that does not make the survival of the United States dependent on decisions made in the Soviet Union. This is essentially an option in which the United States doesn't feel threatened, because it is able either to overpower the Soviet Union or to defend itself. This option is normally considered the "extreme military position" (because it often begins by emphasizing that the more warheads we have the stronger we are); however, it logically would lead to controls on (and reductions in) the numbers of offensive weapons, and to the building of a strong "defense only" system to protect against the few potential attacking missiles that remain. Thus, in a certain sense, this option is getting closer to the one at the other end of the spectrum (option 1). Option 4, however, allows nuclear weapons—which, its advocates argue, represents a relatively stable condition, because of the presence of a capability to defend against them, whereas option 1 would be very unstable unless all nations were to go to zero nuclear weapons.

One view of option 4 is that the United States should have sufficient nuclear superiority so that it would not feel threatened even if it did not have a defensive system. This was the case made by Secretary of Defense Caspar Weinberger at the beginning of the Reagan Administration when he pointed out (reflecting on the 1950s and the 1960s) that "the weapons we had had a degree of superiority that made it eminently clear to them that if they should launch a first strike they would never be able to bear the retaliatory cost that we could inflict. . . . We had this ability, capability. That is one of the strong preservatives of peace, and that was lost. Now we've got to regain it."[12]

As the Soviet Union built up its forces after the 1950s, the United States still felt that, by having an overwhelming superiority in numbers and being able to initiate the first strike, it would "not feel threatened." However, in 1983, President Reagan stated that we must "break out of the future that relies solely on offensive retaliation for our security," and thus initiated the "Strategic Defense Initiative" (SDI). This was not the first time that ballistic-missile defense had been introduced into the nuclear debate. In 1970 the United States was spending about $4 billion a year for missile defense (while spending about $8 billion a year for offensive forces).[13] However, partly because the technology was in its early stages and partly because such a system would have introduced uncertainty into the accepted policy of mutual assured destruction, work on missile defense was dramatically cut back until Reagan's 1983 initiative.

Clearly there are technological problems—perhaps even insurmountable ones—facing the development of an effective strategic-missile-defense system. In addition, such a system would be very expensive to develop and deploy (costs between $200 billion and $1 trillion—over an extended time period—have been estimated). Furthermore, both the technology and the cost of the system are significantly dependent upon the deployment strategy. For example, if the purpose of SDI were to create a more viable second-strike deterrent, then the defense system would be deployed around hardened silos and would be designed to intercept targets at much lower altitudes—which would make the defense considerably easier and cheaper. However, this would not fulfill President Reagan's objective of protecting the population.

Another oddity associated with option 4 is that very few of those advocating SDI have argued for an extensive civil defense program to go with it. Yet a civil defense system would be a highly cost-effective way to save lives—particularly in conjunction with arms limitations and an active defense system, like SDI. (Of course, such a civil defense system would take many years to put in place. The plan designed to protect the entire population of Switzerland will take about 30 years, at a cost of approximately $500 per person.[14])

One of the most interesting strategy questions associated with SDI— frequently said to reveal its greatest weakness—is how to achieve deployment without almost begging your potential adversary to launch his missiles against you before the deployment (because afterward they will be ineffective). From a weapon-system-design viewpoint, this means that an SDI system must be configured in such a way that it can be simultaneously deployed in both the United States and the Soviet Union. For this reason, President Reagan offered in his 1983 speech to give the technology to the Soviet Union.

The above discussion shows how very significantly the requirements placed on individual weapon systems are driven by the strategy options that the policymakers select. The United States today is faced with the problem of having strong representatives of all four of the options, all of them having good, logical arguments and powerful support in Congress, in the press, and even within the executive branch. Thus, there is a tendency to pursue all four options simultaneously in order to satisfy numerous special-interest groups. This tendency is evident in the actions taken in regard to budgets, arms-control agreements, technologies being developed, weapon selections, and so forth. Often the objectives pursued are in direct conflict, and the equipment funded is counterproductive for an alternative strategy. The result is that people have been arguing on the basis of individual weapon systems, rather than on the basis of a broad strategy and the weapons that might flow from it. As Michael Howard has written, "One of the most significant and deplorable developments of the past decade has been the erosion of the consensus reached in the early 1960s (on strategic nuclear strategy), which not only reconciled the often conflicting perspectives from Europe and the United States, but which bridged the gulf between those who believe that the problems of the world could be solved only by general disarmament, and those whose more prudent assessment of the state of international relations lead them to continue maintenance of adequate national defense and deterrent capabilities."[15]

Today there is clearly no consensus between the United States and its allies, or even within the United States. Not only is this true with regard to nuclear weapons; it is equally true with regard to conventional warfare. A simple list of some of the more important strategy considerations, and their implications for weapon systems, will give a clear perspective on the overriding importance of developing strategy *before* discussing weapons. We will return to this issue when we discuss the development of a coherent and affordable national-security posture.

- *Should the United States plan for—and buy equipment for—a "short war" in Europe, or one of extended duration?* The former places heavy emphasis on nuclear use early in the conflict; the latter requires high expenditures for sustained conventional capability.
- *Should the United States plan to fight a war in the presence of chemical and biological weapons?* The Soviets have been designing much

of their equipment for this eventuality. If we were to take this matter seriously, we would significantly change the designs of our weapons, and the changes would raise their costs. (For example, we would redesign our tanks and armored personnel carriers to operate in a toxic environment.)

- *Should the United States develop an anti-satellite capability (as the Soviet Union has)? Conversely, can the United States count on its communication satellites in the presence of the Soviet anti-satellite capability?* The United States has been shifting in the direction of greater and greater dependence on communication satellites. Thus, we should be designing them to be far more survivable than they are.

- *Should the United States depend heavily on troops deployed in Europe and Korea?* There is frequent debate over the wisdom and the expense of maintaining 300,000 U.S. troops in Europe. Some argue that all that is required is a "token"; in contrast, the Senate Foreign Relations Committee has issued a report stating that "any significant withdrawals of U.S. troops from Europe would be seen as punitive and provoke an angry, confused and decisive European reaction from our NATO partners."[16] The difference between these two viewpoints has significant implications for the selection of weapon systems. For example, if significant numbers of our "forward" troops were removed and then had to be rapidly redeployed, we would need a much greater transportation capability than we have today.

- *Should the United States begin the development of strategic weapon systems with non-nuclear warheads?* No technological breakthroughs are required, and the new warheads could even be substituted for the nuclear warheads on some of today's strategic systems relatively rapidly.[17] A move to some non-nuclear strategic forces would bypass the political taboo against the use of nuclear weapons, but it has dramatic implications in terms of the possibilities of escalation. This is a classic example of the need to clarify strategy before developing weapons. In reality, the varying schools of thought are likely to all have their say, and once again it may be difficult to arrive at a policy consensus. The United States is likely to develop the weapons— because it can—and the weapons will then drive the strategy.

- *Should the United States rely on "attrition warfare," or on "maneuver warfare"?* These two approaches to warfare have been debated since

Sun Tzu (around 500 B.C.) argued for maneuver warfare,[18] which is used today by many countries (e.g., China). Maneuver warfare is argued for by the "military reform caucus" in the U.S. Congress. Others, however, state that if we are to "hold the line" at the West German border, we must use an attrition approach—and this has basically been the U.S. (and NATO) posture. Maneuver warfare requires light, highly mobile systems; attrition warfare requires heavier and longer-range systems.

· *Should the United States depend on superior quality of weapon systems, or on superior quantities of weapon systems?* The advocates of quantity note that in World War II the United States "never had a tank that was as good as a German tank—but we had lots more"; the advocates of quality argue that there is no way that the United States can catch up with the overwhelming quantities of Soviet equipment, and thus we must emphasize "making one of ours better than three of theirs." The reality is that, with the Soviet Union having dramatically greater quantity and clearly catching up in quality (see below), the United States is forced to continue its current strategy of technological superiority but to find ways to field significantly greater quantities of equipment (e.g., by using advanced technology and improved management techniques to significantly reduce the cost of each individual weapon system).

· *To what extent should the United States depend on its allies to maintain its security posture?* Clearly, this is a key question—in terms of overall strategy and in terms of the quantities and the types of weapons selected. Some argue that security must be "collective," and that we cannot retreat to a self-sufficiency posture. Yet our current military position is largely one of independence—in terms of planning, programs, and even logistics. The lack of "jointness" has been most evident in operations outside Europe—some of our "allies" have even refused to allow us to land on their territory, or even to fly over it, for fear that it might adversely impact the availability of oil to their nations. (Recall the bombing of Libya and the 1973 Arab-Israeli war.) But equally serious is the lack of sincere joint planning within Europe—where we may be fighting together, yet we can't even communicate with one another.

- *What degree of interservice cooperation should exist in military planning within the United States?* Today, almost all weapons requirements and budgets are determined independently by the four armed services. Clearly this affects which weapons are selected and how much effectiveness we get for the dollars expended. A shift toward the integration of strategy, weapons selection, and budgeting would be a dramatic change in the traditions of the Department of Defense.
- *Must there be a consistent long-term strategy within and among the different services?* For example, what should be the "role of the Navy"? There is even disagreement within the Navy on this question. For example, former Secretary of the Navy John Lehman (and others) argue for a total of fifteen very large aircraft carriers, each manned by 6,000 men and carrying about 90 aircraft and each protected by a formidable "task force" of other (expensive) Navy ships. Part of the rationale for such an increase is that some carrier task forces would be used in northern Norway, off the coast of Russia, to "carry the war to the Russians."[19] However, Admiral Stansfield Turner (a former Director of the CIA, and a former commander of an aircraft-carrier task force himself) says "It is not necessary to send the carriers north for the Navy to protect the Atlantic sea lanes"; thus he argues for fewer carrier task force groups.[20] The difference in the debate cited here represents around $36 billion for three new carrier battle groups. In a similar vein, there is debate among admirals as to whether big carriers—with greater power projection—are better than small ones. Admiral Elmo Zumwalt argues for a "distributed force" involving space-based surveillance and small carriers equipped with cruise missiles and vertical-takeoff aircraft. This "distributed force" would, according to Admiral Zumwalt, improve survivability in an age of guided weapons, and could be geographically distributed so as to provide more of a global coverage.[21]
- *To what extent should the U.S. military shift toward automation?* Good arguments can be made for and against automation, from both military-effectiveness and control perspectives. Manpower costs consume about half of the annual defense budget, so robots and cruise missiles are very attractive. However, decisions about "men versus machines" are value-laden, and there is a great reluctance to even address them.

• *To what extent should the United States depend on reservists rather than full-time troops?* This is discussed in chapter 9.

As can be seen from this brief list of some of the strategy issues that need to be addressed (and all these pertain to high-intensity conventional conflicts, not to regional conflicts or terrorism), it is not at all an easy matter to develop a coherent, credible, and yet affordable national-security posture at either the strategic level or the conventional level. And the politics associated with the various interest groups involved—both within the defense establishment and without—significantly complicate the issue. Nonetheless, this is the challenge that must be addressed if the United States is to have a viable defense posture in this age of insecurity. As Clausewitz stated, "One cannot have a practical theory for the conduct of war unless one understands the relationship between ends and means; in particular, the political end of war and the military means used to attain it."[22] Thus, we must address all the elements in the cycle: political objectives, military strategy, and weapon systems—and the role of arms control in this cycle is becoming more and more significant.

Arms Control

In one form or another, arms-control negotiations (in the nuclear era) have been going on since the early 1960s. However, the rationale has varied widely. Often, arms reductions have been presented as a practical alternative to the arms race, with a clear recognition that significant unilateral reductions are unlikely and that the only way to move away from the escalating buildup—at both the conventional level and the nuclear level—is to shift to mutual agreements on controls and reductions. In the broad sense, as Leslie Gelb has stated, "Arms control is neither sin nor salvation. It is a way—along with diplomacy and military decisions—of managing Soviet/American competition."[23] Clearly—if successful—arms control can significantly increase the credibility and stability of deterrence. It can also have direct military benefits. (As will be discussed below, this was the case for the Intermediate Nuclear Forces agreement of 1988.) Others have argued that arms control and arms reductions are necessary simply on humanitarian grounds—even independent of superpower considerations—owing to the danger of a "nuclear winter." But undoubtedly the most significant driving forces for arms-control negotiations have come from the political arena—and often from domestic rather than international politics. As Christopher Bertran (a European writer) states, "The pressure for arms control is shaped by political opportunism and not by conceptual concern. The short-term threatens to override the long-term. Arms control has become a matter of political expediency rather than being a contribution to stabilize military competition between East and West."[24]

Within the United States, there has been little successful integration of the activities of the Arms Control and Disarmament Agency (ACDA) and those of the Department of Defense (the goal of which would be to come up with a coherent overall long-term strategy). Instead, arms control has become the issue of the "peace" groups, while the Department of Defense has done most of its planning without considering arms control. Often arms control is used as a "budget issue", with concessions being made by the "hawks" to arms-control agreements in order to get increased expenditures for other defense items. For example, in 1981 John Newhouse, a former Assistant Director of the ACDA, wrote: "A restoration of SALT (Strategic Arms Limitation Talks) would clearly help Reagan with the defense budget. The more obvious and urgent military needs lie well outside the area of strategic weapons."[25]

Arms-control agreements (or at least gestures toward them) have also been used by both superpowers to try to influence European opinion.[26] It has often been the Soviets who have gained the most by making symbolic use of arms-control gestures. As Henry Kissinger has stated, "In the West, a conference represents a struggle to find formulas to achieve agreement, while to a revolutionary order it is a struggle to capture the symbols which move humanity. . . . The major weakness of United States diplomacy has been the insufficient attention given to the symbolic aspects of foreign policy."[27]

The United States' basic distrust of the Soviets, which the Soviets have earned by their actions, is the basis for the emphasis on the absolute need for verification of any arms-control measures. Yet verification itself is totally unbalanced. While the Soviets have full insight into all U.S. violations—as disclosed by the American press, the opposition party, the opponents of U.S. arms policies, and others—the United States has no such access to Soviet violations (the Soviet Union being a totally closed society, historically obsessed with secrecy). In fact, it was only in 1987 that the Soviets finally agreed to the principle of on-site inspection (as part of the INF discussions[28]) after over 20 years of SALT negotiations.

By the late 1980s it was generally recognized by both superpowers that each had far more nuclear weapons than were required for deterrence. In fact, the United States had actually been reducing its numbers of nuclear weapons (and its aggregate tonnage) for two decades.[29] Even during the first six years of the Reagan administration, when the United States undertook a massive buildup in defense expenditures and equipment, there was a decline of roughly 3 percent in the American stockpile of nuclear warheads.[30] Since each side has approximately 12,000 warheads in its long-range strategic arsenal, even cuts of 50 percent—such as were proposed in the strategic arms limitation talks of 1988—would leave each side with more than enough for a credible preemptive threat (i.e., a first strike against the other side's missiles). Reaching the level at which each side would retain the capability for a retaliatory strike against the other's population and industry but would not possess the capability for a disarming first strike—a concept long advanced by many arms-control specialists in the West, and one that the Soviet Union began to address in the late 1980s—would require dramatic reductions in both sides' nuclear forces. On one U.S. estimate, the forces on each side would have to be "brought down to about 3,000 to cut into the preemptive capacity"[31]; a semi-official Soviet study of "strategic stability under the conditions of radical nuclear arms reductions" concluded that about 600 mobile, single-warhead, intercontinental ballistic missiles on each side would be sufficient to achieve strategic stability in the absence of anti-missile defenses.[32] Thus, a "non-offensive defense" appears to require between 600 and 3,000 nuclear warheads. This still leaves a significant number on each side, which most people believe to be far more stabilizing than going to numbers so low that small incremental changes would give one side a big advantage. As long as the numbers stay in the hundreds or the thousands (particularly with on-site inspections, such as are specified in the INF agreements), verification is far less critical than it would be if the numbers were to be extremely small.

The INF treaty cut out about 10 percent of the nuclear weapons in Europe. However, this treaty was far more significant for three other reasons. First, it eliminated the direct coupling between war in Europe and "homeland" nuclear exchanges between the superpowers. (The Pershing II and cruise missiles that the United States had deployed in Europe were capable of hitting the Soviet Union, which would have brought an immediate retaliation against the United States). Second, it established a principle of significant asymmetry in arms control—the Soviets took out more missiles than the United States (their logic being that it was in their interest to eliminate missiles that could reach the Soviet homeland, and they were willing to give up a larger number in order to gain that increase in security). This principle of asymmetry will be particularly important in any conventional-arms negotiations, because of the overwhelming numbers of Soviet conventional arms. Third—and perhaps most important—the INF treaty highlighted the fact that the U.S. posture of a nuclear response to a conventional attack by the Soviets lacked a good deal of credibility and thus required NATO to reassess its whole conventional-arms posture. As Senator Sam Nunn stated after the signing of the INF treaty, "There's just not the realization that if we eliminated nuclear weapons—as we've had two presidents aspire to—we would be closer to war unless we did something radical about the conventional balance. . . . Logically, we should have insisted on conventional arms control first."[33] It is very important to recognize that nuclear war is most likely to arise from an escalation of conventional conflict. Thus, reducing the likelihood of conventional war would make strategic-arms reductions much easier to achieve. Yet, even though this position seems to be relatively well recognized,[34] the Mutual Balanced Force Reduction (MBFR) negotiations between NATO and the Warsaw Pact nations went on for 14 years with no progress whatsoever—prior to the signing of the INF agreement (after which attention shifted, at last, to the need for reductions in conventional arms).[35]

In pushing for conventional-arms reductions, particularly in Europe, it is important to recognize that there should be dramatic reductions not only in military personnel (the objective of the MBFR negotiations) but also, and perhaps most important, in "threatening" equipment and in the forward deployment of this equipment. Thus, it would be desirable to remove tanks and other offensive weapons from the front-line areas. Similarly, it would be desirable to stop the military "exercises" that are frequently conducted near the East-West border. Ultimately, the objective of conventional-arms reductions in Europe should be to reduce both sides to balanced forces, of significantly lower numbers, most of which are removed from the borders far enough to require a considerable response time and that are primarily geared toward defensive operations. The negotiators would need to recognize the current asymmetry in both forces and doctrine between NATO and Warsaw Pact forces, and both sides would need to take these asymmetries into account. General Wojciech Jaruzelski of Poland has stated: "We know that the West believes that there is a predominance of the Warsaw Pact in tanks. We believe that the NATO countries have a predominance in certain kind of aircraft, especially bombers. The first steps could be taken with these two categories."[36]

There is a strong relationship—at both the strategic and the conventional level—between arms-control strategy and the decisions on which weapons would make the most sense under the changed conditions. With the current high levels of conventional forces (as was the case in the strategic area), small variations in the numbers of particular forces or equipment would not have a significant impact on the balance (and therefore on the stability) of the forces. Thus, verification—though important—is not critical, and precise issues in this area need not hold up agreements to reduce conventional forces. What is important, however, is to attempt to get control over—and verification of—any technological developments that could have a dramatic effect on the balance, and therefore the stability, of the conventional forces. Clearly, the potential production of chemical and, particularly, biological weapons must be addressed.

In looking back over the answer to the question as to which weapons, and how many of each, the United States should procure, perhaps the most glaring conclusion one could reach is that the answer depends primarily on our overall national-security objectives and strategy and secondarily on the world's balance of forces at the moment. To address the first part of this answer, the United States needs to develop a far more coherent national-security strategy—one that addresses strategic arms, conventional arms, and arms control in an integrated and credible fashion. Today such a strategy does not exist. We will now turn to the second part of the answer, i.e., the status of the world balance.

U.S./NATO-versus-USSR/Warsaw Pact Comparisons

The United States and the Soviet Union have been military "rivals" since the end of World War II.[37] The continued growth of Soviet military power over this long time period has caused great concern and disillusionment in the West. Widely different interpretations for this military buildup have been advanced. Some have seen it as evidence of the Soviet Union's determination to achieve decisive military superiority, and to use it to extend its power and influence; others have viewed it as springing from a deep-seated sense of insecurity—a desire to defend Soviet interests against real or imagined dangers.[38] Thus, the Soviets' aggressive actions—such as have occurred in Eastern Europe and in Afghanistan—can be seen as demonstrating their expansionist objectives or as reflecting their insecurity. Yet, no matter which viewpoint one holds, there is no question that Russia has a long history of militarism, which is deeply rooted in the very structure of the society and which is still very present today.[39] The Russian empire was based almost exclusively on its army, and "no modern state has as uninterrupted a history of warfare as does Russia."[40]

As the Soviet defector Oleg Penkofskiy stated, "If someone were to give an American general, an English general, and a Soviet general the same set of facts and scientific data, it is possible that the American and the Englishman would reach similar conclusions but the Soviet general would arrive at conclusions which would be radically different from the other two."[41] Penkofskiy goes on to say that this is possible for four reasons: First, the Soviet general begins with a completely different set of basic premises and preconceived ideas (his long cultural history, combined with the Marxian concepts of the structure of society and the course of history). Second, the logical processes in his mind would be totally unlike those of his Western counterparts, involving Marxian dialectics rather than some form of deductive reasoning. Third, a very different set of moral laws would govern and restrict his behavior. Fourth, his aims would be radically different.

The difference in military aims is extremely important in any comparison between the Soviet Union and the United States. For one thing, the Soviet leadership sees international relations (politics) and military strategy as closely linked, whereas in the United States military thinking is quite divorced from politics and closely coupled with military technology. Second, the Soviets' balanced force structure (with large conventional forces) results in less dependence on nuclear weapons. In contrast, the United States—since President Eisenhower—has based a significant part of its defense capability on moving quickly to nuclear retaliation, even in response to conventional action. Yet American attitudes profess the "unthinkability" of nuclear war, while the Soviet Union clearly accepts its possibility.[42] Consistent with this, the Soviets equip many of their vehicles to operate in a nuclear environment. The United States, in spite of its stated "first nuclear use" posture, neither equips its vehicles for a nuclear environment nor has plans for what would happen during and after a nuclear exchange. Underlying these differences is the fact that "deterrence in the Soviet context is rooted in war fighting and war survival capabilities, and not, as in American thinking, in the threat of punishment."[43]

Clearly the United States is not going to initiate an "out of the blue" first strike against the Soviet Union. However, we are postured to be able to do this (for example, we have large, accurate, multiple-warhead, fixed-site MX missiles), and in defending Europe—given the imbalance of conventional forces—we might be left with little choice. As Herman Kahn has observed, it is not likely that the Soviet Union would give serious consideration to a deliberate, calculated first strike against the United States, except under the most extreme circumstances: "Cultural, ideological, and analytical factors indicate that the Soviet leadership would act with prudence and caution. The Soviet Union lacks a tradition of successful "wars by calculation"; Soviet ideology stresses patience and warns against recklessness in the long-term struggle with capitalism; and technical uncertainties as to how the military would actually perform in a nuclear war would prompt the Soviets to think very hard before initiating a nuclear attack."[44]

However, if a war does get started, the current U.S. view—owing to the threat of eventual mutual annihilation—clearly emphasizes escalation control. This concept is conspicuously absent from Soviet military writings.[45] Rather, the Soviet concern in the presence of conflict is the "fear of loss of control" over military events and forces.[46] Both sides are concerned about "destabilization"; however, to the Americans this term implies an escalation in power, while to the Soviets it means losing control over your forces.

Another difference in the two countries' views of the likelihood of nuclear war is reflected in their differing views of civil defense. Civil defense is a major part of the Soviets' overall posture. They spend about $4 billion dollars a year hardening factories and command centers and building fallout shelters. The peacetime civil defense program of the Soviet Union involves more than 100,000 full-time military and civilian personnel, and over 16 million part-time personnel.[47] Every Soviet factory, collective farm, and institution has an obligatory civil defense training program.[48] This is a critical "socializing" experience, and also "a constant reminder of the ever-present military threat to the Soviet Union."[49] Such citizen involvement helps the Soviet leaders to justify the allocation of a very large share of the gross national product to defense.

Any attempt to compare the American and Soviet defense budgets— either on an absolute basis or as shares of GNP—must be regarded skeptically. Ruble-to-dollar conversions are inherently tricky, as are any comparisons between command and market economies. In addition, such bilateral economic comparisons overlook the Western European contributors to NATO. Finally, simple tallies of manpower and weapons ignore the superpowers' markedly different security challenges—Moscow must be concerned (for different reasons) about Western Europe, Eastern Europe, and China as well as about the United States. Still, such gross comparisons do provide important insights. At the aggregate level, the Soviet Union spends slightly more money on defense than the United States. However, since the United States' GNP is approximately twice as large, U.S. military spending is about 6 percent of the U.S. GNP, compared with 12–15 percent for the Soviet Union. Therefore, the Soviets' expenditures come at a far greater cost to their economy. In fact, while in the United States the share of the GNP allocated to defense has been declining quite consistently since 1953 (when it was about 12 percent), in the Soviet Union the percentage has increased (from about 10 percent in 1960 to about 14 percent by the mid-1970s).[50]

Additionally, even though the total expenditures for defense are approximately equal in the two countries, the Soviets have dramatically lower manpower costs (they have a draft, and labor in the Soviet Union is relatively cheap). Thus, Moscow can spend from 50 to 90 percent more each year on equipment than the United States (figure 3.1).[51] Even when the large GNPs of the European members of NATO and Japan

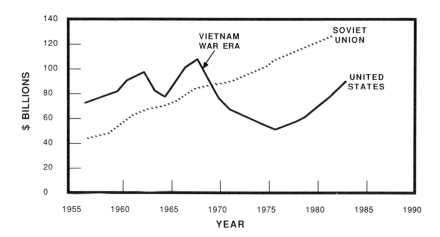

Figure 3.1
Military investment expenditures, in fiscal-1985 constant dollars. (Investment includes procurement, military construction, and research and development. The total for the Soviet Union is an estimate of what it would cost the United States to duplicate the Soviet investment.)

are included on the Western side and the Eastern European members of the Warsaw Pact are included on the Soviet side, the overall investment remains significantly higher for the Warsaw Pact than for the United States and its allies. Clearly, over time, the cumulative difference between these annual investments makes available an enormous amount of additional money for the buying of weapon systems in the Soviet bloc. For example, the difference in the two investment curves between 1970 and 1985 is $500 billion.[52]

As can also be seen from figure 3.1, the Soviets enjoy another very significant advantage: the stability of their budgets. It appears that, year in and year out, the Soviet Union's defense expenditures rose at a rate of about 4 percent annually, in real terms. Eventually, economic difficulties may require a reduction in this growth rate; but it is clear from historical trends that the Soviets will make every effort to maintain it—if for no other reason than because it is built into their planned economy and their industrial structure.

The United States does not need to spend more money for defense just because the Soviet Union does. However, the Soviet Union's continuous buildup of more and better military equipment has had a meaningful effect on the military balance, and for this reason the United States must counter it in order to maintain the relative strengths. Moreover, the Soviet Union's failure to reciprocate the United States' "unilateral disarmament" in conventional forces during the post-Vietnam period (see figure 3.1) indicates that this is not a solution to the United States' defense-spending quandary.

To understand the imbalance in conventional forces— particularly in Europe—one must recognize that the overall numbers of uniformed military personnel are approximately equal—NATO has 5,345,000 and the Warsaw Pact has 4,820,000.[53] Of the NATO forces, the United States provides slightly over 2 million (38 percent); the Soviet Union provides about 3.7 million (77 percent) of the Warsaw Pact forces. A closer look at this manpower comparison usually tends to favor the "quality" of NATO forces, since they generally have better training, leadership, and morale.[54] However, these advantages are somewhat offset by the Soviets' apparently higher ratio of fighting forces to support forces. Furthermore, the various NATO countries have had great difficulty coordinating their military plans.

The latter is obviously not the case in the Eastern bloc, where the Soviet Union exercises strong authority over its "allies." NATO military officials have been trying for years to improve the communications and the coordination of the Western allies' armies and air forces, each of which has different models of tanks, artillery, and aircraft. In fact, war games have revealed that up to half of NATO's aircraft could be shot down by NATO troops. Radio communication is frequently incompatible, and there is no standard "identification of friend or foe" system, so each NATO country would have to either hold its fire or run the high risk of shooting down its allies. Similarly, on the logistics side, different nations use different guns and ammunition. Nor can American fighter planes be refueled on European airfields, because of different fuel nozzles.[55] Clearly this matter requires urgent attention, but to date nationalistic feelings have overridden the obvious need for coordinated military planning.

But the principal military differences between the Warsaw Pact and NATO lie in the area of weapons. Because of the United States' technological superiority, if the existing quantities of weapons and the current rates of production were relatively comparable the NATO allies would have clear superiority. Unfortunately, this is far from the case.

In general, the Soviets have about three times as much military equipment fielded and are producing new weapon systems at approximately three times the rate—as can be seen from figures 3.2 and 3.3. (Figure 3.3 also shows very clearly the significant contribution made by the non-U.S. NATO countries to the overall force balance.)

A commonly heard argument in the United States is that "of course the Russians have more equipment, but ours are better so we will still win." This was true up until the 1980s; however, most knowledgeable people believe that this is no longer the case and that, at best, the overall forces are in balance. In most cases (e.g., land and air forces in Europe), the Soviets' superior quantities of weapons, combined with their growing quality (Soviet weapons are now often comparable, or even superior, to American weapons), will clearly dominate any conflict, and will force the United States to escalate to nuclear warfare.

This imbalance in equipment is a major force behind the United States' high defense expenditures during peacetime.

The Rationale for Large Peacetime Expenditures

One of the most difficult challenges for the Department of Defense, since the Korean War, has been presenting the rationale for the hundreds of billions of dollars of annual expenditures in peacetime. At the end of the trillion-dollar Reagan buildup, the press, the Congress, and the public constantly cried out, "With all the money you have received, how can you still need $300 billion a year?"

History has shown that democracies generally seem to believe that peacetime defense-budget requests are inflated, and that they traditionally underfund defense for that reason. The skepticism is, no doubt, warranted. However, we are living in a "peaceful" era that is unprecedented in terms of worldwide armaments and the potential for destruction. The reality is that, without major changes (such as dramatic conventional-arms-reduction agreements or the development of new technology that would lead to a complete restructuring of our conventional forces), we are required either to increase our annual defense expenditures, just to stay constant in our force capability, or to reduce our worldwide global commitments (or at least, our physical presence in Europe, in Korea, and elsewhere).

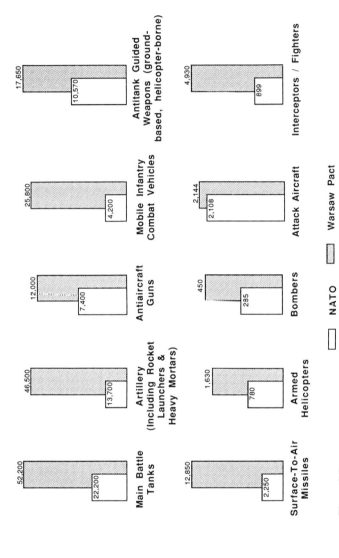

Figure 3.2
Equipment deployed by NATO and the Warsaw Pact countries (ground and air forces from the Atlantic Ocean to the Ural Mountains). The NATO numbers shown here include French and Spanish forces, even though they are not part of NATO's integrated military command, because they are deployed in the region. The Air Forces shown here exclude Naval air forces and bombers assigned to the strategic nuclear forces. The data come from the independent International Institute for Strategic Studies in London, and were presented in the *Washington Post* on December 5, 1987.

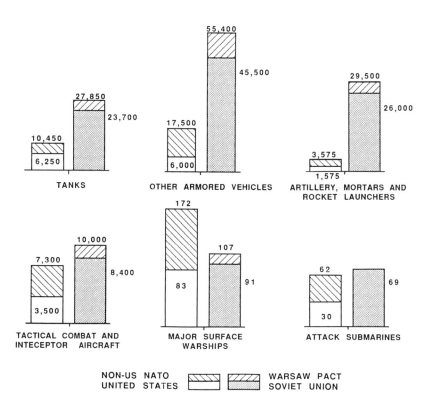

Figure 3.3
Production of selected weapons, 1974–1983. Source: Report of the Secretary of Defense
to the Congress for FY 85 (summarized in "Defense 84" [Washington, D.C., March
1984], page 5).

To understand this, consider four short-term military needs[56]:

- The United States must spend more on the day-to-day operation and maintenance of its forces and equipment simply to "stand still." For example, we must pay for increasing labor costs, and items that age or are lost through accidents and other forms of peacetime attrition and must be replaced.
- Equipment that the United States allowed to deteriorate badly after the Vietnam war must be replaced. Between 1969 and 1975 the defense budget's procurement account plummeted from $44 billion to $17 billion (in real dollars). Normal depreciation and attrition losses were not replaced, equipment aged rapidly, and inventories of munitions and spare parts were used up (and even the Reagan buildup did not replace these losses).
- The United States must continuously improve both the quantity and the quality of its forces in order to maintain its military position relative to the Soviet Union. This should be seen not as a matter of "chasing the Russians" but as a response to a Soviet buildup so massive and sustained that it really does affect the military balance.
- Changes in policy or technology may require changes in defense expenditures. For example, on one hand the capability to deploy forces rapidly in the Persian Gulf or to wage a conventional war well enough to reduce the need to rely on nuclear options can only be attained through increased spending; on the other hand, some forms of arms control and/or some reductions in national-security commitments could allow reductions in spending that would balance those demands. And a technological breakthrough by either side could require a dramatic shift in resources in order to develop the new systems, while the more conventional equipment would have to be maintained during the transition. For example, a breakthrough in armor-piercing munitions would require a whole new generation of tanks and other armored vehicles.

This four-part scheme of defense resource demands is only one way to view the Department of Defense's budget. The official DoD classification sets up four different funding categories: "readiness" (training, spare parts, bullets), "force structure" (the size of the armed forces), "modernization of equipment" (from initial planning and research through production of tactical and strategic systems), and "sustainability" (stockpiling reserves of equipment and improving the responsiveness of the defense industrial base to the demands posed by lengthy conflicts). This methodology allows Pentagon planners to "trade off" annual resources between maintaining the forces at high readiness levels (for immediate conflicts) and upgrading the equipment (for future conflicts). Similarly, it allows tradeoffs in manpower between a smaller force (which would be available immediately) and a larger force with more reservists (which would require a considerable warning time in order to achieve a high level of readiness). It also allows military planners to make tradeoffs between being prepared for "short wars" (through high levels of readiness and deployed forces) and stockpiling munitions, spare parts, and other expendable items that would be needed for longer conflicts.

Obviously, there are a wide variety of ways to look at how the annual budget for military forces should be distributed in peacetime. And it is equally clear that the various approaches overlap significantly, and that they address essentially the same issues. The straightforward approach discussed below focuses on the three major elements of the first methodology—i.e., maintaining the current forces and equipment, making up for the poor maintenance of equipment and inventories during the post-Vietnam period, and improving the American forces as the Soviets continue to build up theirs.[57] This approach provides a simple demonstration of the incremental resource needs, based on the current defense posture. Subsequently, we will look at the potential long-term implications of either increasing or decreasing these budget demands as a result of changes in policy or technology.

Beginning with the issue of the increasing costs of simply maintaining the current forces, and ignoring the Soviet buildup, let us consider the example of fighter aircraft. The United States deploys approximately 6,000 first-line fighters around the world. For military purposes, each lasts about 15 years. Thus, on average, about 400 will wear out and need to be replaced each year (irrespective of obsolescence.) However, during the 1970s and the 1980s, the United States bought only around 300 fighter planes per year. The resulting shortage of 100 airplanes a year drove up the average age of the force. (For example, by 1988, the 200 oldest A-7 attack aircraft were 22 years old, and all 140 of the remaining F-106 fighters were 31 years old.) The problem was even worse in the Navy. The average age of the active ships was going up almost year by year, since the replacement rate was extremely low before the Reagan buildup. In 1980, the average age of aircraft carriers was 20 years, that of destroyers was 13 years, that of nuclear-powered attack submarines was 11 years, and that of mine-warfare ships was 26 years. (The age of the minesweepers was highlighted when they were needed in the 1987 Persian Gulf crisis). The Congressional Budget Office has estimated the value of the U.S. stock of military equipment to be $800 billion (in 1986 dollars). Even if this equipment has an average life of 15 years (longer than those of many commercial "durable goods," such as autos), more than $50 billion of new procurement would be needed each year just to maintain the forces at their original level of military capability.[58] In the post-Vietnam period, these levels were not even nearly maintained; thus, the force continued to age. Even in a high-budget year (such as 1984) the Bureau of Economic Analysis estimated that only about 5 percent of the defense capital stock (valued at about $36 billion) was retired. Thus, the defense budget was falling short of even "rolling over" the inventory by $14 billion per year— ignoring any modernization of forces.[59]

Unfortunately, simply attempting to maintain a constant level of equipment in storage is insufficient. It is necessary to use equipment for training during peacetime, in order for the military forces to maintain their fighting proficiency. For example, during a typical peacetime year, military aviators fly over 7 million hours,[60] and even with improving aircraft safety and maintenance there are still a significant number of aircraft lost each year because of malfunctions and crashes. In 1987, the following losses occurred: ten A-6 attack jets, eight F/A-18 aircraft, eight F-14 fighters, twelve F-16 fighters, one B-1B bomber, ten F-4 fighters, three F-15 fighters, three F-111 bombers, nine UH-1 helicopters, eight UH-60 helicopters, four AH-1 gunships, and four AH-64 gunships.[61] In a typical year, "aviation mishaps" claim from around 160–190 planes and helicopters.[62] The cost of simply repairing or replacing lost equipment—much of which is quite old and therefore not likely to be replaced in kind—runs into the billions of dollars. (One B-1B is over $200 million, eight F-14s are around $250 million, three F-15s over $100 million, and so on.)

In addition to the replacements required for U.S. losses or wearout of inventory, the United States often sells or gives a good deal of its existing equipment to its allies. For example, when Israel lost a large share of its tanks in the 1973 Arab-Israeli war (while the Arabs still had a significant number left), the United States supplied Israel with some tanks that had been deployed in Western Europe. Thus, there was an urgent need to replace the U.S. tanks, and the tank budget was increased significantly.

To replace aging inventories, peacetime losses, and the equipment sold or given to allies, the Department of Defense must either purchase old systems—as item-for-item replacements—or buy new, improved systems. The DoD has chosen to buy the more modern systems, in order to match continued Soviet advancements. Because the generation-to-generation increase in the cost of weapon systems has been consistently rising by 5–7 percent per year (excluding the effects of inflation and the annual variations in the number of weapons purchased), by the end of a 15-year period a 6 percent annual increase in performance-related costs would more than double the procurement funds required to buy the same number of weapons. The $50 billion per year that would be required just to replace the old designs with newer ones (ignoring peacetime losses and sales or gifts to allies) would grow to about $100 billion per year.

Other accounts in the defense budget continue to rise as well. For example, one Act of Congress requires continued growth in retirement pay (which rose from $3.9 billion in 1972 to $14.9 billion in 1982—a 60 percent real increase); salaries for military and civilian Pentagon employees must rise to remain competitive with the earnings of non-defense workers; and the fuel costs rose dramatically during the 1970s and the early 1980s, and by 1983 consumed more than $10 billion of Pentagon funds each year. These non-weapon accounts (including other operation and maintenance costs, such as spare parts) have been rising at about 3 percent per year (without considering the effects of inflation) and together now represent about half of the defense budget. These are not easy costs to eliminate, since they represent such essential items as overhauls of major weapon systems (to avoid the need for replacement). Each year the DoD overhauls 60–70 ships, almost 5,000 aircraft, and about 3,500 combat vehicles. The annual value of depot maintenance alone is approximately $11 billion. Additionally, the annual supply of spare parts costs around $55 billion, and the transportation of military personal property and cargo has an annual cost of around $11 billion.[63] And with the high costs of operating certain equipment (a B-1B bomber cost a staggering $21,000 per flying hour[64]), training hours have been cut in order to keep costs down. Yet, in spite of the reduced operation time, the DoD's budgets for operations and maintenance have been unable to keep up with the growing costs. Congress traditionally under-funds this need, since (unlike weapon systems) it is not directly trace-able to expenditures in a given congressional district.[65]

From the above discussion, it is clear that the overall defense budget must grow at about 5 percent per year (in non-inflated dollars) just to purchase the same amount of capability as was provided in the previous year. The problem has been that such budget growth has not been maintained. Thus, the force levels have gone down and the equipment has been aging at a relatively high rate. Particularly critical to this problem were the years immediately following the Vietnam conflict, when defense budgets fell especially sharply and planners were forced to draw from the dollars available to finance legally required pay raises and unavoidable operations costs.[66] Thus, the needed spare parts and munitions stockpiles were not replaced (a common reaction during periods of defense funding reductions). For example, by 1980, spare parts funding for Air Force airplanes had fallen to only 24 percent of the requirement.[67] In fact, one Air Force officer wrote that even in the high-budget year of 1987 there was "no money available for funding spare parts that would be required for combat sustainability" and noted that "we don't have enough force structure to get through D-Day plus two or three."[68] This was confirmed by an earlier House Appropriations Subcommittee report on defense. The Air Force is so short of parts that F-16 squadrons are assigned extra fighter-bombers (at a cost of $24 million each) solely for the purpose of cannibalizing their equipment.[69] As Secretary Weinberger noted at the time, "We have a long way to go because we had a long period of neglect in the 1970s."[70] Similar prob-lems existed in the munitions area; bullets and bombs used in Vietnam were not replaced. In a 1984 military exercise run by the Joint Chiefs of Staff, it was found that "stocks of conventional munitions were well below the minimum acceptable for even a small war, and a war in Europe would cause still more problems."[71] Similarly, the House Ap-propriations Subcommittee found in 1982 that the Army "does not have the men and material to sustain combat operations in a major contin-gency and the Navy could not sustain full combat operations for more than a week."[72] Even in 1987—after the Reagan buildup—Congressman Jim Courter wrote: ". . . the United States has only three to four weeks worth of munitions at best, and in some categories there are far less . . . nor can our forces rely upon Europe; some of our NATO allies literally have only a few days supply of common munitions."[73] The problem is actually even worse in the area of sophisticated missiles, such as anti-aircraft and anti-tank missiles (which would be used in considerable volume during a conflict). The higher costs of the missiles significantly reduces the number purchased; for example, the Air Force and the Navy have enough air-to-air missiles for only a day or two of intense fighting.[74] Yet, as was demonstrated in the Arab-Israeli wars and in the Falklands, these weapons are extremely effective and can make a dramatic difference in the outcome of a conflict. And, because of the high cost of missiles and the fact that the stockpiles are low, pilots are unable to get the "feel" of these weapons during peacetime. As George Wilson wrote, "an Air Force pilot often goes through his whole fighter plane career without firing a real missile, while his Navy counterpart fires one every two years."[75]

The United States clearly has very real problems with the "readiness" and the "sustainability" of its forces for extended conflicts. In both cases, there is a need for significant increases in peacetime expenditures. The cost of readiness could range in the tens of billions of dollars, and the cost of sustainability could run into the hundreds of billions. Since it will take the defense industry years to build up its production of equipment, the United States cannot afford to wait for the initiation of a conflict to increase the expenditures in these areas.

The Soviet Union faces the same financial dilemma. However, while the United States has chosen (in peacetime) to underfund equipment procurement, the Soviet Union has continued to spend an increasing share of its resources on building up both the quantity and the quality of its forces. As the Warsaw Pact countries phase in new anti-aircraft missiles and improved aircraft, the United States is forced to modernize its equipment. For example, the Army is buying 7,000 of the new Bradley Infantry Fighting Vehicles at about $2 million each, in comparison with $80,000 each for the older M-113; the Navy is buying over 1,000 F/A-18 fighter/attack aircraft, at approximately $30 million each, to replace the latest versions of the A-7, which costs approximately $10 million each; and the Air Force is buying large quantities of the radar-guided Sparrow III missile, at around $169,000 each, to replace the infrared-guided Sidewinder, which cost approximately $59,000 each.[76] Clearly, with such increases in unit costs the United States is going to buy fewer and fewer units of each system. Yet the Soviet Union's production of new weapons far outpaces that of the United States and the NATO allies. (For example, the annual tank production of the Soviet Union exceeds that of the United States by three to one and that of NATO as a whole by two to one, and the ratios are similar in most other categories.) The historical solution to this dilemma has been that the United States has resolved that it would resort to first use of nuclear weapons. As the credibility of that option disappears, the United States must look elsewhere for solutions.

Unfortunately, the world has become increasingly insecure. In the long run, we might look to conventional-arms agreements and/or to dramatic technological breakthroughs as a way out of the dilemma. However, in the short run there is no "easy way out." To handle conflicts such as those that are appearing with increasing intensity in the Third World, or even to address increasing terrorist actions, the United States must increase, rather than reduce, its "peacetime" expenditures. A typical example was the need for significantly increased Naval expenditures in 1987, when the United States decided to escort oil tankers in the Persian Gulf. When the Reagan administration decided to press for the Strategic Defense Initiative, it became an "add on" to the budget and did not, in any way, relieve the need for any of the above-noted "peacetime" expenditures (since SDI was conceived of as not even being deployed for 20 years); since defense dollars were shrinking at the time, this really meant that the DoD was going to be able to do less to maintain its relative military effectiveness in all four of the above-mentioned areas (readiness, modernization, force structure, and sustainability).

Each of the ways out of the continuing need for extremely high and increasing expenditures for defense will be very difficult to achieve. Yet something must be done. Some of the options are mutual arms reductions, changes in the U.S. national-security posture, and changes in the designs of weapon systems. Perhaps some combination of these options will be necessary.

Strategy under Resource Constraints

One of the critical issues the United States will face in the coming decades is the lack of a credible national-security paradigm covering strategic warfare, Central European conflicts, and regional conflicts. Another concern is the lack of a strong relationship between our arms-control policies and our national-security strategies.

A credible national-security posture cannot be developed without a realistic recognition of the fiscal constraints. Even with defense budgets in the range of $300 billion a year, there are not enough funds to address the perceived quantitative imbalance between U.S. and Soviet forces, or even to buy and support the new weapons already slated for development and production. Early in the Reagan administration, Under Secretary of Defense Fred Iklé stated that "even an increase in U.S. military investments as high as 14 percent per year (in real terms) continued for a decade would not close the gap in accumulated military assets between the United States and the Soviet Union. . . . thus there is a need for a defense increase considerably steeper than that which the administration now proposes."[77] Similarly, an Air Force study done at about the same time stated that "even if Congress does not cut the Reagan administration's planned military budgets in the next five years, there will not be enough money to buy the planes, missiles, and other Air Force equipment contemplated in the administration's five-year military plan."[78]

Realism—or at least prioritization—must be introduced both to the defense budget and to the mission of national security. The problem is compounded by the fact that many of the suggested changes (described below) would, at first, require the spending of more money rather than less. Those who argue for a reduction in the United States' dependence on nuclear weapons must recognize that it means an increase in expenditures for general-purpose forces—and at least 75 percent of the defense budget already goes for "conventional" forces and their support.[79]

Most politicians tend to look for simplistic solutions. National debates are held over whether the defense budget should increase by X percent per year or by Y percent, or whether it should be a fixed share of the Gross National Product, or over whether the United States' force planning should mirror that of the Soviet Union, or over some nice round number (such as a "600-ship Navy"). These solutions are very

poor substitutes for in-depth analysis on a mission-by-mission and pro-
gram-by-program basis.

Compromises will be required in evolving a balanced yet affordable
national-security posture. It is fiscally irresponsible for the United
States—as it did in the early 1980s—to simultaneously develop ten new
types of delivery systems capable of reaching the Soviet Union: three
cruise missiles (ground-launched, air-launched, and submarine-
launched), the Pershing II intermediate-range ballistic missile, two
ground-launched intercontinental ballistic missiles (the MX and the
Midgetman), a new submarine-launched missile (the Trident II), and
two intercontinental bombers (the B-1 and the Stealth).[80] Naturally, the
choice of a military strategy will influence decisions about the appropriateness of various systems. (For example, of the above-mentioned
missiles, the Midgetman and the Trident II may be the most invulnerable and therefore the most appropriate for a second-strike capability,
whereas the MX and the Pershing II may be the most appropriate for a
first-strike capability.)

Steps must be taken to close the gap between an unlimited foreign-
policy posture and a limited set of resources. Nine specific steps that
have been proposed are the following: (1) Introduce greater realism and
balance into the planning of the national-security mission. (2) Integrate
arms-control actions with the national-security strategy. (3) Improve
the integration of the U.S. defense posture with those of our allies. (4)
Get our allies to pick up a larger share of the mutual defense costs. (5)
Reduce the permanent deployments of U.S. forces and shift to a more
mobile force structure. (6) Place greater reliance on the use of reserve
forces and on industrial mobilization. (7) Take far greater advantage of
the improvements in military capability and in tactics offered by advanced technologies. (8) Integrate the planning and the war-fighting
capabilities of the various armed services. (9) Stress, in the design of
conventional weapon systems, the importance of increased quantities
and ease of operations and maintenance. Obviously these are not the
only possibilities, nor are they intended to be mutually exclusive. They
serve to highlight some of the important considerations in evolving new
defense strategies under resource constraints. Thus, it is appropriate to
consider each of these measures in more detail.

Introducing greater realism to national-security planning raises two questions: What wars do we plan for? How many dollars do we assume are available for these plans? These two questions must be addressed together, rather than independently (as has often been done[81]).

The strategy of the 1950s and the 1960s was supposed to enable the United States to fight "two and a half wars" simultaneously (one in Europe, one in Asia, and a contingency someplace else). In the 1970s this was scaled down to a more realistic "one-and-a-half-war" scenario. In the 1980s, Secretary Weinberger saw these formulations as "unrealistic" and stated that the United States needed mobile, flexible forces that could fight any place they might be needed.[82] Moving away from the old concept of sizing America's armed forces on the basis of a number of "simultaneous wars" undoubtedly made sense; however, the new formula, with no bounds at all, establishes essentially unlimited goals all over the world, and no realistic amount of money will be able to satisfy these objectives. As Frederick the Great warned, "He who attempts to defend too much defends nothing."

It has always been difficult for the United States to establish an effective, rational, and consistent foreign policy. As Walter Lippmann noted, "the tendency of Americans has been to be extremely pragmatic in our domestic affairs, but idealistic—to excess—in our foreign affairs."[83] Lippmann went on to note that the American penchant for idealism in the practice of foreign affairs often obscures the link between foreign policy and national security and, indeed, often goes so far as to make foreign policy appear to be independent of *any* concept of national security. Thus, it may be difficult for the United States to establish a more realistic, or more clearly defined, set of foreign-policy objectives—and yet this is essential if we are to establish a force structure and a set of weapons based upon "national-security requirements." It is clear that strategic deterrence must be maintained and that Europe and Japan must be kept free and allied with the United States; however, to go beyond such generalities and to define a policy (or a set of priorities) that specifically relates to force structure, weapon selection, and defense budgets is the challenge for those who will have to develop a credible national-security posture for the future.

The dilemma is equally challenging from the budget side. Figure 3.4 summarizes the 1986 debate over five-year defense budgets and broadly highlights the four options that were available. The first option—the

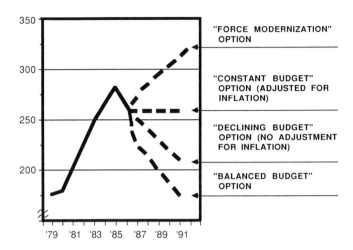

Figure 3.4
Military-spending options for the period 1987–1991, in billions of constant 1986 dollars.
Source: Committee for National Security, "Defense Choices: Greater Security With
Fewer Dollars," *Washington Post*, February 26, 1987. (These numbers do not include
retirement pay for military personnel.)

Reagan administration's proposal for modernization of the forces—
required a modest buildup that would have continued the budget increases that had taken place in the period 1981–1985. The second option, referred to as the "constant budget," would have allowed for the
effects of inflation but otherwise would have kept the 1986 budget level
constant for the subsequent five years. The third option, referred to as
the "declining budget," would have kept the expenditure level the same
as in 1986 but would not have adjusted for inflation and would thus have
resulted in a decline of approximately 3 percent per year. The fourth
proposed option matched the Gramm-Rudman-Hollings "balanced budget" requirement and thus would have effectively brought the defense
budget down, over the five-year period, to the level found at the beginning of the Reagan administration. The issue here is not which of these
four budget options is the "right one" but the enormous difference
among the potential results of the four options in terms of equipment
and force structure. By the end of the five-year period, there is a $150
billion annual difference (or a total "swing," over the five-year period,
of approximately $500 billion) among the four options. Such a large

annual uncertainty (up to 50 percent) precludes an efficient or effective weapons-acquisition program and a credible national-security posture. It is not the number of dollars that causes the problem; it is the large annual uncertainty. Once we pick a multi-year budget plan and stick to it, efficiency and credibility may follow. The United States cannot afford to have this degree of uncertainty in its long-term budget planning, or in the credibility of its national-security posture to its allies and its foes.

The advocates of the second of the broad policy options, *greater integration of arms control into our national-security posture,* frequently point out that without the 1972 ABM (anti-ballistic missile) treaty deployments of such systems would undoubtedly have expanded on both sides—producing significantly more pressure for the development of more and better offensive strategic weapons[84] (for example, maneuverable reentry vehicles and far greater quantities of warheads). In the same vein, many argue that it is necessary for the United States and the Soviet Union to reach clear, verifiable agreements on chemical and biological weapons, in order to prevent rather significant increases in investments related to these (particularly by the United States).[85] Such agreements could eliminate not only the expenditures on the weapons themselves, but also the expenditures required to make existing tanks, armored vehicles, and helicopters operable in the presence of chemical and biological agents.

Unfortunately, few arms-control agreements permit reductions in the overall defense budget. For example, when the 1988 agreement to eliminate intermediate-range missiles from Europe was reached, there was an immediate recognition—both in the United States and in Europe—that the conventional-weapons capabilities of the NATO forces would have to be increased. On the other hand, the agreement also forced an increased emphasis on attempting to negotiate reductions in conventional arms. The potential payoff of dramatic reductions in conventional arms is tremendous; however, they will be extremely difficult to achieve,[86] because we are basically asking the Soviets to help NATO by dramatically reducing the asymmetry in conventional forces in Europe.

Large-scale conflicts in Central Europe must be a high priority in any discussion of potential changes in force structure or in strategy, since a major share of the United States' defense resources is devoted to that region. One of the most obvious objectives should be to *have the United States and its NATO allies do far more integrated planning.* It is a well-known concern of both American and European leaders that NATO seems to have a huge amount of institutional inertia—much of it political in origin—against agreeing on more efficient ways of designing and distributing equipment, manpower, and tactics. Priority must be given to the interoperability of forces and equipment, and changes in the procedures for planning, training, operations, command, and support must be addressed.[87]

The interdependence of the NATO countries presents a dilemma for the United States. American political and military leaders have a great deal of difficulty accepting the fact that the United States is not, by itself, militarily superior to the Soviet Union, and must rely on alliances. Thus, in a sense, the defense expenditures of our allies determine the effectiveness of our security posture. Therefore, *if the conventional forces in Europe are to be strengthened, some of the funding must come from increased expenditures on the part of the European allies.* There should also be a far more effective use of the expenditures of both the United States and its allies.

A common cry heard today in the United States is for the allies to pay a larger share of the mutual defense costs. This is often referred to as "burden sharing." However, the Europeans argue that the United States naturally spends more of its gross national product on defense (table 3.1), because it has far broader global commitments.[88] Additionally, the Europeans often note that, of the forces deployed in Western Europe, the allies provide 90 percent of the manpower, 85 percent of the tanks, 95 percent of the artillery, and 80 percent of the combat aircraft.[89] Nonetheless, it is clear that the United States spends a far larger share of its GNP on defense than its NATO allies, and the resentment is particularly great with regard to West Germany and Japan (in view of their strong economies, and the fact that they are economic competitors of the United States).

A coordinated force is likely to be called upon, in coming years, to protect Western interests in the developing world (e.g., in the Far East

Table 3.1
Defense spending as a percentage of GNP (1986).

United States	6.6
Britain	5.0
France	4.0
Netherlands	3.1
Norway	3.2
West Germany	3.1
Italy	2.7
Belgium	3.0
Denmark	2.2
Japan	1.0

Source: "World Military Expenditures and Arms Transfers" (ACDA, 1988).

or in the Persian Gulf). This burden has been shouldered virtually alone by the United States since World War II.[90] A deployment of forces from West Germany and/or Japan, as well as other parts of the world, will naturally receive some adverse reactions, both from the West and from the Communist countries, but it is highly likely that one will be required—for both political and military reasons.

A more active role for the United States' allies could result in *a reduced permanent deployment of American troops around the world and a shift in the U.S. posture toward a more mobile force.* The United States has occasionally threatened to withdraw some of its troops from Europe as a way to get the European allies to focus on the need for their increased participation in defense. In 1984, Senator Sam Nunn— a stalwart supporter of NATO and, especially, its conventional defense—introduced an amendment to cut the number of U.S. troops in Europe. Although it was defeated by a vote of 55 to 41, the allies took the amendment quite seriously and made a decision to give high priority to items such as aircraft shelters and ammunition (which were high on Senator Nunn's list of NATO's deficiencies).[91]

Although the United States has bases and troops in 19 countries, most of the troops overseas are in West Germany (250,000), Japan (50,000), South Korea (43,000), and Britain (29,000).[92] Though these numbers may come down, it is clear that (perhaps more out of political considerations than out of military necessity) we will maintain a strong presence in each of these countries for some time. Yet the United States clearly needs to increase the mobility of its forces in order to cover its wide variety of military requirements with a limited (perhaps shrinking) number of troops.

With a fixed total number of dollars available, transportation investments are going to be made at the expense of combat equipment; for example, the Air Force will have to pay for transport aircraft instead of some additional bombers or fighters, the Navy for freighters and escort ships rather than force-projection systems, and the Army for lighter equipment rather than heavy tanks and artillery.

In the early 1980s, the Army began experimenting with the concept of a "light" infantry division that could be more easily airlifted but would still have the firepower and mobility to deal with even the largest of the Soviet tank divisions.[93] The Army would have to stock full sets of weapon systems and support equipment and large stocks of munitions in areas likely to see conflict, such as West Germany. Troops would be rapidly flown to these areas, draw the stored equipment out, and move to the front before an attack. It would obviously require a significant airlift capability to be able to move these troops in a timely fashion (defined as between ten days and several months).[94] Traditionally, mobility has received inadequate funding from the services, and the dollars required have had to be "taken out of their hide" by senior civilians in the Office of the Secretary of Defense.

A further step that goes along with a reduction in permanent troop deployment and a shift to a more mobile force is a *greater reliance on the reserves and on industrial mobilization*. Though less expensive than standing forces, this has the very distinct disadvantage that it requires a reliance on political (as distinguished from strategic or tactical) warning and the ability to act on that warning. It is not at all a bad assumption that there would be signs, perhaps over extended periods of time, of any aggressive Soviet policy or buildup of forces. Historically, there has been adequate time to begin industrial mobilization and, particularly, to call up and deploy reserve forces. This is still likely to be the case in the future. The very large unknown is whether the United States and its allies could muster the consensus and the political will. Ways to exploit "warning" and gain valuable time without forcing political leaders into difficult and destabilizing decisions must be developed.

In the past, the United States has relied on the use of warning signals primarily to heighten the readiness of its existing forces. A shift toward greater dependence on mobilization and reserves would mean the introduction of various levels of preparedness of the industrial base as well as of the reserve forces. Throughout its history, the United States has always been able to call up its reserve forces much more rapidly than it has been able to equip them. This problem has gotten worse, because the increasing sophistication of the equipment has led to longer production lead times. It is, therefore, logical that in the late 1980s the United States moved to a system of industrial warning conditions (referred to as Incons).[95] This concept, which makes it possible to "turn on" the defense industry to various levels of responsiveness as a function of world conditions, is considered far less destabilizing than calling up the forces. For example, if it were to be considered likely that a conventional-warfare conflict would take place over the coming months, plans could be implemented to rapidly build "expendable" tactical missiles, which would not have the long shelf life of peacetime equipment but which could be produced rapidly from previously established designs.[96] In order to present a credible deterrent with such a policy, the United States must demonstrate its capacity for industrial surge, and must call up its reserves, relatively frequently and visibly—as Norway and Switzerland do. And to make credible the threat to act on warning, political leaders must be involved in these exercises.

If defense budgets are reduced and/or if equipment and labor costs continue to rise, only smaller quantities of equipment will be affordable and the United States will be faced with one of two choices: either to have a smaller force level, complemented by a shift to greater mobility and greater dependence on the reserve forces, or to have a "hollow" force structure. In the latter case, the military attempts to maintain the overall force structure by greatly reducing the readiness and the sustainability of the forces, with the obvious "hope" that somehow, in future years, money will become available to buy the spare parts, munitions, missiles, and whatever else is needed to raise the levels of readiness and sustainability. The United States began to tend toward a hollow force structure in the mid-1970s, and there was some concern about this happening again in the mid-1980s.[97]

Cutting back on force levels, reducing permanent deployments, and shifting to a more mobile force (with greater dependence on the reserves and on mobilization of industry) is a very difficult choice to make, particularly for military leaders, because it represents a clear dependence on political leaders' willingness to take specific actions based on warning—something they have historically been reluctant to do.

The seventh of the possible broad strategies aimed at significantly increasing force effectiveness under resource constraints involves *taking greater advantage of new military capabilities and improved tactics offered by advanced technologies.* As Senator Sam Nunn has stated,

We now have at hand new conventional technologies capable of destroying the momentum of a Soviet invasion by means of isolating the first echelon of attacking forces from reinforcing follow-on echelons. These technologies . . . capitalize on three major advances. The first is the substantially improved lethality of improved conventional munitions. The second is the growing capability of microelectronics to enhance the rapid collection, processing, distribution, and ability to act upon information about the size, character, location, and movement of enemy troops. . . . The third is improved ability to move and target quickly large quantities of improved conventional firepower against enemy force concentrations.[98]

In the armed services, there is considerable resistance to these new technologies because they affect the various services' traditional roles, missions, and ways of fighting. For example, in the event of a Soviet invasion of Germany, rather than rely primarily on the Army to destroy the enemy's weapons, it might be far better to attack the thousand or so choke points in the network supporting the invasion (road junctions, bridges, air fields, and the like).[99] With the choke points closed off, the aggressor can't support or reinforce his initial forces. Since these choke points are basically all fixed sites, they can be most easily attacked with inexpensive, "stealthy" drones. These remotely piloted aircraft would be much less expensive and much less vulnerable to defensive systems than manned bombers such as the B-1 or the B-2 ("Stealth"), which cost around $200 million and $400 million respectively. Real-time reconnaissance can then be used to ensure that the choke points remain closed. A similar significant difference in cost would result if the Navy were to opt for the deployment of cruise missiles on existing ships (which former Chief of Naval Operations Zumwalt argued would cost about $18 billion over five years) instead of pursuing naval superiority by building new large ships (for example, Navy Secretary Lehman recommended a $50 billion investment for four new carrier battle groups).[100] Alternatively, the Navy's targets (at sea and on land) could often be attacked with ground-launched or air-launched cruise missiles, and even semi-mobile targets such as command centers could be easily targeted using satellite data (if the barrier between the traditional use of strategic reconnaissance satellites and their tactical application by the military services could be broken down).

A revolution in the guidance of weapons and in reconnaissance (both space-based and earth-based) has taken place in recent years. Future military historians may well regard the combination of precision-guided munitions and sophisticated reconnaissance capabilities as a revolution in the fighting of wars approaching in importance the nuclear-weapons revolution of 1945.[101] The newly available ability to locate and destroy targets with unprecedented precision by non-nuclear means must be fully exploited by the West.

The problem here is not one of developing new technologies but one of overcoming traditional institutional barriers to allow the application of the advanced technology, to take advantage of its potential for greatly enhancing our military capability. As the U.S. Ambassador to West Germany, Richard Burt, has stated, the problem is one of "effectively utilizing new weapons technologies, not to just perform old roles better, but to recognize that new technology permits new military tasks to be performed . . . and to understand that the implications of the new technology require . . . a change in tactics."[102]

It must be noted that the concept of using advanced technology to achieve deep attacks into enemy territory, especially when combined with the mobility tactics described above, is often resisted by many West Germans because it has the potential to turn their country into a battlefield. Their preference is for a very strong front-line defense, a war of attrition, and an early cease-fire.[103] Nonetheless, the overwhelming Soviet numbers (unless there are major conventional-arms agreements and very asymmetrical reductions) seem to offer NATO the alternative of either shifting toward advanced technology and deep-attack tactics or committing to huge increases in the defense budgets of both the United States and the European allies.

Each of the seven major changes in strategy considered so far has met with significant institutional resistance that has prevented its effective implementation. The eighth recommendation is one of those most strenuously resisted. It is that *the American military services will achieve synergism only through an integrated approach to resource planning and war-fighting,* and not through their independent capabilities.

As former Army General Bruce Palmer, Jr., has stated, "The National Security Act of 1947 created a Department of Defense . . . by creating a loose confederation of the military services, each continuing to be organized and administered under its own secretary; . . . thus the services were not integrated, but were unified only in the sense that they were placed under a single overall head."[104] Under this system, each of the services puts together its own budget and its own weapon requirements—as though they were planning on fighting separate air, land, sea, and amphibious wars rather than integrated conflicts. It is not that the need to achieve an integrated defense posture is not recognized by all of the military services; it is a question of priorities. For example, the Air Force thinks of "its" mission—deep strikes—as having a higher priority than the mission of providing close air support for the Army, and so it tends not to fund the latter adequately. Similarly, the Army is inclined to try to do "its" air-defense job by itself rather than to count on the Air Force's airborne warning and control system (AWACS) for information on enemy aircraft. Occasionally the services get together and reach an agreement on some particular combined program[105]; however, to achieve an overall optimization of defense resources, rather than a sub-optimization by each individual service, remains one of the greatest challenges for defense reformers.

The ninth point that should be considered in a resource-constrained environment is that *the "requirements process" for conventional weapon systems must be changed to place considerably more stress on the importance of increased quantities, and on ease of operations, support, and maintenance.* An overwhelming share of the total U.S. defense dollars is used for conventional forces, yet the quantities being procured are diminishing each year because of the extremely high unit costs of weapons. Additionally, a great deal of the money is going to the people and spare parts required to maintain and support these systems rather than for the weapons themselves. A report by the National Academy of Arts and Sciences summarized the situation very well:

As the United States shows a diminished capacity to invent and make use of "simple" weapon systems, particularly with regard to conventional arms, substantial military problems are created. The weapons themselves become so expensive, indeed so valuable, that their defense becomes a prime necessity; offensive systems are sacrificed to the proliferation of adequate defenses for intricate weapons too valuable to lose [e.g., the surface ships, submarines, and aircraft required to protect a modern aircraft carrier]. Also, as the systems themselves become more complex, there are growing uncertainties about the adequacy of the military forces that are expected to be able to use these sophisticated arms, as well as their ability to support and maintain them.[106]

The maintenance and support costs of complex weapons are becoming a dominant factor in modern warfare. For example, it takes around 100,000 support troops, with huge amounts of supplies (ranging from integrated circuits to toilet paper), to keep 10,000 troops fighting. To move a tank a mile takes between 3 and 10 gallons of diesel fuel; thus, to move 30,000 tanks 100 miles takes about 15 million gallons. It takes 1,700 5-ton trucks, each with a 1.5-ton trailer, to hold the fuel for one division. Another 3,000 5-ton trucks are needed to haul the ammunition; and on and on.[107] The support problem is further compounded by the maintenance problem. The equipment is not only extremely costly; it is so complex that it requires expensive and extensive maintenance and spare parts. The tradition of keeping equipment in the field approximately twice as long as it was initially planned to be kept requires still higher maintenance costs for old, worn-out equipment.[108] The obvious solution, as General Palmer says, is "to continue to develop quality weapons and equipment that can compete with those of anticipated adversaries, but at the same time stress affordability, reliability, simplicity of maintenance, and producibility as clearly equal priorities. In other words, we must produce good, serviceable weapons that we can afford to buy in the numbers needed."[109] How this can be done, without sacrificing performance, will be discussed in detail below. What is of critical importance here is the recognition that quantity *does* matter, significantly, in military results. As one writer has stated,

No important modern war has been won by the technological superiority of weapons alone. The United States won the Second World War primarily because of its material superiority, while all its technological excellence could not help it in Vietnam. . . . The outcome of wars is relatively indifferent to material technological quality. The two most important factors are non-material quality in short wars [e.g., training, manpower skills, readiness] and superior quantities in prolonged wars. The United States has neglected both of these vital factors [in recent years].[110]

Without question, any of the nine changes in strategy recommended above would be extremely difficult to implement; however, the results could be dramatic. And it appears that the United States will have to implement some or all of these recommendations if the cost of its weapons continues to rise and the resources available do not increase correspondingly.

To summarize, it seems appropriate to consider the following quotation, from a 1985 article on modernization of the Chinese Army, as it might apply to specific changes in the United States' approach to national security:

. . . Remarkably, this improvement has been achieved without an increase in defense spending, [and] without a wholesale re-equipment. . . . It has been achieved essentially by changes in the more intangible components of military power, such as greater realism and threat assessment, improved strategic doctrine, increased military professionalism, and smoother civil-military relations. In the past, it was precisely these components that had been incompatible with the needs of our modern army. . . . The fate of military reforms ultimately depends on the frame of mind of officers . . . on their readiness to break with old ways and to broaden their vision to encompass new developments. However, according to senior military leaders, many officers do not possess these attitudes. They cling to their past, obstructing reform. They have been isolated for a long time and, lacking knowledge of contemporary military developments, are content to stick to their old ways. They pay lip service to reform but fall back on conventional practice when it comes to implementation. They do not believe that new technology has greatly changed the ways of war and are unable to look into the future. . . .[111]

4 Defense Spending and the Economy

"Guns versus Butter"

"Guns versus butter" has become a dominant issue during periods of peace since the end of the Korean war.[1] Before that time, the United States maintained large standing forces only during wartime and disarmed immediately thereafter. The advent of nuclear weapons and intercontinental ballastic missiles, as well as the presence of a permanent adversary with a large and growing military, forced the United States to maintain a significant peacetime military capability, both to deter aggression and to respond rapidly to serious threats. As can be seen from the lower line in figure 4.1, annual U.S. defense expenditures (compensated for inflation) have been around $200 billion since the early 1950s. Fortunately, the healthy and growing U.S. economy could sustain these defense budgets. The share of the Gross National Product devoted to national security actually decreased from more than 12 percent in 1953 to a low of under 5 percent at the end of the 1907s, and was around 6 percent at the end of the Reagan buildup (figure 4.2). Meanwhile, non-defense federal expenditures (the upper line of figure 4.1) grew from a level roughly equal to defense spending in the 1950s to more than three times as much by the 1970s, and are still expanding. Thus, contrary to popular belief, defense is clearly no longer the dominant government expenditure. In the 1950s and the early 1960s, entitlements (Social Security, Medicare, Medicaid, and retirement benefits for federal employees) represented only 20–30 percent of the federal budget, while defense was in the range of 40–50 percent. These two categories became equal in the early 1970s. Today defense is around 25 percent of the total budget, while entitlements represent around 45 percent.[2] In 1988, entitlements alone amounted to $506 billion, while the defense budget was at $291 billion.[3] The next largest category of the federal budget, after entitlements and defense spending, is the net interest payment on the federal debt. Before 1970 this was not a significant number, but by 1988 it had risen to $150 billion per year.

In spite of the significant decrease in the defense budget as a part of the total budget, it remains highly vulnerable to congressional attack—partly because of the still-high levels of expenditure, but mainly because domestic entitlement programs (such as Social Security and Medicare) are politically sacrosanct. However, defense does not provide the bud-

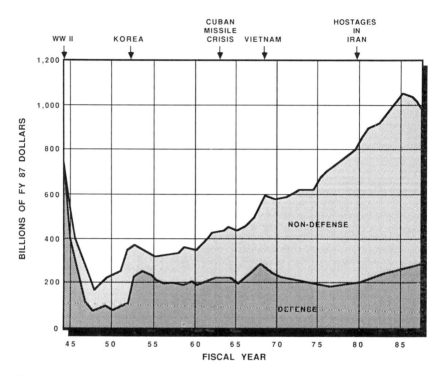

Figure 4.1
Total defense and non-defense outlays, 1945–1987. Source: Report of the Secretary of
Defense to the Congress, February 5, 1986, page 99.

get-slashing potential that Congress would like, or needs, in its effort
to reduce America's growing deficit and the corresponding interest
payments. The dominant share of the defense dollars spent each year
are spent to satisfy military payroll requirements and obligations for
new equipment that were established in past years, and neither of these
can rapidly be reduced. Only 14 cents of each defense procurement
dollar is spent the year it is authorized, 38 cents the following year, and
27 cents the third year. Payments for ships and other major purchases
can stretch out for more than seven years. Thus, when one looks at the
annual defense budget and tries to figure out the effect that an increase
or a decrease might have on *current* employment or inflation, the magnitude of the total dollars is misleading—a reduction of $100 million in

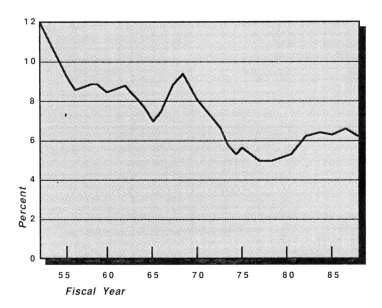

Figure 4.2
Defense outlays as a share of gross national product, 1955–1987. Source: Report of the Secretary of Defense to the Congress, February 5, 1986, page 100.

the procurement account reduces this year's outlays by only $14 million.

Nonetheless, a defense budget of about $300 billion supports, directly and indirectly, between 7 and 8.5 million jobs in the public and private sectors.[4] Moreover, since 1929 the United States has used its full production capacity only during period of armed conflict.[5] The argument that capitalist systems need war to create demands sufficient to absorb the excess goods produced but not normally consumed was raised 200 years ago by the economist Thomas Malthus, and was a major point of Karl Marx's theories. Thus, it is natural, when unemployment rises— especially if international tensions are high—for the government to view defense spending as a possible stimulant to employment (in fact, some refer to this as "defense Keynesianism"). Indeed, each $1 billion in added military spending creates approximately 25,000–35,000 jobs. It is not surprising to find so much political discussion when major weapon systems are under debate. The total investment required for the Trident ballistic-missile submarine program (including 20 submarines and two generations of missiles) will be around $80 billion (in 1987 prices) over 25–30 years, and the investment necessary to develop and construct the U.S. bomber force that will operate into the twenty-first century (including 100 B-1B bombers, 144 B-2 bombers, and the cruise missiles with which they will be armed) will probably come close to $100 billion (again, in 1987 prices) over 20 years.[6] These figures are truly staggering. Defense expenditures of the United States amount to something like $28 million *every hour* (24 hours a day, seven days a week).[7] Such expenditures support over 20,000 prime defense contractors and more than 150,000 subcontractors and parts suppliers.

Debates over whether high defense expenditures have a positive or a negative effect on the economy are heard continually. Needless to say, the literature tends toward extreme and often *a priori* positions. There are authors with substantiation for their case from both ends of the spectrum. The positive side of this perspective is represented by Merritt Roe Smith, who states that "military enterprise has played a central role in America's rise as an industrial power; and, since the early days of the republic, industrial might has been intimately connected with military might."[8] The negative view is typified by Lloyd Dumas's argument that "owing to the disproportionate allocation of scientific and engineering talent to military research, the rate of commercial innovation has declined appreciably since the late 1960s. Rising prices and deteriorating relative quality have made U.S. produced goods increasingly noncompetitive in both world and domestic markets, forcing production cutbacks and plant closures in the U.S. and creating additional inflationary pressures."[9]

Despite the extensive literature, comparisons of the employment benefits of peacetime defense spending with those of other government fiscal or monetary alternatives are highly ambiguous. Some argue that defense is a better stimulus, because it is more capital-intensive and thus creates a greater economic multiplier for the dollars invested.[10] Some analysts in the Congressional Budget Office find that defense and non-defense federal spending have roughly the same job-creation capability.[11] Still other analysts say that defense cannot absorb most unemployed, unskilled workers, and therefore does not stimulate much employment. In fact, defense procurements require mostly skilled labor, drawing disproportionately on the less than 3 percent of workers who are aerospace engineers, computer programmers, and skilled blue-collar laborers (e.g., tool and die makers and machinists).

An alternative choice for the government is to stimulate the economy (and therefore increase employment) through tax reduction and to count on the private sector (especially the non-defense portion of it) to invest the increased dollars. The success of such a program depends on the form of the tax cuts and the state of the economy at the time of the cuts. And the public-policy objective of the economic stimulation is very important. For example, if the objective is to create jobs for unskilled workers, increasing defense spending is a poor way to go about it; the defense sector, with its high skill requirements and high salaries, affects hard-core unemployment very little. (One analysis has shown that, per dollar, military expenditures generate half as many jobs as civilian expenditures but 20 percent more salary dollars.[12]) However, if overall economic stimulation is the objective, then defense expenditures appear to be much more attractive.

Though it would be possible to cite numerous other theories of the macroeconomic impacts of defense expenditures (many of them contradictory), a statement by former Federal Reserve Chairman Arthur Burns may be the best summary: "If the defense sector has stimulated economic development in some directions, it has retarded growth in others."[13] Nonetheless, it is very important to realize that Congress' relative willingness to spend money for "national security" always makes defense spending the most obvious means of stimulating the economy when the needs arises, and particularly in periods of perceived national crisis.[14]

Inflation is the second major short-term issue raised by defense spending. The claim that defense spending fuels inflation because the goods it buys are not useful in the civilian economy and are therefore "unproductive" is an economic myth.[15] Usefulness, it must be emphasized, is a subjective judgment. The economy does not and cannot determine whether automobiles, hula hoops, or gardening services are more useful than tanks. Rather, the production of each of these goods and services generates income for the producer and removes income from the consumer. Government involvement simply requires that the money for the government's purchases come through the secondary mechanism of collecting taxes. The question of whether the government buys food for distribution to the poor or tanks for distribution to the military is not *economically* important (which, of course, does not mean that it is not an important issue). However, public spending of any kind is inflationary if taxes are not collected to pay for it, and non-inflationary if taxes are collected.[16]

The government's ability to pay whatever is required for defense can, when taken to an extreme, preempt ("crowd out") more cost-sensitive production of comparable civilian goods whenever there is a limit on the supply side (as in capital-intensive industries, in the labor market for scientists and engineers, in the fields of electronics and computers, and in the aircraft industry). But such "crowding out" does not take place quickly, mainly because spending defense dollars takes many years and because the factories in defense-intensive production have historically operated well below capacity during peacetime. In fact, Gordon Adams (frequently a critic of defense spending) found "there is no evidence that defense spending actually destroys employment in civilian sectors of the economy."[17] Even a combination of rapid economic growth in the civilian sector and a surge in the defense sector would not produce dramatic effects for about three years. A defense buildup is thus not likely to bring much of an increase in general inflation, as the Reagan buildup proved. However, it *is* likely to have inflationary effects in certain parts of the defense sector of the economy. Some specialized defense parts suppliers raised their prices as defense spending increased in the late 1970s and the early 1980s, and the trend accelerated as the military buildup continued.

Overall prices rose at an average annual rate of 3.7 percent during the first three years of each of the last four military buildups (World War I, World War II, Korea, and Vietnam). However, during such periods, inflation tends to rise much more rapidly in the defense sector than in the overall economy. This is usually explained by the fact (discussed in detail below) that defense tends to use very limited numbers of suppliers—when the demand is rapidly increased, the orders go to the same suppliers, thus causing bottlenecks and increasing the prices of these defense goods.[18] To ameliorate this, the Department of Defense needs to address the inflationary impacts of its own acquisition practices. However, inflation can still be held down if non-defense spending is cut or if taxes are increased—both of which Washington failed to do during the Vietnam war. The fear of increasing taxes when defense expenditures are increased was taken even further by the Reagan administration. The "supply-side economists" argued that increased defense expenditures and *lower* taxes would cause sufficient economic stimulation to more than balance the additional spending. The huge increase in the U.S. deficit was the direct result of this theory's not working out. Many predicted that it wouldn't, particularly because of the time differences between the actual expenditures (which took place immediately) and the anticipated stimulation (which would occur over subsequent years).[19]

Clearly, the reason that defense expenditures are allowed to create inflation rather than balanced with increased taxation is that in a political environment it is much easier to borrow than to tax. However, as Senator Daniel Patrick Moynihan stated, "It will be recorded of us that in the 1980s America borrowed a trillion dollars from the Japanese. . . . Unless we act with far greater clarity than we have shown of late, we will soon learn that the world's largest debtor nation does not decide world policy, and that a deindustrialized America can no longer be the arsenal of democracy."[20]

The major consideration influencing senators' and representatives' positions with regard to defense spending is the impact of defense spending on jobs in the individual legislator's district or state. This will be discussed in much more detail in a subsequent discussion of the defense budget process and the Congress' role therein; however, it is appropriate at this point to recognize that broad macroeconomic issues are not the dominant forces driving these legislators' votes; nor are national-security issues; nor is the goal of achieving some balance between national security and some other priority (e.g., health care). It is far easier to use the national-security "cover" to rationalize one's decision than to be accused of having different motives. To see the effects of employment in local areas, consider the B-1B bomber. After President Carter canceled the program and it was up for consideration in its revised form after the election of President Reagan, there was a large amount of lobbying. The program was essentially being sold to legislators on the basis of "jobs for your district." The program represented 140,000 jobs, "with parts being built by 5,200 subcontractors— in every state except Alaska and Hawaii." The forward fuselage would be built in Columbus, Ohio, the offensive avionics in Wichita, the cockpit in Palmdale, California, the defensive avionics in Deer Park, New York, the air conditioning in Windsor Locks, Connecticut, the tires, wheels, and brakes in Akron, the wings in Nashville, the engines in Avondale, Ohio, the emergency electrical power system in Jackson, Mississippi, the aft fuselage in Dallas, the main landing gear in Cleveland, and the tail in Baltimore.[21] With more than 5,000 suppliers distributed around the country, most states and most congressional districts had jobs depending directly on this $20.6 billion program; and their representatives' views on the national-security issue involved were heavily influenced by these more local issues.[22]

An interesting "fairness" issue comes up in considerations of the politics of defense spending relative to individual states. In that national security is a "public good," all states share in its benefits. However, many legislators wish to also share in its *economic* benefits, and argue that their state should receive an amount of defense business proportional to the federal taxes it pays.

In reality, a combination of other factors—such as the presence of scientists and engineers, the access of shipyards to water, remoteness (for missile testing), and the status of a state's representatives on certain congressional committees tend to control the allocation of defense contracts to the states. In fact, 20 percent of the states receive 60 percent of the defense dollars. California, New York, Massachusetts, Virginia, Washington, Utah, New Mexico, Missouri, Mississippi, Georgia, South Carolina, Maryland, Connecticut, New Hampshire, Alaska, Hawaii, and the District of Columbia all receive more in military spending than they contribute to the defense budget in taxes, while all of the other states receive less than they contribute.[23] In some states (for example, California, New York, and Massachusetts), the employment impacts of defense expenditures have a very significant effect on the overall economy, and thus even "liberal" congressmen and senators frequently find themselves in the position of defending defense expenditures after having promised to reduce them.

A second and far broader "fairness" issue that is often raised concerns the "social impacts" of defense expenditures. A government's spending choices are always value-laden, and discussions of military spending generally draw emotional responses. Critics claim that big Pentagon budgets endanger America's economic health, call for a slashing of military outlays to reduce the budget deficit or to finance social programs, and generate analyses pointing out how many hospital beds could be bought for the price of an MX missile; advocates of more defense spending are equally passionate, and often use menacing images to portray a looming Soviet threat. Unfortunately, these matters do not lend themselves readily to pure cost-benefit analyses. Instead, there is a tendency to immediately relate program resource allocation (which belongs in the economic sphere) to the political sphere, where individuals, groups, and regions argue for their "fair share" of government money on grounds of resource distribution or "distributional justice."[24] Thus, the issue quickly shifts to the world of "public opinion," and Congress often responds to opinion-poll data on the public's attitude toward general increases or decreases in defense expenditures. When Ronald Reagan took office in January 1981, there was overwhelming support for increases in defense expenditures. A *New York Times*/CBS News poll showed 61 percent of respondents in favor of increased expenditures and only 7 percent in favor of decreased expenditures.[25] Five years later this consensus had all but eroded; only 16 percent favored increasing defense expenditures, while 30 percent favored decreasing them and the rest seemed about satisfied with the current levels. In response to this shift in public opinion—which was influenced by a variety of factors, from the deficit to the perception (fostered by stories in the press about "waste, fraud, and abuse," overpriced hammers and toilet seats, and so forth) that there were considerable "management problems" in the use of defense funds—Congress reversed the Reagan defense buildup, even though world conditions had in many respects worsened during this period. Clearly, the "guns versus butter" issue is more "political" than macroeconomic.

Impacts on National Productivity

The arguments about the impacts of defense expenditures on long-term national productivity are similarly complex and ambiguous. Many claim that the low percentage of the gross national product spent on defense in Japan and West Germany accounts for those countries' much higher productivity growth rates. (Figure 4.3 appears to back up this assumption.[26]) However, others argue that nonmilitary factors amply account for the post-World War II economic miracles of those countries. Moreover, no one has demonstrated that defense spending, *per se*, saps a nation's productivity. In fact, during the 1970s the growth in productivity and defense's share of the GNP both declined in the Unites States.

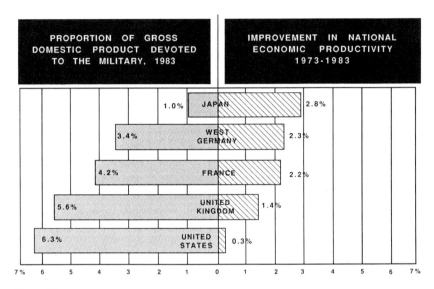

Figure 4.3

Those who investigate the issue of productivity tend to look in detail at three specific areas: manufacturing technology, research and development, and management innovation. For example, the economist Joseph Schumpeter stated that a nation's long-term economic growth is driven primarily by technological innovation in three major categories: process innovation (advanced manufacturing tools and techniques), product innovation (through research and development), and management innovation (through the development and application of new management techniques).[27] If it could be shown that concepts and funding were begun with defense and then spread relatively rapidly throughout the economy, this would "demonstrate" the positive, long-term benefits of defense investments for the economy. The difficulty lies in measuring the effects of dramatic changes in technology on industrial output. (For example, how does one measure the effect on the economy of switching from vacuum tubes to transistors?) As Richard Nelson states, "It is not easy even to specify just how output should be measured, in the relevant industries, so that technological advances can be characterized as enhancing productivity; and it is apparent that actual (traditional) productivity measures are hopelessly inadequate for getting at the effect of such technological advances."[28] Nonetheless, qualitative and pseudo-quantitative measurements have been attempted by numerous authors, and these show that in each of the three areas of innovation defense has played a dramatic role in the advancement of new industrial sectors. Still, there is much debate about whether the effect of defense expenditures was, in the long run, a positive one. Consider each of the three areas individually.

In the manufacturing area, some argue that machine-tool manufacturers have neglected to control the costs of their products because the military—a major customer—stresses performance objectives and does not allow price increases to affect its decisions on purchases.[29] Thus, civilian customers are forced to pay the same high prices for machine tools, and the productivity of the non-defense economy is damaged. Others, however, note that defense's need for high-technology products has spurred major innovations throughout the machine-tool industry. The revolution in numerically controlled machine tools, for example, was sponsored by the military. David Noble argues that during the 1950s the U.S. Air Force "created a market" for numerically controlled machine tools by purchasing, installing, and maintaining "over 100 numerically controlled machines in factories of defense prime contractors."[30] And the Air Force actually paid aircraft manufacturers and various parts suppliers to learn how to use the technology. "Not surprisingly," Noble observes, "machine tool builders got into action, and research and development expenditures in the industry multiplied eight-fold between 1951 and 1957." Thus, the military inaugurated, and sheltered during its initial phases, one of the most important manufacturing technologies of the twentieth century. Yet today, in spite of this boost, the United States imports most of its machine tools.

If the machine-tool industry had developed in a more competitive marketplace, would the United States now be the low-cost producer? German and Japanese machine-tool producers began to introduce cheaper, more flexible numerically controlled machines and software systems in the 1970s, and those countries soon dominated the market. Thus, although the crossover from military to commercial uses occurred in the United States, in the long run it may have worked to the detriment of American tool builders, because their numerically controlled machines were designed to satisfy military rather than commercial needs.[31] Yet it is questionable that, without the defense effort, the United States would have supported its machine-tool industry adequately. We have become a "consumer society" rather than an investment society, and we have tended to shirk our responsibility to invest in long-term manufacturing productivity. For this reason, many still argue that, unless the Department of Defense continues to support the nation's manufacturing-technology efforts, the United States will continue to lag in this crucial area. As will the discussed later, the ideal solution might be for the DoD to continue to stress manufacturing technology but with a far greater emphasis on its effects on product quality and cost.

The long-term effects of the DoD's investments in research and development are equally debatable. There is no question, however, that the DoD plays a major, even dominant, role in America's R&D sector. In 1963, defense represented about 47 percent of all R&D expenditures in the United States. By 1980 this had declined to 23 percent, but it was a very significant factor in the Reagan buildup.[32] In fact, during the 1980s defense R&D quadrupled, while other (non-defense) government R&D expenditures remained at approximately the same level.[33] In some sectors of the U.S. economy, defense's R&D role is even more dramatic. For example, since the Korean war, the DoD has contributed more than half of the R&D dollars in the aerospace field. It contributes approximately one-third of the R&D dollars in the electronics and electrical fields,[34] where there is a great deal of innovation although the DoD is a relatively low-volume buyer.

There is no question that the Department of Defense spends a significant share of U.S. R&D dollars, or that at any given time it is responsible for the employment of between one-third and one-fourth of the nation's scientists and engineers. However, many complain that, because defense R&D displays little or no cost sensitivity and strives to design each weapon system for maximum performance, it does not train engineers for the cost-conscious commercial markets of the world's civilian economy.[35] However, it can be countered (from the Schumpeterian point of view) that military technology has had an overall positive effect by having created or accelerated totally new civilian industries, such as computers, semiconductors, jet aircraft, nuclear power, and satellite communications. Clearly, these major new industries have had a dramatic impact on the overall economic growth of the United States.

The transistor is a good example of the Department of Defense's role in supporting the crossover of technology from the military to the civilian sector. By sponsoring research, subsidizing engineering development, funding the planning for production, being the initial "guaranteed" buyer, standardizing practices, and disseminating the results of such work, the Army Signal Corps played a central role in defining the structure of the early transistor industry. Indeed, the Army's programs increased the pace of transistor development to such an extent that the industry actually experienced a "sizeable overcapacity" by 1955.[36] However, such "pump priming" may well have had some very important negative long-term effects. The military's emphasis on expensive, high-performance devices created a tension between its needs and those of the Bell System and other commercial interests. By 1958, Bell executives had begun to worry that military requirements had complicated and perhaps even compromised their production efficiency. Unfortunately, this trend—initial U.S. defense leadership in advanced electronics, with the commercial world eventually replacing the U.S. producers with foreign sources—continues today. Indeed, the DoD now spends more on electronics ($40 billion per year) than commercial consumers spend on electronics products ($30 billion per year).[37] Yet John A. Young, the president of Hewlett-Packard (a major contractor for both commercial and defense electronics) and the onetime chairman of the President's Productivity Commission, said that military research in electronics is now so exotic and so slow that it offers little commercial use. In fact, the Packard Commission found that the DoD is now a "net user" of commercial research.[38] Again, the solution to this dilemma is for the DoD to take advantage of its significant power in the market by paying attention to quality and cost as well as to high performance.

Management innovation is the third area in which defense expenditures have clearly affected national productivity. Ironically, it is because the Department of Defense has been under continuous pressure from the Congress and the press over its management of public funds, and because of the complex nature of the management of many weapons programs, that much progress and experimentation has occurred. New techniques have been created for controlling and managing spending on weapon programs. Most of the commercially useful post-World War II management techniques were developed by and for the defense sector, in an effort to ensure that the taxpayers would get the maximum amount of security for their dollar. Cost-benefit analysis, operations research, critical-path analysis, program management, program evaluation review techniques (PERT), planning-programming-budgeting systems, and systems analysis are all examples of management tools that were developed by the Department of Defense and later widely applied in the civilian sector.[39] (Within four years of the introduction of PERT in the management of the Navy's Polaris submarine project, 108 of *Fortune*'s top 500 firms in America had installed or were planning to install PERT-type systems.[40]) Yet, in spite of all these management innovations, there is now a clear need for the DoD to greatly improve many of its management techniques—often in the direction of a move toward commercial practices. Once again, the criticism is that the defense sector's techniques are geared more toward achieving maximum performance with advanced equipment than toward improving quality and lowering costs.

Clearly, innovations in manufacturing, in research and development, and in management are going to be required to ensure long-term productivity and economic growth for the United States. In the past, the defense sector has made major contributions in these areas. Those who argue that "if defense had not made these investments they would have been made by the civilian sector" overlook the fact that the United States has no coordinated non-defense program to stimulate industrial development (such as Japan's Ministry of International Trade and Industry). Nor, the record shows, has there been sufficient incentive for private industry to make the very expensive and risky long-term investments. In many cases the choice is not between defense and civilian stimulation, but between defense and no stimulation.

Before we leave this discussion of "guns versus butter" there is one more broad policy issue that must be raised: the balance between a nation's economic strength and its military strength.[41] For many years, advocates of the military route (expansion, conquering territory, or even maintaining the status quo) have vied with advocates of economic strength through development at home and abroad.[42] In recent years, Libya, Syria, Cuba, Vietnam, Iran, and Iraq have pursued the military path. Japan, Singapore, and Switzerland are examples of modern-day trading states. Like it or not, the United States and the Soviet Union have the responsibility for maintaining a stable world environment within which peaceful countries can pursue their chosen paths. This is a responsibility which the Soviet Union has apparently not fully accepted; it has opted to spend a disproportionate share of its resources on its military forces and on the support of countries with military objectives in other parts of the world. Even in the United States there has been a significant, and continuous, battle over the proper allocation of resources between the economic and military spheres. Alan Greenspan, the former chairman of the Council of Economic Advisors, has observed: "I have always thought that an essential ingredient of national security is a viable economy—there are real national security trade-offs between, say, an additional wing of F-16s (fighter planes) and a lower inflation rate. This is not a zero-sum game."[43] Others, equally respected and with the same objectivity, have argued that the effects of defense spending on the economy are not significantly different from the effects of other federal spending—that a dollar spent by the government is a dollar spent by the government[44]—and that if you match an expenditure with taxes it is not inflationary, but if you don't it is. Thus, we return to the difficult realization that there is no "right" answer in this area. As subsequent chapters will show, there is strong argument that the United States should develop a broad and convincing military posture; yet it is equally clear that military strength is of little value without a healthy, growing, and internationally competitive economy. In the past, the United States has had both—even when it was spending 10 percent of its GNP on defense under President Eisenhower or 9 percent under President Kennedy. Yet by the end of the 1980s the United States was spending only 6 percent of its GNP on defense, and still its economy was in relatively poor shape.

The numbers are clear. Reductions in defense expenditures are not the panacea for the record budget deficits confronting the United States. These enormous debt figures result primarily from broad tax cuts (proposed in the first term of the Reagan Administration, and enthusiastically supported by Congress) and from high and growing non-defense spending by the federal government. The defense buildup was a small contributor. Even the largest proposed reductions in defense spending

($20 billion a year) are far too small to shrink the annual $100–$200 billion deficit significantly. Major structural changes in the U.S. economy are clearly required. While outside the scope of this book, they are strongly related to our nation's security and economic strength in the next century.

5 Budgeting and Congress

Having considered the somewhat theoretical (some might say unanswerable) questions of how much is needed for defense and how much is affordable, we now turn to the pragmatic and politically loaded process that links these issues: the annual budget process, involving the executive and legislative branches of the federal government, which eventually results in defense budgets and weapon systems.[1]

Planning, Programming, and Budgeting

Incredible as it may seem, 27 months (more than two years) of official planning, justifying, and debating precede the adoption of each annual United States defense budget. Every January, the president submits his budget proposals to Congress for the fiscal year beginning the following October. During this nine-month period, officials of the Department of Defense make frequent trips to Capitol Hill, explaining their proposals and modifying them at the direction of Congress. To this nine-month period, we must add the 18-month budget-planning process within the DoD that precedes the submission of each January budget proposal. Adding the 12 months of the fiscal year itself, during which the DoD is spending (or obligating itself to spend) the money that has been appropriated, results in a total cycle of *39 months* for *each* annual defense budget.

At any given moment the Department of Defense is involved with three or four different budgets in various stages of development. It is spending according to the current budget, testifying in support of the next one, and planning for one or two after that. Additionally, as thousands of detailed changes are made in the current year's and the next year's budgets as they wind their way through the Pentagon, the White House, and Capitol Hill, there is a multiplicative "ripple effect" of changes continuously taking place in the subsequent year's plans and in the programs themselves. The amounts of time, effort, and money demanded and wasted are extraordinary.

To understand how the United States got into this situation, it is necessary to recognize that before the 1950s the United States fought wars by drafting a manpower pool, arming it, engaging the enemy, and then disbanding the force that had been created. Thus, involvement in national defense was primarily an issue of personal sacrifice and risk of loss of life rather than one of taxes and relative budget priorities.[2] But no longer does the United States fully cut back after each crisis. Rather, $60 billion or more has been spent on weapons each year. Clearly, such levels of procurement require a different approach to peacetime military resource planning. However, when the change to ongoing procurement occurred in the 1950s, the budget was thought of as essentially a one-year budget. Each of the military services specified its needs for the coming year, and little thought was given to "integrated" (i.e., interservice) resource planning. Even within each of the services, planning in response to threat analysis was largely disconnected from budgeting.[3]

In 1961, Secretary of Defense Robert McNamara introduced his famous Planning, Programming, and Budgeting System (PPBS). The objectives of this system were to create a bridge between military planning and budgeting, to integrate and prioritize the resource needs of the various services, and to introduce a longer-term perspective into the planning process. Defense activities were divided into "program elements," each with a current price tag and a five-year projection, and were grouped by "mission function" into "program packages." For example, the Air Force's Minuteman missile and the Navy's Polaris missile were both put into the program package of the strategic retaliatory forces. A considerable effort also was made to define the relative "cost effectiveness" of each weapon system (for example, how many bombs could be delivered on a target per unit cost by one weapon versus another). In this way, it was thought, analysts in the Pentagon could determine the best ways to address particular military missions for the lowest expected costs.

Because the PPBS was oriented toward weapon systems, the people responsible for resource allocation could focus on the point where technology—as utilized in new weapon systems—met the military's perceptions of future threats and their current force-structure weaknesses. Additionally, by extending the planning horizon to at least five years, the PPBS would allow for an initial consideration of a weapon's total cost, in comparison with its effectiveness, rather than just a consideration of its first-year investment cost.

Thus, from its earliest days, the Planning, Programming, and Budgeting System incorporated three major innovations in public budgeting: multi-year visibility, a mission orientation cutting across organizational lines, and an analytically based capability to examine major segments of the defense program in terms of need, rationale, and design.[4]

As the PPBS evolved, major changes were made to it by each administration. Some of the more significant changes were the following.

- At the end of the 1960s, strategic planning was shifted from the Pentagon to the National Security Council. Interagency reviews that examined a wide range of defense strategies, together with their associated force structures and budget levels, became the basis for presidentially approved guidance to the DoD for the planning of strategies and budgets. Unfortunately, these were not continued in later years. In 1986, the President's Blue Ribbon Commission on Defense Management (the "Packard Commission") recommended the reinstitution of a revised version of this approach.

- Next, an attempt was made by the Office of the Secretary of Defense to develop a capability to examine logistics, manpower, and military bases so that these elements could also be looked at in the five-year defense resource plan. The classification schema developed at that time largely survives today, and appears in the Manpower Report required annually of the DoD by the Armed Services Committees of the Congress.

- The concept of "participative management" was integrated into the PPBS in response to concerns about overcentralization of the control of resources by the Office of the Secretary of Defense. Fiscal guidance was provided by the Secretary, and the services would then respond with constrained, service-justified programs. As a result of this decentralization of resource planning, the "out years" of the five-year plan frequently developed large fiscal gaps between the services' plans and the Secretary's budgets, which had to be closed during a succeeding budget cycle.

- In 1970, the Defense Systems Acquisition Review Council (DSARC) was established by the Deputy Secretary of Defense, David Packard, to "discipline" the acquisition of weapon systems. However, since the development of major weapon systems frequently consumed a very large share of the budget dollars, and involved commitments over a very extended number of years, the DSARC process caused confusion in the PPBS. Large out-of-cycle resource commitments made in the DSARC process did not match those made in the budget cycle.

- By the mid-1970s it had become clear that a five-year fiscal plan was inconsistent with weapon-system life cycles that involved perhaps eight years of development and another ten years of production. Thus, the "Extended Planning Annex" concept was introduced to extend the fiscal planning cycle to 15 years. Unfortunately, the budget cycle—especially Congress' part in it—remained focused on the first year. Thus, very little credibility was given to the "out-year" plans, and little attention was paid to the Extended Planning Annex. In contrast, European countries place considerable emphasis on their long-range fiscal plans when doing their budget and weapons-acquisition exercises.

- In recognition of the fact that there were essentially two separate cycles in the planning of defense resources (the PPBS cycle and the weapons-acquisition cycle), a Defense Resources Board was established in the early 1980s to try to integrate all of the various resource planning decisions at a single point. This was chaired by the Deputy Secretary of Defense and gave full participation to the services, along with the Office of the Secretary of Defense. Because of the strong role of the services, this step achieved considerable decentralization of the resource-decision process (in contrast with the intentions of Secretary McNamara when the PPBS was established).

- In 1987, in response to the recommendations of the "Packard Commission," the Department of Defense shifted to a two-year budget—while still maintaining its five-year fiscal-planning horizon. The hope was that Congress also would shift to the two-year budget, and that there would be much more stability and long-range planning in the overall resource-allocation process. Unfortunately, Congress initially chose to treat the budget much as it traditionally had, focusing on the first year of the two-year submittal.

Overall, it can be stated that Secretary McNamara's budget-reform efforts achieved a significant share of their objectives by making the process more rational and efficient and by allowing a far longer view in the planning of resources to meet national-security needs. It changed the focus of the Department of Defense from the traditional categories of budget expenditures (such as "maintenance," "personnel," and "sup-

Table 5.1
Congressional and Department of Defense planning and budget categories

Traditional budget categories	Program categories for defense planning
Military personnel	Strategic forces
Retired military personnel	General-purpose forces
Operation and maintenance	Intelligence and communications
Procurement	Airlift and sealift
Research, development, test, and evaluation	Guard and reserve forces
Military construction	Research and development
Family housing	Central supply and maintenance
Civil defense	Training, medical, and other general personnel activity
Special foreign currency program	Administration and associated activities Support of other nations Special operations forces

plies") to "program" categories (such as "strategic retaliatory forces," "general-purpose forces," and "research and development"). Within these categories, each of the services would have its own specific components; however, they would be evaluated, and their funding levels established, in relation to each service's role in fulfilling the particular mission specified by the program category.

As practiced, the 18-month PPBS process begins with the establishment of "military strategy objectives" by the Joint Chiefs of Staff, and with general fiscal and policy guidance from the Secretary of Defense as to available resources. Then, each service generates a detailed budget proposal within program categories, and strives (in theory, at least) to match the proposal to both the overall strategic goals and the anticipated resources. The cycle ends when the major outstanding budget issues are resolved by the Secretary of Defense or the President, and the budget is submitted to the Congress.

As the second column of table 5.1 shows, the DoD's five-year defense program (FYDP) contains eleven major force elements. These are broken down into a large number of program elements within each service. However, the format used for congressional review still uses the traditional budget categories (shown in the first column of the table).

The defense budgets for 1980 and 1985 are summarized in table 5.2. (Not only does this table give representative numbers; it also highlights

Table 5.2
Department of Defense budget authority, 1980 and 1985.

	Billions of 1985 dollars		Percent change
	1980	1985	
Investment	69.7	133.8	92
Procurement	48.8	96.8	
Research, development, test, and evaluation	17.9	31.5	
Military construction	2.9	5.5	
Military pay	61.5	68.9	12
Military personnel	45.9	68.9	
Retirement	15.5	NA[a]	
Operation and other support	61.1	82.0	34
Operation and maintenance	58.3	78.2	
Family housing	2.0	2.9	
Revolving funds and miscellaneous	0.8	0.9	
Total DoD budget authority	192.2	284.7	48

[a]not applicable (no longer separated out)

the buildup that took place during the Reagan years.) As the table demonstrates, procurement was a major focus of the Reagan defense buildup—during this five-year period, it almost doubled (after adjustment for inflation). A typical procurement-account breakdown appears in table 5.3, from which one begins to get a feeling for the size of the sums involved (in this specific year, over $30 billion for aircraft procurement, over $16 billion for ships, and about $10 billion for missiles). Additionally, over $5 billion appeared in the Department of Energy's budget for the procurement of nuclear weapons.[5] It also must be noted that around $21–24 billion of funding for intelligence activities is "buried" within this overall defense budget.[6] Moreover, there are, within the defense procurement accounts, significant appropriations for "black" or highly classified programs, such as the "stealth" bomber, the "stealth" fighter, and the advanced air-launched cruise missile. During the first seven years of the Reagan administration, the appropriations for classified programs grew from around $5.5 billion to an estimated $22 billion in FY1987 (a 300 percent increase).[7] Naturally, far fewer members of Congress and of their staffs are provided with data on these various intelligence and classified programs. The critics argue that this results in far too little "oversight"; the advocates counter that such secrecy is necessary for national security. It also results in considerably

Table 5.3
Appropriations for procurement, fiscal year 1983 (total obligational authority).

	Millions of dollars
Aircraft	30,350.7
Ships (building and conversion)	16,248.1
Missiles	9,984.3
Weapons and tracked vehicles	7,496.6
Marine Corps	1,977.4
Defense agencies	823.5
National Guard and Reserves	125.0
Other procurement	13,302.5
Total	$80,308.2

better stability and planning, since there is less disruptive "oversight." In fact, these are often said to be among the best-managed programs in the national-security area.[8]

The complicated defense-budget process within the executive branch is nothing more than "preliminary activity" leading up to the congressional budget cycle. Section 8 of Article 1 of the U.S. constitution states that Congress is empowered to raise and support armies, provide appropriated funds, and provide and maintain a navy. Since the Air Force grew out of the Army after World War II and the Marines are contained within the Navy, this is believed to be a sufficiently encompassing empowerment to cover all of the Department of Defense. The constitution also (in Section 7 of Article 1) gave Congress the responsibility for raising revenues; however, it was not until 1974, with the passage of the Congressional Budget and Impoundment Control Act, that expenditures and revenues were brought together under a unified budget. Additionally, by creating the House and Senate Budget Committees, this Act attempted to provide a longer-term (rather than year-to-year) perspective on budgeting, and to establish priorities, within the limited resources, for the overall government in any given year. Interestingly, while the constitution limits appropriations to the Army to "no longer term than two years," the Budget Act, in theory, attempts to establish fiscal guidelines for a three-year budget period. The assumption is that appropriations could be limited to two years, but that the Congress could discipline itself to live within the "top lines" of three-year fiscal plan. (To date, such discipline has not been demonstrated.)

After the president submits his budget proposal, the two houses of Congress conduct parallel sets of committee hearings. First, the House and Senate Budget Committees address overall budget levels. The testimony heard leads to Congress' First Concurrent Resolution, which sets guidelines for overall spending; later, a Second Concurrent Resolution establishes binding budget figures for the coming fiscal year. The appropriate House and Senate Authorizations Committees (in the case of the defense budget, the Armed Services Committee of each house) hear testimony leading to specific authorizations of each program element. Authorizations are made for everything from weapons systems, to manpower, to reserve strength. After this, the Appropriations Committee of each house hears testimony on providing the money for each line item in the budget. In theory, the Authorization Committees are approving the "functions" for which a budget is required, and the Appropriations Committees are approving the funds for those functions. In reality, the hearings are highly redundant.

In addition to these six committees, a number of other committees have "oversight" over specific areas of the defense budget (for example, the Banking Committees in connection with the Defense Production Act). Still more committees have responsibility for various defense practices; for example, the Government Operations Committees have jurisdiction over some defense procurement practices, including buying computers and legislating against "waste, fraud, and abuse."

Although the reforms that have given us the current system were designed to instill orderliness and encourage rationality in the budget process, in many respects these improvements have not yet come to pass. For example, if Congress makes changes in the budget on which it is conducting hearings, there is a direct effect not only on the Defense Department's plans for that year but also on the two other "out-year" budgets that the DoD is concurrently planning. To understand the magnitude of this effect, it must be realized that a typical weapon system takes from 12 to 15 years to evolve; thus, reducing a program's budget for the current year results in a reassessment of the "out-year" budget needs (not only to compensate for the lost money, but also to cover cost increases from the inefficiencies introduced by stretching out the program). The latter change will, in turn, affect the amount of money available for other programs in the "out years"; so this "ripple effect" permeates all future budgets, affecting many more programs than the one changed by the Congress. Needless to say, these effects undermine the coherence of the planning process. Unfortunately, in recent years, some members of Congress (aided by large and growing staffs) have gone beyond making just a few important changes; now they pore over each new budget proposal, line by line, making countless adjustments, redirections, and other "improvements." This detailed "micromanagement" occurs annually, causing dramatic disruptions of the planning process.

Senators and representatives are not the only ones guilty of making frequent, detailed budget changes at the expense of long-term considerations. Officials in the Department of Defense, and some other executive-branch officials with responsibility for preparing the annual budget proposal (for example, some people in the Office of Management and Budget), are also given to tinkering. The tendency is to focus all attention on the budget for the next year. Pressures to economize—from the Congress as well as within the DoD—add to the services' willingness to stretch out weapon-acquisition programs in order to arrive at acceptable figures for a given year. The hope is that somehow the remainder of the needed dollars will be "found" in future years. If the anticipated or hoped-for funding does not appear, defense planners are left with the unpleasant choice of either canceling some programs or further stretching out all programs. The latter is the time-honored approach. Not only does it create a vicious cycle; it also results in such phenomena as a production rate of one every two months for certain airplanes. (It is almost impossible, and certainly very inefficient, to build systems this slowly.) Stretchouts also add to the already-too-long development times for weapons—indeed, since 15 years may pass between conception and deployment, some weapons are obsolete by the time they are ready for the field. Overall, the inefficiencies introduced by the stretching out of programs lead to higher costs, which in turn lead to the need to economize by stretching out programs further. It is the tail of expediency wagging the dog of planning.

Before we turn our attention to possible corrective actions, it is necessary to consider a few subtleties of the current budget process. First is how to budget for inflation. Since budgeting is done in "then year" dollars, when the Department of Defense puts together its budget for the coming year it has to estimate what inflation is likely to be during that year. Obviously, the DoD would like to estimate conservatively—to assume that inflation will be high—in order to get more dollars and to gain some safety if it actually is high. However, the president prefers to have the proposed defense budget project a very low inflation rate—particularly during periods of high inflation, when reducing inflation becomes an important presidential goal. Thus, in a period when the DoD should be estimating high inflation, there is considerable political pressure for lower estimates. For example, from 1978 to 1981 the actual cumulative inflation was 45 percent, while the inflation estimated in the DoD budget was only 28 percent. The DoD had to absorb the difference, amounting to $4.6 billion, in order to live within the dollars allocated by the Congress.[9] In contrast, from 1983 to 1985—undoubtedly as a result of having underestimated inflation for the preceding years—the DoD overestimated the likely effects of inflation by a considerable amount ($23 billion, according to Congressional Budget Office sources). So, in those years, the DoD had a "cushion," which the Congress attempted to get back in the 1986 budget.

A variety of approaches could be utilized to correct the inflation-estimating problem. One would be to remove the political bias from the estimates by having a truly independent assessment of the likely inflation indices for defense goods. An alternative solution would be to simply do the budgeting without inflation and to adjust at the end of the year for the actual inflation indices, if these could be measured for defense goods, independent of the rest of the economy. (If they could not, equivalent overall commercial economic indices could be used.) Because billions of dollars a year are involved, the estimation of inflation is an important issue. Because of the politics involved, it is likely to remain unresolved.

A second subtlety of the budget issue is the difference between the amount Congress authorizes the Department of Defense to spend in any one year and how much the DoD actually lays out in payments during that year. For example, from fiscal 1982 through fiscal 1985 Congress allowed the DoD to allocate a total of $369 billion for procurement. However, actual spending from the procurement account in those same four years totaled only $259 billion (in constant 1986 dollars). Thus, $110 billion more was deposited by the Congress than was withdrawn by the DoD in that four-year period.[10] Such a difference

Table 5.4
Budget authorizations versus outlays (billions of dollars).

Authorizations		Outlays	
Procurement	107.6	Current-year investments	32.8
Research and development	34.0	Prior-year investments	95.8
Operations and maintenance	81.4	Operations	46.0
Military personnel	70.6	Pay	89.8
Other	11.5		
Total	305	Total	264.4

occurs (particularly during a large buildup) because it takes a number of years to manufacture a complex weapon system, and the DoD only needs to pay its bills as the contractors expend the money.[11] For example, it takes about 5 years to build a large combat ship, and a very small percentage of the money is spent during the first year (mostly on engineering design and a few long-lead hardware items). Thus, the DoD essentially builds up a reserve of expendable dollars, and even if the budget gets cut back the program will still have momentum. This is illustrated clearly by table 5.4, which compares authorizations and outlays in a defense budget of approximately $300 billion.[12] From this table we can see that, out of the more than $140 billion authorized for investments (procurement plus R&D), the actual outlays for that period (in these categories) were only around $33 billion. However, because of prior-year commitments, almost $100 billion was expended that year.

Table 5.4 also shows how little actual flexibility there is in Congress' budget reviews. Civilian and military pay are relatively fixed; they are based on the number of people and on any mandated cost-of-living adjustments (e.g., in military retirement pay). The cost of "operations" (keeping the bases open, running training exercises, and so on) is relatively fixed during peacetime periods.[13] Thus, as can be seen from table 5.4, only about 25 percent of the total defense budget is flexible (i.e., allows actual dollars to be "saved" during a particular budget year). The large expenditures for major weapon systems in the "out years" provides most of the flexibility. However, these expenditures are difficult for Congress to cut, since every one of those weapon systems is being built in someone's congressional district.[14]

Table 5.4 also reveals that when Congress is forced to make cuts in the budget for a given year, it actually focuses on reducing outlays in that year. The only way to accomplish this is by cutting "short-term expenditures," which means reducing the readiness and the sustainability of the forces. For example, the first cuts that took place at the end of the Reagan buildup (in 1987) were in the area of spare parts and tactical missiles (the Air Force's funds for new spare parts were reduced by 49 percent).[15] This is clearly very shortsighted. The unstated assumption is that the war won't occur during the coming year, and that thus it is better to pay for "force modernization" (the buying of new weapon systems) than it is to pay for keeping up the current forces.

The final conclusion to be derived from table 5.4 is that the budget-authority categories are significantly different from the outlay categories. Perhaps even worse, the numbers in both of these categories differ from the actual costs of the items procured. Clearly, obligation-based reporting is essential in monitoring the extent to which agencies are making commitments for future payments; and outlay-based reporting is essential in managing fiscal, debt, and credit policies. However, cost-based reporting is essential in determining the actual costs of equipment and services procured. The Department of Defense has a great deal of difficulty relating its accounting to its budgeting, since they are done on two very different bases. In many cases, the timing of obligations, outlays, and costs can vary widely, and these variations can be important because of the multi-year nature of most large defense contracts. Many have argued that budgeting and accounting should be done on the same basis, so that results can be measured against plans.[16] This is not now the case, since budgets focus on programs and projects, whereas the accounting and financial reports focus on categories of expenses (such as travel or personnel) without relating them to the particular programs or projects for which the money was requested and approved. If the DoD is to move to a better management system (one in which results can be compared with plans), it will have to use a common system for accounting and budgeting.

In summary, the characteristics most desired in a defense budget process—rationality, coherence, stability, and accountability—remain the qualities most lacking. It is essential to make changes in the process, and Congress is the place to begin.

Congress

The constitution gives Congress three principal roles in connection with national security: the power to declare war, the power to appropriate money for defense, and the duty to oversee federal acquisition practices. In recent years, while the number of congressional support ("staff") personnel involved in these areas has grown dramatically, Congress' ability to execute policy has deteriorated significantly.

Americans are willing to pay for certain management inefficiencies in order to gain the overwhelming benefits that democracy offers. The framers of the constitution consciously put in extensive checks and balances so that democracy could flourish. It is accepted that the American system was not intended to be the most efficient or effective from the viewpoint of "getting things done"; however, in recent years the ineffectiveness of the legislative branch has approached the extreme.

In the area of foreign policy, Congress was ruled for generations by a few committee chairmen who could bargain with the executive branch and deliver the votes of junior colleagues. In the 1970s this "supremacy by seniority" was shattered by the sweeping changes in the committee structure and in the power of chairmen. As one observer noted, "Mushrooming staffs brought in specialists often able to challenge executive-branch witnesses with equal expertise. The greenest freshman in Congress now may be bold enough to take on the Secretary of State or Defense on issues such as Nicaragua or El Salvador just because the legislator visited there over the weekend."[17] Representative Lee Hamilton (D-Indiana), chairman the House Foreign Affairs Subcommittee on Europe and the Middle East, wrote that "by 1978 Congress was losing effectiveness in foreign policy by its own diffusion."[18] Hamilton noted that 17 of 22 House committees and 16 of 19 Senate committees had "some jurisdiction over foreign policy." In the 1980s the size of the congressional staffs continued to increase, and the chaos in foreign policy got much worse. It provides little consolation to note that Alexis de Tocqueville wrote in 1835, in *Democracy in America*, that "foreign politics demands scarcely any of those qualities which are peculiar to a democracy. . . . They require, on the contrary, the perfect use of almost all those in which it is deficient."[19]

Yet, without a doubt, democracy is the only system for us, and we must make the best of it. This means improving the way Congress deals with the major issues of foreign policy. For example, the chairmen of the House and Senate Armed Services and Appropriations Committees are now given only an annual briefing on the strategic war plan. One observer asks: "Can an hour or so a year provide more than the most generalized notion of the nation's vastly complex nuclear war plans and targeting schemes? The answer seems self-evident."[20] He concludes that "Congress is completely excluded from the war-planning processes." While this may be an exaggeration, it is certainly not far from the truth. In fact, as another analyst wrote, "we have a Congress weaker on the large issues and more intrusive on the small—the opposite of what effective foreign policy-making requires."[21] As a classic example of the "micromanagement" of foreign policy, Senator Sam Nunn (D-Georgia, chairman of the Senate Armed Services Committee) pointed out that in the 1985 defense-program review "Congress changed the number of muzzle bore sights that the Army requested, told the Navy to reduce its request for parachute flares, and instructed the Air Force to make do with fewer garbage trucks."[22]

A similar situation exists in the area of the constitutionally mandated congressional budget process. Article I, Section 8 reads: "The Congress shall have the power to raise and support armies, but no appropriation of money to that use shall be for a longer term than two years." Making appropriations more cumbersome, and therefore less efficient, was the explicit objective of this clause. Alexander Hamilton, James Madison, and John Jay all agreed that this was the major purpose of this section of the constitution,[23] and dealt with it in eight of the Federalist Papers. As will be seen below, the current budget system certainly operates in the way the founders (particularly Hamilton, in Federalist 26) described it—but to excess, with so many checks and balances that it has almost ground to a halt.

In considering the constitution's intent with regard to Congress' third role (to oversee the procurement process), we must go back to the 1700s and recognize that "waste, fraud, and abuse" in defense procurement were a problem even then. As Thomas Jefferson expressed it in the Kentucky Resolutions of 1798, "In questions of power let no more be heard of confidence in man, but bind him down from mischief by the chain of the Constitution."[24] Unfortunately, by the end of the 1980s Congress' oversight had gotten out of control. Congress was passing "procurement-reform legislation" at the rate of over 150 bills a year. As

Representative James Courter (R-N.J.) stated, "Congress is not the answer to waste, Congress is the problem. They mean well but reformers are too often the cause of what's wrong with the military."[25] Courter was not alone in his views. Senator Nunn and some Republican senators, including Pete Wilson (R-California) and Dan Quayle (R-Indiana), have also criticized Congress' role in the acquisition process. Undoubtedly, a major cause of this problem is Congress' failure to recognize that it is an integral part of the acquisition process, as well as being responsible for overseeing it.

Congress must change its "way of doing business," from dwelling on small details to looking at the big picture. Such a change would have a direct effect on the way in which the Department of Defense approaches its role. Thus, changes in the congressional management process can make for dramatic improvements throughout the national-security arena.

In 1974 Congress recognized that it needed to take a longer-range and more integrated view and established (through the Congressional Budget and Impoundment Control Act) a major new approach to the overall management of the government's resources: It set up the Budget Committees. Many years must pass before the full effect of any such dramatic change can be assessed, but it is clear by now that the implementation of this act was both desirable and significant for the effective operation of the government. Yet it is equally clear that more steps are required if Congress is to "get its act together."

Congressional self-improvement is needed in four major areas: the adoption of a longer-term perspective, a reduction of redundancy in the system, improved timeliness in congressional budget actions, and a shift toward addressing the "mission need" of each executive-branch department (Defense, Energy, etc.) rather than voting for local (district or state) "pork-barrel" projects.

In comparison with parliamentary systems, the U.S. government has great difficulty in achieving a long-term perspective. Although Congress sets three-year "targets" for funding in the "concurrent resolutions" considered by the Budget Committees, the second- and third-year figures are not binding on either the executive or the legislative branch. Thus, "goals" notwithstanding, the system is focused primarily on the one-year budget; it practically ignores the other two years, both at the "total obligation authority level" and at the level of individual programs.

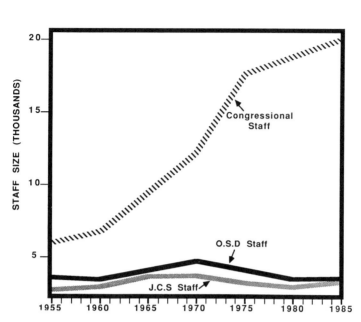

Figure 5.1
Trends in congressional staffing and in staffing of Office of Secretary of Defense and Office of Joint Chiefs of Staff, 1955–1985.

Figure 5.1 illustrates the dramatic growth in the congressional staff[26] from 1955 to 1985—from 5,000 to 20,000.[27] (This total does not include the thousands of additional analysts available to the Congress through various other agencies, such as the defense specialists at the General Accounting Office, the Congressional Budget Office, and the Office of Technology Assessment.) From this figure it can also be seen that the corresponding staffs within the Pentagon (those who have to "answer the mail" from Congress) have remained relatively small during the same period.

Of the 20,000 congressional staff people, some are highly experienced, often having more experience than their executive-branch counterparts; however, the vast majority are quite young and inexperienced and are simply putting in a few years of hard work on Capitol Hill in order to "learn the business." For example, about 40 percent of the legislative assistants (the "worker bees" of most House offices) have

Table 5.5
The growth of congressional micromanagement, 1970–1985.

	Number				Percent increase, 1970– 1985
	1970	1976	1982	1985	
Requested studies and reports	36	114	221	458	1,172
Other mandated actions for DoD	18	208	210	202	1,022
General provisions in law	64	96	158	213	233
Number of programs adjusted					
In authorization	180	222	339	1,315	631
In appropriation	650	1,032	1,119	1,848	184

held their positions for less than a year, and two out of three have less than two years' experience in their posts.[28]

All these staffers, unfortunately, do not make for a better "big picture policy." Rather, they make possible—or encourage—a great deal more involvement by members of Congress in the details of each and every item that they review. This impact is reflected in the data in table 5.5.[29] Notice that the detailed involvement of Congress (and its large staff) has affected not only the number of studies and reports requested but also the number of general provisions in law (often in procurement bills) and, most significant, the number of detailed adjustments made to defense programs as the budgets went through the authorization and appropriation process.[30] As Representative Courter stated, "It is small wonder that last year's [1986] authorization bill was 169 pages long with 354 pages of report language; just ten years ago, the bill was only 15 pages long with 75 pages of report language. . . . What is disturbing is the truly trivial, parochial, and intrusive activities that masquerade as legitimate oversight functions. No one can credibly contend that all these actions will result in a better defense for America, although they may result in a better economy for certain key congressional districts."[31] These continuous changes in the defense budget and in the management process bring instability, uncertainty, inefficiency, and reduced effectiveness for the taxpayers' dollars.

One possible corrective action is to make the Congressional Budget Committee's out-year budget targets binding on Congress and the executive branch, even though there is a constitutional question as to whether Congress can truly bind itself to specific appropriations beyond a two-year period. The idea here is to encourage a longer-term perspective in the budget process. If necessary, the third-year ceilings could be made binding only on authorizations, leaving specific appropriations on a two-year schedule.

Many object to a multi-year budget process, since it takes away a great deal of the annual "flexibility" of both the legislative and executive branches. But, of course, that is exactly the intent; flexibility is the inverse of stability. If there are good reasons (a technological breakthrough, a change in world conditions, or even a war) for rapidly increasing or decreasing our allocations to defense, then the levels of defense expenditures could change (even during the budget year), and the multiyear plan could be adjusted accordingly.[32] In 1986, Senator Dan Quayle pushed through a bill (containing a concept known as "enterprise programs") according to which Congress, at the beginning of a weapon system's development and again at the beginning of its production, would commit to the full funding required for either the development or the production of that program. These dollars would then be built into the subsequent years' authorizations and appropriations. This Congressional action is a move in the right direction; however, it does not keep the "top line" of the defense budget predictable from year to year. Thus, without knowing the total dollars available, the DoD is reluctant to commit many programs to this concept. A multi-year budget would introduce the needed stability.

This multi-year budget—subject to broad annual review by Congress—should apply at the "total obligation authority" level (the "top line" of the budget) and also within the major budget and program categories. This would require the executive branch to submit a budget for subsequent years that would be consistent with the previous year's "concurrent resolution"—something that is not done today.[33] If the president chose to either reduce or increase the budget for an agency for one or both of the "out years," he could submit an optional or alternative budget along with the budget he would be required by law to submit in January. This change would force both branches to look at the long-term implications of revising the budget. For example, a short-term budget "fix" that might look attractive in the first year would appear very unattractive if the out-year budgets were binding.

It must be reemphasized that, according to any of the multi-year budget proposals, Congress would still have some form of an annual review but would also be looking further ahead.[34] For example, with a three-year budget, a fourth year could be added annually to replace the expiring year. This overlap would force the executive and legislative branches to plan for the longer term—something that neither of them is able to do today. (In contrast, it is not uncommon for a European parliament to be debating the sixth year of a five-year fiscal plan.)

The argument for an annual budget process may have made sense when the federal budget was relatively small, when the lead time for procurement of most items was relatively short, and when there were no budget committees to resolve and unify the government's cash flow. However, it is now time for a change, as the Grace Commission[35] and the Packard Commission both highlighted. There is no need, and no excuse, for the multi-billion-dollar cost of instability in the defense budget process to continue. Congress will have to give up a little of its precious "flexibility" in order to improve the efficiency and effectiveness with which it spends the taxpayers' money.[36]

The implementation of a multi-year budget is clearly the most important congressional budget reform; however, three other reforms should be addressed: reducing the redundant reviews (and the associated unnecessary workload of Congress), completing the budget cycle in a timely fashion (so as to allow the executive branch to operate effectively), and shifting the process to a "mission orientation."

It might be possible to justify the annual (and even, in some cases, semiannual) review of the defense budget by six different congressional committees if these committees would stick to their specialties. However, the members of each of the various committees and subcommittees—and, to an even greater degree, their staffs—view the process as an opportunity for delving into every "line item" of the budget. This encourages the members of Congress to devote almost all their attention to the budget, leaving little time for other legislative responsibilities. Instead of line-item reviews, Congress could attempt to analyze the relationship between national policy objectives and the budget.

On the other hand, one frequently hears the complaint that the chief occupation of senior members of the executive branch is to appear before one or another committee or subcommittee to testify in defense of their budgets. In 1983, 1,306 DoD witnesses testified, for 2,160 hours, in hearings before 96 committees and subcommittees (a 357 percent increase since 1975). In that same year, there were approximately

85,000 written congressional budget inquiries to the DoD, and 21,753 pages of supporting documents were submitted by the DoD to justify the fiscal 1984 budget request (an increase of over 300 percent since 1975).[37] The Department of Defense estimates that "roughly 200 hours of staff time in preparation and follow-up are required for each hour of testimony" by senior DoD officials.[38] All of this is on top of the more than one million congressional "inquiries"—in non-budget areas—that are sent yearly to the Department of Defense.[39] The vast majority of these involve nothing more than passing on a constituent's letter to the DoD and requesting a response; however, a number of others require significantly more analysis and preparation.[40] Thus, the Office of the Secretary of Defense and the services are forced to maintain large staffs whose principal function is to respond to congressional mail.

There are three ways to help solve the problem of congressional-committee redundancy, all difficult to implement.

The first is to combine some of the existing committees. Many who argue that when the budget committees were created in 1974 other committees were not eliminated have proposed combining the budget and appropriations committees, or the budget and finance committees, or the appropriations and authorization committees. Each of these proposals has some merit; however, it is crucial that the budget committees themselves remain intact—otherwise, progress made since their creation will be jeopardized. The political difficulties of combining committees are obvious: Some members of Congress would find their influence diminished.

A second approach to the redundancy problem would be to force the various committees to perform only the functions for which they were intended. For example, the budget committees would look only at the top-line dollars in a given area, rather than at each detailed line item. (Of course, this is the stated objective today. However, it is not being followed. The tendency is toward review in greater and greater detail by all the committees and their staffs.) It is questionable that this change could be brought about, since Congress would, in effect, be putting out a directive saying "Do what you are supposed to do."

The third approach would be for some combination of the Budget, Armed Services, and Appropriations committees in each house of Congress to hold joint hearings rather than separate hearings. This would seem to be the easiest reform to implement, but in fact political obstacles remain (such as the question of who would be the chairman of each session).

Clearly, each of these means of reducing redundancy would decrease the workload of the Congress and of the executive branch.

A complementary recommendation that has been made is to make drastic cuts in the congressional staffs, regardless of which of the above techniques is utilized to reduce redundancy. One former congressional staff member recommended "slash[ing] the congressional staffs in half" so as to "restore Congress as a deliberative body rather than a staff-driven public-relations machine."[41] Many on Capitol Hill realize that the present process hurts the Congress and the nation, but to date there has not been the leadership to correct it.

The next major problem with the current budget process is Congress' notorious inability to release money to the executive branch at the scheduled times in the budget cycle. The rules are unequal. The president must submit his budget on time; however, Congress has not felt compelled to meet its own mandated schedules—even after giving itself an annual three-month extension when it revised the budget calendar in 1976. Congressional delinquency has been with us for a long time. As of 1984, a Defense Appropriations Act had been approved by the beginning of the fiscal year it was supposed to govern in only three of the prior 32 years. The DoD has not yet reached the point of operating the whole department for a full year on the basis of "continuing resolutions," whereby the preceding year's budget is "temporarily" extended into the next fiscal year to allow the continued operation of the government. Yet in fiscal year 1983, six of the eleven categories of the overall defense budget were not authorized by the *end* of the fiscal year.

Not only does operating under a continuing resolution cause uncertainty and instability; in addition, the law's prohibition against raising the funding on any single line item means that programs that call for an efficient increase in funding are instead stretched out and funded at the prior year's level—thus causing large increases in the programs' future costs. For efficiently planned programs that involve multi-year contracts, the consequences are even more extreme. The money Congress thinks it is saving through delay is spent many times over in future years. For example, in March of 1986 (the sixth month of that fiscal year) Congress required the DoD to take a 4.9 percent reduction in each of almost 4,000 programs, projects, and activities, for a total cut of

$13.6 billion in budget authority and $5.2 billion in outlays.[42] These automatic across-the-board cuts allowed no analysis and no management judgment about priorities or their effect on defense programs and forces. The results were devastating.

This trend toward congressional procrastination must be reversed. The move to a multi-year budget will help, but greater discipline on the part of Congress is still required with respect to timing. Congress must force itself to behave in the same way that it requires the executive branch to behave. If the total budget, in its vast detail, can be put together on time by the executive branch, there is no legitimate reason why Congress cannot review it on time.

The last of the congressional changes—perhaps the most obvious yet most difficult one—is a shift in the congressional budget debate from *where* things are bought to *why* they are bought. This means that Congress must spend more time on the "mission need" of the agency making a budget request and less on local politics and "pork barrel." Huge sums of money are involved, and it will not be possible to eliminate local considerations. But it is not wishful thinking to attempt to create proper incentives for Congress.

Unfortunately, during the 1980s the incentives actually moved in the opposite direction. Contributions to political action committees (PACs) from defense contractors more than doubled in the first four years of the Reagan administration, and the top 20 defense firms poured $3.6 million into the 1984 congressional and presidential campaigns.[43] The purpose of most of this lobbying is to protect old, inefficient programs or firms in order to preserve employment in a particular district or state. At the other extreme, "public-interest" lobbying is invariably anti-business. "Public-interest" groups are the ones responsible for much of the recent "waste, fraud, and abuse" legislation, which (as is discussed below) has hamstrung the procurement process.

It would be unrealistic to assume that any individual member of Congress would vote against a program that would bring dollars to his or her state or district, or against spending as much as possible there. The real problem in this regard arises when all the other congressmen and senators, fearing retaliation against their own pork-barrel bills, fail to exercise their responsibility to the nation and instead allow wasteful locally oriented spending to be approved.

The Department of Defense knows that Congress rarely will stop a major weapon-system program once it gets started. As Senator Thomas McIntire (D-New Hampshire) stated back in 1971, "I have discovered, much to my own frustration, that the present viewpoint seems to be that we are committed to a system's ultimate production as soon as we have sunk virtually any money into it. This is an attitude we will have to change."[44] Unfortunately, his warning was not heeded. Almost 15 years later, Representative Dave McCurdy (D-Oklahoma), an influential member of the House Armed Services Committee, stated: "Once a weapon system gets into the procurement stage, it develops a life of its own. There's no way you can make much of a difference except on the margins."[45] What is discouraging about this is that Congress clearly recognizes the problem, yet fails to act. As Senator Dan Quayle commented, "From a political point of view, Congress cannot and does not cut procurement programs; it is what is known as the camel's-nose-under-the-tent syndrome, and it is adroitly practiced by military planners."[46] In fiscal year 1986, twelve weapon systems were voted to be dropped by one committee or another in the House or the Senate; by the time the bill got through, all twelve had been restored to the defense program.

A classic example of Congress' actions in this regard is the MX missile program. The rationale for this weapon system was that the silo-based Minuteman missiles were vulnerable to Soviet attack, and that therefore a new mobile ICBM was required. When the DoD had great difficulty explaining how a very large missile with ten nuclear warheads could be moved around, a "compromise" was reached to "initially" spend about $20 billion to build 100 MX missiles and place them into the same silos that had been used for the Minuteman. In spite of the DoD's inability to "sell" a basing concept (they tried trucks, hardened silos, railroad cars, and other possibilities), and in spite of the fact that, as Senator Lawton Chiles (D-Florida) stated, "the MX probably doesn't have the support of even one-third of the Senate,"[47] by 1985 the MX had survived for 11 years, through 30 votes in Congress, and had consumed over $13 billion out of the defense budget. As one writer commented at the time, "The missile survives as a ten-warhead monument to Congress' inability to say no to a president seeking a major new strategic weapon system."[48]

In cases like that of the MX, the Department of Defense fully supports the representative or senator who wants to help keep a program alive. However, there are some congressional programs that even the DoD doesn't support, and yet they are in the budget every year. These are the so-called congressional "add-ons" that are appended each year when the DoD tries to end the production of a weapon system whose production Congress feels should be extended for the sake of national security. For example, in 1981 the Carter administration requested no funds for the Cobra/TOW helicopter, but the delegation from Texas (where the helicopters were made) put 17 of them into the budget, at a cost of $44.5 million. In the same year, the Carter administration did not request funds for the A-6E Intruder attack plane, but the New York delegation saw to it that 12 planes were included in the budget, at a cost of $186.7 million.[49] These two aircraft were produced with astonishing inefficiency—the A-6E at the rate of one per month and the Cobra at the rate of 1.5 per month.

At least these congressional add-ons buy the Department of Defense a few more weapon systems, even if they are not the best or the most cost-effective. In the case of those congressional programs that are "pure pork" the DoD has to pay for things that have little or no military value. Anyone who has the time and the interest to plow through the hundreds of pages of the annual defense appropriations bill will find it almost humorous reading. There are, buried within these pages, programs for almost every state and every district. Consider the $13.5 million that Senator Edward Kennedy (D-Massachusetts) put in for a noncompetitive contract for "military research" to build what the senator referred to as "a high-technology resource center" at Northeastern University in Boston. Anyone else would have referred to this as a "library," and Kennedy's testimony suggests its main purpose was "provide construction jobs and thus help the economy of a poor community where the site is to be located."[50] This item and similar programs for nine other schools were buried in the defense budget and totaled $56 million. The Senate first voted 58–40 to reject these programs. Three weeks later it voted 56–42 to support them, in spite of the objections of the American Association for the Advancement of Science and the National Academy of Science that Congress should not award academic research money without competition or merit review. Senator John Danforth (R-Missouri) looked into the issue and found that three of the nine universities "never even had submitted proposals to the Department of Defense at the time the congressional committee on appropriations put the earmarking in for these proposals." Of the remaining number that had applied, "the Department of Defense found that four of these earmarked universities did not have the research capability to do the job." Thus, seven of the nine universities either had not submitted proposals or had been judged unfit. Yet the Senate approved the overall program. Equally interesting in this particular case is the fact that when the bills went to the Senate-House Conference Committee, the House had only two of these nine projects in its bill and the Senate had none. Thus, the compromise reached by the House-Senate Conference Committee should have come out someplace between zero projects and two, since the conference committees are only authorized to address issues that come up in one or the other of the houses. As Senator Jeff Bingaman (D-New Mexico) stated, "The result $(2 + 0 = 9)$ was a moment of 'numerical creativity' in the Congress."[51] The *New York Times* estimated that in 1985 "more than $5 billion of such pork [was] inserted by Congress."[52] Representative James Courter commented that "this hodgepodge of pork barrel amendments cannot fairly be called responsible legislation."[53]

Another example of expensive congressional tinkering with the defense budget is the refusal to allow inefficient military bases or depots to be closed, even though the DoD requests such closures every year. Numerous studies have shown that the savings from closing such inefficient bases would amount to at least $3 billion a year.[54]

Advancement of social objectives and other agendas is also part of the defense appropriations bill. For example, a study on the effects of tobacco on military personnel was once ordered—just in case the studies on civilians might have overlooked something. Alcoholic beverages for a military base must be purchased in the state where the base is located, floating storage of petroleum products for the armed forces must be done in U.S.-flag merchant ships, and the Department of Defense is prohibited from purchasing foreign coal. Finally, there is a large amount of legislation promoting the employment of special-interest groups. For example, the DoD is encouraged to award contracts to, and take other actions that will benefit, American Indian labor, areas of high unemployment, minority-owned firms, and "disadvantaged" small businesses. Many of these congressional actions do, in fact, have significant social benefits. However, they drive up the cost of defense, and there is little control over them. As Representative Courter stated, "The situation has reached epidemic proportions, and more exposure clearly is needed."[55] The press (with over 15,000 newsmen in Washington) might provide such exposure; however, as John Tower (former chairman of the Senate Armed Services Committee) stated, "The press holds the President's feet to the fire, but does not focus on the congressional reforms that are badly required."[56] In fact, the effect of press coverage is almost perverse—by giving publicity to a senator's or a representative's efforts to channel money to his state or district, the press actually encourages such efforts. The answer, therefore, is to restructure the budget process so that Congress will be forced to vote on "top line" (i.e., total budget) dollars for the various "mission areas" rather than on the details of specific programs and projects that are clearly identified with districts and states. Such a move would restore Congress to a deliberative body acting in the national interest rather than a staff-driven special-interest machine whose members see each budget action as a way to raise reelection funds and/or to obtain jobs for constituents.

These four changes in the congressional budget process would go a long way toward increasing efficiency in the defense arena, but they must be matched by corresponding changes within the Department of Defense. Currently, as we have seen, the DoD is at least as guilty as Congress of making annual, detailed, line-item changes in the budget. Although the DoD now generates both five-year and fifteen-year resource plans, these are largely ignored in the rush to fit everything into the binding one-year budget. The move to a multi-year budget—begun in fiscal year 1988 with the first two-year budget[57]—will force the DoD to *use* these long-range plans. If Congress follows suit, it will also force the DoD to submit (and to tailor its plans to) realistic out-year budgets based on the levels of the binding concurrent resolutions, rather than to indulge in planning on the basis of optimistically high levels (such as the 22 percent increase hoped for in fiscal year 1985), which are invariably revised downward at the last minute. A multi-year budget will also encourage more realistic cost estimates in each defense *program* budget, since a program manager will no longer wishfully assume that next year the budget will be increased. Realistic long-range program budgeting could then be enforced by the DoD.

The absolutely critical question for defense budgeting is the following: Is such cost realism—both in terms of the "top line" of the defense budget for future years and in terms of the "expected" cost of a weapon system—likely to be utilized in the environment that Congress and the executive branch have created, or is this game of "optimistic planning" inherent in a representative democracy? Perhaps the solution lies in two directions: first, understanding the enormous impact that budgetary inefficiency has on the United States' defense capability; second, creating new structural mechanisms that will generate incentives for more realistic planning by Congress and by the Department of Defense.

The Importance of Stability

The best-known and most troublesome problems associated with defense acquisition are cost increases ("overruns") and schedule slippage.[58] Numerous studies by the General Accounting Office (and others) have shown that the cost of the average defense program increases between 50 and 100 percent, depending on how inflation and changes in quantity are accounted for. Annual cost overruns on weapon systems are measured in billions of dollars, and the schedule slippages that generally follow these overruns delay delivery by an average of about 30 percent. Cost growth and schedule stretchout are interrelated and reinforce each other. As increasing costs confront a fixed or decreasing budget, the only way to "fit" the higher costs into the budget is to stretch out the program, by extending its development time and/or by buying fewer production units each year.

The critical questions are these: What causes these cost overruns and these delays? Can steps be taken to reduce or eliminate them? A common belief is that overruns and delays are caused by unforeseen technical problems and/or by the government's inability to accurately project the costs of development and production. However, numerous studies by the Department of Defense and by independent research organizations show that, of late, the principal causes of cost growth and schedule slippage have been "instability" (i.e., frequent changes) in program budgets and/or in weapon-system requirements (performance requirements, quantity requirements, etc.). These studies indicate that program instability is costing the DoD over $15 billion each year.

In a 1983 study, the Air Force Systems Command reviewed over 100 weapon-system programs covering 30 years of Air Force acquisitions in order to identify the major factors in cost growth and schedule slippage.[59] The common assumption that most program problems are technically based was found to have been true in the past, but it was found that recent cost overruns and delays have tended to be attributable more to "external management" and to "funding instability"—two factors that are very much interrelated. "External management," in this context, means nonbudgetary changes external to the program, such as changes in the services' "requirements" (in connection with quantity, desired performance, new technology, and newly discovered threats). "Funding instability" is caused by frequent budgetary changes made by various offices within the service, by the Office of the Secretary of Defense, by the Office of Management and Budgets, or by Congress.

Similarly, a 1985 study of cost growth and schedule delay in nine Army programs revealed the three principal causes to be (in descending order) "changes in requirements" (to accommodate perceived changes in threat, new technology that promises better performance, and changes in quantity), "funding instability," and technical problems.[60] This study found dramatic annual fluctuations in the number of units of a given system ordered. As might be expected, a strong relationship was found between available funding, quantities ordered, and unit costs, and it is difficult to separate these items into causes and effects.

Thus, the three chief sources of instability are (1) annual or even more frequent departures from the expected or planned level in the top line of the DoD's or the service's budget; (2) externally generated changes in an individual program's budget, quantities, and/or technical requirements; and (3) changes generated from within the program (for example, because of low initial cost estimates or technical problems for which no contingency funds had been budgeted). All three of these sources cause cost increases that cannot be covered by the authorized budget for the program.

Figure 5.2 illustrates the combined effects of this instability. The service (the Air Force, in this example) starts off assuming (based on what the president and the Secretary of Defense have provided as initial guidance) that a certain number of dollars will be available with which to procure certain quantities of various weapon systems. Then, typically, the total obligational authority (TOA) is reduced—often by the president first, and later by Congress. The proper way to handle such a budget cut, in order to maintain the efficiency of the remaining programs, would be to assign priorities and then to defer or cancel enough

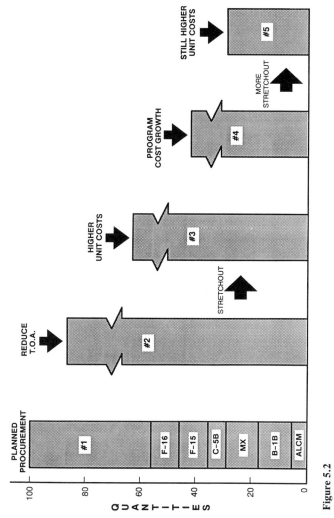

Figure 5.2
The effect of instability on quantities acquired. (TOA: total obligational authority.)

lower-priority programs that the cuts could be absorbed. Historically, both the DoD and Congress have been reluctant to cancel programs; the approach has been simply to buy fewer units of each system "this year" and to stretch out *all* the programs, hoping to purchase the rest of the units in later years.

This approach has serious consequences. As annual quantities decline, unit costs rise. Equipment must be built at a less efficient rate, and all the "fixed" costs of plant, equipment, and management must be absorbed by fewer units. Thus begins the spiraling of costs. When unit costs increase, still fewer weapon systems are bought (as shown by bar 3 in figure 5.2). Significantly fewer units are procured, even if the programs themselves are otherwise perfectly managed. However, as history has shown, costs within most DoD programs have a tendency to grow (for reasons discussed below); thus, if unit costs in each program grow, and total dollars are fixed, the quantities of each system that can be procured are smaller yet (bar 4). This causes further reductions in annual production rates, a corresponding increase in unit costs, and still another reduction in quantities procured (bar 5). The effect on the armed forces is clear: they get fewer weapon systems, and they get them later. This is a well-documented, generally accepted fact of weapon-system procurement. Not so well known, or so well accepted, is the fact that without this instability the DoD could get a lot more equipment for the same dollars (because the process illustrated in figure 5.2 would stop at bar 2).

Two cases, one from the Air Force and one from the Army, illustrate the problem discussed above. As shown in figure 5.3, the original plan for the Air Force's F-15 aircraft was to produce about 150 per year—an efficient use of the factory capacity. Principally because of cost overruns ("bottom-up" cost growth) and cuts in total procurement dollars ("top-down" reductions), the Air Force decided to stretch the program out by about three years and to produce an average of fewer than 100 F-15s per year. Independent analyses by the manufacturer and the Air Force[61] show that (with all other variables held constant) the cost of the three-year stretchout and the reduced production rates was about $2 billion—excluding the effects of inflation on the stretched-out program. This was equivalent to the cost of procuring approximately 83 additional F-15s. In other words, the United States lost more than a "wing" of aircraft because of the production stretchout. Many people

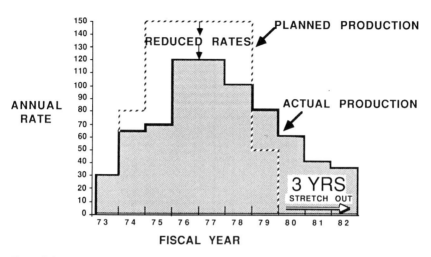

Figure 5.3
Stretchout.

believe (members of Congress included) that, by buying fewer units each year and stretching out the program, the DoD is simply buying the same total number of aircraft over a longer period of time. This is clearly not true.

The Army's Patriot missile program similarly illustrates the high cost of stretchout. The missiles and the "fire units" were produced at lower average production rates than had been planned. The stretchouts for these two main elements of the system were two and three years, respectively. An independent analysis showed that these stretchouts added approximately $1 billion to the total costs of the program.[62] If the original schedules had been maintained, 1,760 additional Patriot missiles could have been bought for the same dollars. When the Army later decided that it needed to procure that many more Patriots, it had to pay approximately $1 billion more for them. Had program stability been maintained, the taxpayers could have been spared this large extra expense.

The few weapon-system programs for which the schedules have been maintained have shown little cost growth. The Navy's submarine strategic missile program has, for many years, been a model of a well-executed program. Schedules and budgets established years in advance

Table 5.6
The combined effects of stretchouts and cost increase (one-year examples).

	Fiscal year	Quantity	Price for one	Percentage increase in unit cost
M1 tank	1987	800	$2.3 million	
	1988	600	$2.6 million	13
Blackhawk helicopter	1987	82	$5.2 million	
	1988	61	$6.5 million	25
AV8B Harrier jump jet	1987	42	$16 million	
	1988	32	$20 million	25
EA6B electronic-warfare plane	1987	12	$36 million	
	1988	6	$59.6 million	64
E2C Hawkeye warning plane	1987	10	$44 million	
	1988	6	$66 million	50
Sidewinder air-to-air missile	1987	627	$ 57,000	
	1988	288	$150,000	163

have been maintained, and the total program cost growth has been only about 6 percent (as compared with 50–100 percent on the typical defense program). The Army's AH-64 Apache helicopter program also maintained its production schedule for the first 446 units, and actually *underran* its production cost estimate (in constant dollars). So it can be done—the Department of Defense *can* run stable programs. However, this is not the norm. In fact, there are continuous stretchouts, from year to year, on almost every weapon system. Table 5.6 shows what happened to six typical weapon systems that were reduced in quantity and stretched out between fiscal years 1987 and 1988.[63] From these data it is clear that, as the quantities are reduced in order to fit each of the programs into the budget, the unit cost increases significantly. In aggregate, this leads to low—and extremely inefficient—rates of production. Even at the peak of the Reagan administration's buildup (1983–1987), half of 40 weapon programs reviewed by the Congressional Budget Office were being produced at rates below what the Department of Defense itself defined as the lowest efficient rate of production. For example, the minimum rate of efficient production for the F-15 fighter was defined as 120 per year, yet from 1981 to 1986 the Air Force bought only 41 aircraft a year.[64]

To understand the basic causes of the continuous changes in the

Table 5.7
Planned numbers of ships and submarines to be procured, versus actual numbers.

Year of budget request	Year ship would be purchased				
	1984	1985	1986	1987	1988
1983	21	24	32	38	
1984	17	21	28	28	31
1985		23	27	22	24
1986			23	20	24
1987				21	24
1988					20

dollars available and/or required for a given weapon system, one must be aware that two sets of erroneous budget estimates are used in the planning process: the estimate of the "top-line" dollars that are likely to be available to the Department of Defense (and, therefore, to the services) and the estimate of the likely cost of each weapon system.

To address the first of these problems, it is necessary for the president and his advisors (the National Security Council, the Secretary of Defense, and particularly the Office of Management and Budget) and the Congress to focus on the long-term stability of the defense budget rather than only on "this year's budget." Unfortunately, most of the long-term estimates that are made are overoptimistic. For example, in FY 1988 the total defense budget was approximately $290 billion. Five years before, when planning how many ships, planes, and tanks were going to be bought, the Department of Defense assumed that in 1988 the budget would be $425 billion—47 percent higher than it turned out to be. Naturally, these unrealistic five-year plans are reflected in the services' budgets. For example, the Air Force's plan for FY 1984 assumed an increase, over the next five years, of 240 percent. At about that same time, the authors of a different Air Force study, known as "Air Force 2000," stated that "planning for continued substantial increases in almost all appropriations and major force programs reflects unbridled optimism unsubstantiated by either an analysis of the economic and budgetary environment or historical funding patterns." If the services continue to receive such guidance from the top, they will continue to make such unrealistic assumptions. This overoptimistic planning has a direct impact on defense-industry planning. Consider (table 5.7) a shipyard looking at the Navy's five-year plan for the years 1983–1988, as contained in the 1983 and 1984 fiscal plans. The management of the shipyard assumes that by 1987 or 1988 there will be a dramatic buildup in ship construction, and takes this as a signal to invest in new capital equipment. However, by 1986 the number of ships actually ordered is not the anticipated 32 but only 23 (almost a 30 percent reduction), and by 1987 it is not 38 but only 21 (a reduction of over 40 percent). Thus, long-range military or industrial planning becomes essentially impossible. (On the military side, because the Navy, while attempting to build up to its 600-ship objective, received significantly less money than it originally expected, it may—according to the Congressional Budget Office—end up with too few airplanes for its new aircraft carriers.[65])

The other set of erroneous assumptions mentioned above consists of overoptimistic projections of the sums of money that will be needed to develop and procure given weapon systems. The typical approach is to assume—based on actual experience—that if a program can get into the budget it will stay in, even if it has to be slowed down. Unrealistically low initial cost estimates can help a program "get its nose in the tent." Thus, the military service budget can be made to contain more programs than it would if each program was realistically budgeted (for example, ten programs can be included in a budget that can adequately fund seven). And the problem will only get worse. An ever-present, ever-increasing "bow wave" of planned versus actual expenditures is typical of most defense programs. Figure 5.4 plots the sum of the original production financial plans for seven large defense programs, which were "expected" to peak at around $4.5 billion per year in the 1976–1978 period. By the early 1980s, the planned costs for these seven programs were at much higher levels and deliveries had slipped considerably. In the mid-1970s, the DoD was arguing that even with approximately $150 billion a year there was not enough money to cover the existing programs. After the defense buildup of the mid-1980s, and with a budget of $300 billion a year, the DoD was still saying that there was not enough money in the defense budget to cover existing programs. In the interim, new programs were added; however, they were underfunded and stretched out, raising costs needlessly and reducing the quantities procured in almost all programs.

The budget instability is further compounded by the services' historic tendency to "protect" military force structure (manpower) in times of

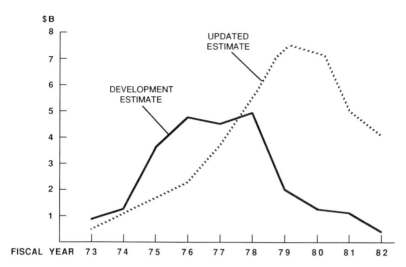

Figure 5.4
Changes in procurement funding for seven representative weapon systems.

total-dollar cutbacks. For example, between the time the Army submitted its FY 1985 initial budget estimate to Congress and the time the final FY 1985 appropriation was made, there was a total Army budget cut of 5 percent. To maintain its force structure in the face of inflation and rising costs, the Army decided to make most of its cuts in the acquisition area. This resulted in a 20 percent cut in the procurement account and a 35 percent cut in the R&D account.[66] Changes of this magnitude are extremely disruptive to the development and production of weapon systems and, if just a few minor programs are terminated, can only be absorbed through significant, across-the-board program stretchouts. Contracts originally written so as to allow production at an efficient rate now have to be rewritten after renegotiation. For example, in FY 1986, when the Army received from Congress a 4.9 percent cut in all its procurement-budget items, it had to renegotiate over 50 percent of its contracts for hundreds of weapon systems.[67] As figure 5.5 shows, from FY 1981 to FY 1986 the average production program suffered a quantity decrease of 17 percent and a resultant cost increase of 22 percent.[68]

In addition to these budget changes, significant changes in military "requirements" lead to program stretchouts and cost increases. This

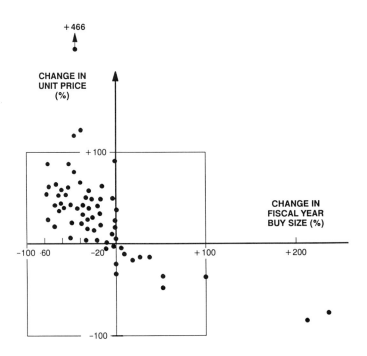

Figure 5.5
Production-rate instability and unit-price growth for 30 representative weapon systems
and 85 annual buys, fiscal years 1981–1986.

problem seems to stem from the military "users'" lack of any real fiscal
responsibility. The separation, in the services, between "developers"
and "users" (operators) causes the users to ask for financially unconstrained "requirements," and the developers to do their best to satisfy
them regardless of the costs. As a result of this "requirements process,"
the DoD tries to get the best weapon systems technology can offer. The
prices are so high that only a few can be purchased each year. This
creates, in the requirements process, the same kind of vicious circle
that exists in the budget process. The development cycle, which once
averaged 4–5 years, now averages over 8 years and in some cases
stretches to 15. During this cycle new technologies and new components come along that the users would like to incorporate into the
system, so they change the "requirements" in order to add a new missile
to an airplane, a new electronic system to a ship, or a new fire-control

system to a tank. At the same time, intelligence analysts pick up a new Soviet R&D activity and hypothesize "threat changes," for which new "requirements" are generated and more adjustments are made to the ongoing U.S. program. "Requirements" are also affected by budget realities. Having fewer total dollars or finding that programs cost more than was planned, the services are forced to reevaluate their "priorities" each year. Often they decide to "live with" fewer weapons of each type in order to keep all the other programs in the budget. So the quantities "required" often change from year to year, causing great instability and inefficiency in industrial production. A true commitment to a stable set of priorities and to programs that the services can not only "sign up for" but also "live with" over a number of years is essential to the correction of the flaws in the requirements process.

Stability in program priorities and requirements for individual weapon systems must be combined with far greater realism in the estimating of costs—specifically, in the estimating of the future "top line" of the DoD's and the services' budgets and of the likely program costs of the individual weapon systems. The latter must include sufficient "contingency funds" for the probability that technical problems *will* develop on these high-risk, advanced-technology weapon-system programs. It is not that the DoD doesn't know how to make realistic estimates; however, it prefers to assume that budgets are likely to grow, and that the particular weapon program at hand will be different—that no problems will arise and maximum efficiency will be achieved. This optimistic approach has been extremely costly, as is evident from table 5.8 (which is based on an analysis by the Congressional Budget Office comparing the five-year plans for 1981 through 1985 against the actual results). During these first five years of the Reagan administration, the overall procurement account rose very dramatically. The amount of equipment procured did not increase correspondingly. In fact, as table 5.8 shows, the primary result during this period was a significant increase in the unit costs of weapon systems. The first row of table 5.8 shows that in the five-year plan submitted in 1981, the Army had planned to buy approximately 3,800 tanks for about $6 billion. By the end of the five-year period it had, in fact, bought approximately 3,800 tanks; however, the actual cost was $9 billion. Both numbers are in constant 1985 dollars, to remove the effects of inflation.) In many of the cases cited in the table, the performance of the weapon system actually

Table 5.8
Procurement plans vs. actual results for selected weapon systems, 1981–1985.

	Planned[a]			Actual			Percentage change		
	Quantity	Funds[b]	Unit cost	Quantity	Funds[b]	Unit cost	Quantity	Funds[b]	Unit cost
M1 tank	3,891	6,332	1.63	3,804	8,966	2.36	−2	42	45
M2/3 fighting vehicle	3,720	3,591	0.97	2,855	4,522	1.58	−23	26	64
AH-64 attack helicopter	284	2,615	9.20	315	3,955	12.56	11	51	36
F/A-18 fighter aircraft	656	13,692	20.90	375	12,387	33.00	−43	−10	58
F-15 fighter aircraft	90	2,764	30.70	195	7,379	37.80	117	167	23
F-16 fighter aircraft	660	8,717	13.20	714	11,713	16.40	8	34	24

a. As contained in FY81 budget and five-year plan.
b. In constant 1985 dollars.

procured was significantly better than what was in the plan; however, the increase in numbers acquired, which was the rationale for the budget increases, was not commensurate with the increased dollars.

To correct these problems, both Congress and the executive branch must make a far greater commitment to achieving stability—from the time a program is authorized to enter full-scale development until production is completed. Such a commitment could yield cost savings of from 5 percent (based on the average of the data in figure 5.5) to 12 percent (based on the F–15 and Patriot examples discussed above). In addition, the "ripple effect" of instability (the effect of a change in one program on another program in the same budget) probably adds 3–5 percent to the second program's costs. Thus, the overall cost of program instability is somewhere around 10–15 percent.

To put this in dollars, let us assume that such stability is introduced not only into the few large programs that dominate defense spending (for example, the ten or so programs that receive over 40 percent of the DoD's acquisition dollars) but also into many smaller programs, whose percentage of instability—and therefore cost growth—is frequently far greater. Since the DoD will neither achieve stability in all programs nor achieve it fully in any one program, perhaps a reasonable dollar estimate of the potential long-term savings is around 10 percent of the acquisition budget, or *well over $15 billion* each year. This figure assumes significant changes in the way the system operates—changes that will take years to implement and become effective. These changes are clearly required, and must be initiated now.

Linking Strategy, Budgets, and Weapon Selection

As the chairman of a Defense Resource Management Study wrote in a 1979 discussion of the Planning, Programming, and Budgeting System, "There is broad agreement that the first P in PPBS is silent."[69] Unfortunately, that statement is still largely true today. Historically, the linkages between strategy, budgets, and the selection of weapons has been missing in the defense resource process. Similar ideas were expressed in 1986 by the President's Blue Ribbon Commission on Defense Management:

. . . there is a great need for improvement in the way we think through and tie together our security objectives, what we spend to achieve

them, and what we decide to buy. The entire undertaking for our nation's defense requires more and better long-range planning. This will
involve concerted action by our professional military, the civilian leadership of the Department of Defense, the President, and the Congress.

Today, there is no rational system whereby the executive branch and
the Congress reach coherent and enduring agreement on national military strategy, the forces to carry it out, and the funding that should be
provided—in light of the overall economy and competing claims on
national resources. The absence of such a system contributes substantially to the instability and uncertainty that plague our defense program.
These cause imbalances in our military forces and capabilities and
increase the cost of procuring military equipment.[70]

Because it takes so many years to develop and then deploy new
weapon systems, and because those systems are likely to be in the field
for decades, and because the existence of those systems will directly
influence our potential strategies, we must think out this process—the
closed cycle from strategy through budgets through weapon selection
and back to potential strategies (based on the weapons deployed)—on
a very long-term basis. The introduction of "affordability" constraints
is the only way to realistically link the issues of which strategies are
credible, which weapons we can buy, and in what numbers we can buy
them. It would also help to justify to Congress and to the public the
large expenditures that might be required. In other words, budgets and
weapon systems would be justified on the basis of their military value
in the context of a resource-constrained overall national-security
strategy.

At the risk of oversimplifying, it may be said that the hallmarks of a
viable national-security posture should be *affordability, balance,* and
credibility. Unfortunately, these three characteristics have been absent
from the national-security posture of the United States in recent years.
What is needed is an *integrated* national-security posture that displays
all three of these fundamental characteristics, that accepts the geopolitical structure and the military balance that exists in the world today
(there is no way to "return to the 1950s"), and that takes full advantage
of the United States' strong points and assets—including advanced
technology, political freedom, industrial might, competitive markets,
voluntary allies, international trade, and flexibility.

Alliances and arms control should be crucial elements in an integrated
national-security posture. It is essential that we consider the priorities,
interests, and perceptions of our allies as we formulate our defense

planning. Recognition of the fact that "the greatest danger [i.e., risk] for the Soviet Union is that the various centers of power in the world will combine against it"[71] means that our planning must be not only consistent with but, in many cases, *integrated* with that of Europe, Japan, and China. Similarly, treating arms control as an integral and crucial part of our evolving national-security posture, rather than as if it were in conflict with it, will add to the coherence of our overall plans.

In developing a new national-security posture, we should *begin with a doctrine and work toward force structure and equipment,* rather than begin with equipment and force structure and work toward a doctrine (as is done today). But this cannot be a one-way path. Proper planning requires a defined strategy, a long-term affordability constraint, and the constant iteration of the two, as well as a recognition that, for many years to come, the potential strategies will be largely limited to those that can be achieved with the forces already available.

A balanced defense posture will also require tradeoffs between the marginal gains provided by major investments in one area and the marginal gains that could be provided for the same dollars in another area. For example, the incremental gain in strategic deterrence that would be achieved by spending approximately $40 billion for 100 B-1B bombers and 100 MX missiles might be compared against what that $40 billion might add, as a marginal benefit, to the nation's conventional war-fighting capability in potential regional conflicts. (Indeed, in 1988 a special advisory board, which had been set up to help the Reagan administration evolve a future defense strategy, concluded that in order to achieve a more balanced capability for regional conflicts the United States should spend more on conventionally armed, high-accuracy missile systems.[72])

To develop long-range resource plans linking strategy, budgets, and weapon selection will require changes within Congress, within the White House, and within the Department of Defense.

The president must get involved not only in the one-year decisions but also in the long-range planning process regarding strategy, in the top lines of future defense budgets, and (particularly) in the relationship between strategy and the budget. The president must then "sell" a long-range program to Congress in order for the concept to work. Neither the involvement nor the selling will be easy. Both are essential if we are to achieve cost realism, program stability, and greater coherence in the overall process.[73]

The changes required in the Department of Defense begin with the establishment of a long-range resource plan (or set of options) that will be closely tied to national-security objectives, will be fiscally constrained, and will treat the various services in an integrated way. This plan should address not only the quality (performance) of specific weapon systems, but the quantity as well. Such a unified plan—with resources allocated to major military mission areas—would enable the Department of Defense to be certain of precisely where its priorities lie.

Creating this plan, and following it, will require a shift in responsibilities within the Department of Defense. Currently, each of the services develops its own resource plans and its own requirements for new weapon systems and then, after approval from the Office of the Secretary of Defense and Congress, implements these plans. But this practice of each service largely going its own way ignores the evolution of technology, which has created enormous overlaps in the roles and missions of the services. (For example, long-range Army missiles serve the same mission as Air Force aircraft and air-to-ground missiles, and there is also overlap in strategic nuclear forces, in close air support for ground forces, and in the military uses of space.) Additionally, and perhaps most critical, there are some missions that tend to fall outside the services' definitions of their "primary" responsibilities and, as a result, do not receive sufficient funding from any one service. "Strategic mobility" (airlift and sealift capabilities), command and control (particularly between services), close air support of the Army by the Air Force, "special operations" in regional conflicts, and hostage rescue are examples of this problem. These all tend to get low priority, and therefore low funding, from the services. Finally, inadequate resouces are provided for the "joint" (multi-service) planning, training, and exercises that are required to achieve an effective integrated force. Yet, in almost any foreseeable military conflict there will have to be joint operations among the services. A battle in Central Europe would involve air, land, and space operations, and an amphibious operation in the Persian Gulf or the Caribbean would of course involve the Navy as well. Even a more ambiguous case, such as an at-sea operation by the Navy, would probably involve satellites and land-based missiles or aircraft. Since the various services would have to fight together, it is desirable to establish resource plans and weapon-system requirements, and to select weapon systems, on a multi-service basis, in order to get the most war-fighting capability for the dollars available.

Long-range resource plans, in the presence of realistic 5-to-15-year fiscal constraints, will force the military to set up long-term priorities rather than to leave this role to the civilians in the Office of the Secretary of Defense or to Congress. With changing world conditions, the levels of defense funding may change in future years; therefore, there must be plans for fluctuations in weapon-system procurement. But broad changes in funding will not be frequent, and they will certainly not be annual or even semiannual, as they are now. If properly planned, they need not affect almost every budget line item, as they now do. The objective is to focus the Defense Department's weapon-selection process—and its establishment of priorities for program funding—on a period of 5–15 years, rather than on next year's budget.

Such plans would have the additional advantage of addressing in advance the issue of how many weapons are to be procured over, say, 15 years. If the total dollars for a mission area, and thus for a weapon system, were allocated (and fixed) on the basis of a long-range, priority-ordered plan, then tradeoffs between quantity and quality would be considered during the resource-planning process. This would give proper consideration (now often missing) to the significant military value of having increased quantities even if each individual weapon system performs at a slightly lower level than is theoretically obtainable.

If the Office of the Secretary of Defense were to become the policy and oversight organization that it is intended to be, then the generation of this jointly developed long-range plan would logically be the responsibility of the Chairman of the Joint Chiefs of Staff. In the past, such planning has not been within his purview. In fact, it was not until 1987 that the Chairman of the Joint Chiefs of Staff was, in any significant way, involved with either the defense-budget process or the weapon-system-requirements process. At the recommendation of the Packard Commission, and on the basis of internal studies done by the Senate Armed Services Committee, Congress passed the Goldwater-Nichols Department of Defense Reorganization Act of 1986, which established a Vice-Chairman of the Joint Chiefs of Staff and put the Chairman directly "in the loop" of the resource and requirements processes. The Goldwater-Nichols Act also calls for the establishment of a staff for the Chairman that will be far more independent of the services. Naturally, these steps will take considerable time to achieve. The parochialism of the services will have to be overcome, and the strong support of the Secretary of Defense, the president, and the Congress will be necessary.

A recommendation that has been made in a variety of forms by General David Jones (former Chairman of the Joint Chiefs of Staff), by General Edward Meyers (former Chief of Staff of the Army), and by the National Military Command Structure Study calls for the Chairman of the Joint Chiefs, following fiscal and national-security policy guidelines provided by the Secretary of Defense, to submit an integrated long-range resource plan to the Secretary.[74] It would be up to the services and to the Chiefs of the Unified (multi-service) and Specified Commands, acting through the Chairman of the Joint Chiefs, to establish the priorities, the requirements for new systems, the quantities of systems to be procured, and the ties between these factors and national-security objectives, with continued and strong oversight by the Office of the Secretary of Defense.

Historically, the fear of a strong "general staff" is rooted in a fear that the military might come to dominate the elected and appointed civilian officials in matters of national security.[75] Many cynics claim that Congress uses this fear of the military taking over as a way to prevent the executive branch from developing an integrated policy, since Congress can achieve much more control over the executive branch by keeping it divided and dealing with the separate services. The military services oppose an integrated approach because it would weaken their control over the budget and the weapon-selection process. However, in the late 1980s many members of Congress, and even some people within the military, have begun to recognize the value of an integrated military plan. The Goldwater-Nichols Defense Reorganization Bill was a very positive step. Even with further movement in this direction, concern about a "military takeover" will have little credibility in the United States. As we move toward the need for a far more integrated war-fighting capability, the traditional autonomy of the armed services is more and more unacceptable. General Maxwell Taylor, Chairman of the Joint Chiefs of Staff between 1955 and 1959, wrote—after noting a long list of items on which the Joint Chiefs could not concur—that all these issues were "obviously important," that "the bulk of those upon which they agreed were unimportant," and that "on important matters artificial agreement was probably the prevailing pattern."[76] That was in the 1950s. In the 1980s, former Chairman of the Joint Chiefs of Staff David Jones lamented the same situation. However, the need for joint military operations, force planning, and resource planning had increased greatly over that 30-year period. General Jones concluded that "the results of [the] tedious defense budget process is a defense budget that is derived primarily from the disparate desires of the individual services rather than from a well-integrated plan based on a serious examination of alternatives."[77]

For the Goldwater-Nichols Bill to work, the Chairman and the Vice-Chairman of the Joint Chiefs of Staff must truly exercise independent judgment. To do this, they will need a strong and independent staff, selected and trained so as to achieve a multi-service perspective and to develop genuine cross-service priorities. Over time, such a more independent view could be established by the chairman and his staff—especially with the greater role in the resource-allocation process that would be assigned to the Commanders-in-Chief of the Unified and Specified Commands. This change would not require that the actual development and procurement of new weapon systems, or the responsibility for the associated budgets, be under the control of the Chairman of the Joint Chiefs. These matters could be totally decentralized. The implementation of the decisions of the Chairman and the Secretary of Defense could be left entirely to the services (which already have the manpower and the capability for this management role). Also, this change need not mean that all new weapon systems will be standardized. Rather, it would mean that they would all be consistent with a jointly developed overall plan. In practice, it seems likely that there would be more multi-service weapon systems; however, needs for individual-service weapons would certainly be considered.

Overcoming the obvious tendency of the services to favor their traditional weapon systems and to ignore nontraditional ones will require guidance from the Office of the Secretary of Defense to encourage (and/ or "hedge" funds for) the adoption of nontraditional systems. Nevertheless, it is more likely that nontraditional systems will be recommended from a set of jointly developed requirements than from a set of individual-service requirements.

The new planning system recommended herein is beginning to take shape within the Department of Defense at the end of the 1980s. Its full implementation will take many years—if, indeed, it is ever to be achieved—since it represents a basic "cultural" departure from the traditional individual-service-based approach to planning and budgeting. Any degree of success will take enormous pressure on the services from the leadership in Congress and the executive branch. Three things stand out as the principal requirements of this set of planning and budgeting changes, and all three must be achieved since they are so highly interrelated: *realism* in long-term defense budgets and long-term program cost estimates; *improved military planning,* with far stronger ties between strategy and resources and far greater inter-service integration of military planning (in regard to strategy, resources,and weapon requirements); and *increased stability* in overall military plans and priorities and in the requirements and budgets for individual programs. These improvements will be difficult to achieve, but their combined effect will make an enormous difference in the effectiveness and the efficiency with which the defense budget is utilized to provide national security.

However, even if we can significantly improve the process of planning, programming, and budgeting, there remains the question of the execution of the weapon-acquisition process: How do we go about developing, producing, and supporting the weapons we have chosen to buy?

6 Buying Military Equipment

In April 1986, the President's Blue Ribbon Commission on Defense Management, headed by the industrialist and former Deputy Secretary of Defense David Packard and composed of a bipartisan group of experienced former government officials, issued a report stating that

All of our analysis leads us unequivocally to the conclusion that the defense acquisition system has basic problems that must be corrected. These problems are deeply entrenched and have developed over several decades from an increasingly bureaucratic and overregulated process. As a result, all too many of our weapon systems cost too much, take too long to develop, and, by the time they are fielded, incorporate obsolete technology. . . .

In general, we discovered these problems were seldom the result of fraud or dishonesty. Rather, they were symptomatic of other underlying problems that affect the entire acquisition system. Ironically, actions being prescribed in law and regulation to correct [the problems] tend to exacerbate these underlying issues by making acquisition procedures even more inflexible and by removing whatever motivation exists for the exercise of individual judgment.[1]

Senator Dan Quayle (R-Indiana), who in 1984 was chairman of the Special Task Force on Selected Defense Procurement Matters for the Armed Services Committee, had reached a similar conclusion:

I am concerned that we have not looked at the most fundamental and central questions that the [acquisition] system's operation raises. For example, the U.S. Army spent the same amount of money on tanks this year as it did 30 years ago, but 30 years ago that $2 billion purchased 7,000 tanks while this year it bought only 700. In 1951 the Department of Defense ordered 6,300 fighter planes at a cost of $7 billion (in 1983 dollars). This year we will spend $11 billion to build only 322 planes. I am fully aware of the fact that weapon systems today are hardly comparable with systems 30 years ago, but that does not change the reality of trends towards far higher unit costs and far smaller quantities, trends that must be of concern to anyone who cares about our national defense.[2]

The public's perception of the defense acquisition process is, perhaps, just as important as the views of these "insiders." Certainly the taxpayers' willingness to support a strong defense establishment depends in large measure on their perception of the effectiveness and efficiency with which the funds are spent. Thus, it is quite significant that an extensive survey conducted by the Packard Commission showed that "respondents think almost 50 percent of the annual defense budget is lost to waste and abuse," and that "aerospace contractors are suspected of a proclivity towards fraud."[3]

To understand whether these perceptions are valid (even if only partially so), and what should be done to improve the system, we must look at six very broad and highly interrelated issues:

- We must understand the procurement process, from its objectives and its theory through its actual implementation.
- We must consider the performance, the costs, and the quality of the weapons procured.
- Since competition—the essence of the market economy on which the overall U.S. system is based—is also the underlying theory behind the defense acquisition process, we must study the form of competition that exists in the unique defense environment and consider ways to improve it.
- Since the overwhelming proportion of items purchased by the Department of Defense are much like commercial items (fruitcake, towels, and so on), we must understand how these items are bought, why there is extensive use of "military specifications," and what improvements can be made in this area.
- Because of the frequent "horror stories" in the press, and the resultant negative public perception, we must face head-on the issue of "waste, fraud, and abuse" in the procurement process.
- We must look at the competence and experience of the thousands of people who are involved in the acquisition process.

Before addressing these six matters, we should put the acquisition system into perspective in terms of size and performance. It is not an exaggeration to state that defense acquisition is the largest business enterprise in the free world. Annual purchases by the Department of Defense total around $170 billion (more than the combined purchases of General Motors, Exxon, and IBM). The DoD's research and development expenditures alone are $7\frac{1}{2}$ times the combined R&D expenditures of France, Germany, the United Kingdom, and Japan. Defense acquisition involves almost 15 million separate contract actions each year, implemented through over a thousand buying offices around the world. More than 300,000 industrial supplies are involved, and about $4\frac{1}{2}$ million different kinds of items are purchased each year. The DoD employs more that 165,000 people (civilian and military) to manage this vast array of R&D, procurement, and logistics and support activities. (Some argue that it is over 500,000, depending on who is included.) It takes over 27,000 people just to administer contracts. Per working day, there are 56,000 contract actions and over $700 million in expenditures.[4]

With such numbers, it is not at all surprising that there are occasional errors. For example, an Army clerk once made a one-digit error on the 13-digit order number and ended up ordering a 7-ton anchor instead of a $6 incandescent lamp.[5] Naturally, such errors make headlines and are frequently followed by legislation. In each particular case, the new law ensures that the mistake is not likely to recur. However, there is then one additional step to be taken in ordering each of the 15 million contract items the following year. That the cost of the "corrective action" may greatly exceed the cost of the one error is rarely, if ever, considered.

What is surprising, in view of the size of the system, is how *few* such errors occur. Numerous independent studies by the Congressional Budget Office and other organizations have found the DoD to be one of the best-managed of all government agencies, and it is often used as the model when new procurement practices are to be established elsewhere. And in terms of cost growth, defense programs compare quite favorably with many other public-sector and private-sector activities, as figure 1.1 shows. Nonetheless, there is ample room for significant improvements in the way defense business is done—and there is an urgent need to initiate these improvements now.

Procurement in a Unique Market

In trying to understand the defense procurement system, it is most important to recognize that two major categories of items are purchased each year: major weapon systems (high-technology, performance-driven, and purchased in small quantities at high unit costs) and commercial-type "standard" items (highly price-sensitive, and bought in large quantities at low unit costs).

An overwhelming majority of the contract actions involve standard items, but the overwhelming share of the defense dollars go for a few major weapon systems. For example, in 1976, 98 percent of the contract actions (all under $10,000 each) took approximately 11 percent of the total defense dollars, while 2 percent of the actions took 89 percent of the dollars.[6] It is interesting to observe that a similar distribution exists within various defense buying commands. For example, over 50 percent of the dollars spent by the Air Force Systems Command (which buys the Air Force's weapon systems) during the first half of the 1980s went to only four major systems: the B-1, the MX, the F-15, and the F-16).[7] Similarly, in 1985 the Air Force Logistics Command (which buys all the spare parts for the Air Force) spent 78 percent of its dollars on 3 percent of its contracts, while 74 percent of the contracts took only 1.7 percent of the dollars.[8]

With this sort of a distribution of contract actions versus dollars, it is not at all surprising that numerous examples of mispricing, and other abuses, occur within the category of standard items, and that most of the procurement laws and regulations have been written with this category in mind. Congress often fails to recognize that such legislation also affects the costs of the major weapon systems. The Department of Defense and the Congress must fully acknowledge the dramatic difference in complexity and sophistication between standard items and weapon systems, and must provide management flexibility and experienced personnel to supervise the procurement of weapon systems. Such recognition is gradually evolving, but there is still a long way to go. Additionally, there is a need for the DoD to change its procurement of more "standard" items so as to make greater use of commercial equipment and practices, in order to take advantage of the lower costs and the higher quality that are to be found in this far larger market.

Perhaps the best way to understand the process of acquiring a weapon system is to briefly review it step by step, placing emphasis on the problems at each step.[9]

The process begins with the perception of a "military requirement" for a new weapon, which predates the weapon's development. "Requirements" arise from two directions: The so-called "user pull" is based on the services' perceptions of deficiencies in their current weapon systems or of likely future Soviet threats. (The equivalent in the commercial world is the "market demand" for new products.) The "technology push" comes from a recognition that a new technology may offer a military advantage over a potential adversary. The way the process currently works, both of these sources of perceived military requirements lead to significant errors. In fact, it is from this false start in the weapons-acquisition process that many of the downstream problems have historically evolved.

Usually, the "user pull" that induces the military services to state what they would like to have in the next generation of equipment to overcome the inadequacies identified in their current equipment does not sufficiently involve participants with a sophisticated knowledge of the cost and schedule implications of the technical improvements required to satisfy these desires. This often leads to "gold plating"—the inclusion of features that may be very desirable but whose costs far exceed their real military value. More than likely, if the future users of the equipment understood the impact of "requirements" on the schedule, quantity, and maintainability of their weapons, they would demand something simpler. They might even opt for modification of their existing equipment, which is attractive in terms of cost and schedule and which often yields acceptable results. Generally, there is not enough of a compromise between performance and costs. Instead, it is assumed that military requirements are "pure" and must be satisfied. The fallacy of this position is twofold: there is no recognition that, in a resource-constrained environment, quantity of weapons is being traded off for performance of each individual system; and there is no skepticism about the extreme predictions of what the military threat environment will be 25 years hence (which no one is in a position to make with any degree of certitude).

Similar errors arise from "technology push," which begins when a government team, an industry team, or (frequently) a government-industry team conceives of a new or advanced technology that could have considerable military potential and tries to persuade the services to define requirements that will exploit this new technology. Most of the really significant leaps in military capability come from "technology push" rather than from the pull of known military deficiencies (as would be expected, since until a technology is demonstrated there is no defined "need" for it). Radar, jet engines, and atomic weapons are all examples of how "technology push" has changed force structures and war-fighting capabilities dramatically. However, it is clear that the engineers developing a new technology tend to push the technology for its own sake, and that this approach also often results in "gold plating." Worse still, "user pull" and "technology push" often combine into what has been euphemistically referred to as the "technological imperative" ("because we can have it, we must have it").

Once military requirements have been defined, the next step is to

assemble a small team to first define what kind of weapon system would
meet these requirements and to then get funding for its development
authorized. A military service will take the lead in this effort, with
significant help from potential industrial sources. They basically are
trying to "market" the new system within the government, in a highly
competitive environment where other new weapon systems, and existing ones, are vying for the same budget dollars. This competition is
highly desirable, so that (one hopes) only the best ideas survive. However, it does not encourage realistic estimates of costs and schedules.
Invariably, when a program finally receives budget approval, it embod-
ies highly overstated requirements and greatly understated costs. As
the director of the Procurement and Systems Acquisition Division of
the General Accounting Office stated in 1979, "The planning estimates
(sent through the DoD and on to Congress) are not honest. I think they
are highly optimistic for a specific purpose, and that is to get the program started."[10]

Once funding has been approved, the weapon system must be specified in detail. A large program team is assembled for this task within
the Department of Defense. Such specifications for a major program
typically run to thousands of pages, not counting the general military
specifications that are included by reference. (The latter fill up book-
shelves of backup documentation.) Potential bidders from industry are
usually involved in this process, and they try to influence the specification of particular design characteristics. Such government-industry
joint efforts have the potential to help the government find out what can
be done for the lowest possible cost; however, this is frequently not the
result. Instead, the "best of each" often becomes the "requirement" in
the detailed specification. (For example, one contractor may say "I can
give you a weapon that will fly at a certain high speed," while another
may say "I can give you a weapon for a very low cost." The specification may end up saying that the government wants a high-speed, low-
cost weapon—which, in fact, could not be produced.) Unfortunately,
this detailed system specification effectively becomes the surrogate for
the already overstated military requirement, and the basic "military
mission need" tends to fade from direct view.

The next step in the process is the competition among firms for the
responsibility to develop and produce the weapon system. The basis
for this fierce competition is the overdetailed system specification. In

order to win the competition, a contractor must demonstrate that it will meet this specification for the lowest cost. Asking that the specification be modified or pointing out its fallacies is not only discouraged but may even cause a firm to be considered "nonresponsive" and ruled out of the game. Thus, the process is designed to encourage improvements within the specification, and it effectively eliminates compromises between performance and cost (on which normal commercial competition is based). Since each contractor must say that it will fully satisfy the requirement, the competition is based principally on the bidders' optimism with regard to both performance and cost. The eventual result is frequently that there are too few dollars to achieve the performance promised; yet a low bid is necessary to win the competition. Each time, both the DoD and the industry hope that perhaps "this program will be different" and that the system will be delivered ahead of schedule, cheaply, and with no problems.

After the selection of a contractor, the burden then shifts back to the DoD program manager, who must now accomplish the improbable task of managing his overspecified and underfunded program to a successful conclusion. His success becomes still less likely when he discovers that he has very little management authority over his program, and that 40 or so line and staff people (over or around him) have veto power over his efforts (for example, they can insist that he use certain military specifications, certain reliability requirements, certain maintainability requirements, and certain small-business and minority-business requirements). None of these people have responsibility for the ultimate schedule, cost, or performance of the program; however, they have "functional authority" over their areas of responsibility, and they are sure to take the safe course (with no requirement to price out the implications of their edicts). None of the positions that these "special-interest advocates" take are undesirable in themselves; it is just that the program manager has no room to trade off their demands against the overall program's cost and schedule objectives. Clearly, in such an environment, no one can really be held responsible for the management of the program, and the program manager's usual path is to accept the added requirement and try to figure out how to pay for it later.

Throughout this process, Congress is fully involved. In the yearly budget activities, the program manager has to "sell" the program to all the "relevant" committees and subcommittees. Additionally, problems with the program offer opportunities for senators and representatives to grab headlines, and so thousands of Capitol Hill staffers are constantly traveling to DoD field offices to search for such problems.

The continuous uncertainty in the budgets for individual programs keep the program manager "on the road" selling his program, rather than at home managing it, and make it likely that his program will be cut back and stretched out almost every year.

Predictably, there is a high incidence of cost overruns on major weapon-system programs. Equally serious is the unreasonably long acquisition cycle (10–15 years) for a typical major weapon system. This long cycle leads to unnecessary development costs, to increased "gold plating," and to the fielding of obsolete technology.

In view of these underlying problems, it is no surprise that the DoD's acquisition process ends up putting too few weapon systems in the field for too many dollars expended. What is amazing is that only a few weapon systems are in serious trouble; this is a tribute to the dedication and professionalism of many of the people involved.

To better understand the procurement process, its scope, and the challenges and problems that it introduces, let us consider a specific high-technology subsystem: the guidance system required to accurately place a warhead from an MX strategic missile on a target at intercontinental range. This is an extremely challenging mission that would make great demands on the skills of both technologists and managers in any environment, yet it is a relatively typical defense program for the period it covers (the 1970s and the 1980s).

The initial "requirement" was a combination of a perceived military need for a missile with extremely high accuracy to replace the Minuteman and a "technological opportunity": the development of an advanced type of guidance system at the Instrumentation Laboratory of the Massachusetts Institute of Technology. This self-contained guidance system (known as an inertial measurement unit), developed over many years, promised to satisfy the need for greatly improved accuracy. It should be noted, however, that it had been designed in a university environment rather than an industrial one, and not as a low-cost system. The MX missile itself was justified to Congress as a weapon that was "required" because the silo-based Minuteman had become vulnerable to the Soviet Union's increasingly accurate missiles. Congress approved the initial plan on the understanding that the MX was to be a mobile missile, moving covertly in special vehicles. Again, because of the high priority that strategic weapon systems receive, cost considerations were not a major factor.

The Northrop Corporation was selected as the winner of the competition for the guidance-system contract.[11] Northrop's annual revenue of approximately $5.6 billion can (and still does) come almost entirely from the U.S. government. The contract for the MX guidance system was worth roughly $1.6 billion over its duration, and the overwhelming majority of those dollars went to Northrop. (No other firm was contracted to produce this system.)

Each inertial measurement unit contains more than 19,000 parts, ranging from microchips that are barely visible to the naked eye to large metal hemispheres machined to extremely close tolerances. Many of these parts had never been produced before. It would have been inappropriate to plan on producing them on automated production lines designed for high volume, since the Air Force wanted only 239 complete guidance systems (including spares and replacement units for the planned 100 missiles). Many of the parts were not actually made at Northrop; more than 500 subcontractors were used. Most of these subcontractors are small businesses, without the financial resources to underwrite the high risk of advanced technology (but the government would essentially assume that risk).

As the House Arms Services Committee stated, "Northrop was behind schedule before it even started"—which is not surprising, in view of the above-described process for establishing costs, schedules, and performance. In addition the Air Force was unwilling to delay the MX's deployment date, and therefore it continually pressed Northrop to speed up production. It was very clear to Northrop that the MX program faced considerable annual uncertainty in the budget fights on Capitol Hill; and for Northrop to have established an efficiently run program, it would have to get all of the "bugs" out of the system and then commit to volume production (both in its own factory and in those of its suppliers). The Air Force wanted to get as many systems out the door as quickly as possible and to play down the program's technical difficulties; however, it was unable to guarantee the stability of the budget.

During the time when the MX program was being phased in, Northrop's Electronics Division was growing rapidly—from a research house employing 500 to a production facility employing over 5,000. The DoD's stress on performance versus cost led to the selection of a research operation to build this equipment, rather than an existing production operation. Thus, while the system was still being developed by the engineers, the company had the extremely difficult job of moving from laboratory benches to full production. Again, however, price was not a consideration, and there was no competition as to who would do the production. The normal process in the defense world has been to go with the same firm from development into production.

When the program began to encounter schedule problems, and the first production deliveries were late, the Air Force placed the blame on Northrop and sent a scathing letter stating that the problems were "a direct consequence of inadequate planning and management response" and demanding that Northrop "give direct, forceful, and immediate attention to the problems." In a typical response of a defense firm to pressure from a service, Northrop replaced about 30 top executives in a single year because of the problems of the MX and other programs.

The first inertial measurement unit was delivered 203 days late. A month before that, payments to Northrop were reduced as "an incentive to get the shipments back on schedule." Yet a year later, even as contracts were being signed for additional units (since the government had no one else to buy them from), an Air Force evaluation of Northrop's compliance with production rules found continuing serious problems. By that time, the Air Force had withheld about $130 million worth of payments to punish Northrop for missing its schedules.

On the basis of assertions by Northrop employees of irregularities at the plant, the Department of Justice initiated several criminal investigations of Northrop's role in the MX program. The accusations, published by the *Los Angeles Times* and aired on the CBS television program "60 Minutes," came from "whistle blowers" who were pressing lawsuits under federal fraud statutes and who stood to receive considerable shares of the monetary awards for damages if the cases were upheld. This example is a relatively extreme one, since it ended in criminal investigations; however, it is not unusual in many of its other characteristics, and it certainly highlights the complexities and potential pitfalls of the weapons-acquisition process.

If we step back and consider the overall acquisition process, we see that there are basically three ways to operate it. The first (the preferred

American system) is to allow the "invisible hand" of the free market to operate and to use market incentives to achieve the necessary efficiency and responsiveness. The second is the Soviet way, involving a fully planned economy and government-owned facilities. The third is the regulated economy, which is usually the model used when there is a monopoly on the supply side (as in the utilities or the communications industries).

Interestingly, defense is never listed among the "regulated industries" in the U.S. economy, because here the monopoly is on the demand side. Similarly, while some critics accuse the defense sector of being a totally "planned" economy (in which someone at the Pentagon selects which contractor's "turn" it is to get the next award), there is ample evidence (as will be discussed in detail below) that this is, in fact, not the case. It is also interesting to note that almost every congressional speechmaker, in discussing the defense industry, preaches the virtues of the free market—yet in reality defense is a totally regulated market where Congress, as a part of its "control over public funds," has been the instigator of most of the regulation. The framers of the constitution warned that "the internal effects of a mutable policy are calamitous. It will be of little avail . . . if the laws [are] so voluminous that they cannot be read, or so incoherent that they cannot be understood; if they [are] . . . revised before they are promulgated, or undergo such incessant changes that no man who knows what the law is today can guess what it will be tomorrow. . . ."[12] Yet, in spite of this warning, by the mid-1980s the Pentagon's book of purchasing rules had grown to more than 7,500 pages,[13] with an additional 30,000 pages of accompanying "policy guidance." In discussing a trial involving DoD procurement, Los Angeles U.S. District Court Judge Ferdinand Fernandez stated that he found a "web of laws and [DoD] rules that almost defy understanding."[14]

To see how we got into this mess, it is necessary to go back to the Armed Services Procurement Act of 1947. This act was intended to consolidate and reconcile the various military services' regulations (which had proliferated in the 1940s) by creating a single set, called the Armed Services Procurement Regulations. However, by the early 1960s, an independent assessment found that "technical performance, cost, income, and reputations are being affected adversely by over-regulation, conflicting regulations, ineffective administration of regula-

tions, close and not always capable government surveillance of [pro-
curement] activities, and burdening of the procurement process with
socioeconomic objectives."[15] In fact, things got so bad that a special
Commission on Government Procurement, established in 1972, found
that "procurement regulations, practices, and procedures are relatively
uncoordinated and often inconsistent. The volume of expensive paperwork swells yearly, and procurement procedures grow more complicated with each passing day. . . ."[16] As a result of this commission's
findings, the government instituted the Federal Acquisition Regulations
designed to govern almost all federal acquisitions (not just those of the
DoD). The intent was to "eliminate redundancy and conflicts, reduce
paperwork, [and] cut the volume of regulations in half." Originally
scheduled to take 18 months, this set of regulations took over 5 years
to complete. It was finally published in September 1983; however,
within a few months Congress began to pass major procurement legislative actions which, when combined, would take years to assimilate
into the procurement laws. First there was the Competition In Contracting Act of 1984; then came two more major procurement bills: the
Defense Appropriation Act of 1984 (PL98-525) and the Small Business
and Federal Procurement Enactment Act (PL98-577). In April 1986, the
Packard Commisision concluded that "the legal . . . regime for defense
acquisition is today impossibly cumbersome. . . . 394 different regulatory requirements in the federal acquisition regulations and the DoD
supplement are pegged to some 62 different dollar thresholds. . . . at
operating levels within the DoD, it is now virtually impossible to assimilate new legislative or regulatory refinements promptly or effectively. . . ."[17]

The Department of Defense's procurement system places four layers
of requirements upon the government's contracting personnel. First
there is the basic Armed Services Procurement Act (Chapter 137, Title
10, United States Code), which has been, over time, supplemented by
numerous laws and authorities, including the following:

Buy American (41 U.S.C. 10a–d); Noise Control Act (42 U.S.C. 4914);
Convict Labor Act (18 U.S.C. 436); Humane Slaughter of Livestock (7
U.S.C. 1901); Recycled Material (42 U.S.C. 6962); Conservation of
Energy (42 U.S.C. 6962); Gratuities (10 U.S.C. 2207); Officials Not to
Benefit (18 U.S.C. 431); Preference for U.S. Flag Vessels (10 U.S.C.
2631); Preference for U.S. Flag Air Carriers (49 U.S.C. 1517); Covenant
Against Contingent Fees (41 U.S.C 254(a)), (10 U.S.C. 2306(b)); Small

Business Subcontracting Requirements (15 U.S.C 631–647); Walsh-Healey Act (41 U.S.C. 35–45); Copeland "Anti-Kickback" Act (18 U.S.C. 874); Examination of Records (10 U.S.C. 2306); Preference for Domestic Speciality Metal (Annual DoD Appropriation Act); Preference for Domestic Food, Clothing and Textiles (Annual DoD Appropriation Act); Preference for Domestic Hand Tools (Annual GSA Appropriation Act); Required Source for Jewel Bearings (National Policy).[18]

During the mid-1980s—the period of headlined "horror stories" on spare-parts procurements—members of Congress were falling all over one other trying to pass legislation that would "reform" defense procurement. In any given year there were approximately 150 bills going through the Congress, and a significant number of these resulted in significant changes in the procurement laws. The impact of these changes was never assessed prior to their implementation, and in numerous cases they were contradictory to each other or to existing laws.

From the basic legislative framework—the Armed Services Procurement Act, its numerous amendments, and the many other laws and authorities (which come through separate laws as well as through annual additions to the various appropriation bills)—the executive branch must issue regulations and guidance to the people who actually implement the buying of goods and services for defense. In theory, these regulations are intended simply to implement the legislation; however, there is always the question of interpretation, and in numerous instances the executive branch implements them in such a way as to impose even greater restrictions of its own making. These regulations—which began as the separate services' regulations, then evolved into the Defense Acquisition Regulations, and then evolved still further to cover the whole federal government (the Federal Acquisition Regulations)—now are the basis for the executive branch's procurement activities. Just for example, out of the thousands of pages of regulations, consider the following:

Review and veto over "make or buy" decisions (Section 3-900); Subcontracting procedures (Section 1-800 and 707); Which firms to use as subcontractors (Sections 7-203.8); Which products to buy domestically (Section 6-100); What internal financial reporting system to use (Section 3-800); What industrial engineering and planning system to utilize (Section 1-1700); What minimum and average wage rates to pay (Section 12-601); How much overtime work to authorize (Section 12-102.3); What safety rules to be followed (Section 7-600).[19]

With thousands of pages of detailed regulations and then tens of thousands of pages of "policy guidance," it is incredible that the defense industry is not listed as a regulated industry. It is equally astonishing to find that the people who administer the DoD's procurement program— with its high technology, its complexities, and its billions of dollars— are not considered by the Office of Personnel Management as "professionals" and therefore are not required to have extensive education or experience.

Defense buying is extremely decentralized. Each large program office has its own buying people, and the smaller programs go to a local buying office for their procurement activities. Thus, the Department of Defense has thousands of people all over the world who, with only local supervision in most instances, make important procurement decisions on a daily basis, with large amounts of public funds at stake.

It must be emphasized that a very significant share of the defense procurement legislation is passed by Congress not to improve procurement, but to achieve some social or political objective. The argument made is that public funds should be used to achieve both national-security objectives and other objectives, such as helping small businesses, areas of relatively high unemployment, or minority-owned firms. There are over 50 such legislative requirements. While desirable from a socio-economic viewpoint, they reduce the Department of Defense from a very strong buyer, capable of driving quality up and prices down, to a buyer whose hands are tied because it is not allowed to take advantage of normal market forces. Many argue that Congress should either allow the DoD to use its market position to save public resources or acknowledge what it is doing and adjust the DoD's budget to compensate for the cost of using defense procurements as a means of subsidizing other social objectives. The cost of these subsidies has been estimated at between 15 and 30 percent of the DoD's total spending.[20]

Another very important point to recognize about these laws (and their derived regulations) is that the large defense contractors are accustomed to operating in such a totally regulated environment and to all the DoD "paperwork" and its legal implications. However, a large share of the business in the defense industry is actually done by the various subcontractors and material and parts suppliers working for the large defense firms. On the average, about 55 percent of the business given to the prime contractor for a major weapon system is subcontracted out to his suppliers. The problems arise when the prime contractor passes on all the detailed regulations and specifications to all his suppliers, who have great difficulty understanding and applying them. Because of this, many smaller firms choose not to go into the defense business at all. Others find that the implementation of military regulations throughout their operation causes them to be no longer price-competitive in the commercial world; thus, they become "specialists" in defense work. From the DoD's viewpoint, neither of these results is desirable. Defense-only suppliers become very high-cost as a result of their not having the far larger commercial base to absorb their overhead costs (facilities, management, etc.). Interestingly, some analyses have shown that the prime defense contractors place their own additional requirements, on top of the government's, on their suppliers. Often these specifications are far more extensive and restrictive than the government's. Although this gives the prime contractor a safety factor in his attempt to meet the government's requirements, it makes things much worse for the subcontractors.[21]

Perhaps the two things that come as the greatest surprises to people who begin to look into the way the defense market operates are the amount of time consumed by the acquisition process and the numbers of dollars involved in individual procurements.

Addressing the time scale first, let us consider a "typical" program. The program itself is preceded by relatively low generic expenditures for research and exploratory development. However, years may be required to develop materials or components for a new weapon system (for example, we could not have had space travel without the miniaturization of electronics). Thousands of contractors and university researchers are involved in small-dollar-value projects at this stage, and even the total dollars in this area represent a relatively insignificant share of the total defense acquisition budget. Often this generic activity continues through the evaluation of a subsystem in a prototype demonstration. The weapon program itself does not begin until the *program definition* phase is reached. Here, multiple contractors are usually funded, again at relatively low levels, to take the advanced technology and try to match it to a military mission need. This phase is basically one of "paper studies," although a great deal of computer simulation and modeling is usually done and in some cases there may be feasibility demonstrations. Typically this concept-exploration phase takes from 3 to 8 years.[22] At the end of this phase a major decision is made to build a prototype of the weapon.

The next phase is known as the *demonstration and validation* phase. Here the dollar values are still relatively small; however, the commitment to the program itself begins to get firmer. In the past, a single contractor was often selected to build the prototype, and then that contractor would almost always be the one to take the program through its subsequent phases. More recently, there has been an emphasis on attempting to get two competitive contractors to develop prototypes, as an incentive to better performance and timeliness. Depending upon the complexity and the amount of technological advancement required, the prototype phase typically takes between 2 and 7 years.

Next comes the major commitment to the *full-scale development* of the weapon system. Although the Department of Defense has argued that its decision-making process is basically "incremental," the reality is that a commitment to full-scale development is almost always a commitment to production. The number of programs canceled after full-scale development can be counted on one hand, and the cancellations have almost always come not from the military services but from the executive branch or from Congress. This phase involves large sums of money and, historically, a single contractor. The concept is, basically, to "prove out" the design that will then be used in production. This typically takes between 2 and 8 years, depending on the complexity of the technology and on the magnitude of the differences between the prototype and the production model.

At the end of full-scale development, a system goes through engineering testing and "initial operational testing" to assess its design and its military effectiveness. After this, the system is said to be ready for *production,* which usually begins at a low rate so that the "producibility" of the item can be proved. The low rate of early production delays the attainment of "initial operational capability" in the field (for example, the first deployment of a "wing" of aircraft) by an additional 2–5 years. Thus, the total time, from the conception of a weapon system through the initial deployment of a small quantity, is in the range of 11 to 19 years.

Even after a weapon system has gone into full production, the rates are very low because the units are very expensive. Therefore, the production time is very long, and it often lasts for more than 10 years.

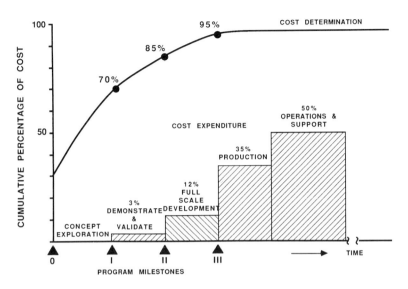

Figure 6.1
Expenditures on weapon systems contrasted with far earlier cost determinations.

Finally, the high costs of weapon systems make it impossible to replace the deployed systems with more modern ones at the planned date. Thus, some will stay in the field—and will have to be supported—for more than 20 years. (In the mid-1970s, vacuum tubes were still in use in many weapon systems, and no one could manufacture replacements for them because the rest of the users of electronics had shifted to semiconductors.)

The histogram in figure 6.1 represents the approximate percentages of dollars expended on a "typical" weapon system in each phase. Notice that the largest share of the dollars is used in operating and maintaining the systems, and the second largest share is associated with production. To have a significant impact on the costs of weapon systems, the support and production costs—not the R&D costs—must be dramatically reduced through a combination of improved design and improved management techniques. Advanced technology must be used in the early phases of a program in order to reduce the subsequent costs of production and support. The focus should not be on the development costs associated with the system. The time that passes between when costs are designed in (at the beginning of a program—see the curve in figure

6.1) and when money is expended (during the later phases of the program) must be recognized in any significant changes that are introduced into the weapons-acquisition process. This is a hard lesson to learn. It means spending a little more money "up front" in order to save millions or even billions of dollars later on.

There is a clear trend toward fewer programs, more expensive programs, and fewer weapons produced per program. This is very dangerous, both in terms of military needs and in terms of the impact on the economy. Yet spending more money "up front" means having to cancel a few weapon systems in order to make the needed dollars available—obviously a difficult political action.

The Department of Defense buys its weapon systems very slowly; in large dollar units; very carefully (under public scrutiny); with standardized, inflexible regulations and procedures; through decentralized offices; and in a very different manner from what is seen in the commercial world. It is to this last point that we now turn to get a better understanding of the unique market structure that exists in the defense arena.

Many have attempted to describe the very special buyer-seller relationship that exists in the realm of defense. The economist Walter Adams called it "a closed system of buyer and seller, interrelated for common interest" that "defies analysis by conventional economic tools."[23] The economist James McKee said that "it is a relationship of 'participation'" in which "the large buyer has a direct influence on the policies and decisions of the large seller," and that "what we observe is a kind of behavior that is not adequately described by any of the commonly employed 'models' of market relationships and economics."[24] The consumer advocate Ralph Nader emphasized "the institutionalized fusion of corporate desires with public bureaucracy, where the national security is synonymous with the state of Lockheed and Litton."[25]

The differences between the free market and the defense market are detailed in table 6.1, where each of thirty important assumptions of free-market economic theory is completely countered by a reality of the defense market.[26] As George C. Lodge of the Harvard Graduate School of Business Administration noted in discussing the U.S. government's role in saving the Lockheed Corporation in 1976, "It is a dangerous delusion to keep mumbling the old myths of free enterprise when they are irrelevant. Ethics requires calling a spade a spade. If we are to

Table 6.1
Some "market imperfections and failures" illustrated by comparing practices in the defense market against tenets of free-market theory.

Free-market theory	Defense-market practice
Many small buyers	One buyer (DoD)
Many small suppliers	Very few, large suppliers of a given item
All items are small, and bought in large quantities	Each item is extremely expensive, and bought in very small quantities
Market sets prices	Monopoly or oligopoly pricing—or "buy in" to "available" budget dollars
Free movement in and out of market	Extensive barriers to entry and exit
Prices are set by marginal costs	Prices are proportional to total costs
Prices are set by marginal utility	Almost any price is paid for desired military performance
Prices fall with reduced demand to encourage buying more	Prices rise with reduced demand, owing to cost-based pricing
Supply adjusts to demand	Large excess capacity
Labor is highly mobile	Greatly diminishing labor mobility
Decreasing or constant returns to scale (operating difficulty)	Increasing returns to scale (in region of interest)
Market shifts rapidly with changes in supply and demand	7–10 years to develop a new system, then at least 3–5 years to produce it
Market smoothly reaches equilibrium	Erratic budget behavior from year to year
General equilibrium—assumes prices will return to equilibrium value	Costs have been rising at 5–7 percent per year (excluding inflation)
Profits are equalized across economy	Wide profit variations between sectors; even wider between firms
Perfect mobility of capital (money)	Heavy debt; difficulty in borrowing
Capital (equipment) is mobile with changing demand	Large and old capital equipment "locks in" companies

Table 6.1 (continued)

Free-market theory	Defense-market practice
No government involvement	Government is regulator, specifier, banker, judge of claims, etc.
Selection is based on price	Selection is based primarily on promised performance
No externalities	All businesses working for DoD must satisfy requirements of OSHA, EEO, awards to areas of high unemployment, small-business set asides, etc.
Profits are a return for risks	Profits are regulated, primarily as a percent of costs
All products of a given type are the same	Essentially, each producer's products are different
Competition is for a share of the market	Competition is often for all or none of a given market
Production is for inventory	Production occurs after sale is made
Size of market is established by buyers and sellers	Size of market is established by "third party" (Congress) through annual budget
Demand is sensitive to price	Demand is "threat-sensitive," or responds to availability of new technology; it is almost never price-sensitive
Technology is equal throughout an industry	Competitive technologies
Relatively stable, multi-year commitments	Annual commitments, with frequent changes
Benefits of the purchase go to buyer	A "public good"
Buyer has the choice of spending now or saving for a later time	DoD must spend its congressional appropriation or lose it

save the noblest and best of free enterprise and strengthen the force of market competition, we must be clear about where it is relevant and where it is not."[27]

Recognition of the fact that the "free market" does not exist in the world of defense is an essential first step in any possible corrective actions. However, the absence of the "invisible hand" does not mean that we can throw out all economic theory in establishing defense policy. In an environment of a single buyer (monopsony) and, largely, either single suppliers of individual products (monopoly) or a very few highly specialized suppliers of these products (oligopoly), there are significant aspects of economic theory that are applicable. At the general level, the "theory of the second best" should be used for analyzing the desired market characteristics[28]; at the detailed level, "bargaining theory" applies.

In simple terms, the theory of the second best says that if some of the conditions for the traditional free market (the "first best") do not apply and cannot be created, then creating some additional free-market conditions or moving more in the direction of free-market conditions may not improve efficiency. In the case of defense it is clear that some of the obstacles to the operation of a free market cannot be removed; thus, it follows that all policy actions in the defense sector must be made with the theory of the second best in mind. Each case is a "special case," and actions must be evaluated on their own merits rather than on the basis of any universal theory. Unfortunately, many do not accept this statement. For example, one senator commented at a public meeting that there was "a dangerous story going around Washington to the effect that it would be a good idea to close some aircraft plants."[29] He noted that "this would clearly reduce competition" and that, therefore, it would be wrong. This statement, based upon traditional free-market economic theory (mixed with politics), neglected the applicability of the theory of the second best to the case at hand. In fact, fewer bidders and less excess capacity would still represent more than sufficient competition in the aircraft industry (ample firms would still remain); yet it would result in a more efficient industry, since the remaining firms would have sufficient business to justify modernization of their facilities.

Interestingly, there are analogies, at least in some respects, between the defense marketplace and the commercial world. For example, as the economist Barry Bosworth pointed out, "The defense market structure is very similar to General Motors buying from its suppliers—yet defense does it totally differently."[30] General Motors is a dominant buyer in its market, and in most critical areas it has only one or two suppliers; yet it works closely with them. And GM has the definite objective of achieving mutual benefits for both the supplier and the buyer, since, in this case, the buyer clearly recognizes the importance of having a healthy, innovative, and responsive set of industrial suppliers.

In the commercial world, good contractors are rewarded with more business and bad contractors are punished by not receiving more business.[31] In the defense world, it is almost exactly the opposite. Public

Table 6.2
Traditional business contracts contrasted with weapons-procurement contracts.

Traditional contracts	Weapons-procurement contracts
Fixed scope (in terms of specifications, cost, performance, quantities, and schedule)	Constantly changing scope (in terms of specifications, budgets, desired performance, quantities, and schedules)
"Arms-length" (i.e., distant) relationship	Involvement in every step of the process
A change terminates or fundamentally alters the contract	Changes are treated as administrative matters, and appropriate adjustments are made to the contract
Results are easily measured, and blame is placeable	Results are hard to identify and measure. Placing blame is difficult because of the strong relationship between buyer and seller
What is bought is, basically, a product	Contract is as much for the service of producing the system as it is for the product itself (again reflecting detailed government involvement)
Short term	Long term (often decades)
Disputes are litigated	Disputes are resolved by adjustments that preserve contractual relations

accountability and regulation are the dominant characteristics in the defense market, and those incentives that do exist (as will be discussed below) are often perverse, encouraging higher costs rather than driving costs down. There is even the fear that the appearance of good working relations between the government and industry will be misinterpreted as indicating the abuse of public funds. Thus, when it comes to the contractual relations between the government and its industrial suppliers, the relationship is largely an adversarial one. And, because of the lack of trust, there are detailed regulations covering every aspect of the relationship, and thousands of auditors to probe every aspect of a supplier's performance (during and after the work). Indeed, because of the continued "belief" in the existence of a free market in the defense arena, a second "myth of the market" exists: that the contractual relationship between buyer and seller is the "traditional" legal relationship. As table 6.2 shows, contracts are dramatically different in the defense world.[32]

At the detailed level of the contractual relationship, what exists is basically a "bargaining" relationship between a single buyer and either a few suppliers or a single one.[33] In this form of decision making, it makes a very significant difference where the center of power lies. Thus, it is interesting to observe that, in the defense market, the government has all the power when it is running a competition between multiple sources (even when there are only two competitors). The government can use the "oligopoly game"—it can play the contractors off against one another to extract promises of high performance, low cost, and early delivery. But once a winning developer is announced, the tables are turned; now the "sole source" is in an increasingly powerful position. As time goes on, the government becomes more and more dependent upon this contractor for a product which is (or is believed to be) badly needed but for which it would take many years to develop a substitute product or an alternate source. From this point on, the contractor is in a position to go to the government with "explanations" of "government-introduced" problems that are raising costs, causing delivery delays, and so forth, and to bargain for higher prices. Thus, there is a great inducement for a firm to "buy in" with a low initial bid and then, after it is in a sole-source position and the government is dependent upon it, to figure out ways to get the contract changed. In general, the basic view of each of the firms is that, since there will only be one program awarded every 5 or 10 years, it is far better to be the low bidder and win than it is to be a realistic bidder and not have a program (especially when the winner can "get well" through subsequent changes to the program). The contractors know full well that there are likely to be thousands of changes in a program during its many years of evolution—often as a result of changes to the budget or the program introduced by Congress or the DoD, but also possibly as a result of "threat changes" or shifts in priority among various defense programs. If the government (Congress and the executive branch) was a less fickle customer and could stick to its commitments over an extended period of time, as commercial customers generally do, then not only the buyer-seller relationship but also the efficiency and effectiveness of the acquisition process would be better.

Before discussing the more desirable alternative mechanism, namely the creation of "incentives" to replace the "controls" in the defense marketplace—we must note two other characteristics of this unique market.

First, the government often owns significant amounts of the plant space and the equipment used by the contractor.[34] For example, the government owns most of the plant space and the equipment of the prime contractors in the munitions and strategic missile industries, one-third in the aircraft industry, and a significant share of the overhaul and repair sector of the shipbuilding industry (but very little in the new-construction shipbuilding industry). This government ownership presents a conflict, since the government wants to keep "its plants" in full use whether or not they are the most efficient locations for the orders at hand. This leads to situations in which the government and the industry compete to do the work. For example, when the government decides to modify an aircraft, it can choose between government-owned-and-operated facilities and a contractor's facilities (which may also be partly government-owned).[35] If such work were awarded competitively, and on the basis of price (or, preferably, price and quality), this mixture of public and private ownership might be a very desirable means of increasing competition. In reality, the "in-house" bids are always significantly lower, since the government's way of bookkeeping does not consider depreciation of plant and facilities, retirement pay, or profit. One might expect that Congress would resolve the issue of public versus private ownership; however, legislation in this area is sufficiently ambiguous to justify actions in either direction.[36]

The second unique characteristic of the defense marketplace worth emphasizing is that the barriers to entry and exit are extremely high. This will be discussed in considerable detail in chapter 8; however, it should be noted here that the entry barriers are due to (among other things) government regulations, special bookkeeping, security requirements, and special production procedures, and that firms with long-duration government contracts (and the associated high overhead) have great difficulty diversifying into the commercial marketplace. Thus, there is a mutual dependence between the defense firms and the Department of Defense. The present defense firms are (at least at the plant or the division level) a "specialized" set of suppliers. If one were going to attempt to change this market, one would have to be able to induce a dramatic shift from the current regulated environment to one built on incentives. Yet this is an "either/or" situation. One cannot have a totally regulated environment and, simultaneously, create incentives for independent action. This crucial point is rarely recognized by those legislators who constantly preach the idea of creating incentives for improved performance by the defense industry, but who attempt to accomplish this through additional regulation. The need is just the opposite: to create incentives, one has to have an environment in which the various suppliers are free to innovate and to manage. Thus, for successful implementation of the incentive approach, one needs to look at each sector of the defense industry and "create" an environment in which incentives for desired industrial performance can be maximized in the absence of regulation, yet one in which, for each specific sector, the incentives will be to the government's benefit rather than to its detriment.

Compare the normal operation of a free market against the government's buying practices. In a free market, if a supplier achieves unit-cost reductions, quality improvements, or shortened delivery times, his efforts may stimulate a demand for additional units, and his reward would be a greater market share. However, in the case of defense procurement, the number of units to be built is fixed by Congress as part of the budget process, and a firm's market share is usually either 100 percent or 0. In the commercial sector, reductions in the unit cost usually result in significantly improved profits for the supplier (an obvious incentive). In the defense sector, if the costs go down, then the following year, when the contract is negotiated for the next annual buy, the prices are based on the lower costs, and the supplier's profits will actually be reduced (certainly a perverse incentive). Finally, in the commercial sector a firm has a significant incentive to invest in new plant space and equipment and in labor training, to lower cost, or to improve quality in order to obtain future contracts. In the defense sector, contracts are awarded on the basis of the original agreements contained in the proposals submitted for the *development* of each new weapon system; thus, there is very little incentive for a sole source to make productivity-enhancing investments. (The alternative model—of continuous competition in defense contracting—will be discussed below.)

It is appropriate here to note briefly that one of the underlying principles of the defense procurement process[37] is that the government will "use the type of contract appropriate for a particular procurement." For example, when a contract involves high risk (as in the case of advanced technology), the government is better off having a "cost plus" contract, under which the contractor is paid on the basis of his cost. In this case, a fixed-price contract would have to include so many dollars for contingencies that the price would more than double. In contrast, when the risks have been reduced and a program is ready for production, then the contract should be a "fixed-price" one, and the cost quoted, especially in a competitive environment, should be the minimum cost; thus, the government should get the best deal for its money. Additionally, under a fixed-price contract, if problems develop in the production process, the contractor pays the increased cost; as a result, the government has limited liability and need only budget for the basic contract value—with no "insurance" dollars required.

This all sounds very rational, and it would make a lot of sense if defense business were similar to commercial business (particularly after a contract is awarded). However, there is a dramatic difference between the two kinds of business in the area of "changes" to a program after the initial contract. There are logical reasons for the DoD to want to be able to change a contract at any time and, therefore, to have a provision in the contract for unilateral changes of schedule, budget, or performance requirements. In the case of schedule, there are situations in which the government might want to increase the speed of a delivery because of some international crisis. In the case of cost, it is very possible that Congress will not give the DoD the dollars it had planned to have available for a program in any given year. In the case of performance, a potential threat might alter needs; for example, the discovery that the Soviets were using a new radar frequency might require the United States to modify some of its systems. In all three cases, the government needs to have the flexibility to modify the contract, and the contractor is entitled to bill the government for the impact of the change. Were only one or two changes to be made in a program during its many years of development and production, such a system might work quite well. Unfortunately, this is far from the case. For example, on a single class of submarines, there were over 35,000 changes made in the first seven years after the contract award,[38] and during the lifetime of the F-111 aircraft program there were a total of 394,922 changes.[39] The implementation of all these changes is priced by the contractor in a sole-source environment. Thus, it is not surprising that the supposedly fixed-price contract for the Maverick missile grew from $90 million to $360 million in 3 years, thanks to almost 300 changes.[40] The Navy's F-14D fighter plane had a "fixed-price" contract for $984 million that grew by $260 million.[41] Boeing's "fixed-price" contract to modify the B-52s rose from $575 million to $852 million.[42] And, in looking at a large number of Navy contracts for ship repairs, the GAO found that "of 75 so-called fixed price contracts valued at some $594 million, between 1982 and mid-1985, they wound up costing 63 percent more than at the outset. . . . for cost-based contracts, the increase was 35 percent on a total of 30 contracts worth $539 million in total."[43] Thus, surprisingly, and certainly contrary to the traditional theory, the overruns on the "fixed-price" contracts were almost twice as large as those on the cost-based contracts.

With hundreds of millions of dollars in changes to contracts, there is bound to be a question as to who is at fault in causing these cost increases. The government will say that the industry was not capable of managing the program well; the industry will say that the government was "messing up" the program. It is such issues that keep the 30,000 lawyers in Washington busy.[44] In the mid-1970s, every shipbuilder in the country had the Navy in court over cost increases. Perhaps even thornier are the questions as to who is at fault when a product that satisfies the contract, or for which the terms and conditions of the contract have been waived by the government for the sake of more rapid delivery, fails to meet its performance objectives. Under such conditions, the contractor often blames the failure on conflicting specifications written into the contract by the government. Such was the case when the Air Force had to pay the Lockheed Corporation $1.5 billion to put new wings on its giant C-5 transport airplanes after studies showed that the old wings, which Lockheed had built, were in danger of cracking.[45] It was also the case when the Air Force paid Pratt and Whitney nearly half a billion dollars on a multi-year "Component Improvement Program" aimed at "improving" the F-15's engines to meet their original durability goal.[46] Getting the original contractor (Rockwell International) to correct various design problems afflicting the B-1B bomber was expected to cost the Air Force an extra $3 billion.[47] In such cases, both parties—the government and the contractor—are obviously at fault, but the basic problem rests with the overall acquisition system.

If the government were interested in running its programs efficiently and effectively, it would estimate the *most likely* cost of each program and then budget its funds accordingly—even if fewer programs would then be funded. Each contract then would be awarded at a realistic cost level, in order to allow the contractor to focus on delivering the product rather than on figuring out ways to change the contract to "get well" financially. Contrary to this desired approach, however, the GAO found (in a 1986 analysis) that "71 of the 75 fixed-price contracts and 24 of the 30 cost-based contracts were awarded at prices *below* the government's own 'estimates' of expected costs of these particular products."[48] Needless to say, such results are highly predictable in the environment in which they occur. It is also true that they need not occur. Some programs—such as the Navy's development of the Polaris, Poseidon, and Trident missiles—have been budgeted and contracted for realistically (with sufficient provisions for contingencies), and there have been few if any overruns on these programs year after year.[49]

One last, unique aspect of the acquisition process that must be highlighted is the way in which the government pursues high quality in its weapon systems. Here, too, the government has fallen into trying to solve problems through firm contracts or detailed regulations rather than through good business sense. The government's method seems to be to make sure that a product meets its specifications by continuously inspecting it and running tests on it. The contractors, however, recognize that if they "satisfy the contract" they will get paid, and that their performance on their current contracts (in terms of the quality of the products) has almost nothing to do with whether they will get future contracts. In contrast, the Japanese commercial manufacturers, and then the American ones, discovered that the right approach is to make continuous efforts to reduce the costs associated with poor quality, by using statistical monitoring to detect any failures early (when it is cheapest to fix them) and by revising the production process to prevent the failures from recurring. As one reporter observed, "military suppliers have been slower than others to adapt production efficiencies popularized by Japanese companies, such as factory automation and worker participation . . . moreover, the Defense Department rarely penalized companies for providing substandard equipment."[50] As the above example of the $3 billion B-1B repair indicates, fixing a system after it has been deployed is extremely expensive.

To follow the Japanese model, one needs to look at the "total cost of poor quality" throughout the life cycle of a product—including the cost of rejections and reworking in the factory and the cost of failures that occur in the field and have to be repaired there. Extensive studies of commercial systems show, as one would expect, that those items on which a large share of the cost of achieving high quality is spent on design, prevention, and in-process appraisal have much lower total costs than those on which most of that "quality cost" is spent on trying to test and appraise systems after they are built or trying to fix them after they are in the field.[51] For U.S.-made commercial systems, it is estimated that the "quality cost" per unit of sales may be 25 percent or more. However, one top Pentagon official estimated that some defense equipment may have a "cost of quality" of 50 percent or more[52]—which means the waste of billions of dollars.

Notice that the emphasis in the new approach to quality is on spending *less money* overall and yet getting much *higher quality,* which is quite contrary to the traditional defense argument that "we know we're spending more, but we have to do it to get the quality." In this area, as in many others, we need first to recognize that there is a problem, and then to make dramatic "cultural changes" in the way the Department of Defense does its business. The challenge lies in figuring out how to get higher quality at lower cost.[53] This is a *management* challenge. Not only do the process and product technologies exist; they have been demonstrated in the non-defense world.

The Results Achieved

There are generally two approaches to measuring the effectiveness of the weapons-acquisition process. The first is to look at the long-term trends from generation to generation of weapon systems and to determine whether performance has improved and costs have gone down— the combination being a clear indication of improvement. The second is to look at an individual weapon system's development and production and to determine whether the cost and performance objectives that were established for that system at the beginning of (say) a 20-year time period have been realized. These two measures are very much interrelated; however, they are driven by different processes within the overall acquisition system. The results measured by the first method are controlled more by the requirements and planning processes and by the way in which technology is utilized; those measured by the second method are controlled more by the procurement process and by the effectiveness with which the Department of Defense manages individ-

Table 6.3
Costs of selected weapon systems (millions of 1988 dollars).[a]

	Unit cost	Number	Program cost
Nuclear aircraft carrier[b]	$3,046	2	$ 6,092
Trident II submarine	1,486	11	16,350
Aegis cruiser	987	27	26,658
B-1B bomber	261	100	26,142
C-17A cargo aircraft	126	211	26,607
Trident II missile	36	845	30,451
F-15 fighter	33	1,286	41,904
F-16 fighter	16	2,737	43,147
UH-60 helicopter	6.5	1,121	7,233
M-1 tank	2.5	7,857	19,947
Harpoon anti-ship missile	1.2	4,023	4,996
Sparrow anti-aircraft missile[c]	0.19	14,309	2,724

a. All data in this table are from the DoD's Systems Acquisition Report (SAR) to Congress, December 1986.
b. This price excludes the aircraft and weapons on the carriers.
c. This is for total procurement by both the Navy and the Air Force.

ual programs. Before we consider the actual results determined through these two methods, a few general remarks are appropriate.

Historically, the military has primarily emphasized the *performance* of weapons. The schedule of delivery has received secondary attention, and there has been very little emphasis on the unit cost of systems. Thus, it is not surprising to find that the performance of individual weapon systems has been improving from generation to generation. Each generation of tanks has been significantly better than the last, and the same can be said for ships and aircraft. Unfortunately, this performance increase has been achieved at an extremely high cost. As table 6.3 shows, a single program often runs into the billions of dollars, with each individual weapon costing an enormous amount of money. As we go down the columns in this table, the unit costs decrease but the quantities required increase significantly.

The effect of the increasing unit costs of weapon systems has already had a significant impact on America's defense posture, in terms of the amount of equipment that can be bought each year for the dollars available. For example, in the 1950s the United States bought over 2,000 fighter planes a year. In the 1960s the number dropped to around 600, and in the 1970s it was down to 300. It was only because of the doubling of the defense budget that the DoD was able to keep on buying over 300 fighters per year in the 1980s. The long-term trend is clear. As Norman Augustine has pointed out,[54] if this trend continues, by the year 2054 the United States will be able to buy only one fighter plane a year. (The performance of this single aircraft will be outstanding, of course.) Such results are clearly unacceptable. Something must be done to reverse the declining quantities. Therefore, something must be done to reverse the increasing unit costs of individual weapon systems.

If we use the second measure of effectiveness in the acquisition of weapon systems, namely the comparison of results with objectives, the performance is somewhat more encouraging.[55] In comparison with many other organizations, the DoD does a *relatively* good job of controlling cost overruns. However, the cost overruns in the area of defense are quite significant—historically, they have been in the range of 40–100 percent for entire programs (from initiation through completion). Obviously there is a great deal of room for improvement; however, the DoD could not necessarily obtain twice as much equipment if there were no doubling of the program costs, since it might well be that the cost estimates were unrealistically low to begin with, and that a considerable portion of the cost growth, as the program evolved, was simply a recognition of this fact.

The overall effects of the rising costs of weapon systems on the United States' security posture were dramatically demonstrated during the period of the Reagan buildup in the first half of the 1980s. As dollars were rapidly increased to buy greater quantities of weapon systems, we found, surprisingly, that we did not get the corresponding increases in quantity. For example, a comparison of the dollars spent in 1977–1980 with those spent in 1982–1985 shows that the dollars spent for tanks and Army vehicles went up by 147.4 percent, but the number of tanks and vehicles actually purchased went up by only 30 percent. For missiles, the dollars increased by 91.2 percent but the numbers went up by only 6.4 percent. For aircraft, the dollars went up by 75.4 percent and the numbers by only 8.8 percent.[56] Clearly, the desired objective—increased quantities of systems for the dollars spent—were not achieved in the Reagan buildup. To understand these results better (and, therefore, to be able to make recommendations for corrective actions), let us look in greater detail at the two broad categories of weapon-system costs.

In analyzing the results from generation to generation of weapon systems, the initial issue is the length of time it takes to develop a system. In 1958, one report concluded that "one of the major weaknesses in our strategic posture has been our inordinately long weapon system lead times."[57] In the 1960s, Merton J. Peck and Frederick M. Scherer wrote that they considered long lead times to be among the most serious problems in defense acquisition.[58] As figure 6.2 shows, despite the DoD's efforts to try to improve on the lead times for weapon-system development (as the military's need for systems utilizing the increasing technological evolutions became more urgent), the trends have gotten worse in almost all categories.[59] In the 30 years covered by this figure, as weapon systems became much more complex, the average development cycle for these systems got significantly longer. The 6 or 8 years taken to develop a weapon system was much longer than the development time for a typical commercial system of comparable complexity.

Improvements in performance from generation to generation of weapons must also be considered. Figure 6.3 traces the performance of 79 different types of U.S. fighter and attack aircraft.[60] The trends in this chart are extremely positive, and reflect the high level of emphasis given to improving performance in the military environment. In fact, a comparison of these data with performance results of Soviet systems (see chapter 7) indicates that these American fighters significantly surpassed their Soviet counterparts of the time. But overall military effectiveness is not measured only in terms of a single weapon's performance; *quantities* matter, too. Many military theorists argue that quantity has an even greater effect than individual weapon performance. Looking at the costs of 38 different fighter and attack aircraft (figure 6.4), we see that increased performance has been paid for by an even higher rate of increase in unit production costs.[61] (Again, costs are adjusted for both the effects of inflation and the effects of reduced quantities.) Comparable curves showing increasing performance and increasing unit production cost could be drawn for each and every category of weapon systems.

Perhaps equally to blame for the high and rising cost of national defense is the extremely high cost of operating and maintaining modern

Buying Military Equipment   173

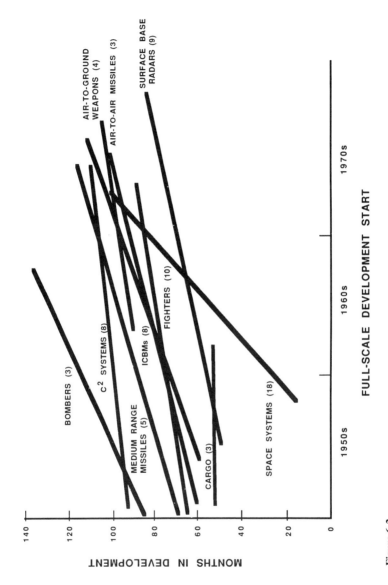

Figure 6.2
Development time trends. (Numbers in parentheses represent numbers of systems.)

Figure 6.3
Performance potential versus time, for fighter and attack aircraft.

weapon systems—both in "direct" costs and in manpower costs. An hour's flying time for a B-1B bomber costs $12,000, a squadron of sixteen B-1Bs requires 84 crewmen and 1,493 mechanics and other handlers,[62] one aircraft carrier costs $593,000 a day to operate,[63] and the annual cost of operating one Naval Carrier Task Force is $1 billion.[64]

The Department of Defense does not set out to design expensive weapon systems, yet that is clearly the result. To see why, one need simply think back to the "requirements" and the budget process. If military "requirements" are written without any fiscal constraints and with nothing in mind but the best possible system to counter the Soviet threat, and if the planning and budgeting systems are based on the assumption that there will be ample dollars available in future years to cover the increased cost of the systems in the required quantities, then clearly the process is not fiscally constrained. Additionally, there are

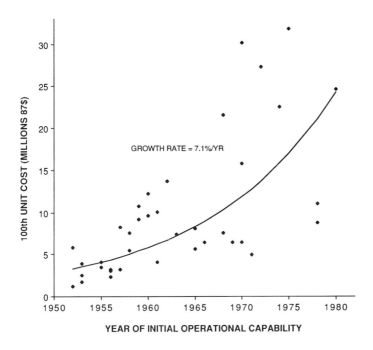

Figure 6.4
Cost of hundredth unit versus time, for fighter and attack aircraft.

no incentives to reduce costs at either the design phase or the manufacturing phase.

Nor does the defense industry have much of an incentive to reduce the costs of weapon systems (even those in production), since in most cases there is only one firm building each system. Instead of introducing productivity-enhancing, cost-reducing innovations, the defense contractors have been adding more "indirect" labor costs (many of them attributable to engineers and administrators in the industrial facilities). In General Dynamics' Fort Worth plant, where the F-111 and the F-16 have been built, 72 percent of the labor force was involved in "hands-on" production operations in the mid-1950s; 30 years later, with a work force of the same size, only 30 percent were involved with "hands-on" labor.[65] In 1985 only 14 percent of the Hughes Aircraft Corporation's work force was involved in production, while engineers and technicians made up more than 50 percent.[66] In 1984, 75 percent of Northrop's new hires were engineers.[67] During the Reagan buildup, when production orders to the industrial plants increased dramatically, one would have expected the overhead burden (the indirect costs to support the factories, such as facilities, supervision, and utilities) to go down as a percentage of the work, since more of the work should have been associated with direct manufacturing. However, such was not the case, since there was little incentive for the factories to cut back on their indirect-labor pools. In fact, with the increasing volume of work, the percentage of indirect costs actually went up—in direct contradiction to economic theory.[68]

From this discussion it should be clear that if the basic costs of weapon systems are to be reduced, significant changes must take place in the requirements process, the budget process, the procurement process, and the structure of the industrial base that supplies these goods. These are the four essential changes that are the focus of this book.

We now turn to the second broad category of weapons costs: the management of programs already initiated. Perhaps the best summary of the historical data in this area is the following statement from a 1979 General Accounting Office report:

Since 1969, the initial (planning) estimate (submitted by the DoD) has turned out to be approximately 100 percent below the actual cost of major systems. The later, more refined, development cost estimate given Congress prior to full-scale development has proved to be approximately 50 percent below actual procurement costs. The review . . . failed to find one example where the DoD accurately estimated or overestimated the cost of any major weapon system. And once initial funds have been provided, it was found that a program is terminated only when the most extreme cost increases have occurred.[69]

This study confirmed a 1972 GAO study.[70] An Air Force study done in June 1981 found that things were even worse, and that for the programs covered by the study the cost growth had been almost 100 percent from the initiation of full-scale development to the completion of the program.[71] Of course, 100 percent cost growths are not anything new; Gibbon points out that an aqueduct being built for Hadrian around the year 100 "more than doubled the estimate,"[72] and Norman Augustine notes that in 1794 the Congress had to cut back the number of large frigates authorized from six to three because of cost overruns.[73] However, to discourage the impression that a 100 percent cost growth is some immutable law of nature, it should be pointed out that—in a period when the defense budget was rising rapidly and inflation was extremely low—the Department of Defense reduced its cost overruns from an annual rate of about 14 percent in 1980 to less than 1 percent in 1984, and the Congressional Budget Office acknowledged that defense-program cost estimates actually *fell* for the year 1985.[74] Again, it must be repeated that the DoD has a relatively good record in the area of cost overruns. A 1982 report by the General Accounting Office revealed that 137 DoD projects did better, on average, than 239 civilian projects being carried out by government agencies. (The GAO found that the average cost increase for the defense programs was 43 percent of that for the non-defense programs.[75])

As was noted above, on any given weapon system, the DoD is likely to attempt to give performance requirements the first priority; the schedule comes next, and the cost of the program comes last. As a result, it is quite typical for a system's performance to come very close to that originally required; however, schedules run about 30 percent late.[76] And since schedule slippages increase costs, the long-term effect is the production of weapons at extremely inefficient rates. A typical production line will have an "optimum rate" as well as a minimum and a maximum "economically efficient rate," beyond which the costs become prohibitively high on either end. Surprisingly, even during the Reagan buildup (1983–1987), the Congressional Budget Office found that half of the 40 largest weapons programs were purchasing weapons in numbers below the minimum requirements for economically efficient rates. For example, the minimum rate for economically efficient production of the Air Force's F-15 fighter plane is 120 per year; however, the DoD was buying F-15s at an average rate of 41 per year.[77] To point out how drastically these program stretchouts affect production, Senator Bingaman pointed out that "of the 26 combat aircraft production programs authorized for fiscal year 1986, nearly 45 percent will produce aircrafts at a rate of fewer than two per month. Indeed 11 of these programs . . . will manufacture aircraft at a rate of fewer than one per month."[78] Clearly, the DoD has chosen to keep all these programs at very low (and inefficient) production rates.

Unfortunately, the basic cause of these problems is built into the DoD's procurement and management practices. As described above, this system encourages a great deal of "optimism" in bidding and in budgeting, and there is almost no incentive to put in management reserves for likely risks or problems that will occur with high-technology, advanced-development items. It is always assumed—unrealistically—that growing budgets in future years will provide the needed dollars. Therefore, it is not surprising to find overruns occurring on these programs—they were predictable at the beginning. In fact, in an analytic study looking at the variations of overruns from contractor to contractor and program to program, Frederick Scherer found that "the incidence and magnitude of overruns and underruns appear to be explained more by differences in the degree of optimism or pessimism negotiated into contract cost targets than by variations in contractor efficiency."[79] The solution to this problem is relatively clear: to adequately budget and realistically plan these programs even if it means that there will be fewer programs in the overall budget. However, the military services feel that even an expensive item, in smaller quantity, is better than none at all; a senator or a representative certainly doesn't want to cancel a program in his state or district; and the press is constantly criticizing the DoD's management when a program is canceled.[80]

Traditionally, one of three techniques has been used to "correct" the problem of cost overruns on weapon systems: increasing congressional regulation, adding layers of management in the DoD, or firing the industrial managers believed to be responsible. All three techniques have been shown to have perverse results.[81] For example, the Packard Commission found that having many layers of management between a program manager and the senior acquisition executive in the DoD (often up to 40 people, including staff people with veto power and "line" people above the program manager) usually caused turmoil in a program, and thus introduced significant inefficiency, without providing any greater management oversight or any improvements.

Finally, there is basically no incentive for either the DoD or Congress to eliminate weak firms from a "sick industry" (one having "capacity much in excess of current and probable future needs, and rigidities which retard the reallocation of capital and or labor toward growth industries"[82]).

In summary, the acquisition process is too slow, overcautious, inflexible, overregulated, unstable, driven by the quest for performance at the expense of high costs, and far too different from the commercial world; and there are few incentives to change any of these characteristics. To fix what it called the "disastrous effect the process is having on

the cost and efficiency of the system," the Packard Commission recommended (in its Final Report) a number of significant "cultural
changes" in the way the Department of Defense does its business: to
streamline the organization and the procedures, to use technology to
reduce costs, to balance the cost and the performance of each weapon
system, to stabilize the programs, to expand the use of commercial
products, to increase the use of "commercial-style" competition, and
to enhance the quality of acquisition personnel. We will consider each
of these points, beginning with competition.

Competition

Competition is, perhaps, the one thing that most differentiates the
defense and civilian markets. In the civilian world, if one car manufacturer doubles the price of its car, then people buy their cars from
someone else. In the world of defense, if a supplier significantly raises
the price of a particular aircraft, the Department of Defense has no
choice but to attempt to negotiate the price down. It is not that competition is not intended to be the normal way of doing defense business;
in fact, competitive procurement of defense goods and services has
been required by law since the Armed Services Procurement Act of
1947. Nor is it that there is never any competition present in the case
of defense procurement; to the contrary, there is usually fierce rivalry
for the initial award for the development of a weapon system. But once
the initial award has been made, a weapon system is generally developed, produced, and "supported" by a single firm, over many years.
The absence of a buyer's alternative—in other words, the sole-source
environment—makes the critical difference in the defense market.

The acquisition of a major new weapon system usually begins with
competition for a research-and-development contract. This award is
based primarily on the projected technical capability of the weapon.
Often the only price used in the selection process is development cost;
the big dollars associated with the production program are largely ignored. Hundreds or even thousands of industry people are involved in
writing a proposal for a major weapon system.[83] Prototypes are often
built and tested as part of the proposal effort.[84] The cost of the proposal
effort often runs into the millions of dollars.[85] The proposals are then
evaluated by the DoD in a very detailed source-selection process, which

involves hundreds of government employees and takes at least six months and often more than a year. The evaluators know that the award will be subjected to enormous public scrutiny, and will attempt to take the safe route by making the award to the contractor who promises the most and offers the lowest price.[86]

One big reason why the competition for the R&D award is vicious is that very few major weapon-system programs are initiated in the course of (say) a decade. In essence, the government is making an "all or nothing" choice. Because of the long duration and the high cost of an R&D competition, only a few firms have the resources to compete. These competitors usually strive to propose unique ways of meeting the DoD's requirements. Because there are few bidders and highly differentiated products, the economist Frederick Scherer refers to this competition as "differentiated oligopoly rivalry."[87]

Not only do the contractors know that the DoD is searching for the best possible performance for the dollars available; they also know the DoD's budget for the development program well in advance, since it is published as part of the budget submitted to Congress two years before the program is to be initiated. Again because of the severe competition for these few, large programs, there are two principle incentives for bidders to be "optimistic" in their technical claims and in their bids. First, they know that the winner will have to promise very high performance, since the military officials involved in the selection generally place a premium on projected technical achievements. Second, they recognize that there are almost no financial penalties for competitive optimism,[88] so they have much to gain and little to lose from an optimistic bid.

Additionally, each proposal is viewed as basically a new event, and there is little if any consideration of a company's record on other contracts. This is one of the major differences between competition in the commercial world and competition for government business. In the private sector, a supplier's record is perhaps the most important consideration. A supplier who does a good job is usually rewarded with more business; one who does a poor job is not. In order to move in that desirable direction, the government should allow those who award contracts to exercise "management judgment" (i.e., judgment of prior performance) and to reject low bids from firms with poor records.

Perhaps the best concise comparison of the government's source-

selection process with the commercial approach is the following com-
ment by Alan Polsen, president and chief executive officer of the Gulfstream Aerospace Corporation:

I personally believe that the C-20 aircraft program procurement could
have been completed in a 2–3 week period instead of the 8 or 9 months
spent in proposal preparation and source-selection activity. The C-20
proposal and source selection cost Gulfstream over $1.3 million, and
we delivered over 4,000 lbs. of written material and data. I'm sure the
government also incurred considerable expense in concluding this procurement. Compare this to the hundreds of customers, including foreign
governments, that buy our aircraft on a 133-page detail specification
and a 23-page contract![89]

Polsen might have added that his corporation's reputation also influenced the confidence with which people would buy his aircraft in the
commercial environment, whereas in the defense environment he could
have been competing with any firm that wanted to be in the aircraft
business and could get a congressman to vouch for its responsibility.[90]

One of the most misunderstood aspects of competition in defense
procurements is that, in most cases, having a few highly qualified bidders creates a more effective competition than having a very large
number of bidders—in contrast with a normal free-market environment,
where, as the number of bidders increases, the competition becomes
more intense. Because of the uniqueness of the defense environment,
the "second-best" solution appears to be the answer. The use of "limited
competition" among qualified firms should be encouraged, particularly
in competitions involving new ideas (e.g., research and development;
professional-services awards). The use of "limited" rather than "free
and open" competition was recommended by the Government Procurement Commission in 1972.[91] A firm will tend to put more of an effort
into its proposal if the probability of winning appears to be very good,
and to make a significantly smaller effort (or even to drop out) if the
number of bidders is large. One study has shown that a prime contractor
initially solicited bids from ten potential subcontractors and received
no good proposals until the number of competitors was limited to three.
Initially, each firm perceived its chance of winning as too remote to
warrant a strong effort. The study concluded that "competition in the
limiting case of only two rivals may be just as effective, from a behav-
ioral standpoint, as competition among a few firms."[92]

Unfortunately, Congress has moved closer and closer to legislating that government procurements must be awarded solely on the basis of "free and open competition."[93] Congress argues that, since the goal of competition is "fairness," it should provide everyone the opportunity to sell to the government. However, this kind of thinking considers competition only from the *seller's* viewpoint, whereas "effective" competition considers it from the *buyer's* (that is, the government's) viewpoint. Congress argues that letting everyone bid must be better—and it certainly allows constituents the maximum opportunity. However, from the DoD's viewpoint it makes no sense to take the time and spend the dollars to evaluate fifty bids for a few-hundred-dollar item.[94] Not only do the administrative costs exceed the cost of the item being purchased, but the chances of securing any cost savings from allowing fifty firms to bid (rather than five high-quality firms) are probably minimal.[95] By shifting the emphasis from efficient and effective procurement (as seen by the government) to "fairness" and "free and open" competition (as seen from the perspective of the many potential bidders), Congress also opens up the risk that the DoD will end up with a low-quality product from a "cheap" and often unproven producer. To reduce this likelihood, Congress has passed numerous rules and regulations to "protect the government" from unqualified or even unscrupulous bidders and to help protect the inexperienced bidders (again, all in the name of "fairness").

Perversely, the excessive amount of regulation, which often includes socio-economic requirements, greatly *restricts* the amount of effective competition (for example, small-business and minority "set-asides" do not allow the majority of experienced bidders to compete). Actually, since the laws favor the many weaker potential suppliers, the DoD is unable to obtain the most effective weapons for the lowest costs—which, as a very strong buyer, it should be able to do. In fact, increasing regulation is the antithesis of increasing competition. Yet nearly every member of Congress speaks not only of doing things to increase competition but also of passing more and more regulations to make sure that the competition will be "fair" for his constituents. Interestingly, when the Postal Service (in 1987) tried to simplify and improve the effectiveness of its purchasing, it introduced a "new policy to obtain adequate competition from qualified sources, rather than maximum competition."[96] This was allowable because, under the terms of its organization, the Postal Service is not subject to the requirements of the Federal Property and Administrative Services Act, which govern the contracting procedures of most government agencies. It is too bad that similar freedom to have effective competition could not be provided to the Department of Defense.

Collusion is one of the concerns often expressed about limited competition—especially in the case of segments of the defense industry in which there may be only two or three qualified firms. However, no serious study of the defense industry[97] has ever yielded any data to show that there is any form of conspiracy among the defense suppliers. In normal markets, concern about conspiracy stems from a high concentration of sellers, from homogeneity (interchangability) of products, from a low concentration of buyers, from the importance of price competition, and from the use of sealed bids—all but the first of these are factors not present in the defense sector. The many reasons for the lack of collusion (or even "dominant firm" behavior) in the defense sector[98] include the following:

- The monopoly buyer can play firms against one another.
- The monopoly buyer can bring in other firms. (The mechanisms are in place.)
- If no other firms are available, the government itself may enter the market.
- Public visibility—especially of costs—is high.
- "Custom-designed" products are not substitutable; therefore, there is no market to "share."
- The demand is unpredictable; therefore, it is hard to divide up the market.
- The "lumpy" nature of demand (all-or-nothing awards) makes it hard to divide up the business.
- Awards are very infrequent; 10 or 15 years is too long to wait for one's "turn."
- Competition is on technology rather than on price, and rapid technological changes make it hard to collude.
- A new "leader" can emerge at any time; all it takes is a technological breakthrough and a large investment.

It should be clear from the above discussion why the normal antitrust criteria[99] (market power, collusion, etc.) do not apply in the defense market. It is the customized nature of the products that is most significant here, as Assistant Attorney General Douglas Ginsberg noted in

1986 when he was looking for bid rigging. Ginsberg specifically commented that he would be looking at "off-the-shelf products" but not at "complicated weapon systems that have to be built to specifications."[100]

The concept of "market shares" has no meaning in the defense sector.[101] As was stated in a 1973 Ralph Nader report, "The Department of Defense determines, by its procurement decisions, whether there will be more or less concentration."[102] Yet there is no regulation relating to the allowable degree of concentration. In fact, as Walter Adams noted, "The Pentagon creates more monopoly in one day than the Anti-Trust Division can undo in a year."[103] Recently, the DoD has even encouraged—and sometimes required—the formation of industrial "teams" or partnerships to bid against other teams for the sole development contract on a new weapon system.[104]

In holding competitions for complex, high-technology weapon systems, the government is attempting to do more than simply get the cheapest item. In fact, other considerations often properly outweigh costs. For example, competition has often brought higher quality, greater realiability, faster delivery, reduced risk, improved performance, tighter cost control, better assurance of supply, and an enhanced mobilization base. It is the combination of these considerations, along with cost, that should be the basis for the awarding of government contracts.[105] However, evaluating these various considerations is very difficult. The government is often under pressure to award a contract to the low bidder, and this is considered to be the "safe" approach by the government's procurement people. Newspaper articles and congressional speeches are constantly highlighting, as an "abuse" of competition, the fact that an award was made to someone other than the low bidder. Nonetheless, the commercial approach—and the correct approach—is to place more emphasis on "total value" and less emphasis on price (particularly in a competition of ideas). The Government Accounting Office has upheld awards that were made to a more highly qualified bidder rather than to the one with the lowest price.[106] In the Competition in Contracting Act of 1984, Congress specified that contracts should be awarded on the basis of best value, stating that in many cases "quality may be the dominant factor, and cost may be secondary in source selection decisions."[107] Until the government learns to award the typical high-technology defense contract on the basis of a combination of quality and price rather than solely on the basis of price, it will fail to receive the best value for its money.[108]

It was noted above that the DoD's historical approach has been to hold a competition *for* a contract award, without the continuous presence of an alternative after the award. As we have seen, even this appears to be beneficial *if the competition is run with an emphasis on past performance and quality*. Unfortunately, the normal mode of competition in defense is that of holding an "auction" for the award and then having a sole source for the development and production of the weapon system. A very attractive way of increasing the benefits of competition in defense is to have two sources through the development phase, and then possibly two through the production phase as well—that is, to maintain an alternative source at all times. When this technique has been tried, the performance improvements and the net cost reductions have been quite striking.[109]

Funding two suppliers for the development phase (prototypes and/or full-scale development) will clearly result in additional costs for the DoD. However, this phase accounts for only a small portion of the cost of the program (the big dollars go to the production and support phases), and the significant gains in performance and the long-term cost reductions that may be realized from dual-sourcing at the R&D phase(s) should more than offset the early costs. Indeed this has been found to have happened in every case that has been analyzed. When dual-source development was used, the weapon's performance was significantly enhanced and the government's risk significantly reduced. (In the case of one program, only the second source was able to successfully complete the effort.) And as long as production cost was a major factor in dual-source competition for development, there was a dramatic drop in the subsequent production costs. A typical defense program nearly doubles in cost over the acquisition cycle, but a study of seven Army programs that were dual-sourced in development found that their production costs came out almost on target.[110] The explanation for this is that the *production* costs are basically "designed in" during the development phase, and that in a competitive environment this aspect can be sufficiently emphasized that each of the competing firms will "design in" a lower per-unit production cost.[111] In spite of the empirical data, however, the DoD often feels that it cannot afford the additional development costs.[112]

The idea of using two sources to *produce* an item has also been tried a number of times by the Department of Defense and has also yielded significant improvements in quality and reductions in cost. Here, the idea is that once a design has been proved then a second contractor (in addition to the original source) is selected to produce the same item, and the two share the production each year as a function of the quality and the cost of the preceding year's buys. Again, it is not intuitively obvious why such an approach works. After all, the extra production equipment, facilities, and overhead associated with the second source have to be paid for, and the original source will obviously produce the item in smaller numbers than if it had been the sole source (and will always claim that it could produce the larger quantity for a lower unit cost, because of "labor learning"). In theory, economics of scale should apply. Thus, on most defense programs—since the volume is relatively small and the manufacturing is quite capital-intensive—one might expect monopoly to be justified.[113] The basic flaw in such thinking is that in the normal sole-source environment of defense production there is very little incentive for the producer to drive down his costs, and almost an incentive for him to *raise* his costs (since the subsequent year's production negotiations will be based on the preceding year's actual costs). Thus, in case after case a sole-source producer goes through a relatively flat learning curve (of unit price versus cumulative quantity), and when a second source is introduced it changes the whole environment of the procurement by putting the government in a very powerful (monopsony) buyer's position, with the two sources competing as oligopoly suppliers. (See figure 6.5.) There are some "startup" costs for the second source (often between 1 percent and 6 percent of the production program's costs), but then in every program that has been analyzed—and there have been many—the second source (if it is a high-quality producer) has always had a significantly steeper learning curve than the first source. Thus, within a very short period of time, the second source's costs have gotten down below those of the first source. The first source reacts by lowering its costs (shown in the figure as a downward shift in the solid curve), and both producers go down the steeper learning curve. When the quantities are at all significant, and when there is sufficient labor content in the production process, the *net* effect of such continuous competition in production (after the nonrecurring costs of starting up the second source are subtracted) has been

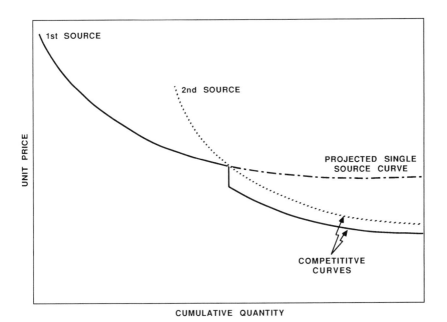

Figure 6.5
The impact of production-phase competition.

average savings in the range of 12–30 percent (depending upon the assumptions used in the analysis).[114] For example, the Shrike anti-radar missile system was selling for $19,500 each when it was sole-sourced. After competition, the first producer's price dropped to $4,480 (a 77 percent reduction) and the second source's price to $3,850.[115] Similar results were found when this acquisition strategy was used on critical subsystems of a weapon system; for example, the unit price of the computer on the HARM missile system dropped from $260,000 to $52,000.[116]

Even more important than these dramatic price reductions is the fact that with dual-source development and/or production, when quality producers were selected, the performance and reliability of the systems and subsystems increased significantly. Though the Sparrow III anti-aircraft missile system was dual-sourced to improve its reliability (since the first source was having trouble in this area), the result was not only a dramatic improvement in reliability but also a significant lowering of costs. The Air Force's decision to dual-source jet engines in the mid-1980s is projected to save $3 or $4 billion in maintenance costs while also reducing production costs significantly.[117] However, the DoD has historically been reluctant to engage in dual-sourcing because of the startup costs and the difficulty of getting money for the initial investment.[118]

The benefits of continuous competition in defense procurement have been recognized for many years. In 1964, Frederick Scherer published findings which showed that during World War II the learning curves for bomber production were much steeper when there was dual-sourcing than when there was single-sourcing.[119] By the late 1970s it was known that programs such as the Navy's dual-sourced FFG-7 "patrol frigates" had much steeper learning curves than any other ships being built for the Navy. Yet there was still a great reluctance to introduce the concept of dual-sourcing in either development or production, because it was believed that the quantities were not large enough or that sufficient contractual incentives existed to ensure that the sole producer would achieve the desired results. However, in 1984 Congress passed the Competition in Contracting Act (CICA),[120] and followed this with a number of amendments to defense bills which put increasing pressure on the DoD to devote more attention and more resources to competition in future procurements. The CICA required that "Competition Advocates" be established in the armed services.[121] It also recognized that the use of sealed bids was inappropriate for most defense procurements, and that "negotiated competitions," in which quality and price could be balanced, would be a perfectly acceptable form of competition. This act also defined a limited set of conditions under which sole-source awards would be appropriate.[122]

Since the CICA was passed there has been a significant increase in competition for defense procurements. From 1984 to 1987 the percentage of competitively awarded contracts went up from 37 percent to 58 percent.[123] In response, defense firms began cutting their costs. By 1987, Pratt and Whitney stated that it had reduced its supervisory staff by 10 percent, Boeing said it had cut overhead costs by 25 percent, and General Dynamics claimed to be aiming for a 40 percent reduction in overhead.[124] In many cases, even the "threat" of competition seemed to have a significant impact on prices.[125]

As expected, the bargaining position of the government had changed dramatically. However, this was not all for the good. Since Congress now required an annual report on the amount of defense competition, there was a strong tendency to overemphasize competition (even when it didn't make sense) and to stress bid price as the sole award criterion (rather than quality and value). Because of the ease of making awards based on low bids, there was great concern that—particularly in R&D and professional services, the "ideas" sector of the industry—quality was being driven down in order to improve the competition score-card.[126] Further, there was no recognition that (as Scherer stated) "too much competition can discourage rather than stimulate vigorous effort."[127] Worse still, as the bribery scandals of 1988–89 showed, all-or-nothing competitive awarding of contracts on the basis of low price creates enormous incentives for a firm to do anything to be the winner.

Competition for its own sake is clearly wrong; however, when competition makes good management sense and when "best value" is emphasized, that is a different story. The issue is whether or not the Department of Defense can exercise the necessary management judgment, and whether Congress will allow it to do so. What is perhaps most needed is a recognition of the importance of the DoD's being able to reward good work by giving a contractor follow-on business and to punish poor performance by withholding future business. These are the greatest incentives in the commercial world. To date, the DoD has had difficulty using them—particularly when it comes to making source selections.

Buying Commercial Items

At the beginning of the discussion of buying practices, we divided defense procurements into two major categories: the few major weapon systems, which take the overwhelming share of the billions of dollars spent annually, and the millions of small items (food, clothing, spare parts, and so on), which use few of the dollars but which account for the overwhelming share of the DoD's procurement actions. It is to the latter category that we now turn.

The DoD buys 13 million undershirts, 6 million pairs of green socks, 51 million dozens of eggs, and 7.6 million pounds of coffee per year.[128] Why shouldn't it buy these items in much the same manner as any normal consumer? Since defense procurement is decentralized, shouldn't the buyers on military bases be able to go out and purchase these items, and even receive a volume discount? Unfortunately, the problems with such an approach become evident when one begins to think more deeply about the process.

Consider the famous purchase, in 1985, of 12 tons of fruitcakes for the troops overseas at Christmastime.[129] In the free market, the DoD's buyer would simply call up the "brand-name" producers (whose names he would have obtained by going to a supermarket and looking on the shelves) and ask them for bids. However, such a large order would attract the attention of "potential fruitcake producers" all over the United States. Many of these people might never have produced fruit-cakes, but they would write to their representatives in Congress saying that they wanted the opportunity to bid on the contract and that they were fully capable of making excellent fruitcakes. Naturally, Congress wants to be "fair" to the constituents, and therefore it has passed numerous laws prohibiting the government from simply buying "brand names" and from limiting competition to a few qualified sources. In fact, the laws require that "anyone" be allowed to bid (as was noted, this is called "free and open" competition).

The change in the rules, from the buyer deciding who should bid (as long as there is adequate competition) to all potential suppliers having an opportunity to bid, alters the market conditions dramatically. It is the first and most crucial step toward military specifications for fruitcakes.

The DoD's fruitcake buyer is now likely to receive hundreds if not thousands of bids for the opportunity to produce some or all of the fruitcakes. Now, the question is how to decide who should get the award(s). If price were the only consideration, the troops would get inedible and perhaps dangerous fruitcakes, supplied by low-cost fruit-cake makers who may be inexperienced. One solution might be to ask for "bid samples." This is a relatively common technique, but it in-volves setting up a laboratory and establishing very clear criteria for determining which fruitcakes are "acceptable." This leads to one of the DoD's more difficult decisions (essentially the same one it is forced to make when writing a military weapon's "requirements"): On what basis should the procurement decision be made? The broad choices are these: (1) the best possible fruitcake; (2) a good-tasting but reasonably priced fruitcake (the "best value"); (3) a "minimum acceptable" fruitcake at the lowest possible price. For some weapon systems, option 1 is clearly the necessary choice; however, option 2 is usually the best choice for both weapon systems and fruitcakes. In fact, it is the one that consumers use in food stores when they are looking for the "best value" and are willing to pay a little bit more to get a better taste. Unfortunately, in the case at hand, the low-cost fruitcake producer will, after losing, write to his congressman and state that he was treated unfairly, since he offered a lower price for what was (he will claim) an acceptable fruitcake. In the commercial world, where procurements are based on the "uniform commercial code" and where the best-value judgments of commercial buyers are accepted as the rule, there is nothing that losers can do. In the case of defense procurement, however, Congress has given losers the right not only to protest but also to hold up the procurement until the protest is ruled on. Thus, for the price of a stamp, anyone can initiate litigation over the award of a contract—probably with the full support of his congressional representatives, and with a virtual guarantee of press coverage.

In 1984, with the writing of the Competition in Contracting Act, Congress *encouraged* losers of defense competitions to protest. The number of protests went from a few hundred a year to over 3,000 a year within four years of the law's passage.[130] This made the procurement lawyers in Washington happy, but it increased the delays and bottlenecks in the procurement system. Worse still, it brought more of an emphasis on low bids rather than best value.

The end result of the DoD's commercial procurement process is a detailed specification. Military specification MIL-F-1499F describes, in 18 pages, exactly what must go into a fruitcake, how it must be made, how long it must be able to sit on the shelf, what types of fruit it should contain, how it should stay together when cut, and how it should be wrapped—all "foolish" from the perspective of how the normal consumer purchases fruitcake, but all perfectly understandable when it is recognized that, if one item is left out of the specification, then, in trying to be the low bidder, each of the bidders is likely to "cut corners" on this aspect of his fruitcake.

The same specification process is applied to every purchase of a common item. For example, there is a 20-page specification for towels, a 20-page specification for underwear, a 16-page specification for plastic whistles, a 17-page specification for olives, a 20-page specification for hot chocolate, and a 17-page specification for chewing gum. Some of these would be outstanding material for a stand-up comic—for example, military hot chocolate is prevented from containing large chunks through a specification stating that "when washed with petroleum ether, not less than 98 percent, by weight, shall pass through a U.S. standard No. 200 sieve."

Foolish as all this sounds, in many ways it does achieve Congress' objective. It even yields acceptable products, and (often) *apparently* low prices. The 12 tons of fruitcakes were purchased under competitive contracts at an average price of $1.51 per pound. Of course that price excludes the costs of the government's buyers, inspectors, laboratory testers, storehouses, shipping, sales clerks, etc., which are covered under other DoD accounts (discussed below); nonetheless, fruitcakes were going for $3.50 per pound[131] in supermarkets, so at least the apparent price was attractive. Perhaps even more important, the fruitcakes were of reasonable quality—which was ensured by the government's inspectors. Since the DoD is probably the largest buyer of food in the world (spending over $5 billion per year[132]), such cost and quality considerations are extremely important. The other thing the current process attempts to do is minimize the opportunities for improper judgment. By having a detailed specification and then making sure that each of the suppliers satisfies it, the government is in a position to simply pick the low bidder, without having to make "management judgments" (such as the ordinary consumer is forced to make whenever he goes to a food store and has to choose from a large variety of items differing in quality and in price). The government *could* allow its buyers to make management judgments if the buyers were free from the threat of protests (as the consumer is) and if they were capable of making such judgments—even on complex items.

The "ridiculous" nature of military specifications is not, however, the biggest problem here. Consider also the fact that the price paid by the DoD for a fruitcake excludes all the "overhead" costs that a supermarket has to cover (employees' salaries, inventory costs, facilities costs, etc.), which typically more than double the cost of an item. (The profit markup at a supermarket is only around 1 percent on food goods.) All these additional costs are borne by the taxpayers under various DoD budget categories. Even worse, in the case of something like fruitcake, is that the overwhelming majority of the sales are to commissaries, which are primarily frequented by military retirees and their families rather than by those currently in the military.[133] These funds are appropriated by Congress to cover the DoD's "operating and maintenance" costs, and thus they are "buried" within the $300 billion defense budget. A second disadvantage of this system is that it develops a class of suppliers who are purely "government suppliers."[134] Since these suppliers don't have to meet the test of the commercial market, they become totally dependent on doing business "the defense way." Conversely, the DoD often becomes dependent on these suppliers; their specialized factories and and their experience with military specifications makes it hard for other firms to compete with them. Further, many highly qualified commercial suppliers simply don't want to put up with government paperwork; as long as they can get enough business elsewhere, they refuse to deal with the government.[135] However, perhaps the worst result of this process is that it really doesn't "pay" a supplier to do a good job and to provide high-quality goods or services, since the procurement process basically starts over with each new bid; prior performance does not matter at all, and there is a built-in incentive to cut corners. Thus, the government often ends up with marginal goods. Indeed, sometimes a supplier finds a way around the specifications and produces *inferior* goods. Particularly discouraging is that, on the next invitation for bids, these same suppliers will be treated just as though they had done outstanding work on previous contracts. The "invisible hand" is not at work here as it is in the commercial world, where good performance is rewarded and poor performers are forced to drop out.

The Department of Defense should move toward buying standard commercial items by standard commercial practices. Such a move will require specific actions on the part of Congress. Although Congress has been the source of many speeches in favor of greater use of commercial products and of much mockery of military specifications, it has passed the laws that *require* the DoD to do its business in the present manner. As Representative James Courter has stated, "Congress is not the answer to waste. Congress is the problem. They mean well, but reformers are too often a cause of what's wrong with the military."[136]

The proper approach is not to legislate the price of every single commercial-like item, as Congress did in the case of a toilet seat.[137] Such overregulation works in exactly the wrong direction with regard to the market. Rather, Congress must move in the direction of removing restrictions on the effective operation of the market. The place to start is with the numerous restrictions that offer a major impediment to small businesses that want to bid on small-dollar items. If Congress were to establish a $25,000 minimum for contracts to which the various socio-economic programs should be applicable, the DoD would be able to buy small-dollar items using normal commercial practices—i.e., purchasing from market-tested suppliers, and negotiating only the price and the delivery schedule. This recommendation has been made repeatedly by the General Accounting Office,[138] by numerous other government commissions, and in private studies. Although the expenditures in question are small, under-$25,000 contracts constitute from 70 percent to 98 percent of most defense agencies' procurement actions. Thus, the removal of the above-mentioned restrictions would dramatically reduce administrative costs and greatly encourage small businesses to bid. Limitations could still be placed such that if only one bidder responded to the request then, in order to ensure adequate competition, the old requirements (or, better, less complex ones) could apply.

A more general solution would be to apply the Uniform Commercial Code to most of the DoD's purchases of goods and services. Obviously, special-purpose military equipment would have to be excluded, but the overwhelming majority of items could be purchased in a commercial fashion. As was noted above, this would entail allowing "best value" judgment by the government buyer and no protest by the losers (except in cases of illegality). It also means that, as long as the prices being bid were established by the commercial market, the supplier would not be required to provide a detailed price breakdown (because this is very commercially sensitive) and the government would conduct no auditing (again, as in the commercial world). Finally, and perhaps most important, the prior performance of a supplier should play a major role in the evaluation. A supplier that has done a good job should be given favorable treatment, and one that has done a poor job should not be considered for the next procurement.

For these changes to take place, there would have to be congressional action—in some cases, new legislation; in others, a statement of the "intent of Congress."[139] Senators and representatives will have to accept the fact that their constituents will be unable to bid on some procurements because there are already enough qualified suppliers who have done good work on earlier contracts. They will also have to recognize that there will occasionally be some errors of judgment, and that tolerating a few such errors over millions of annual procurements is far better than trying to regulate all of them. Fraud, of course, will still be prosecuted, and there will still be "watchdogs" (people from Congress and the press, the DoD's inspectors, and selected DoD auditors) to make sure that the system is operating well.

Such changes would dramatically increase the use of commercial items, decrease the use of uniquely designed "special-purpose" items, and obviate many ludicrous military specifications. Allowing and encouraging the use of commercial items by making their procurement easier would encourage the use of such items wherever possible. This would make for a dramatic shift in the Department of Defense's whole way of doing business.[140] It is time for those in Congress to stop giving speeches on the "ridiculous" specifications for ketchup and fruitcake and to begin looking seriously at the possibility of changing the laws so as to allow the DoD to buy commercial items in a commercial fashion.

"Waste, Fraud, and Abuse"

In the midst of the Reagan defense buildup, almost every day's newspaper contained a story about "waste, fraud, and abuse" in defense procurements. However, these articles were not about millions or billions of dollars' worth of cost overruns, or about ineffective weapon systems (two subjects that have periodically gotten attention in the press); rather, they were about fantastic prices paid for familiar items— $9,609 for a wrench, $748 for a pair of pliers, $7,400 for a coffeepot, $436 for a hammer, $1,075 for a bolt, $1,118 for a plastic cap on a stool leg, and $640 for a toilet seat.[141] In each case, the government offered a "rational" explanation (see below), but the public would have no part of it. A survey[142] found that Americans consider waste and fraud in defense spending a large and serious national problem—on average, they believe that almost half of the defense budget is lost to waste and fraud; they believe that fraud accounts for the loss of as many dollars as waste; and they believe that anyone involved in defense procurement (especially a contractor) is likely to commit fraudulent and dishonest acts. Essentially, people knew the price of a commercially purchased hammer and assumed that, since the Department of Defense was paying over $400 more per hammer, the defense contractors must be making enormous and illegal profits. They also assumed that these same abuses were directly extendable from the hammers to major weapon systems.

In the summer of 1988, these public perceptions were "confirmed" as the "Pentagon bribery scandals" captured the nation's attention. A two-year FBI investigation of bribery and conspiracy, involving high-level Defense Department officials, former officials, and defense contractors, unfolded daily and was exploited by representatives and senators anxious for election-year attention.[143] Clearly, criminal actions had occurred, and they deserved to be punished; but was this a case of a few "bad apples," or was the system fundamentally flawed? The truth, of course, was somewhere in between. Some people had abused the system; but the mid-1980s trends toward low-bid, winner-take-all, "you bet your company" auctions for a few multi-billion-dollar contracts had encouraged the use of every possible means to "win," since the losers would be out of the game.

A scandal in defense procurements is certainly nothing new. In the mid-1930s there were the famous "merchants of death" hearings of Senator Gerald Nye,[144] and in the early 1940s there were Senator Harry Truman's "war profits hearings." But what was different about this set of "scandals" was that it could be easily understood by the common man, and the message was passed to Congress that something had to be done. The result was a period of wild "procurement reform," with almost every member of Congress proposing a "curative" bill. Before we consider the government's actions, we must put the issue in perspective. To begin with, it is important to differentiate between *waste* (the inefficient and ineffective use of government money through poor management), *abuse* (unintelligent, "wrong," but not illegal actions), and *fraud* (the actual performance of illegal actions).

A headline in the *Washington Post* of July 19, 1985, read "Defense Audit Uncovers 'Questionable' Purchases." Eight paragraphs into the story, the statistics appeared. Some 330,000 procurements had been reviewed, and "372 purchases were deemed questionable." That means that, out of the 15 million contract actions a year by the Department of Defense, perhaps one in a thousand might be considered "questionable." However, "questionable" does not mean improper or illegal. In his annual report to the Congress for 1984, the Secretary of Defense reported that, out of 24,380 cases investigated (these would be equivalent to the "questionable" cases mentioned above), two out of three were found to involve no actual problem and were dropped; of the remaining cases, some required administrative actions (e.g., changes in procurement procedure) and some were referred for prosecution.[145] That year there were 657 convictions, which means that fewer than three out of every hundred "questionable" cases resulted in convictions. If these two sets of statistics can be roughly generalized, they mean that, of the 15 million annual procurement actions, perhaps 1,500 involve illegalities.

The same ratio of one in 10,000 is found when we look at the dollars. The Secretary's report to Congress for 1984 said that in fiscal 1983 $5.2 million in penalties, restitutions, and recoveries had been collected by the Justice Department, and $9.6 million by the DoD. Thus, $14.8 million was recovered, out of an annual procurement budget of around $170 billion—again about one part in 10,000. And, although $14.8 million is certainly not a small amount, it is relevant to point out that, in the same year, it cost the government far more (for the salaries of auditors, lawyers, and other people in the Department of Defense and the Justice Department) to recover those dollars. The issue here is not one of economics but one of ethics and legality; however, the economics do not argue for more auditors and lawyers.

The worst cases, of course, are those of bribery. Here, the focus of the investigation was the Navy procurement community, where it was alleged that perhaps up to six (high- and low-level) officials were involved, out of approximately 70,000—about one in 10,000. As Norman Augustine observed, relative to the approximately 3 million people involved in the military-industrial complex, "Is there any city, with even a small percentage of that number of people, without a jail?"[146] That, of course, does not justify bribery. It is clearly against the law, and the offenders must be seriously punished. In fact, an example must be made of them, to discourage others. But the ultimate challenge is to create incentives for proper performance by the personnel involved, particularly on the large-dollar items.

Another way to get some perspective on waste, fraud, and abuse is to consider the following observation (from the *Washington Post*):

Many arms makers' misdeeds seems to differ little from the infractions of corporate America at large, from Exxon overcharging customers by $900 million (according to a May 1985 court ruling) to the Crocker

National Bank failing to report to the government $4 billion in cash transactions. Those responsible frequently are mid-level managers, not motivated by greed, but under pressure to meet corporate profit goals.[147]

The difference obviously, is that in the defense world public funds are involved; thus, like Caesar's wife, the defense firms must be beyond reproach. It is not acceptable to say that similar problems occasionally occur in the non-defense world, and that therefore one should expect them in the world of defense. Appropriate corrective actions and great diligence are required.

If spending more for a weapon system than you have to is waste, then we are wasting billions of dollars. In 1985 the Grace Commission found 104 categories of alleged waste in the Department of Defense.[148] Of these, by far the largest were *high overhead charges by defense contractors* (due to the absence of incentives for cost reduction in the management of weapon systems), *instability in the budgeting and procurement process* (which leads to uneconomical production rates), and a *lack of cost-consciousness in the designing of weapons* (and, correspondingly, in the requirements process). Thus, we should focus on the broad structural issues of the weapons-acquisition process.

If a weapon system doesn't work, it is a terrible waste.[149] As Richard DeLauer, former Undersecretary of Defense for Research and Engineering, stated in 1985, "The number one weakness of the Defense Department is the poor workmanship common to a great cross-section of weapons rolling off an assembly line."[150] The estimates of the cost of this poor quality range from 25 percent of the cost of a weapon to much higher figures for many defense goods.

Excessive regulations is another major category of waste. The Grace Commission placed the cost of paperwork at around 2 percent of the cost of the items procured (over $3 billion annually); others have placed it significantly higher. The cost of the socio-economic programs is far greater—estimates run up to 20 percent of the cost of the items.[151]

Poor inventory control gets considerable press attention. Since the DoD stocks more than 4.5 million different items and fills roughly 30 million orders each year, there are bound to be a few mistakes. The DoD contends that it can track the whereabouts of items in its inventory with about 95 percent accuracy.[152] However, independent studies by the General Accounting Office indicate that the accuracy is considerably lower, ranging from 44 percent for the Army's Tank Automotive Command to 68 percent for the Air Force's Logistics Center and 69 percent for the Navy's Supply Center. Some of the losses make for interesting reading—for example, in 1985 a million-dollar aircraft radar was "lost" during an inventory check at the Navy Supply Center.[153]

The press seems particularly fond of reporting waste connected with the ordering of too few or too many spare parts. It is clearly a waste to ground aircraft and helicopters as a result of not having spare parts available.[154] It is also clearly a waste for the government to be over-stocked with spare parts that are not needed because the parts in use did not fail as had been predicted.[155] (This appears to be a "no-win" situation.)

This discussion of "waste" could go on for some time, and might touch on the expenses associated with canceling a program after it has been started,[156] the cost of "buy American" trade barriers,[157] and the cost of "bailing out" many small defense firms that have received contracts because of socio-economic set-asides.[158] Now, however, it seems appropriate to move on to the category of "abuse." However, we will return to this category of "waste" when we address the needed corrective actions.

The gross overpricing of commercial-like items—already discussed above—comes under the heading of "abuse." The Department of Defense refers to most of these items as "spare parts," since they are meant to replace worn-out or broken small parts of major weapon systems.

In the mid-1980s, during the period of the "spare part scandals," the DoD was managing over 4 million different types of spare parts and spending about $22 billion a year for them. Thus, one could certainly expect to find "abuses." Nonetheless, the headline stories brought on numerous investigations and "corrective actions." The problems fall into six major categories[159]:

- *Closed production lines* Because the DoD keeps its equipment so long, and because the life of the equipment is often extended because of budgetary constraints prohibiting replacement, the DoD sometimes finds itself procuring spare parts after the production line has closed.[160] Reopening such a line—especially for the very small quantity of items usually ordered—is an extremely expensive process, involving retooling and retraining. Naturally, the supplier has to pass these costs on to the government, and the unit price for the small quantity procured is extremely high. But the alternatives—to order large numbers of parts when the production line is open or to throw out the whole weapon system because you can't get the parts—are even less attractive.

- *Custom-made items* Because of detailed specifications, there is often only one supplier who is certified to produce an item. This sole supplier can charge a high price for the otherwise unattainable item. However, shifting from the use of detailed military specifications to the procurement of ordinary items would bring on the problems of "commercial-item procurement" described above.

- *Low-quantity buys* Because of funding constraints and the desire to avoid having unneeded parts, and because of highly distributed operations, the DoD may often buy the same parts in very small quantities a number of times each year.[161] These small, unpredictable orders compel the producer to operate at very inefficient rates of production and to charge the DoD for the additional costs associated with the interruption of other work.

- *Government accounting procedures* Many of the apparent abuses are due to the government's historical approach to the "allocation" of costs. Spare-parts costs include the "direct" costs of labor and materials, the indirect costs associated with production (e.g., plant and equipment), and the direct costs associated with the processing of the part through the procurement operation of the buying firm. The indirect costs (for example, those associated with the procurement people, the inspectors, the supervisors, the corporate management the facilities, the utilities, insurance, and taxes) cannot—by definition—be easily assigned to specific parts. To simplify accounting practices and to reduce paperwork, the government has its contractors allocate the same average indirect costs to each item, regardless of its share of the overall contract. This arbitrary distribution of indirect costs significantly raises the unit prices of low-value parts while lowering the unit prices of high-value parts. There is no change in the total costs paid by the government for these indirect costs; but the effect is a great distortion of the cost of a very-low-cost item, since a part that might cost only a few cents now has many dollars' worth of overhead allocated to it. The obvious fix for this problem is to have a large number of detailed overhead pools, so that the proper charges can be allocated to each item. This requires keeping track of which items people work on at any given moment, so that their charges can be more appropriately allocated—a time-consuming and expensive process, but one that would make the final price paid for an item match the commercial-market price more closely.

· *Multiple layers of order processing* The government normally orders its weapon systems from its large prime contractors; they, in turn, order subsystems from their suppliers, who order parts from their suppliers. When a part is required, each of the members of this chain passes on its costs (associated with processing the order, inspecting the part, and so forth) and its profit on these costs. Though each of these firms is charging for work that it does, there is no question that there is redundant "markup" associated with the buildup of the cost to the government.[162] The corrective action for this is for the government to order directly from the vendor—but then the government has the responsibility and the costs for all the purchasing, inspection, and record keeping associated with this process.

· *Poor judgment by government buyers* In certain instances, the government's procurement personnel have emphasized "ordering" instead of "buying" or have checked for "accuracy" rather than "reasonableness." In other cases they have been unable to successfully challenge, or ineffective in identifying, the excessive prices being charged. Generally, this poor judgment has been due to limited information about the item, insufficient training, inadequate technical and management support, and improper contract procedures. With the thousands of people involved in this process, improving it so that "management judgment" can be effectively applied—rather than a more automatic ordering process—will require significant investment in personnel, in training, and in computer-based information systems.

In many cases, the excessive prices that made headlines resulted from some combination of the six causes listed above. The $7,400 coffeemaker for the C-5A transport aircraft was a unique item produced by a sole-source manufacturer in a low quantity after the original production line had closed. In the case of the $110 diode (normally a 4-cent item), the DoD had bought a high-value electronic amplifier along with the diode in the same contract, and the accounting method called for an equal distribution of the overhead costs of the two items. This accounting procedure artificially inflated the price of the diode and understated the price of the amplifier; however, the total price of the contract was not affected. The "excessive" charges for numerous other spare parts have similar explanations. Nonetheless, the appearance of incredibly high prices being paid for "standard" items, and the assumption that such abuses were uniform throughout the DoD's equipment purchases, demanded immediate action from the DoD and legislative "fixes" from Congress.

The government began buying more spares with the initial production runs; contracting for more spares on an annual basis; allocating indirect costs in proportion to the inherent value of the part; purchasing spare parts directly from the original manufacturer; challenging the supplier's proprietary rights to technical data (from sole-source producers of spare parts); providing improved technical information and better support to the government's buyers; actively pursuing refunds for overcharges found; and hiring more than 6,000 additional people for pricing, contracting, and auditing. These "fixes" did reduce the number of "horror stories" and increase the government's attention to these issues; however, they also had their costs. Every analysis done has shown that "the cost of finding these cases [was] much more than the resultant savings."[163] Finding the few "abuses" means searching through the thousands of routine cases, and the costs of this are significant. And these searches have a significant time impact on the ordering of spare parts. The above-mentioned changes doubled the procurement lead time for spare parts[164]—in itself a significant cost, since one has to either be able to predict much further in advance or to order twice as many parts in order to cover the longer lead time. Furthermore, some of the apparent cost savings from the actions taken are not "real"; they only replace industry costs with government costs. For example, ordering parts directly from the vendor means that all the costs of procurement and inspection are now government costs and risks rather than industry costs. The fact that these government costs are paid by the taxpayers under different "line items" in the defense budget gives the appearance that the part is much cheaper; in reality, however, it may be much more expensive, because the government may be not only less efficient at processing the paperwork but also be less effective in negotiating with the suppliers. One Air Force study found that 25 of 36 different types of spare parts purchased from the vendors through the prime contractor were much cheaper than if the Air Force had bought them directly from the vendors, and that the government was generally paying 50 percent more than the prime contractor for the same part[165] (clear evidence of the difference in buying experience and skills.) Perhaps the most important error here is the disproportionate allocation of the government's limited oversight resources to the small-dollar items. If the 6,000 people addressing the "pennies" spent on spare parts had been devoted to the "dollars" spent on weapon systems, there might be a significant overall benefit. However, the public's perception of the management of defense spending had to be addressed, and Congress had to respond to the headlines.

Some defense contractors charge "questionable" items to the allowable overhead accounts and then include these charges in the price of the goods charged to the government. In the non-defense commercial world, it is totally up to a firm to establish what items it puts into its costs. In the case of government contracts, however, prices are subject to auditing, and occasionally the auditors turn up some charges that the taxpayers might not expect to pay (even though they would not be so unusual in the context of the commercial practices of large firms). The government has paid for country club memberships for corporate executives and, in one of the more famous cases, for the kenneling of a General Dynamics executive's dog while the executive attended a business conference.[166] Obviously, such charges represent a trivially small portion of a defense contractor's overall costs (at most, thousands of dollars out of billions of dollars of contract costs). In the past, such charges were simply disallowed when detected by auditors, and the companies then paid for them out of their profits. With the publicity that such items began to receive in the mid-1980s, the government shifted to a policy whereby a company could be held criminally liable for such charges.

The last broad category of "abuses" in defense contracting includes the abuses that often take place in well-intended government socioeconomic programs. It is certainly hard for anyone, conservative or liberal, to object to programs intended to stimulate "minority capitalism." Such programs are continuously pushed by Congress, and the share of defense dollars required to be "set aside" has been increasing quite significantly. A 1987 law called for the Department of Defense to almost double the amount of business it set aside for small and disadvantaged contractors.[167] The *Washington Post* (normally a strong supporter of such programs) observed in an editorial in 1988 that the minority set-aside programs have "produced a steady trickle of corruption. Some minority firms have been false fronts; some contracts have been politically guided."[168] The "Wedtech scandal," which centered on contracting by the Army under the set-aside program, is an example.[169] One senator commented, regarding the set-asides, that "the program cannot be allowed to continue to operate as it has. The program's history is a record of major legislative interventions over the years, mostly driven by abuse or due to poor or inconsistent program management." The *Post* summarized: "As it stands, the program does a disservice to the cause it is meant to help."[170] Yet, largely for political reasons, the program not only continues but receives increased funding, with no significant changes. Thus, abuses of it are likely to grow.

All the above "abuses" are still within the law. Fraud clearly is not. Fortunately, it accounts for only a small share of the overall problem we are considering here. Even the DoD's Inspector General (whose job it is to dig out as many improper actions as he can) has stated a belief that "for every dollar wasted at DoD, . . . only 2 cents are stolen; the rest is lost because of mismanagement."[171] Nonetheless, as the "horror stories" started to build up during the first half of the 1980s, one of the DoD's reactions was to increase the intensity of its reviews and try to turn up as many examples of "questionable" behavior as it could. In addition, according to many in the defense industry, there was a shift toward assuming that contractors were guilty and suspending them from defense contracts until they were proved innocent. Actual suspensions and debarments from defense contracting went from approximately 50 cases in 1980 to almost 900 cases in 1986,[172] and that year no fewer than 45 of the nation's top 100 defense contractors were under investigation or indictment.[173] However, a GAO study showed that between 1982 and 1985 fewer than 10 percent of the cases under investigation resulted in prosecution.[174] Of these, the overwhelming share involved not personal avarice but improper and illegal behavior by firms, usually due to efforts by middle-level management people to improve their performance records.

The largest share of these fraud cases (over 30 percent) involve contractors allegedly charging work to the wrong contracts.[175] Such "labor mischarging" usually involves charging costs against a cost-reimbursement contract when they should have been part of a fixed-price contract; as a result, the government ends up paying for costs that otherwise would have been profit losses against the fixed-price contract.[176] Other major categories of fraud include providing the DoD with inflated estimates of goods and services that led to excessive payments (11 percent),[177] substituting inferior goods for those required by the contract (9 percent),[178] and conflicts of interest (8 percent). The few cases in which *individuals* received financial rewards involve "kickbacks" to a government buyer from a supplier (usually on low-cost, commercial-like items),[179] or more likely to a prime contractor's buyer from his suppliers.[180] All these kinds of fraud must be prosecuted. More important, ways must be found to reduce their occurrence still further.

One of the first reactions of the government to the perceived increased incidences of waste, fraud, and abuse was to amend the False Claims Act (an 1863 statute aimed at Civil War profiteering) by strengthening the government's investigative powers and increasing the likelihood of civil cases against contractors for fraudulent claims.[181] The amendments provided for subpoena power, investigation, prosecution, and the conduct of trials outside the federal judiciary. The last of these provisions is an acknowledgment that the Justice Department couldn't handle many of the fraud cases developed by other federal agencies. As Associate Attorney General Stephen Trott stated, "the defense procurement system is one of the most complicated processes with which we have ever been confronted."[182] Finally, the government emphasized the use of *qui tam,* a legal concept of paying individuals who bring to justice those who are defrauding the government. This provided additional incentives for rightful and wrongful "whistle blowing." (Unfortunately, it encouraged individuals to make frivolous—and even vindictive—accusations with the hope that the government would find something and give the accuser a large financial reward.[183]) Along with this, the government considerably increased the number of contractor suspensions (from all defense work), sometimes without due process, and in many cases (particularly in cases of poor or allegedly poor work) the government withheld financial payments to the contractors as additional leverage. However, the most dramatic change was an enormous increase in the amount of government auditing. Congress increased the Defense Contract Audit Agency's staff of auditors from 4,023 to

5,230,[184] and the General Accounting Office resumed its auditing of defense contractors after a lapse of more than 20 years.[185] With the staffs of the various Inspector General offices figured in, one estimate was that the total number of auditors for defense business went from 19,000 to 24,000 in the time period from 1984 to 1987.[186] As if this was not enough, in addition to the many government program representatives and auditors located in the industry plants, the number of government personnel visiting defense plants increased dramatically. One major defense contractor counted about 57,000 government visits to his corporation in 1985.[187] Obviously, such visits, in such numbers, can be highly disruptive to the operation of any facility, particularly if the people making the visits or doing the auditing are inexperienced.[188]

During this period (the mid-1980s), a basic breakdown of the "social contract" between the government and the defense industry was taking place. A climate of mistrust developed. One study showed that half of the men and women doing the Defense Department's buying believed that defense contractors could not be trusted.[189] Government employees, afraid of appearing in the headlines, shifted to an overcautious view of their job, and the procurement process slowed down dramatically.[190] There was a significant shift in responsibility from the normal role of the contract officer (as the intermediary between the government and the industry) to the auditors (whose objective is not to get the work done at a reasonable cost, but to ensure that there are "zero defects"). And there was a strong anti-industry flavor to many of the laws and regulations that came out during that period (for example, reduced and delayed payments for work done, the introduction of a reduced-profit policy, and a shift toward placing more and more of the financial responsibility on the industry). As one senior government official stated, "Suddenly the critics and the discontented are the drivers of the administration rather than the doers and the risk takers who create through action. The premium now is on being legally clean and above investigation, not on taking action and risks necessary to get things done. The power now goes to the parasite rather than the producer."[191]

The industry's perception was that litigation, adverse publicity, and intimidation were now thought of as the ways to handle contract issues and settle claims.[192] In an attempt to reverse the obvious deterioration, the Packard Commission, in its final report to the president, strongly recommended the initiation of a program of "corporate self-governance in the defense industry" as a way out of the situation.[193] The underlying idea was that those firms that had programs for improving their ethical conduct, and could demonstrate the results of such programs, would experience much better relations with the government. (By 1988, a similar initiative was being taken within the non-defense business community, because of the increasing concern about ethical behavior in that sector.)[194] By the end of 1988, over 45 large defense firms had signed up for a specific (and quite rigorous) self-governance program,[195] and many more had set up their own programs. Naturally, there was a great deal of skepticism over whether corporate self-governance could substitute for detailed government auditing and inspections—especially when the bribery scandals hit the headlines in the summer of 1988. However, the concept does not require a hands-off view on the government's part; rather, the intention was to shift more of the responsibility for the industry's actions to the industry, and then to have the government perform fewer audits and reviews on those contractors who show that they can assume the responsibility. Ultimately, the objective was to move toward a "self-certification" program, with government oversight. Such a program would be most effective in an environment in which there were market incentives to reduce waste and abuse, and strict enforcement of the laws against fraud. More regulations to "not waste money," and more government auditors (requiring more paperwork and more time-consuming reviews), are *not* the way to improve government procurements. To reward good work and punish poor work is the only way to improve the procurement system. Increasing the professionalism of the acquisition workforce will also be crucial.

Acquisition Managers

In 1986, the President's Blue Ribbon Commission on Defense Management reported, as one of its major findings, that "lasting progress in the performance of the acquisition system demands dramatic improvements in our management of acquisition personnel at all levels within the Department of Defense."[196] The personnel they had in mind were the political appointees at the top of the acquisition process, the managers (both civilian and military) of major weapon-system programs, the military officers who serve in the acquisition community, and the civilian specialists who serve in the acquisition world.

As Hamilton warned in the Federalist Papers, "A government ill executed, whatever might be the theory, is in practice poor government." It is the public administrators' responsibility for the day-to-day operation of the "wheels of government" that makes the difference in whether the policies achieve their goals. In the words of Elmer Staats, "It is in the nation's interest, the public interest, that the political leadership recognize the fundamental value of obtaining and motivating the caliber of people needed in the interest of all."[197] Yet almost every politician today runs "against Washington" and "against the bureaucrats." When it is time to make budget cuts, both presidents and congressional leaders find it most easy to attack the salaries and benefits of those in the executive branch who must implement the policies of the government. With relatively low salaries and continuous attacks, it is not surprising that it is becoming increasingly difficult to recruit and retain high-quality people in public service. In commenting on this matter, former Federal Reserve Chairman Paul Volcker observed that "the idea that the public would accept mediocrity in public service is, in time, an invitation to mediocrity as a nation."[198] This truly is a critical issue for the United States, and particularly for the Department of Defense.

The solution must begin at the political-appointee level. Here, the dozen or so top people in the acquisition pyramid (particularly in the Office of the Secretary of Defense and at the top of the military services) make the major decisions on acquisition policy and on particular weapon systems—decisions that determine how effectively and efficiently the DoD uses its billions of acquisition dollars. Unfortunately, this story is not a very positive one. A survey by the National Academy of Public Administration of 536 presidential appointees in the last five administrations found increasingly rapid turnover in top jobs, longer delays in Senate confirmations, increasing reluctance to make the required financial disclosures (which have become much worse as a result of the post-Watergate changes), a widening gap between salaries of top government executives and their private-sector counterparts, longer work hours, and an increasing number of appointees who said their government jobs had caused stress in their personal and family lives.[199] The NAPA report went on to note that the average length of service for presidential appointees is "just a shade over two years" and that one-third stayed for 18 months or less. Not only is this turnover inefficient, but (as the 1985 Senate Arms Services Committee staff report on Defense Organization stated) "in many instances the defense management credentials of senior OSD officials seem to have been given low priority in their selection by the Executive Branch. In many cases, political debts (often to members of Congress) were apparently the pivotal consideration. . . . "[200] To top off this inexperience and rapid turnover, there is essentially no training provided to them. Even those appointees who have some management experience in the defense industry have difficulty adjusting to a "way of thinking that is different from what they have been accustomed to."[201] The head of a corporation has a lot more leeway than a political leader. In industry, such freedom is thought to lead to a more efficient operation; in the government, Americans would rather see less efficiency than give up checks and balances.[202] The ideal candidates for acquisition-related political appointments are people who have had experience in the industry *and* in government management; however, such people run right into the conflict-of-interest laws.

Most of the conflict-of-interest laws in this area were written to prevent military or civilian career government personnel from working for the government on a given contract and then going to work for the contractor immediately after leaving the government. These laws greatly restrict the ability of the government to get experienced people to take crucial high-level acquisition positions (because they deal with large numbers of contracts, and therefore essentially all defense contractors). Another law that has the same negative effect requires an appointee to sell any stock he may hold in a defense firm,[203] and thus to incur heavy capital-gains taxes at the very time when his salary is about to go down sharply. Then the appointee is told that he may not go back to the defense industry upon leaving the government. This compounds his financial loss if he accepts the job. Each year, more such restrictions are introduced; thus, each year it becomes less likely that people with the necessary experience will accept acquisition jobs in the government. Obviously, the potential for conflict of interest must be addressed—people coming into the government from industry must not get involved in helping firms that they have recently left. However, this would be better accomplished by simply requiring an individual to eliminate himself from any considerations involving his former employer.

In 1987 the National Association of Public Administration, in a report

entitled "Leadership in Jeopardy: The Fraying of the Presidential Appointments System,"[204] made 23 specific recommendations for improving the recruitment of senior-level executive-branch personnel. These
included simplifying the financial-disclosure requirements; establishing
a procedure for periodic salary adjustments; setting up thorough briefing and orientation procedures; limiting the period by which any senator
can delay a nomination to five working days; banning any solicitation
or discussion of future private employment by any presidential appointee, but providing three months' severance pay; allowing presidential
appointees to defer capital-gains taxes incurred when they sell assets
to comply with conflict-of-interest provisions; and an annual 10 percent
bonus for appointees who remain for more than three years. Surely it
should be possible to develop special legislation to cover the few people
who are critical to the efficient and effective operation of our multi-
billion-dollar defense acquisition process. Thomas Jefferson once wrote
to a friend, criticizing him for not taking a greater part in national affairs:
"There is a debt of service due from every man to his country, propor-
tioned to the bounties which nature and fortune have measured to
him."[205] Many defense-industry executives recognize this obligation.
Congress simply needs to make it not quite so hard for these individuals
to take four to eight years out of their lives to serve. Helping the
individual is not the issue, rather, it is the ability to help the nation get
its money's worth for its defense expenditures that must be addressed.

The Packard Commission concluded that far greater centralization of
acquisition decision-making was needed, and recommended the creation of the new position of Under Secretary for Acquisition as the
number-three position in the Department of Defense. Clearly, if the
decision-making is to be centralized, then the people making these
decisions must be extremely well qualified.

The Packard Commission also recommended that "the day-to-day
execution of the development and production of weapon systems" be
decentralized, down to the level of the program manager. The program
manager fills a critical position in the acquisition process and must be
capable and experienced. Unfortunately, here too inexperience and
high turnover are common. Over 90 percent of the program managers
in the roughly 240 program offices within the Department of Defense
are military officers[206] (usually Army, Air Force, and Marine colonels
or Navy captains, but occasionally generals or admirals). The services

argue that military officers are in a better position to understand military needs and thus more capable of making performance-versus-cost trade-offs during the evolution of a weapon system. (Essentially, the services fear that military performance will be given up for lower cost.) The problem is that senior military officers also believe, as former Under Secretary of the Army J. Ronald Fox has written, "that the weapons acquisition process can be managed by military officers like themselves, whose primary training and experience has been in military field operations unrelated to the complex tasks of procurement and program management that the process involves. . . . Most military chiefs see little need to get program managers more specialized training or development."[207]

Still worse, military officers see program-manager jobs as career dead-ends. The armed services reward and promote people with "operational" experience, so an ambitious officer who becomes a program manager wants to "get back to the field" as quickly as possible. The GAO found in a 1986 survey that the average tenure of a program manager (including his experience as a deputy program manager) was just a little over 2 years.[208] Thus, during the 8–12 years of its development, a weapon system is not unlikely to have four or five different military officers as program managers—an extremely inefficient way to "run a business." In contrast, both the GAO's survey and a detailed study by J. Ronald Fox and James Field found that program managers in industry are given program-management responsibility only after extensive acquisition-management experience, remain as a program's manager for extended periods, and continue to be promoted within that field.[209]

The above problems affect the military officers scattered throughout the acquisition process as well as to those in program management—if there is no advantageous career path for them in the field of acquisition, they will choose not to go into that field, or else not to remain in it. The Army is perhaps the worst of the services in this regard. One study showed that the average Army program manager had a total of only five years' experience in the acquisition world, including his program-management experience.[210]

The excessive layers of management above the program managers are often, unfortunately, filled with people who also lack acquisition experience. Thus, a program manager is placed in a position in which he has little flexibility (since he is constrained by the requirements for performance, cost, and schedule) and numerous layers of people above him who are "helping" and "overseeing" him. The typical program manager reports that he spends 50–70 percent of his time "selling" or "defending" his program at higher levels. Some report that they have to go to 40 meetings to get any significant decision made on a program. With such lack of authority and so few opportunities for promotion, it is no wonder that many military officers consider this an undesirable position.

There are two alternative ways to address this problem: to shift to civilian program managers, and to alter career paths in the armed services so as to encourage top officers to go into acquisition and stay there. When John Lehman was Secretary of the Navy, he issued an edict that 40 percent of all future admiral positions would be reserved for officers specializing in weapons procurement or management rather than in command at sea.[211] Such a step is an essential one to stick to if the problem of program managers is to be solved. [212] What is really required is incentives—including promotion—for the best people to choose these career paths. Congress has passed legislation requiring a person to have at least eight years of acquisition-related experience before becoming a program manager, and to stay in the job at least four years. But experience is desirable only in the hands of the best people, and the best people will go into program management only when they know that they can get promoted from it and when they can be sure that they will not find someone from a field command placed over them.

Sweden now allows an added salary increment for crucial acquisition positions. A colonel serving as a program manager can receive a significantly higher salary than other colonels and even the Director General of the agency. This provides prestige, and it does in fact get high-quality, experienced people to become and remain program managers.[213]

Yet another problem with the American system is that a military officer is forced to retire at just about the time when he has accumulated enough experience to hold a key program-management position. The solution to this is to allow someone to stay in the service and remain a colonel or (in the Navy) a captain in order to allow him to run a major acquisition program.

And clearly the many layers of management above the program manager should be eliminated so that the program manager can exercise proper authority and concentrate on running the program, rather than on briefing his superiors.[214]

The fourth category within the acquisiton community is made up of civilians, who constitute 89 percent of the acquisition work force[215] (in positions such as contract administrator, buyer, engineer, and comptroller). Here, rigid pay grades and the seniority-based promotion system of the federal Civil Service act as strong disincentives to outstanding performance and to the retention of high-quality people, who can rise faster in industry. Greater flexibility in promotion and pay is required.[216]

Of the more than 24,000 members of the DoD work force who specialize in awarding and administering contracts, 85 percent are civilians. These people have the authority to enter into and administer contracts in the name of the United States Government, and they are required to master an extensive, complex body of knowledge, encompassing materials and operations management, contract law, cost analysis, negotiation techniques, and industrial marketing. Yet the Office of Personnel Management designates these employees as "administrative" rather than "professional."[217] This designation prohibits the establishment of any business-education requirements. As a result, only half of the contract specialists have college degrees, which may or may not be business-related.[218] Both the GAO and the Packard Commission have recommended a minimum education and/or experience requirement for the contract specialists.[219]

Because it will take a considerable number of years before there can be a broad upgrading of either the military or the civilian personnel in the acquisition community, a short-term corrective action has been suggested: put industrial people, with experience in management, engineering, manufacturing, and so forth, into some of the key program-office and functional-management positions on a temporary basis. These are the jobs that provide day-to-day management of the overall acquisition activities but are below the political-appointee level. There are only a few hundred of these acquisition-management positions, and they could be selectively filled with experienced industrial managers without creating any conflict of interest (either on their way in or on their way out).[220] A majority of the key acquisition positions below the political level would still be reserved for career personnel (civilian or military)—a very necessary requirement in order to provide career-path incentives for such people. However, especially over the first few years while the government is building up its corps of experienced acquisition professionals, a group of experienced industry personnel would provide the needed complement to the career professionals that is so obviously absent today.[221]

If we don't have top-notch people involved in the acquisition of military equipment and supplies, the system will not work no matter how good the policies and practices are. As the Packard Commission stated, "Whatever other changes may be made, it is vitally important to enhance the quality of the defense acquisition work force—both by attracting qualified new personnel and by improving the training and motivation of current personnel."[222]

7 Research and Development

The Soviet Union invests far more money in arms than the United States, produces more than twice as much military equipment in most categories, is deploying weapons that increasingly match their U.S. counterparts in quality, and spends a large share of its resources on military research and development.[1] The relative strength of the United States lies in technological and industrial advantages—the subjects of the next two chapters.

Heavy expenditures for research and development (both defense-related and civilian) are essentially a post-World War II phenomenon in the United States. Before 1940, the combined R&D expenditures of industry and government were only about $1 billion per year.[2] However, in the 40 years after the end of World War II, investment in R&D grew to almost $100 billion per year. Approximately half of this R&D is government-sponsored. By 1985 the Department of Defense alone was spending over $30 billion per year for R&D on defense systems.[3] Furthermore, in the post-World War II era R&D has been taking an increasingly larger share of defense dollars. After 1945, the ratio of defense R&D expenditures to defense production expenditures increased gradually from around 5 percent to a peak, in the mid-1970s, of over 50 percent,[4] with cyclical variations during periods of conflict and periods of rapid force buildup. In 1989, it is still 47 percent. Typical civilian-sector industries have R&D-to-production expenditure ratios of around 2–10 percent, not 30–50 percent.

The DoD has stressed the importance of "technological superiority," and its heavy investment in R&D appears to have paid good dividends in two respects. First, the United States has been able to maintain significant technological superiority over the Soviet Union. Each generation of American weapon systems is considerably better than the comparable Soviet systems, and American weapons are the envy of the world in this regard. Second, there has been a very significant "fallout" in civilian-sector industries from this large DoD investment; it has generated and/or stimulated a number of major commercial industries (including jet aircraft, computers, and communication satellites). Thus, stressing R&D has paid dividends not only for the DoD but also for the U.S. economy in general.

However, over time, the emphasis on R&D has engendered criticism. President Eisenhower, in his famous "military-industrial complex" farewell address, stated that "in holding scientific research and discovery in respect, as we should, we must also be alert to the equal and opposite danger that public policy could itself become the captive of a scientific-technological elite."[5]

History has shown that scientists and engineers do not often oversell technology. Lawyers, economists, journalists, and politicians are more susceptible to the technocratic temptation.[6] Thus, the danger is that technology might become the dominant force behind U.S. national-security strategy and doctrine.[7]

Other critics have wondered about the very high ratio of R&D to production in defense and have evidenced concern that not enough equipment is being bought. As Representative Samuel Stratton (D-N.Y.)—a member of the House Armed Services Committee—stated, "It's a weird logic that you should abandon weapon systems which are finally made to work and sink all of your billions into dream weapons of the future."[8] Still others have argued that the continuous emphasis on technology at any cost has driven the costs of weapon systems, ammunition, and spare parts so high that unacceptably small numbers of these items can be purchased—and that those systems that are being purchased are too difficult to maintain and to operate. This school (known as the "military reform group") has argued for lower technology and greater quantities of systems.[9]

Though the critics' concerns may be extreme, there is certainly some basis for each of them. Thus, one must step back and ask whether there is a way for the DoD to do better with its $30 billion a year of R&D. In particular, can the R&D effort be redirected so as to yield more total force effectiveness from the $300 billion a year spent on national security? This question is especially critical as we look forward to the 21st century, when a whole new generation of weapon systems will be evolving—"ceramic tanks," "plastic aircraft," intercontinental ballistic missiles with conventional warheads and near-perfect accuracy, space-based high-energy lasers for shooting down ICBMs, and other advanced weapons yet to be unveiled. If historical trends continued, such weapons will offer great military advantages at extremely high costs. The challenge is to reverse the cost trend so that the next generation of weapon systems will offer higher performance with higher quality and lower costs. That is the technological challenge to which we must now turn.

Historical Problems

The first, and undoubtedly the most critical, of all R&D issues is the basic question of which weapon systems should be developed. This question is the core of the "requirements" process. In theory, the military services establish "mission area needs" to address current or projected deficiencies in their ability to carry out national-security objectives.[10] However, these "requirements" must be based on new weapon systems that are within the current concepts of war-fighting or within the current limits of technology and are likely to be "incremental" advances, such as a "faster plane" or a "more heavily armored tank." (How could one write a "mission need statement" for an atom bomb, or a high-energy laser, if it had not yet been invented?)

The technological advances that have evolved through the funding of military R&D fall into two distinct categories.[11] The first are those that fit within the current paradigm of the "military-industrial complex," which involves institutions, organizations, force structures, historical equipment, military tactics, and industrial R&D and production facilities. These technological advances usually are aimed at previously stated "mission needs"; alternatively, since they fit within the existing "system," they can easily be used to justify new "mission needs." For example, if someone invents a way to make a better jet engine that allows a plane to fly faster or maneuver more rapidly, the military will instantly begin to develop a new weapon system, which will eventually go into production (as long as an even better engine doesn't come along in the meantime). Because the military wants to have the maximum possible performance for its systems, each of these new "incremental" changes is greeted with considerable enthusiasm and support. Thus we have what many refer to as the technological imperative: because we can have it, we must have it.

Another form of technological opportunity created by military R&D (and the more significant of the two) involves "nontraditional" changes of the sort brought about by some totally new type of weapon system that breaks down some part of the traditional paradigm of the military-industrial complex. In this case, advanced technology is defining *possible* new military strategies, equipment, applications, and/or institutional structures. Unfortunately, these tend to be resisted enormously by both sides of the military-industrial complex. The Navy resisted anti-ship missiles for years,[12] because of their obvious implications; the Air Force resists pilotless aircraft (such as cruise missiles and reconnaissance drones)[13]; and all the services tend to resist new technology that requires changes in their roles and missions.[14]

Thus, a dialectic conflict is created by technological advancement. On the one hand, technological opportunities that result in incremental changes (within the traditional paradigm of the military-industrial complex) are rapidly accepted and enthusiastically pushed forward—perhaps too unquestioningly. On the other hand, those technological opportunities that offer revolutionary changes are often outside the paradigm; thus they meet with extreme institutional and structural resistance, with every effort made to reject them.[15] As a result, the "requirements" for equipment tend to perpetuate themselves because of parochial interests, both in the military (for example, tank officers do not want tanks replaced by unmanned vehicles) and in the defense industry (tank makers don't want tanks to be considered obsolete). Before becoming Secretary of Defense, James Schlesinger, referring to the DoD, said that "large hierarchical organizations tend to be remarkably efficient mechanisms for the suppression of new ideas and alternatives."[16]

As long as the United States enjoyed military superiority, the cultural tendency to oppose changes and to view them as threats to the current establishment was not a serious problem. However, in view of the trends in both numbers and performance of new Soviet equipment, it is crucial that the United States reevaluate this resistance. This will be difficult, and it will require significant structural and organizational changes within the military service.

The second of the major problems with defense R&D is that once it has been decided that a given weapon system will be developed, the requirements for the new system tend to be driven almost exclusively by the desire for high performance. Contrasting the DoD's approach with the approach taken to the development of a new system in the commercial world will help to clarify this issue. A number of years ago, when Texas Instruments was going to develop a new hand-held calculator, it listed a set of technical characteristics for the unit. Then, it specified that the production cost per unit must be under $100, since that was the "value" that the potential users placed on such a device.

In essence, this was an affordability constraint. If the DoD had been ordering the calculator, there would have been an extensive set of military requirements written for it. The requirements would have been similar to those for the commercial calculator; however, they would have been based on what the "state of the art" allowed, rather than on what would be "acceptable." The resulting calculator would probably have been a better-performing calculator than the commercial one, but the added 5–10 percent of performance would have resulted in a 30–50 percent increase in cost. Therefore, in a resource-constrained environment, far fewer of the military calculators would have been built—and that would have driven the price even higher. Furthermore, the military calculator would have encountered many more problems during its development stages;[17] therefore, the development time would undoubtedly have been much longer.

As would be expected, the third major R&D problem is that weapons are designed so as to be too expensive and, therefore, cannot be produced in sufficient quantities. It is not that too much money is spent in the production process. Rather, high cost is inherent in the design. This, in turn, makes the production process expensive and results in the production of too few systems.

The fourth problem is that the complex designs created in the quest for high performance result in low-quality production, and high rejection rates in the production process lead to high production costs. For example, one Navy official reported to the GAO that the numerous defects in the Phoenix missile were due in part to an overcomplicated design, which made assembly too difficult.[18] In addition, the complexity of certain systems appears to be highly correlated with the fact that they fail more often in the field and with the fact that they are difficult and expensive to maintain.[19] And because these weapons are so expensive, fewer of them can be tested.[20]

The fifth of the R&D problems is that it simply takes too long to develop new weapon systems. Limited resources lead to a refusal to fund programs realistically so as to cover the obvious risks that are likely to come up in development. Furthermore, multiple approaches to advanced technology are considered wasteful and thus are not funded, even though they clearly would reduce risks. Finally, it is always believed that, in any given area of weaponry, there will only be one new system for a decade or more; thus, all new technology is poured into that system—even technology that has not been completely demonstrated. As a result of this, the advancements become too complex and the R&D schedule has to be extended farther and farther. As Robert Costello, the Under Secretary of Defense for Acquisition, noted in 1987 about the DoD's development program for very-high-speed integrated circuits (VHSIC), "While over 60 systems have VHSIC products in their plans, VHSIC parts are only in one current deployed system. . . . the technology is available and proven and the Japanese are already using equivalent technology in commercial applications. . . ."[21] Comparisons between other (similar) technologies for commercial systems and military systems in the United States indicate that the military systems take much longer to develop.[22] The United States loses a significant amount of its technological superiority over the Soviet Union because of this. American engineers invent an item long before it becomes available in the Soviet Union, but the Soviets manage to go through the "technology insertion" phase much more rapidly, and then into high-quantity production—so the two countries often get the advanced technology into the field at almost the same time.

The sixth of the major problems in U.S. R&D today is the overemphasis on the full-scale development of weapon systems at the expense of the crucial long-term development of a strong technology base at the level of components, materials, and processes. As the development of individual weapons became extremely expensive, resources for the technology base were reduced (both on an absolute and on a percentage basis).[23] In the past, the DoD had counted on the civilian sector for a lot of basic research, since it was applicable to both military and commercial products.[24] Unfortunately, as the American stock market placed greater and greater emphasis on quarterly earnings, there was a clear shift in the civilian sector toward a short-term emphasis in the R&D area, and a simultaneous move toward offshore procurements and production for the short-term economic benefits. Thus, there was a simultaneous reduction of civilian-sponsored generic R&D and DoD-sponsored development of the technology base.

An additional effect of the channeling of more R&D resources toward major weapon systems is that the money tends to go to the large prime contractors; therefore; less is available to innovative small firms. Though there is much controversy, the data seem to show quite clearly that small firms contribute more innovation per R&D dollars.[25] The Small Business Innovative Research Program[26] was created in 1982 to correct the maldistribution of R&D money. Unfortunately, there are considerable opportunities to abuse this program and, particularly, the many other legislated small-business programs. An easier way to correct the problem would be to simply devote greater resources to the more basic technology activities (on which the smaller firms are often working).

The seventh R&D-related problem is the growing difficulty of luring American students, at both the undergraduate and the graduate level, into science and engineering.[27] The effect of this can be felt both in the universities and in the workplace. The percentage of foreign students in the engineering and science programs at American universities has increased dramatically, from around 17 percent in 1975 to 30 percent in 1985.[28] In 1984, fully 56 percent of the doctorates in engineering awarded by American universities went to foreigners.[29] And many foreign students, particularly those from the more developed countries, return home.

The shortage of American students in science and engineering is of particular concern to the Department of Defense, which needs people to perform classified research; but it is also a problem across the entire U.S. economy. In 1981, for example, there were ten jobs for each new degree holder in computer science and four for each new nuclear engineer. Defense analysts also cited shortages of aeronautical engineers and of people to work on avionics, computer software, and electrical systems.[30] With such a severe shortage of scientists and engineers, the competition for them becomes quite intense. As a result, it is difficult for the DoD to hire these people to work in the government R&D organizations, since salaries are constrained by the Civil Service system. Those who go into industry find their salaries bid up dramatically; this drives up the cost of defense R&D, which is extremely labor-intensive.

These seven adverse trends in defense R&D, if allowed to continue, will have dramatic effects on the long-term security posture of the United States. To date, the United States has been able to maintain its technological superiority in the military sphere, though at a high and increasing price. Reversing these adverse trends, over time, will allow the United States to use its innovative capabilities to achieve a stronger defense posture with fewer dollars.

The Importance of the Preliminary Design Phase

The most crucial phases in the evolution of a weapon system occur before the major development efforts actually begin. As figure 6.1 showed, a trivial amount of money is spent during the concept-exploration phase, and only about 3 percent of the program dollars are spent during the demonstration-and-validation phase (i.e., on the prototype efforts). However, it is during these early phases that the overwhelming share of a weapon system's costs (i.e., the amounts of money to be spent in the production and support phases) are "designed in." Approximately 85 percent of the total life-cycle cost of a weapon system has been committed, through the design of the system, by the time full-scale development begins. It is also during these phases preceding full-scale development that much of the "cost growth" of a weapon system is built in. Typically, in order to get a prototype of a weapon system initially approved ("onto the drawing board"), a very optimistic "planning estimate" for the total cost of the program will be made. Then, as the design evolves—driven by the performance requirements—there is a tendency for the cost of the program to increase by 50 percent before the initiation of full-scale development.[31]

To take advantage of the importance of the preliminary design phases, the Department of Defense must recognize that the concept-exploration period is not simply a time to convert a requirement into a technically feasible design; rather, it is a time to go through an iterative process in which performance is traded off against quantity. The crucial point here is that the important costs are not the development dollars; they are the production and support costs being "designed in." Thus, it is necessary to continuously iterate preliminary design performance against estimated production and support costs.

Another important point about the concept-exploration phase is that there ought to be a relatively clear operational concept for the weapon system. Too often this is missing at the early stages; the weapon-system requirement is technology-driven and essentially unconstrained. The commercial world has found that R&D produces the best results when it is "market-driven."[32] The defense-sector equivalent of market-driven R&D is for the likely operational users of a weapon system to write down what they actually need and how they will use it (i.e., a functional performance requirement). This approach has often been recommended[33] but has rarely been followed. Following it would mean that a new airplane would not be described in terms of its detailed design characteristics, or even in terms of an airplane, but rather in terms of the *military mission* the new weapon system is expected to achieve.

The demonstration-and-validation phase constitutes the second half of the preliminary design activity. The objective here is to demonstrate, with prototypes of either systems or subsystems, three things: that the system is technically capable of satisfying the functional requirements, that it can be used in the military mode implied by the operational concept, and that it will be affordable when it is developed and produced. Traditionally, the DoD has bothered with only the first of these points. The second could be addressed through operational testing of prototypes. However, affordability can be addressed only by taking the preliminary design sufficiently far along to determine how much it is likely to cost to produce the system and to support it in the field. This affordability issue is a very serious engineering challenge, and one that many engineers are not adequately prepared for; they often believe that their job is simply to design things that will work, and that it is someone else's job to price them.

How far to push technology is one of the biggest questions that should be answered before full-scale development of a weapon is begun. The DoD's answer has often been "as far as it will go." It would be much wiser to constrain the technological push by requiring a very short development cycle. This latter approach—which is the norm in the commercial world—forces the designer to make two assumptions: that he will utilize only technology that has been demonstrated (at either the system level or the subsystem level) when he begins full-scale development; and that since the technology will continue to advance, improvements will be held up and introduced into the weapon system through subsequent modifications (often called "block changes" or "pre-planned product improvements"). Having a short development cycle with planned product improvements has proved to be the lowest-cost, lowest-risk approach whenever it has been tried.[34]

The Department of Defense often does plan on relatively short development cycles. However, the DoD rarely is able to stick to these plans, because they are not based on proven technology and because the budgeting for the uncertainties and problems in the development program has rarely been adequate. One of the best techniques for covering risk on a development program is to fund parallel approaches and to assume that some of these will fail, but that through alternative technological approaches or multiple contractors pursuing similar technologies (or both) the areas of risk will be covered.[35] This can often be done at the component level or the subsystem level. Of course, by its very nature, advanced R&D work is highly risky. One should *expect* some failures. Thus, the only way to be sure of maintaining a short development cycle (for the sake of both low cost and early deployment of superior-performing systems) is to adequately fund the high-risk areas and to ensure that alternatives are available to cover the likely areas of failure.

One important way to see the benefits that can be realized through the use of relatively "proven" technology is to examine a concept known as the "high/low mix."[36] If we define the "high end" weapon systems as those that were designed to incorporate significant technological advancements and the "low-end" systems as those that were based on previously demonstrated technical capabilities, we can plot the cost histories of a series of weapon systems by taking the aggregated cost trends that were detailed in chapter 6 and splitting them between the "high-end" and the "low-end" systems. This is done in figure 7.1. As can be seen, there is a significant difference in unit costs between the "high-end" aircraft (such as the F-15A and the F-111A) and the "low-end" aircraft (such as the F-16A and the A-7A). As has already been discussed, the difference between these two categories is based not on actual performance but rather on the state of the technology when it was applied. In fact, there is not a dramatic difference in performance[37] (see figure 7.2). The data suggest that the first operational units of a "high-end" system reach a given level of performance only about 5 years sooner than their "low-end" counterparts. Therefore,

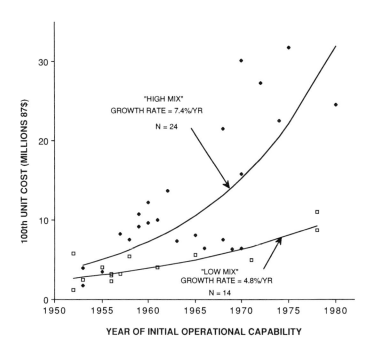

Figure 7.1
Cost comparisons of "high-end" (♦) and "low-end" (□) U.S. fighter and attack aircraft.

"high-end" technology should be chosen only when it is crucial to get maximum performance a few years earlier, since the "low end" is much less expensive and therefore will allow far greater quantities.

Equally significant is the performance comparison in figure 7.2 between U.S. and Soviet aircraft for the same initial-operational-capability time period.[38] This comparison shows that the United States maintained technological superiority in aircraft between 1950 and 1980. However, it also indicates that the United States could have maintained that technological superiority using the lower-risk, lower-cost approach represented by the low end of the high/low mix.

A quantity-versus-quality choice was, in fact, made in the mid-1970s when Secretary of Defense James Schlesinger offered Air Force Chief of Staff General David Jones a choice between a fighter force made up of only F-15s and one with a mix of F-15s and F-16s (with significantly

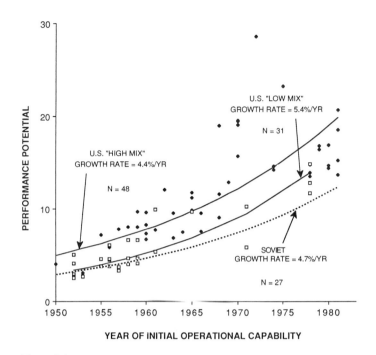

Figure 7.2
Performance comparison of "high-end" (♦) and "low-end" (□) U.S.
fighter and attack aircraft and Soviet aircraft.

more aircraft—three whole "wings" of F-16s).[39] Buy dozens more units
by having a high/low mix is exactly what the commercial world does
when it applies "price elasticity" (the principle that as prices fall, greater
quantities are procured). Quantity-quality tradeoffs of exactly this sort
must be made by the military services in the early "affordability" analysis of the next generation of weapon systems.[40]

A common misconception during the formulation of the concept for
a new weapon system is that forcing two military services, or two allied
nations, to jointly develop the same system will significantly reduce
costs, since they will be sharing the R&D costs and gaining the benefits
of higher-volume production. Unfortunately, the data on multi-service[41]
and multi-nation[42] programs suggest that these potential savings have
not been realized for two reasons. First, and perhaps more important,
when two services or nations get together to establish the requirements

for a program, they almost invariably "compromise upward" and design a system that satisfies the requirements of both parties, rather than truly compromising. Therefore, they drive up the inherent costs of the weapon system.[43] Second, as a joint program evolves, it is extremely difficult to maintain either the requirements or the budget (owing to changes in "perceived" needs and priorities). A comparison of R&D cost control, production cost control, and schedule control for single-service programs versus joint-service programs show that the joint programs' annual costs and schedule growths were 217 percent, 103 percent, and 150 percent larger, respectively.[44] Such historical data should not be interpreted to mean that multi-nation or multi-service programs do not have the potential to offer significant savings. However, the way in which this potential has been realized in the past is by having a single service develop a weapon system and then having a second service or country sign up to buy large quantities of the identical system or a slightly modified version. In this way, the requirements are not driven up by a combination of inputs, and the economies of scale can be realized through increased volume. Such a result could also be realized by the two services of two countries working together on the initiation of a development program; however, as described above, they would have to use cost constraints as a key part of their requirements process and their preliminary design process.

Cost as a Technology Issue

A typical American engineering student (graduate or undergraduate) is taught how to design the "best system." Using computers, sophisticated mathematics, and all their engineering skills, these students set out to design systems that will achieve the maximum performance. If they enter the commercial world, they are taught that their designs should be modified to reduce the likely costs of production and operation. However, if they enter the defense world, they continue to use the design practices they learned in school, and cost-cutting becomes an exercise for the manufacturer. The results of these two different approaches to design are, as would be expected, significantly different.

In both worlds, performance has gotten better and better as technology has evolved; however, in the defense world costs have risen along with performance. For example, military radars have been increasing

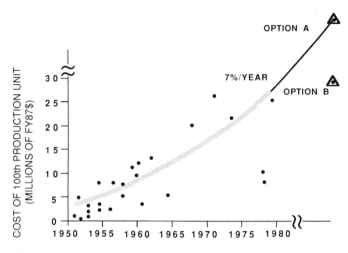

Figure 7.3
Cost versus time for U.S. fighter and attack aircraft.

in cost and performance at a rate of about 7 percent per year (in constant dollars and constant quantity). Yet commercial computers, televisions, and other items that use similar technology have improved dramatically in performance and gone down dramatically in price. In the latter case, advanced technology has been used both for cost reductions[45] and for performance improvements. Similarly, U.S. tanks have improved in performance at an annual rate of around 5–7 percent, with the cost of a tank doubling from the Sherman to the M-60 and then tripling from the M-60 to the M-1. (These numbers are based on constant dollars and the price of the 1,000th unit, so they are adjusted for both inflation and quantity.) Yet the automobiles produced over the same 30 years have improved enormously in handling, safety, gas mileage, and other aspects while their cost (in constant dollars) has remained essentially the same.[46]

For a specific example of how the DoD should approach the use of advanced technology so as to get both cost reductions and performance increases, consider the curve in figure 6.4. In figure 7.3 that curve is extended into the time period when a new fighter might be under consideration. If the designers of this plane had been given the task of designing the "best possible fighter plane for the early 21st century," it

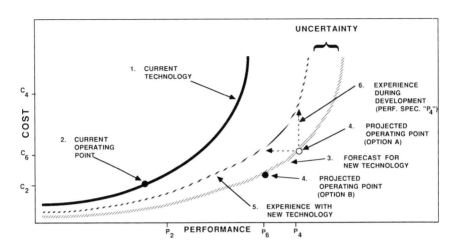

Figure 7.4
Impact of uncertainty on acquisition cost and performance.

is likely that this aircraft would have followed the historical cost-growth curves and come out costing well over $100 million each.[47] The plane would be an outstanding performer, but it is highly likely (again on the basis of historical trends) that the United States would be able to buy only a few—probably not enough to represent a credible air-superiority capability under most conditions. Clearly, one would like to "move off the curve" and come up with a high-performance aircraft with a cost closer to that shown as option B on the figure. The challenge is to figure out how to achieve that.

For the answer, let us turn to the cost-versus-performance curve shown in figure 7.4. Curve 1 shows that as performance increases, cost increases gradually until we start to approach a limit, at which point, if we want to get much more performance, we face a dramatic cost increase (30–50 percent in order to get the last 10 percent or so of performance increases). A well-trained engineer would operate "below the knee of the curve," at point 2. Now imagine that a new technology comes along—one that is forecast to bring significant performance increases and to shift the curve far to the right, as shown by curve 3. We can now take the two operating-point options from figure 7.3 and project them onto the new-technology curve as the "projected operating point" for either option A or option B. Notice that the projected cost and the promised performance for option A point are considerably higher than for option B. However, in both cases the projected performance is dramatically higher than that for the current operating point (with the older technology). The choice is simply whether one feels compelled to move to the higher performance requirement of option A or whether one would be better off having the slightly lower performance of option B and being able to buy significantly more of the systems (the choice discussed earlier in connection with the "high/low mix" option). In the commercial world, one would probably move still farther down the curve to what might be considered option C, which is lower in cost but still higher in performance than the current product. This explains why commercial electronics products continue to improve in performance, generation after generation, and at the same time continue to drop in cost.

The DoD has generally chosen to aim for option A as the projected operating point, explaining that this is "required" for the "likely threat" that will be seen over the 25-year life span of the weapon system. Unfortunately, the problem does not typically stop at this point. The performance-versus-cost-curve forecast for the new technology does not get fully realized when the equipment is built and put into the field. What is realized is frequently closer to curve 5. However, the DoD usually holds firm to its performance "requirement"—since, by this time, the operating performance (point P_4) has been solidified as a specification to the contractor developing the weapon system—and, as a result, sees the cost rise from C_4 to C_6. The alternative would be to hold firm to the design cost (C_4) and follow the horizontal dashed line, which would move the performance down slightly (from P_4 to P_6) but would hold firm to the specified "design cost." This approach would allow the planned quantity of these advanced systems to actually be built. Thus, the "design to cost" approach yields far greater numbers of weapon systems without a significant reduction in performance—in fact, with a dramatic increase in performance over the prior-technology weapon system (from P_2 to P_6). This is not simply an academic exercise; it is the exact choice that the DoD is forced to make every day on each of its new weapon systems. Traditionally it has always chosen first to go to the option A projected operating point as its preliminary design requirement and then, as the system evolves through its development, to hold firm to this performance (P_4) and see the cost rise significantly (from C_4 to C_6). Until the DoD introduces affordability constraints into its requirements process and shifts from a design-to-performance approach to more of a design-to-cost approach, it will procure fewer and fewer weapon systems each year, and eventually the United States will not have enough modern systems to present a credible defense posture.

As a necessary complement to the design-to-cost approach, the engineers in the defense industry must begin to achieve a far greater integration of the design process with the manufacturing process. If proper planning and funding are available during the early design efforts, then the engineers can make the transition from computer-aided design through computer-aided manufacturing into computer-aided logistics in a smooth and continuous process. In fact, this overall shift toward computer integrated manufacturing promises to reduce development time and cost dramatically, as well as to yield great savings in the production and the support of future systems. This approach should encourage the use of "flexible manufacturing technology"—a particularly attractive alternative for the relatively small quantities of production that are typical of defense equipment. However, this approach requires the integration of engineering, production, and support *in the early design phases*. It also requires that the design, as it evolves, be continuously modified in order to take producibility and maintainability directly into account. Additionally, process technology (i.e., manufacturing technology) must receive equal emphasis during the early design phases, and adequate funding must be put into manufacturing technology if both the cost advantages and the schedule advantages offered by these new R&D programs are to be realized.

Another way to realize dramatic reductions in the costs of defense equipment would be to shift from military specifications to commercial specifications, and to make greater use of commercial equipment in defense systems. The DoD was historically driven to the increased use of special military specifications because the performance and reliability of commercial equipment had lagged significantly behind. However, in recent years, particularly in the electronics area, this is no longer the case. For example, today's automobiles have semiconductor devices hard-mounted to their engines. These operate in environments very similar to, and in some cases worse than, the environments encountered by military equipment. Yet, *for comparable environments,* table 7.1 clearly demonstrates the far lower cost, far higher reliability (fewer

Table 7.1
A comparison of mil.-spec. and commercial semiconductors (comparable part, comparable environment).

	Mil. spec.	Commercial
Part cost: Bipolar digital logic	$15.78	$1.67
Bipolar linear	$11.40	$0.42
Reliability failure index	1.9–4.6	0.06
Lead time for new part (months)	17–51	1–12

failures), and far greater performance (as represented by the lead time to put more advanced parts into a system) of commercial semiconductors.[48] For the above reasons, both the Packard Commission and the Defense Science Board[49] strongly recommended that the DoD make greater use of commercial components.

The fact that commercial parts are produced in far greater quantities is the primary reason for their much lower cost and higher reliability. By using them, the DoD would be able to benefit from this fact. A Defense Science Board Study found that systems built with commercial components would have lower overall costs (by a factor from 2 to 8) and comparable or better reliability. And if proven, off-the-shelf commercial components were to be used, the DoD could acquire its electronic systems from 2 to 5 times more rapidly.[50] Since most of today's weapon systems have between one-third and one-half of their cost devoted to electronics (and this ratio is growing), a shift to commercial components would make a dramatic difference in cost, quality, and schedule. However, before this shift can be achieved, the government must learn how to buy commercial systems and components through its existing procurement operation.

Characteristics of a Successful Program

The twelve characteristics that always stand out in studies of successful high-technology development programs should be emulated in the evolution of any new management approach to be taken by the Department of Defense[51]:

1. *Short and stable schedules* for both development and production, with a continuous flow into production.

2. *Experienced, small staffs, with clear command channels and limited reporting* (essentially, "decentralized execution," down to the program manager, after a "baseline" has been established for performance, schedule, and cost by top management).

3. *Cost realism* throughout the development and production phases, with full funding of all needed resources.[52]

4. *The presence of a continuous alternative*—often with different technologies and/or different contractors maintaining options in critical technology areas—at the system level and/or (particularly) the subsystem and component levels. This does not mean that competitive sources were maintained in all programs all the time; rather, some alternative existed to both minimize risks as well as to create incentives for the achievement of maximum performance at a reasonable cost.

5. *Unit production cost and low support cost used as significant design requirements.*

6. *Good communications maintained with potential future users.* This is particularly important during the early phases of a program, when tradeoffs between performance, schedule, and cost are made.

7. *Prototyping,* at both the system and the subsystem levels, for early demonstration of technical feasibility, likely production and support costs, and operational utility.

8. *Early and extensive testing,* including early operational testing by the user community. Successful systems viewed testing and evaluation as an integral part of the development process (finding problems, fixing them, and testing them to be sure that they were corrected).

9. *Early, development-phase funding for production and support.*

10. *Maximum use of proven technologies, components, and subsystems, with planned product improvements after the system has been deployed.* This means standardizing interfaces so that improvements can be "plugged in," and it means beginning subsystem improvements in parallel with the system.

11. *Maximum use of commercial components, subsystems, and specifications.*

12. *An emphasis on quality*—rather than lowest cost—as the driving consideration in all major development, production, and support decisions. There is a tendency to believe that one has to "pay for quality," but the Japanese approach to quality has taught us that if

one can achieve high quality then the savings will be dramatic. Thus, it is worth paying "up front" for quality—in terms of design, prevention, and (especially) process control—in order to avoid all the high costs associated with failure, reworking, and retrofitting.[53]

Long-Term R&D Strategy

Since World War II, American military strategy has been based on technological superiority. Innovativeness and responsiveness are the strengths of the American economy, particularly in comparison with the Soviet economy. However, the U.S. Department of Defense, as a monopsony buyer, needs to develop a long-term R&D strategy–a strategy clearly stated, clearly understood, and recognizing the "mixed" (government/industry) nature of the overall defense R&D economy. The development of such a strategy will require industry's support. As the economist Richard Nelson stated, "To think that an industrial policy can successfully be imposed on an industry is a mistake. To be effective, a policy requires a degree of cooperation and participation from the industry."[54]

Naturally, the defense industry, as well as the military, has a strong institutional bias toward continuing to do things the way they have always been done. Thus, any recommendations for change contained in the DoD's long-term strategy will have to be instilled in the industry as well as in the military. The successful implementing of the necessary changes is going to depend on leadership, and this leadership is going to have to come from the top levels of the DoD, where both the mission and the resources are known.

The Defense Department's long-term R&D strategy must encompass

• a shift in emphasis toward technological advances that are likely to provide truly significant military advantages and/or dramatic improvements in quality and cost,

• a shift in overall R&D funding to address the "front end" of research and advanced technology as well as R&D support at the "lower tiers" of the defense industry,

• a greater emphasis on the quality of personnel, in the universities, in the government's laboratories, and in the management of the R&D programs, and

• changes in the DoD's organizations and procedures that will facilitate the implementing of the long-term R&D strategy.

To get the maximum for its R&D dollars, the DoD will have to stop pushing traditional weapon systems and will have to focus more on "breakthrough" technologies that can make a qualitative difference in military advantages[55]—for example, inexpensive, "smart," non-nuclear weapon systems. Naturally, the next tank, the next airplane, and the next ship always receive funding and support; however, at present there is little institutional support for less traditional systems. Special organizations will have to be created to encourage work on such systems. It will also have to be recognized that, if the undersirable trends in weapons-acquisition practices are to be reversed, low-cost technologies must receive as much emphasis as high-performance ones. Advances likely to improve quality and to lower production and supports costs must receive sufficient resources and management attention. Clearly, large numbers of inexpensive, smart weapons could make a very significant difference in the outcome of a conflict, as could improved intelligence, communications, and conventional-warhead lethality. And there should be a parallel effort to get industry to shift its emphasis toward higher quality and lower cost by creating appropriate incentives. It will be an expensive undertaking to shift from current manufacturing technology to (for example) flexible manufacturing integrated into the design process; but it will result, if properly implemented, in great benefits to both the DoD and the industry.[56]

The shift in technological emphasis (toward cost and quality) must be accompanied by a shift of funding toward the "front end" of the R&D cycle.[57] In addition the DoD must move from emphasizing R&D at the weapon-system level to emphasizing R&D work on components, materials, and subsystems—the items that will determine the quality, cost, and performance of the next-generation systems (for example, we could never have had communication satellites without microelectronics). R&D on these items, on an individual-project basis, is much cheaper to fund; therefore, the way to do it properly is to fund multiple technologies and multiple contractors. This will create a more competitive lower-tier environment and will allow technology to evolve more rapidly and to be focused on the desired quality, cost, and performance objectives. At the same time, both the DoD and the Congress must recognize that failure is one of the *desired* characteristics of advanced research and development—if there aren't some failures, the technology isn't being pushed hard enough. Research, by definition, is risky, and in order to maintain technological superiority we must do research in the areas of high-risk technologies. Finally, with the increased emphasis on R&D in the lower tiers and the more generic (less weapon-system-oriented) technologies, the rest of the U.S. economy should benefit from investments in defense-related R&D. The DoD will be operating more in the area of "dual-use" technologies—technologies that will be of benefit to the civilian economy as well as to the DoD.[58]

Shifting the focus of defense R&D toward "dual-use" technologies is not meant to replace private-sector funding of non-defense R&D; it is meant to complement it. As was noted above, this is an area where the overall U.S. economy has not maintained its position, and there is a need for the government to assist in order to place the United States back in a stronger position in terms of international competitiveness.

Civilian and military technology are moving closer together. More and more of the unclassified work done at universities and in industrial research laboratories has major military implications, while work performed at the government's national laboratories (which receive an annual federal investment of close to $18 billion[59]) is moving more and more in the direction of civilian-sector usefulness. And the DoD's investments of $650 million in work on very-high-speed integrated circuits,[60] $200 million or more per year in work on advanced manufacturing technologies (flexible and computer-integrated manufacturing),[61] $600 million in a prototype semiconductor plant ("Sematech"),[62] and $150 million in R&D to "develop the required processing and manufacturing capabilities" for superconductivity[63] have obvious military implications but have equal, if not more important, implications for the civilian economy. Without the DoD's investments, it is questionable whether these projects would have been adequately funded. Unfortunately, these projects have been initiated and managed largely on an *ad hoc* basis. Their proper management requires organizations and industrial linkages that currently do not exist.

The shortage of science and technology manpower, on both sides of the military-industrial complex, is the third of the major long-term R&D issues to be addressed. Clearly a growing problem for the United States, it starts in the high schools with insufficient incentives for students to take the more difficult courses in mathematics, science, and computers, and continues in the colleges where there are inadequate resources for proper engineering education and inadequate salaries to lure the most qualified people into teaching. The salary structure in industry is also at fault; someone who merges and acquires companies can make millions, while someone who invents and produces products in those same companies can make only a relatively small salary. The DoD cannot change this overall structure by itself, but it can do more—particularly at the university level—to make it desirable for Americans to study science and engineering. Research grants, scholarships, and salary structures are within the proper domain of the DoD. Driving down prices on engineering proposals in order to buy the "lowest-cost engineer" is clearly not in the government's long-term interest.[64]

The recognition that a particular set of skills will not last an individual throughout his or her working life is of great importance. Technology is evolving rapidly, and retraining is essential. The vast majority of today's engineers completed their education more than five years ago and are, therefore, basically obsolete. Incentives must be created for these people to maintain their technological currency.

Finally, there will have to be "institutional changes" in organizations and procedures relating to R&D. Besides the basic shifts toward stability, dual sourcing, design-to-cost, product improvements, and technology insertion, there will have to be specific R&D activities that can focus on nontraditional technologies, and organizations to promote these activities. This will require greater coupling between the DoD and industry, in the form of advisory boards, joint research activities, and even collaborative efforts where the DoD will hold positions on some boards and provide some of the sponsorship.[65]

Many of the initiatives to redirect U.S. technology into nontraditional areas will have to overcome large institutions on both sides of the military-industrial complex. (As Alvin Toffler stated, "Bureaucracy must be overcome with ad hocracy."[66]) The DoD will have to select key areas of technology and set up special organizations to push for R&D in those areas. The people in some of these organizations should be rotated every few years to prevent the organizations from becoming rigid.

The first such organization the DoD set up was the Defense Advanced Research Projects Agency (DARPA), which was created in response to

Sputnik.[67] As Secretary of Defense Neil McElroy stated at the time, "I want an agency that makes sure no important thing remains undone because it doesn't fit somebody's mission." DARPA was to ensure that the United States would maintain technological superiority, help prevent technological surprises, and support research and technology that would have multi-service applications or would fill in where the services were not focused.

It may be necessary for DARPA to expand its mission, or to create other organizations (either within the services or as divisions of a centralized agency). Recently the DoD created the Strategic Defense Initiatives Office (SDIO), which is outside of the traditional organizational framework in much the same way that the Manhattan Project was. Such independent organizations can create the financial and personnel support that R&D in a nontraditional area requires; however, after the R&D phase every such program must be put back into one of the services for operation and must also become part of an existing R&D institution. Therefore, it is necessary that these *ad hoc* organizations be staffed with people who can take the programs back to their service afterward, and can guarantee that the program will not lose support in the transition from nontraditional R&D back into the traditional organization. Obviously, it is necessary to carry nontraditional R&D at least through the prototype-demonstration phase in order to convince the military services of the value of the product. Furthermore, the *ad hoc* organizations must be given enough flexibility (in procurement techniques, military specification waivers, and so on) so that they an operate with as much freedom as possible. One of the most successful programs ever undertaken by the Department of Defense was the development, in the 1950s, of the simple yet effective air-to-air missile known as the Sidewinder. That program was "kept from meddlesome Navy and Pentagon officials in Washington."[68] Such a program would be impossible today, because of the restrictions that have been placed on both government and industry operations. Yet such freedom must be provided to innovative organizations. For example, they must be allowed to take maximum advantage of the commercial market in order to achieve "dual-use" applicability of their discoveries. Such organizations will not be easy to set up, or to keep alive within the DoD–especially when the budget is tight. However, they will be necessary.

8 The Industrial Base

The United States spends over $100 billion a year buying equipment from its defense industry and is not getting its money's worth. The peacetime efficiency and effectiveness, the crisis responsiveness, and the technological innovativeness of the defense industry can all be improved significantly.

Many argue that the current problems of the defense industry are very similar to those of other important U.S. industries, such as steel and autos[1]: excess capacity; obsolescence of capital equipment; a short-term focus; a declining emphasis on manufacturing; low quality; a cutback on basic research; a focus on mergers and acquisitions instead of on growth through production; low productivity growth; a loss of worldwide competitiveness; and adverse effects of incoherent government policies, overregulation, and a lack of proper government incentives for good business performance.

The problems of U.S. industry, and the potential corrective actions, are beyond the control of the Defense Department. For America's overall industry to be positively affected, broad changes in education, industrial management, and government policy are required. Beyond these changes, specific actions unique to the defense sector need to be taken as a compliment to the broad revitalization of American industry.

Understanding the uniqueness of the corrective actions requires a historical look at the defense industry. As figure 8.1 shows, the defense industrial base must be viewed in three dimensions. In one dimension, the large prime contractors or weapon suppliers (normally known as "the defense contractors") are at the top, the second tier is made up of the major subcontractors (many of whom manufacture electronic devices, such as computers and radars), and the lowest tier is made up of the suppliers of parts and material. It is at the lowest tier (the level of the semiconductor producers, the metals fabricators, etc.) that a great deal of commonality exists between the defense industry and the rest of the economy. This is often referred to as the "dual-use" tier of the defense industry, and emphasis should be placed on the desirability of increasing the use of commercial firms for defense work at this level.

The second dimension shown in figure 8.1 is made up of the numerous distinct major sectors of the defense industry (aerospace, shipbuilding, munitions, and so on). Although many firms operate in multiple sectors of the defense industry, there are dramatic differences between these sectors—for example, building ships is somewhat like building houses

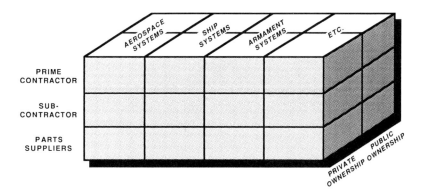

Figure 8.1
The composition of the defense industry.

(i.e., a one-by-one production process), while making bullets is a mass-production operation. Therefore, the Department of Defense should deal differently with each sector, and the incentives for the various sectors should differ correspondingly.

The third dimension of figure 8.1 shows that the defense industry has a mixture of private ownership and public ownership, varying significantly from sector to sector. All the shipbuilding yards (for new construction) are in the private sector; approximately one-third of the plant and equipment in the aircraft industry is government-owned; in the munitions industry, almost all of the final-assembly operations are in the public sector. Again, this difference should be recognized by the DoD when it is dealing with any defense firm or sector—for example, in some cases private firms must make all of the investments in equipment, while in other cases all the equipment is government-owned, so the firms' risks vary widely.

The structure of the defense industry is the result of a historical evolution, which in some cases has been going on for 200 years. A study of this history[2] indicates significant features, all leading directly to many of the current problems and pointing, therefore, to directions for future corrective actions:

- *The extremely cyclical nature of defense procurements* Since 1776 the nation has gone through periods of large increases in defense expenditures—in times of crisis, or apparent crisis—and then followed these with dramatic reductions, often leading to a total breakup of the defense industrial base. Yet planning in defense is traditionally based upon the assumption of relatively constant defense expenditures. If the cycles are likely to continue, then action must be taken to reduce the inefficiencies that they create, i.e., to plan an industrial structure which assumes that there are likely to be fluctuations in the demand for military equipment.

· *The lack of structural planning* From the inception of the defense industrial base until the present, its evolution and its status at any point (for example, the mix between government-owned and privately owned facilities) has been based largely on chance.[3] Even such issues as the ability of the government to create competition and the existence of an adequate number of firms in a given sector have not been addressed in a systematic fashion. It has generally been assumed that the "free market" would achieve the necessary desired structural characteristics; however, this has not been the case.

· *The inadequacy of industrial-preparedness planning* Historically, when emergencies have developed, there had been an absence of peacetime planning to meet these crises. Such efforts are usually postponed until the crisis occurs—at which time it is too late.

· *The lack of actual industrial readiness* The result of the lack of industrial-preparedness planning has been that in all its wars—for the 200-year history of the United States—the nation has been able to mobilize men much more rapidly than it has been able to equip them. Because of the increased sophistication of equipment today, the lead times are far longer. Thus, without proper planning, the response to a crisis today would be far slower in spite of America's overall industrial strength.

· *The importance of technology and research in defense* As was noted in earlier chapters, in the post-World War II era the United States has counted heavily on technological superiority as the basis of its military posture. This has pushed the defense industry in the direction of greater and greater emphasis on the use of advanced technology to achieve maximum performance in each weapon, rather than on quality and cost, and it has encouraged industrial management to focus its attention on new systems under development rather than on those in production or already deployed.

· *The differences among the industries that make up the defense indus-*

trial base In spite of the significant differences that have historically evolved, the government continues to pursue—and Congress insists upon—"uniform procurement practices" across all these sectors. For example, there is a "uniform profit policy" in spite of the dramatic differences in the percent of government ownership in the different sectors. Thus, the application of the same "corrective actions" to sectors having different structural characteristics actually amplifies the differences.

· *The high concentration within industrial sectors* Each rapid buildup and rapid "selloff" has increased the concentration of the share of the business in a few large firms. (This was particularly true after World War II.[4]) The complex nature and the extensive capital-equipment cost of modern technology (both in R&D and in production) have further contributed to this concentration.

· *The heavy dependence on international assistance* Although one normally would think of defense as an issue that should be considered in a closed domestic economic system, the facts—throughout America's history—indicate the contrary. This trend continues today, with the defense industrial base increasingly dependent on sales of military equipment abroad, and on shipments from foreign countries of critical components and materials for almost every piece of U.S. military equipment.

An important set of analyses that appeared in November of 1980 indicated growing problems at all levels of the defense industrial base.[5] At the prime-contractor level, the reports noted unhealthy financial conditions, aging plants and equipment, excess capacity, and the high cost of weapon systems. At the lower tiers, they showed a diminishing number of sources, growing foreign dependency, and the development of bottlenecks. Even though defense procurement dollars were more than doubled during the Reagan administration, conditions in the defense industry had actually grown worse by 1988. Not only had the DoD ignored the problems in the defense industrial base during the buildup; almost in a perverse manner, Congress and the DoD had made a series of "attacks" on the defense industry. Initially brought on by the "waste, fraud, and abuse" headlines, these attacks intensified as the defense budget began to flatten out in the late 1980s. From 1985 on, the DoD attempted to shift the risk of the budget actions from its own shoulders to those of its industrial suppliers. A series of "industry bashing" actions,[6] both legislative and regulatory, resulted in a deterioration of government-industry relations and had a significant financial impact on the defense industry. These actions included a greatly reduced profit policy; delayed and reduced progress payments for work completed; 3–4-year delays for auditing and payments on completed work; "cost sharing" on high-risk research that was applicable only to the DoD; long stretchouts in the time to award contracts; delays in awards, due to new protest procedures; abuse of suspension and debarment procedures; fixed-price contracts on high-risk developments; increases in "disallowances" for costs incurred on government contracts; abuses of industrial proprietary data rights; and making competitive contract awards for "low bids" instead of "best value." The overall effect was that defense firms deemphasized quality and innovation for the sake of their very survival. Some firms were forced to make large zero-profit bids,[7] while others were forced into investing hundreds of millions of dollars in competitive programs when there was a reasonable chance of not only losing the competition but having the program canceled.[8] In the area of R&D and professional services, the "low-bid" approach to contracting was forcing firms to bid engineers at salary levels less than what secretaries were making at the same time—thus obviously placing little emphasis on quality or innovativeness in these critical "idea" areas of the defense industry.[9] Projecting the likely effects of all these actions (especially when compounded over time, and with a declining defense budget), the stock market began to significantly downgrade the value of defense stocks, thus making it even more difficult for these contractors to maintain their financial position.

Clearly, an unhealthy defense industry is neither good for the DoD nor good for the nation. Yet the assumption made was that the market would correct these effects. This "free-market myth" has historically been one of the primary causes of the problems of the American defense industry. The basic belief has been that a normal free market was operating in this area and would maximize industrial efficiency and responsiveness. Yet the prevalent condition for defense procurement is essentially a single buyer (the Department of Defense) and only one or two suppliers of any given weapon system. Thus, in this unique market environment, it is necessary for the government to exercise its monopsony power in a responsible fashion by *creating* the proper incentives for the effective operation of the industrial base. And since individual firms will (properly) act in their own self-interest rather than in the interest of the nation, the government must, when required, take the actions necessary to speed up essential structural changes in order to make the defense industrial base efficient, effective, responsive, and innovative.[10] It is crucially important for government policymakers, both on Capitol Hill and in the executive branch, to recognize the conflict that exists between their historical assumptions about the operations of the market and the reality of the defense industry's market (i.e., a unique market dominated by the government as a monopsony buyer and in which there are large barriers to entry and exit). Because of the lack of such recognition, policymakers continue to take steps that are counterproductive to the government's best interests.

Large Defense Contractors

Thinking about the defense industry normally brings to mind the giant defense contractors who supply the ships, the planes, and the tanks that constitute America's military arsenal. These are all familiar names. The top twenty (in 1985) were McDonnell Douglas, General Dynamics, Rockwell, General Electric, Boeing, Lockheed, United Technologies, Hughes, Raytheon, Martin Marietta, Grumman, Westinghouse, Textron, Honeywell, IBM, Sperry, ITT, LTV, General Motors, and Litton. These firms, and a few others, appear year in and year out as the major defense contractors. Their annual sales to the DoD each exceed a billion dollars, and they cumulatively capture around 50 percent of the DoD dollars each year.[11] Among this group, there are clearly two types of firms. Those whose work is almost exclusively in defense are highly sensitive to the ups and downs of defense funding and contract awards. Others, such as General Motors, General Electric, IBM, ITT, and Honeywell, are primarily commercially oriented but have divisions that do significant amounts of defense work. Some of the latter firms have policies constraining the amount of defense business they will perform, in order to prevent their being significantly influenced by the cyclical nature of defense business.[12] Even among those firms, however, there is very little integration at the plant level or the division level between the defense operations and the civilian operations. The result is, for either type of firm, a largely specialized sector of American industry that is heavily dependent on the DoD for business and on which the DoD is heavily dependent for supplies. President Eisenhower, in his famous farewell speech on the "military-industrial complex," warned the country about this interdependency; however, he was also aware of the positive features of this close working relationship between the industry and the DoD: "The lessons of the last war are clear. The armed forces could not have won the war alone. Scientists and businessman contributed techniques and weapons that enabled us to outwit and overwhelm the enemy. Their understanding of the Army's needs made possible the highest degree of cooperation. . . ."[13]

As in the commercial world, the buyer-seller relationship in the world of defense must be neither adversarial nor conspiratorial; rather, it must be an honest business relationship, with joint interests, in which the buyer gets a good product at a fair cost and the seller makes a decent profit. Unfortunately, while the desirability of such a relationship is fully recognized in the commercial sector, there are many in Congress, in the DoD, in the press, and among the public who are suspicious of its appropriateness in the defense sector. Occasional actions by the defense industry in which it appears to take advantage of the govern-ment certainly add to this suspicion.

Since World War II, the U.S. defense industry has performed very successfully in providing what the Department of Defense has most demanded: technological superiority over the Soviet Union. This over-emphasis on advanced technology and on high performance led to the paying of high prices for weapon systems and may have had a negative impact on the overall economic competitiveness of the United States. The challenge for the future is for the defense industry to maintain its innovativeness and technological superiority while shifting toward a greater emphasis on higher quality and lower cost.

The defense industry is relatively concentrated; the top 100 firms do about 75 percent of the business (a ratio that has held since the late 1950s).[14] However, this is no more concentrated, and perhaps slightly less so, than most segments of the commercial sector.[15] However, actual defense contracting becomes extremely concentrated because most of the defense firms tend to specialize, not just (for example) in missiles, but in very specific types of missiles (e.g., air-to-air, anti-aircraft, radar-guided, homing missiles). This specialization, combined with the government's "lumpy" buying practice of buying a weapon system of a certain type only once every 10 or 15 years and awarding the contract (usually) to only one contractor, results in higher concentration ratios for selected weapon areas than are found in typical commercial sectors. For example, the percentages of business done in the military market by the top four firms are the following: surveillance and detection satellites (100%); nuclear submarines (99%); space boosters (97%); fighter aircraft (97%); attack aircraft (97%); missile inertial guidance systems (97%); aircraft inertial navigation systems (96%); missile reentry vehicles (95%); aircraft fire-control systems (95%); transport and tanker aircraft (94%); helicopters (93%); jet aircraft engines (93%).[16] These concentration ratios are extremely high by any measure of "non-free-market behavior."[17] Among the few firms that are already in any given sector of defense business there is fierce competition for any new awards; however, one of the most distinguishing characteristics of defense business is the presence of extremely high barriers to entry and exit.[18] The barriers to entry include a unique environment; high capital investments (of highly specialized equipment); "brand loyalty" (by the military services); the need for high levels of engineering and scientific capability (due to the R&D emphasis in initial contract awards); the need for large cash reserves (e.g., for writing proposals that cost millions of dollars); specialized reporting requirements (accounting, management reports, drawings, inspection, etc.); the required knowledge of detailed federal regulations; security clearances; and political considerations (such as congressmen trying to keep work in their district[19]). The barriers to exit and/or diversification to civilian business, even when the market has shrunk dramatically and a comeback is unlikely, include the following: government sponsorship of R&D; the large overhead required for defense work (which makes a firm's prices unattractive in the commercial world); the specialized nature of the capital equipment (which often prevents it from being used for diversification); the government's tendency to accept "low bids" (thus allowing a firm to stay in the business even when it doesn't have the qualification to do so); the specialization of labor (especially the large percentage of scientific and engineering labor used to design the high-cost weapon systems); the specialized nature of the marketing force, which is not usable in the civilian market; the "comfort" (familiarity) with military specifications, which are expensive and difficult to convert to the practices of the commercial world; the partiotism (the "duty to the nation" that may firms in the business definitely feel).

In order for market forces to operate more effectively in the defense sector, many of the barriers to entry and exit must be greatly reduced or eliminated. At the very least, the large defense firms need to be able to move more freely within the major segments of the defense sector. For example, in the two major defense sales activities ("aircraft," with approximately 50 percent of the sales, and "electronics and missiles," with over 25 percent) there are probably already too many firms for the few programs and the small quantities likely to be procured in the future. Thus, those firms that remain in the defense business will have to work on many different types of defense equipment and/or to diversify (at the factory level) in order to be able to absorb the high cost of their overhead and still be competitive. Others will, undoubtedly, be forced to become defense subcontractors. A typical defense prime contractor subcontracts between 40 and 60 percent of a weapon system to its lower-tier suppliers; most certainly there is ample business at this level that can be performed by some of the firms that are now prime contractors.[20]

The various segments of the defense industry tend to differ dramatically from one another, even though they share many of the broad, unique, and non-free-market characteristics of the overall defense industry. Therefore, the only possible corrective actions are "second-best" solutions tailored to the special circumstances of particular industry segments. For example, in the tank industry there is only one industrial firm, which runs the two tank "arsenals." A possible corrective action here might be to create a competitive market by having two firms involved and letting each run one of the plants. In contrast, the aircraft industry undoubtedly has too many firms in the business to adequately maintain valid competition (without extreme "buy-ins" and bankruptcies). The government should encourage some of the firms to leave this segment by not awarding them contracts when they make "buy-ins" or, perhaps, by restricting competition to firms that have up-to-date facilities that could clearly be competitive in the next round. Also, the government could attempt to change some of the buying practices that encourage firms to be so highly specialized and thus make the market more competitive overall.

The DoD could also make significant improvements in the efficiency of the defense industry by addressing the "factors of production" (labor, capital equipment, and money). Defense work tends to be extremely labor-intensive, and there is a lot of instability in the labor force. As expected, defense budget cycles have a direct effect on the total employment in the industry. However, this is greatly amplified by the award, or the completion, of a large contract. The curve shown in figure 8.2 is typical of most defense facilities. The plant in question—owned by the government but run by General Dynamics—has done relatively well in the post-World War II era, having been awarded six major contracts to build airplanes and the subsequent contracts to modify these aircraft (shown in the "other" category). Nonetheless, it can be seen not only that there have been dramatic periods of hiring and firing during the more than 40 years shown on the figure, but also that there have been few periods of relative labor stability. Unfortunately, efficiency in a production facility is achieved through labor stability—"learning" by workers, using trained workers, achieving group unity, and having supervisory continuity. Obviously, in an environment such as the one summarized by figure 8.2, it would be extremely difficult to achieve such efficiencies. Also, it must be emphasized that this figure is not at all atypical of defense plants, from shipyards through missile facilities.[21]

Compounding the instability caused by the broad fluctuations in the defense budget and by the awarding of contracts from plant to plant is the basic instability of the labor force in selected segments of the defense industry, even over the short term. For example, in shipbuilding there is an annual turnover of approximately 75 percent of the labor force; often, after receiving training in the shipyards, workers leave for private-sector construction jobs.[22] As will be discussed, this overall high labor instability results in defense contractors' having to pay approximately 20 percent more for their workers (even after adjustment for the higher skill requirements).[23]

The B-1 bomber program is a typical example of this phenomenon. After North American Rockwell was awarded the contract for the B-1A, they proceeded to build up a labor force in the Los Angeles area. When the Carter administration canceled the program, over 8,000 employees were laid off immediately. Eventually, 17,000 had to be laid off, and the plant in Los Angeles was sold. Then, when the Reagan administration brought the program back, about 7,000 new jobs were created

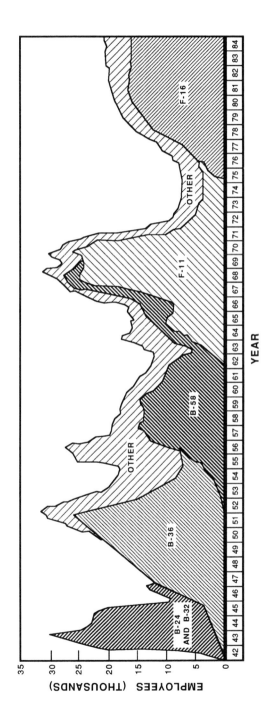

Figure 8.2
The employment history of Air Force Plant 4 (Fort Worth, Texas).

in the Los Angeles area and a new plant was built at Palmdale, where another 4,000 people were hired. In addition, Rockwell had to hire about 2,000 new workers in their Tulsa facility, and a facility at Columbus, Ohio, was totally modernized and about 7,000 people hired.[24] When Rockwell's manager was asked by *Fortune* magazine if the company would have any trouble hiring these large numbers of people, he stated: "It will be expensive, but the taxpayers will pick up the bill. In any case . . . manpower won't be a problem."[25]

Since the number of skilled engineers and technicians available for such jobs does not increase instantaneously, especially in a given geographic area, the only way one can hire them is to bid them up and lure them away from other firms. Thus, the Reagan administration's dramatic increases of the defense budget created a significant need for additional labor, which caused the price of the labor force (particularly the professional and highly skilled workers) to be driven up quite significantly, and resulted in high "inflation" in the costs of the equipment produced. This has been particularly troublesome in the scientific and engineering areas, since (as was noted in chapter 7) the United States has had difficulty encouraging its young people to go into these fields,[26] and because there is a growing need for scientists and engineers in the civilian sector. Thus, there ensues a "bidding war" for scientists and engineers between the civilian and the defense sectors—which defense frequently wins (at least in terms of the quantities of people) by offering higher salaries. The very best people, however, frequently pick the commercial sector, because of the greater stability and growth potential.

One might hope that the problem of high labor costs in the defense industry would, over time, be ameliorated through the introduction of automation. Unfortunately, this has not been the case. For example, from 1970 to 1985, both the "total number of workers in the aircraft industry per aircraft built" and the "total number of production workers per aircraft built" rose almost by a factor of 2.[27] Increasingly, as the defense industry produces fewer but more sophisticated items, the additional emphasis placed on scientists and engineers (rather than on production workers) results in even higher total labor costs. The long-range solution to this problem would be for the defense industry to move toward computer-integrated design and manufacturing, and toward "flexible manufacturing systems" (which allow multiple products to be automatically produced in the same plant efficiently and in low volume). However, this requires significant initial investments, and most government weapon-system managers and individual firms (with a single program) will be reluctant to make such a large one-time investment. Thus, a long-term, overall government strategy is essential.

To produce complex, high-quality, low-cost systems requires very modern automated manufacturing equipment. This brings us to the matter of capital equipment. The situation today in the defense industry is far from desirable. A 1987 investigation showed that the Grumman Corporation developed and produced the highly complex F-14 jet fighter on equipment whose average age was 34 years; in fact, "most of the equipment had been provided by the government during World War II."[28] And Grumman was producing these planes basically as it had been doing for 30 years: almost entirely by hand. For example, after tracing a pattern onto aluminum sheets, workers would guide the sheets through 30-year-old band saws, and then any required holes would be drilled manually.[29] The scrap rate resulting from such manual operation is extremely high; one defense plant reported 70 to 80 percent scrappage because of outmoded machine tools, and another noted that only three electronics boards out of every ten produced were acceptable. As expected, the cost and quality of systems produced on such old equipment are not what would be desired. Not only are such operations extremely expensive; they also take a lot longer, which compounds the cost. The problem is that there are inadequate incentives to encourage defense firms to make the long-term capital investments necessary to drive down costs and improve quality. In fact, significant disincentives to such long-term investments are built into the DoD's way of doing business.[30]

Numerous studies have found that defense contractors invest in new manufacturing equipment and technologies at only about half the rate of comparable commercial firms.[31] In an attempt to get defense contractors to increase their capital investment, the DoD, in 1977 and again in 1987, shifted to a new profit policy that allowed higher profits for those firms that made greater capital investments. However, a follow-up study (to the first change) done by the Air Force in 1982 found that "while profits had increased significantly, relative investment did not change."[32] In fact, a few years later, a DoD review stated: "Profit policy in and of itself is insufficient to bring about productivity-enhancing improvements. Other methods are required."[33] Thus, more basic structural changes appear necessary to encourage the defense industry to increase its capital investments sufficiently in the future. These would have to include long-term government commitments and timely rewarding of defense contractors if they produce high-quality and low-cost goods.

Now it is time to turn to the third of the factors of production, namely money (generated either from the financial community or through DoD progress payments and profit). As was noted above, Wall Street has placed defense firms at a relatively low price-to-earnings multiple (in the mid-1980s at about 50 percent of comparable non-defense firms); also, the DoD is making progress payments for work completed at a slower and slower rate (having shifted from 90 percent progress payments in the early 1980s down to 75 percent by the middle of the 1980s). Thus, profits are the key to understanding the defense industry's money situations. Here, it would be expected that, with extremely heavy concentration of producers and with contracts often awarded to single sources, the industry would be able to extract "monopoly profits."[34] The criterion the DoD uses as the profit measure for the defense industry—return on sales—is a good start in analyzing the situation.

The negotiated, pre-tax profit rate depends on the type of the contract and the overall economic conditions relating to defense, from a "firm, fixed-price contract" at the high level (such as at the peak of the Vietnam war) of around 11 percent down to a low level (as in the early 1980s) of around 5 percent for a "cost-plus-fixed-fee" contract.[35] In general, the average level has been around 6.5 percent. However, these negotiated levels (at the start of a contract) are largely meaningless; what matters to the industry is the actual results achieved at the end of the contract period. The average realized (pre-tax) return-on-sales rate for the Vietnam war period was around 4.9 percent,[36] and it dropped to about 4.7 percent for the post-Vietnam period.[37] Thus, the realized profits were significantly less than the negotiated profits. This difference can be attributed to the contractor's initial "buy in" to win the award, or to technical and schedule problems that developed during the contract, or to "changes" imposed by the government on the contractor but not fully compensated, or to costs "disallowed" after the fact through government auditing (typically about 2 percent for "unallowable expenses").

When one compares the average profits of defense firms with those of similar manufacturing firms in the civilian sector (having high concentration ratios and the same types of products), the return on sales for the defense industry is about half that achieved in the commercial world by "defense-oriented" companies, around one-third that of purely civilian firms,[38] and about 25 percent less than that of durable-goods manufacturers (often compared with defense firms).[39]

In addition to the above-noted explanation of the relatively lower realized profit, when compared to negotiated profit, a more structural perspective would provide a far greater rationale as to why profits are so low in the defense sector. "A monopsonistic buyer can control the seller's profit to be under that which would come from a market economy,"[40] and, in this case the government's high leverage is actually complimented by the extensive public scrutiny of defense firms' profits. Congress gets great pleasure out of highlighting this issue, and the press picks this up, since both realize that the public (understandably) has great revulsion to "war profiteering." This public perception is mirrored by the DoD's contract negotiators, who appear to feel considerable pride when they can negotiate a low profit rate. A 1976 survey of government contracting officers confirmed that they felt it was their job, in protecting the public's interest, to attack the profits of the suppliers.[41] This is the wrong perspective for these negotiators to have; rather, they should be attempting to reduce the total price of the equipment, of which profit is only a small percentage. If the cost base could be reduced significantly (perhaps even by allowing slightly higher profits), the government and therefore the public would be far better off— particularly if incentives could be created to encourage reinvesting the increased profits in the higher productivity needed for a healthier, more effective defense industrial base.

When one considers return on investment (the primary profit criterion by which industry assesses the success of an operation), the picture is much less clear.[42] Part of the problem is that return on investment may be measured in terms of equity or in terms of assets; part of it rests on how each of these is determined. Studies by the Government Accounting Office and by independent researchers have come up with a wide variety of answers; however, no matter what the answer is, it always draws significant attacks from the other side of the argument. Furthermore, those who have conducted the various studies have chosen different time periods for their samples, and it appears that during some periods the defense industry had slightly higher return on assets than, say, the durable-goods industry, while in other periods its returns were slightly lower.[43] Undoubtedly the biggest part of the problem, however, lies in the question of what industry data set is used. If one uses only the large defense firms (especially the aircraft and missile companies who have a significant amount of government-owned plant and equipment), then defense profits tend to look significantly higher[44]; if one takes the shipbuilding industry (which supplies much of its own capital) or the majority of the other defense firms, the returns will appear to be relatively low.[45] Overall, this question of what should be a fair and reasonable profit for the defense industry is an extremely difficult one. It could be said that the industry's return on sales is far too high in comparison with that of supermarkets but far too low in comparison with that of electric utilities; however, its return on *equity* turns out to be essentially the same as that of supermarkets, and quite comparable to that of electric utilities[46] (a regulated industry whose profits are generally assumed to be fair and reasonable). In reality, the public will always think that the defense industry's profits are too high, while the industry will always think that they are too low. Yet the basic issue is that profits are a misleading indicator of an industry's efficiency and effectiveness, particularly in comparison with the costs and the quality of the industry's products. Unfortunately, it is likely that the debate over profits will go on forever and will detract from the more basic structural problems that must be corrected before the incremental effect of the DoD's profit policy can begin to have any significant impact on the performance of the defense industry.

A major problem in addressing the issue of efficiency is that the DoD has very little insight into the costs of its major contractors. The accounting system the DoD uses for its contractors is based on the job's "direct labor" content multiplied by some "overhead ratio" associated with all the principal "indirect" costs of the firm (facilities, management, etc.). Direct labor is defined as the "touch labor" on the factory floor or in the engineering organization, and all other costs are essentially "indirect"; however, as factories and design activities move more and more toward automation, the normal "indirect" category takes a larger and larger share of the costs. In a highly automated factory, direct labor may be only 5 percent or less of the total costs; but even this includes primarily setup and supervision rather than actual processing of the output. To correct this problem, the defense industry must shift to "total cost" visibility and, particularly, to a system of which the focus is the total cost of quality (or the lack thereof). All costs should be included— not just those within the production process (for "down time" on machines, and scrappage) but also the maintenance costs, the repairs, and the failures of the equipment in the field.[47]

What trends are likely in the defense industry? In the aircraft industry (the largest segment of the defense industry), even with the increase in dollars during the Reagan era, the trend has been to build fewer and fewer aircraft each year. As a result, fewer firms are needed. In the case of a particular airplane, fewer dollars are being spent on the airframe and more on the subsystems (particularly the electronics). Thus, it is highly likely that the future will see the addition of new electronic devices to existing airframes, and also that more of the aircraft companies will go into the electronics business (often by acquiring electronics companies).[48] Unfortunately, similar acquisition trends are evident across the U.S. economy. In 1985 alone, U.S. firms spent $180 billion for mergers and acquisitions, versus $120 billion on R&D and $50 billion on net capital investment.[49] Mergers in the defense industry can have a particularly deleterious effect, since defense firms traditionally treat each of their plants as a separate entity with its own engineering, marketing, and management staffs. For example, when McDonnell Aircraft (the sixth largest aerospace firm) acquired Douglas Aircraft (the eighth largest), the two plants (in St. Louis and California) continued to operate separately without real consolidation; thus, a firm was eliminated, but not a plant. Economists refer to such mergers, which reduce competition without reducing costs, as *unrationalized mergers*.

Another significant trend that is likely to increase is the "teaming" of defense firms to bid on the few available contracts for weapon systems. Large defense firms are often encouraged by the government to team up so that they will be able to share the high-investment risk as well as to keep a large number of them in the business.[50] In these teaming arrangements, a number of the prime contractors become subcontractors to one another on various parts of a weapon system. Not only does this raise the question of overall efficiency (with so many firms and people involved in the design and production of the system); it also raises the following question, asked by one very knowledgeable aerospace-industry stock analyst: "Are we doing anybody a favor by trying to keep everybody alive with a teaming arrangement? The principal benefit which competitive U.S. industry has always realized—superior technological capability—is being deliberately dissipated by teaming; because you are freezing everybody into one technology approach."[51] Perhaps the best summary of the data in this case states, "There are no indications that joint ventures have a beneficial effect, either on market competition or on the competitiveness of the participating firms."[52]

Finally, as expected, there has been a slow decline in the number of defense-oriented firms. With the reduced total volume being produced, this shrinkage of the industry is warranted—and it probably should occur at a much higher rate. However, it is worrisome that the firms with large amounts of civilian business and only a few divisions in the defense area are often choosing not to bid on new defense business and to focus their attention and resources less and less on defense work. Unfortunately, these are the firms that are most needed in defense work, because they have the commercial base for overhead absorption and the cost consciousness that is so crucial to the future of the defense industry. IBM,[53] Allied Signal, and the Eaton Corporation are among the defense contractors in this category that, by the late 1980s, had chosen to reduce their risk on defense programs by not entering some of the competitions for future DoD business. This is a loss that the DoD cannot afford. Positive actions are required to encourage such firms to return to defense work.

At the prime-contractor level, the defense industry shows definite signs of a "sick" industry. The firms operate in a weakening market with heavy debt, difficulty of borrowing, considerable excess capacity, low cash generation, high (and growing) risks, old production equipment, too little capital investment, relatively low productivity, mixed quality, and rapidly rising prices. Clearly, the defense industry is vitally important to the nation's economy (one of every ten production workers and one of every three engineers and scientists are in the defense area), as well as to the nation's security. However, the *wrong* cure is for the government to "bail out" firms, as it did Lockheed, General Dynamics, and McDonnell Douglas.

Rather, the government should begin by recognizing that a major contract award directly alters the structure of the defense industry.[54] In these contract-award decisions, and many others affecting the industry, the Department of Defense and the Congress must take responsible actions to ensure the evolution of a healthy, responsive, and innovative industrial base to meet the nation's needs in the 21st century. The National Cooperative Research Act of 1984, which allows industrial firms to collaborate in generic R&D initiatives without fear of prosecution under the anti-trust laws,[55] is a good example of such an action. It encourages long-term research; and it does not reduce competition, since the actual development and exploitation of the research will be done, on a competitive basis, by the firms that took part in the collaborative generic research. (This technique has long been used, quite successfully, by the Japanese.)

Whatever corrective actions are taken (and many are possible; see below), it is clear that there must be a restructuring of the defense industry. As former Air Force General James Mullins has written, "we now have a private-sector defense industry set up to produce large numbers of new systems, when we no longer buy large numbers of new systems."[56] The answer lies in evolving a few competitive firms in each segment of the industry, each producing multiple products efficiently by making full use of computer-integrated manufacturing and having flexible operations. The industry itself is highly unlikely to achieve this broad structural adjustment, since each firm is bound to feel that the other firms are the ones that should either change or leave the industry. Thus, it is up to the Department of Defense to create the incentives for this change.

Subcontractors and Part Suppliers

The defense industry is basically a "dual economy," with an upper level (the large defense contractors) and a lower level (the subcontractors and part suppliers).[57] The differences between the two levels are not simply matters of degree; rather, the two levels are almost totally different in many respects, such as the way in which business is done, the basic industrial structures, and the problems (which are almost exactly opposite). Yet legislation, regulations, policies, and procedures primarily written for the giants of the defense industry (the prime contractors) are passed down and applied equally to the small contractors. This amplifies the existing problems and differences. The Department of Defense and the Congress must recognize the differences between the two sectors and take the appropriate actions to correct the relevant problems at each level. These actions will, necessarily, differ.

Typically, between 40 and 60 percent of the dollar value of a weapon system is subcontracted by the prime contractor to its suppliers. Small, inventor-lead firms have made many of the qualitative breakthroughs in military technology. Yet the DoD has historically ignored the lower level of the defense industry[58] by assuming that the prime contractors would ensure its continued viability. Unfortunately, the prime contractors do not tend to show much concern about the viability of the lower-tier suppliers and subcontractors, and the result is a clear deterioration of that portion of the defense industry, both in terms of numbers and in terms of a growing dependency on foreign producers.

Warnings of the growing problems in the lower tiers of the defense industry were heard at the end of the 1970s,[59] but not until the late 1980s did Congress, the DoD, and the prime contractors begin to gather data on these problems and to take corrective actions. For example, in 1988 the president of IBM's defense activities stated: "We have run a variety of surveys looking at the supply base for critical components and parts we use in our systems. We found we are losing second and third tier suppliers—and if that trend continues, we and other prime contractors can be significantly hurt. . . . The traditional make-or-buy decision facing [prime contractors] on major subsystems now involves more than just economics. In many cases, [prime contractors] are being forced to make critical parts themselves, often at higher cost, simply because of a lack of suppliers."[60] This was a continuation of earlier trends; for example, in 1980, *Electric Engineering Times* estimated that "50 percent of small, high technology defense contractors [were] either going bankrupt or dropping out of competition for government contracts, largely due to growing regulation." From 1967 to 1980, the number of aerospace suppliers alone had dropped from 6,000 to 3,000.[61]

The result of the shrinkage of the lower tiers is that in many crucial segments of the defense industry there are only a few suppliers remaining. Table 8.1 lists some important subsystems and parts for which the DoD now has only one or two suppliers (and in almost all of the cases where there are two firms there is usually only one plant that is tooled to supply a particular part or subsystem). Many of these suppliers are operating at or near full capacity and have substantial backlogs. Thus, an increase in demand, due to either a defense buildup or a crisis,

Table 8.1

	Number of suppliers
Airborne radar systems	2
Aircraft engines	2
Aircraft navigation systems	2
Infrared systems	2
RPV/missile/drone engines	2
Gun mounts	2
Doppler navigation systems	2
Aluminum plate	2
Aluminum tubing	2
Titanium wing skins	2
Titanium extrusions	1
Special ball bearings	1
Needle bearings	2
Radomes	2
Image converter tube	1
Special lenses	2
Optics coatings	1

results in bottlenecks at these critical part suppliers. These bottlenecks dramatically increase lead times and prices whenever there is any significant step-up in orders.[62] For example, in 1974 Congress authorized a doubling of tank production to replace the tanks the United States had given to Israel, which had lost almost all its tanks in the 1973 war. The sole plant producing the M-60 tank had a large amount of excess capacity and had assured the Army that increasing the production of tanks rapidly, should it ever be required, would not be difficult. However, over a period of years the Army had gradually forced the reduction of armor-casting subcontract firms to a single source (due to the reduced quantities of M-60s procured in the post-Vietnam era), and that plant was operating at close to full capacity. Thus, when the orders doubled, all the casting supplier could do was try harder. Costs increased significantly, and it was a long time before the armor castings, and eventually the tanks, could be produced in increased quantities. Unfortunately, this is a typical case. Surge capability, through excess capacity (including extra capital equipment) was built in at the prime-contractor level, but at the lower level there was neither sufficient capacity nor competition. Thus, both the benefits of peacetime competitive efficiencies and the benefits of wartime surge capability were totally lost. Perhaps most surprising, the DoD had failed to notice the problem.

An analysis of the growing problems and the reduced number of suppliers at the lower tiers leads to the conclusion that subcontracting is simply an unattractive business. Unfortunately, the prime contractors, the DoD, and Congress make it even more so. The following is a list of items, in no particular priority order, that contributed to the decline of this portion of the defense industry.

- The government often adjusts the prime contractor's contract according to the program's risk, but the subcontractor receives much more difficult terms and conditions. One study found that in more than 85 percent of the cases where the prime contractor had a cost-plus-fee contract, the subcontractor had a firm fixed-price contract.[63] Yet usually the subcontractor has the higher technical risk.
- Prime contractors are reluctant to "pass down" favorable contract clauses (such as "unusual inflation" clauses, which are intended to cover the risk of inflation-based cost increases[64]) to their suppliers and subcontractors, and the government does not require them to do so.
- The government often makes capital-equipment, manufacturing-technology, and facility investments at the prime-contractor level while making few (if any) such investments at the lower tiers.
- Prime contractors are afforded legal rights and remedies against the government which the subcontractors do not have against the prime contractors.
- The prime contractor is often assured of continuing as the sole producer on a weapon system, but a subcontractor often has no such assurance. His product often is later opened to competition, or else the prime contractor may choose to make the item instead of buying it from the supplier.
- Prime contractors can often leverage the subcontractors (during negotiations) by playing an opportunity on one program against another; but, since the government is decentralized in its buying, this is usually not done to the prime contractor. Of course, a small subcontractor usually is in a very weak bargaining position, relative to the prime contractor, in the first place.

- A prime contractor often imposes more stringent specification interpretations on a supplier than on its own internal operations, in order to have a "safety factor" when supplying the final product to the government. Therefore, the specification (which undoubtedly was already difficult) becomes that much more so for the supplier.
- While the prime contractors have staffs to handle all the government paperwork, the small, relatively unsophisticated firms at the lower tiers of the defense industry have far more difficulty handling the detailed regulations, procedures, accounting systems, socio-economic legislation, inspection requirements, and technical manuals associated with defense business.[65]
- The actual profits realized by the prime contractors are significantly higher than those realized by the subcontractors and part suppliers.[66] And when a large prime contractor has gotten into financial trouble, the government has traditionally bailed that firm out[67]; such has not been the case for the small subcontractors and part suppliers.
- Defense prime contractors are often not in a very strong financial position (relative to their "borrowing power" with banks or Wall Street). As a Conference Board study concluded, "defense subcontractors are in a more perilous situation than the primes."[68] In many cases, the subcontractors do not receive progress payments in the same way that the primes do, yet they have to do more borrowing than the primes (since they do not receive capital equipment from the government).
- Even when prime contractors receive multi-year contracts, they are often reluctant to pass these on to their subcontractors. This increases the annual uncertainty at the lower tiers, where it can least be afforded.

Thus, it is not at all surprising that many firms have been exiting the lower tiers, or that (especially with the low volume of defense business) commercially oriented firms have not been entering. In fact, not only are commercial firms discouraged by the facts listed above; they are also discouraged by many additional barriers to entry, such as the significant marketing differences, the specialized tooling and test equipment required, the extensive reporting requirements, the inelastic demand (even if prices are lower, the volume remains the same), and the heavy concentration on engineering and scientific capability (since a subcontractor usually enters a program during the R&D phase).[69] Thus, only a few suppliers remain in the lower tiers of the defense industry, and they are highly specialized. The specialization of these firms in defense subcontracting means that the DoD loses the economies of scale that could be realized by combining defense and non-defense production in the lower tiers of the industry, since the few items produced in these companies' specialized plants now have to absorb all of the overhead.

Congress, recognizing that the overwhelming number of businesses in the United States are small ones, and considering the valid argument that small businesses have been the country's greatest source of employment growth and innovation, has passed legislation requiring that "a fair portion of the total purchases in contracts or subcontracts for property and services for the government be placed with small business enterprises."[70] As a result, many contracts are set aside to be awarded to small businesses that can show their prices to be "reasonable and competitive."[71] Owing to the difficulty of working on defense contracts and the high technology usually required, it is not uncommon for these small firms to have cost overruns, make late deliveries, or default on contracts, and to then ask the government for "relief." In fact, the turnover rate among high-technology small businesses is around 50 percent, and it is among these small lower-tier contractors that a large share of the "abuses" and illegal actions occur. Unfortunately, much of the small- and minority-business legislation does not actually help the nation's security posture. In effect, the DoD is paying for political considerations rather than for potential innovativeness.

It is this innovativeness that must be captured. Small, high-technology, inventor-led firms have played an important role in the evolution of American industry and technology. Because of the flexibility and innovative genius of their founders, they have often been able to capitalize on small inventions. For example, much of the pioneering development work on power steering, power brakes, ball joints, alternators, and transistorized ignitions was done by the part suppliers to the "big three" American auto companies.[72] In the defense sector, the DoD has often been the source of the R&D funding for such firms, since the founder-inventors have often lacked the capital. In 1982 Congress passed the Small Business Innovation and Research Act (Public Law 97-219), the objective of which was to set aside a significant number of small R&D projects to help small firms get a "foot in the door" and get started on a research project in preparation for having to compete with the larger firms at the later stages of the defense R&D process. There is a need for much more reform legislation in the small-business area, as was noted in chapter 6.

More broadly, the crucial lower-tier supplier base of the defense industry must be strengthened. Three steps are required. The first is to achieve insight into the details of the problems in this area. (As the DoD itself has stated, "The nature and health of the subcontractor industrial base is not well understood."[73]) This does not mean getting data on every piece of, and every supplier of parts for, each weapon system; rather, it means identifying the crucial technologies on which the DoD is heavily dependent and for which there are only a few domestic suppliers. Having done this, the DoD should be able to gain the needed insight and to take whatever actions are required to ensure the future viability of these suppliers. Second, the DoD needs to spend far more of its R&D and manufacturing-technology dollars at the lower tiers of the defense industry.[74] Such investments would bear fruit not only in the military sector but also in the civilian sector—particularly if the DoD were to take the third step of invoking specific actions (described later in this chapter) to remove the barriers that have historically separated the civilian and defense sectors of American industry.

Responsiveness to Crises

The most common rationale for the economically inefficient structure of the defense industry is that it must be tolerated since it provides for industrial mobilization in time of war.[75] However, the United States today is not capable of achieving a rapid surge in the production of defense goods.

World War II is the most commonly considered example of industrial mobilization, and that example is best summarized in terms of the "five M's": manpower, materials, money, manufacturing, and morale.[76] Historically, the United States has maintained a large, active reserve of military *manpower.* There has always been concern about the availability of raw *materials* from foreign sources; during World War II, this became such an acute problem that the United States decided to maintain stockpiles of crucial raw materials. Today these stockpiles are worth billions of dollars but are in desperate need of updating to meet the needs of today's weapons.[77] *Money* is usually available once Congress recognizes that there is a crisis, and the public's positive attitude toward defense in times of national emergency helps to boost *morale*. Thus, *manufacturing* is crucial.

Inadequate planning for manufacturing results in unacceptably long lead times for the weapons needed in a time of war or crisis. Even with the less sophisticated equipment produced during World War II, it took about 3 years for the United States to reach its full capacity to produce airplanes and bombs, and $2\frac{1}{2}$ years to reach 25 percent of that.[78] It took more than 2 years to achieve any significant buildup in equipment deliveries during the Korean war.[79] With today's more complex military equipment, the production process is more difficult, the skill levels required are higher, the material lead times are frequently longer, and the parts tolerances are much tighter. Thus, without proper planning, the lead times might be even longer in any future crisis. Unfortunately, numerous studies[80] have shown that today there is little planning for a production surge in a crisis situation, or for the industrial mobilization that would be required to sustain an extended conflict in Central Europe. The studies have also confirmed the lack of potential industrial responsiveness. Even during the extensive Reagan defense buildup, the focus was entirely upon "force modernization"; little was spent on industrial preparedness.

The belief that there will not be an extended, intense non-nuclear conflict, because the United States will be forced to use nuclear weapons in a very short period of time, is clearly one of the reasons for the absence of interest in industrial preparedness. It is argued that industrial planning would be "irrelevant." Unfortunately, this is a self-fulfilling prophecy with regard to any Central European scenario; the absence of a sustained "conventional" capability would in fact force the United States to "go nuclear." But there are also many other reasons for developing a capacity for surges in defense-related production. Arms control is the most obvious of these. The more the United States and the Soviet Union move in the direction of agreeing to reduce weapons, the more crucial production capacity becomes. American surge capacity would be stabilizing; it would allow the American military to feel more comfortable about arms-control agreements, and it would discourage the Soviet Union from "breaking out" of these agreements. It would also enable the United States to quickly acquire the increased quantities of special-purpose equipment that might be needed in order to contain a regional conflict.

Traditionally, to satisfy the potential need for a production surge or a mobilization, the DoD has focused on storing old machine tools (so that production lines[81] for certain weapon systems could be set up quickly) or on maintaining existing plants and equipment in a greatly underutilized or even idle condition. However, as the mid-1970s inability to "surge" tank castings clearly showed, the limitation to a rapid buildup in tank production was not at the prime-contractor level but at the part-supplier level. Analyses of other military equipment have reached to same conclusions. For example, a study of the ability to increase the production of the F-16 fighter plane found that—even with a plant that, at maximum production of the F-16, was only using about one-third of its overall capacity—it would take over 3 years to increase output significantly. The reasons were (primarily) the inability to get critical parts of the aircraft and (secondly) a few production-line bottlenecks where a very expensive machine was already being fully used on three shifts and no additional machine was in the inventory. Thus, the DoD has been paying for big empty plants and for the stocking of old machine tools without actually receiving any benefit in terms surge capacity for the production of modern military equipment.

The appropriate action would be to analyze each of the items for which a production surge might be required and to make the small investments that are necessary for a significant change in production responsiveness for those particular items. For example, an analysis of the TOW anti-tank missile showed that a $16.2 million investment in long-lead-time parts would eliminate a significant bottleneck in production, and that—since the extra parts procured could be used at the end of the production operation as spare parts—this investment would not increase the net cost. The money for this was appropriated by Congress in fiscal 1985. Additionally, it was found that the consoles used to test the TOW were being utilized on three shifts and there was no room for any increase. Congress appropriated $22 million for additional consoles in fiscal 1986. The combined effect of these two small investments (on a multi-billion-dollar program) was that the United States could, if necessary, double the production of TOW missiles in 6 months and sustain that higher production rate indefinitely. Without these investments, it would have taken over 2 years to achieve a significant increase in production.[82] Obviously, to plan surge capacity for *all* weapon systems would be extremely expensive and, undoubtedly, not worthwhile. For example, such planning for new ship construction (which in peacetime takes perhaps seven years per ship) would require a lot of new capital equipment and would not be worthwhile. However, there are many items that would be rapidly used up during the early months of any conflict and for which the costs of preparedness planning and preparedness actions are relatively small (as was the case with the TOW missile). These expendable items include munitions, short-range missiles, and spare parts for the larger weapon systems. The United States' national-security posture (especially in terms of "sustainability") could benefit greatly if money for the production of these items were to be included in the peacetime budget.

In order to prepare, in peacetime, for a possible conventional conflict, the United States basically has two choices: to take the actions and make the investments to have a responsive defense industry, or to stock enough military equipment (known as "war reserve materiel") to sustain a conflict for the several years it would take the defense industry to get up to speed.[83] Historically, the military has been extremely reluctant to provide funds for war reserve materiel, and even less enthusiastic about providing funds for industrial-preparedness measures; it has preferred to modernize major equipment and to worry about sustainability later. As was seen in the TOW missile example, the costs of industrial preparedness measures are dramatically less than those for war-reserve-materiel actions; and even the latter are significantly less than the cost of the primary weapon systems themselves. Thus, the issue is not one of having sufficient available resources but rather one of establishing priorities in military planning. Essentially, the need is for the military to begin to think of the defense industry as an equal partner, in its national-security strategy, to its strategic and tactical forces. This approach makes the assumption that there would be some reasonable warning time before a conflict, as has always been the case even though the United States has often not acted on the warning. Most people today believe that a "bolt out of the blue" is highly unlikely, and that there will be adequate time to "turn on" the industrial base; however, our industrial response must be planned, and we must act on the warning.

Traditionally, American military planners have assumed that, upon the initiation of a conflict, the United States would simultaneously mobilize both its manpower and its industry. However, the manpower has always been available well before the equipment. In order to correct this—and not to have the action appear to be too provocative—it is necessary to separate industrial-responsiveness actions from manpower and military actions. The DoD has long had a system of "defense readiness conditions" (known as "defcons") corresponding to various states of heightened tensions. The idea of an industrial equivalent to the defcons ("indcons," for industrial alert conditions) was summarized by Secretary of Defense Frank Carlucci in his posture statement of 1988:

To insure that our industrial base can respond in an adequate and timely fashion to a broad range of potential emergencies, we are testing a new concept of industrial mobilization responses linked to early warning indicators. Under this concept, the readiness of our industrial base would be progressively increased, as intelligence suggested, in increasing probability of hostile actions directed against U.S. interests. To support this concept, in peacetime, planners will identify and catalog relevant industrial capabilities, prepare specific response options, and create a series of graduated responses to be implemented within existing capabilities at a time of crisis.[84]

The concept involves six industrial alert conditions, ranging from the status quo (indcon 6) through the expanded production of long-lead items (indcon 4) to total industrial mobilization (indcon 1).[85] This concept, and its effective implementation throughout the DoD's planning and budgeting process, would be a major step forward in enhancing America's national-security posture at a relatively low cost.

The obvious danger with this system, as with all systems that act on warning, is the possibility of false alarms. Adequate measures are required to ensure that we move up to the higher indcons only when there are real crises. Having so many steps allows for a graduated response and makes it less likely that huge amounts of resources will be wasted if an ambiguous warning turns out to be false.

Internationalization of the Market

As a basic tenet of its military posture, the United States has always assumed that its industrial base can be viewed as self-sufficient and treated in isolation. However, 200 years of American history have shown otherwise. Today is no different; but perhaps the situation is even more acute, since all of U.S. industry—and defense is no exception—has become international.

In viewing the current situation, we must revert to the "dual economy" model. Again, the issues, problems, and solutions are different at the prime-contractor level than at the lower tiers. At the prime-contractor level, the *selling* of U.S. equipment overseas is the primary issue; at the lower tiers, the issue is the *buying* of foreign parts and subsystems for almost all U.S. weapon systems, and the resulting dependence on foreign sources.

First, considering the worldwide weapons market at the prime-contractor level, it is clear that sales of American weapons to foreign clients have a major positive impact on the United States' balance of trade. In recent years, the annual net balance of exports over imports for aerospace products alone has ranged from $10 billion to $13 billion.[86] However, trade and jobs are intended to be only secondary considerations; by law, the sole valid justification for all military assistance (whether through the federal government or directly from U.S. companies) is its value to the overall defense posture of the United States.[87] Yet the selling of military equipment overseas has long been a difficult, politically loaded issue for the American people. The conflict between the desirability of foreign trade and employment in U.S. industry and the image of "arms merchants" has resulted in ambivalence within Congress and, thus, in a deficiency of congressional control over arms sales.[88]

The big change in the area of foreign military sales occurred in the 1970s. Before that time, most foreign arms sales involved prior-generation equipment and offered little in the way of advanced technologies. Such sales had the advantage of keeping American production lines "warm" in the event that they might be needed for wartime mobilization, and the transfer of advanced technology was a relatively minor issue. Additionally, the annual level of foreign arms sales was under $2 billion—small in comparison with U.S. military procurement. However, by the mid-1970s, partly because the oil-rich Middle East nations had dramatically increased their demands, the annual level of foreign military sales had jumped to $12–14 billion. At the same time, domestic purchases had fallen dramatically, from a high in 1968 of $44 billion, to a low in 1975 of $17 billion. Not only were foreign military sales almost equal to domestic military procurements, but the foreign customers were now demanding "first-line" equipment.[89] In many cases, foreign buyers paid for the development of new weapons that were to surpass the requirements of the U.S. Department of Defense.[90] There was also an increasing demand by foreign countries for engineering and manufacturing technology, co-production, "turn-key" factories, training, and military construction. Concern about the growing "dependency" of U.S. defense firms on foreign military sales[91] and about the effects of technology transfers led many to think that there should be more control in this area. Thus, the Reagan administration attempted to introduce significant "technology transfer controls." However, during the 1980s foreign demand for military equipment, from countries in the Persian Gulf, Europe, Asia, Africa, and Central and South America, and also from a wide range of terrorist organizations, continued to increase dramatically. In addition, since the market became flooded with more and more suppliers, it essentially became a buyer's market. Not only were the "traditional" nations (the United States, the Soviet Union, France, Britain, Italy, and West Germany) continuing to sell their arms, but now the market was booming with Third World producers. China, South Korea, North Korea, Israel, Brazil, Egypt, Pakistan, South Africa, India, and Singapore[92] are some of the leaders, and many of them are offering high-quality items at lower cost and with far fewer political strings than either the Western or the Eastern-Bloc suppliers.[93] China sells ballistic missiles to Saudi Arabia; Brazil sells aircraft to Honduras and missiles and armored vehicles to Iraq, and indirectly supplies Iran through sales to Libya.[94] If the United States, for political or humanitarian reasons, refuses to sell to someone, there are more than enough countries willing and able to sell similar equipment or to offer even more attractive packages.

As expected, U.S. foreign military sales began to drop significantly. By the mid-1980s, they were down to half what they had been at the end of the 1970s.[95] And whereas foreign military sales had been a high-profit business, the shift to a buyer's market had undercut profit margins and forced sellers to offer much more than simply a top-quality product in order to make the sale. With considerable excess capacity having been built up in many countries, and with jobs as well as economic development heavily dependent upon foreign military sales, the packages became more and more attractive. Common techniques included barter[96] (e.g., arms for oil); offset agreements (in which the seller agrees to buy other products from the buyer, sometimes in amounts equal in value to a significant percentage of the selling price[97]); the offer by the selling government to "share" costs with the arms producer in order to ensure the export sales[98]; co-production of equipment in the seller nation and the buyer nation (which often increases the cost of the equipment to the selling country[99]); "turn-key" factories (i.e., the selling country builds a new plant and does not take an equity position, but simply sells management, technical know-how, and prototypes); co-development of new equipment[100]; pure technology transfer (the selling of product technology and, particularly, process technology to other countries, including highly developed countries such as Japan[101]); licensing of foreign production of U.S.-designed systems (by 1981, 44 different U.S.-designed systems were being produced in more than 20 different countries, under more than 120 different agreements[102]); and the old, tried and true method: bribery.[103]

There is growing international concern about the many nations (especially in the Third World) that have been selling sophisticated systems with few or no political or ethical controls, and about the impact that such sales could have on future regional conflicts and even terrorism. However, the large number of nations involved and their heavy economic dependence on such sales make it highly unlikely that controls will be successful and increase the likelihood that U.S. forces may face such weapons in future conflicts.

The increasing U.S. dependence on foreign-made equipment (particularly critical military parts) is the other issue of growing concern. American policymakers have long been concerned about the danger of American dependence on foreign sources for many important raw materials[104] and have spent billions of dollars stockpiling materials such as chromium, cobalt, and manganese, which come primarily from South Africa, Zaire, and the Soviet Union.[105] Only recently, however, have American officials begun to address the potential ramifications of the nation's growing dependence on offshore producers of components (a trend that the commercial world has been seeing for some time, but which the Department of Defense largely ignored until the mid-1980s).[106] Traditionally, the DoD focused on prime contractors and had very little insight into the growing dependence on sole-source offshore producers, who are now providing components, and even subsystems, for almost every American weapon system.

In 1985 the Congressional Defense Joint Oversight Committee on Foreign Dependency looked into the Navy's Sparrow III air-to-air missile and found that the guidance system contained integrated circuits and transistors from Japan, a ferrite phase shifter from West Germany, a memory chip assembled in Thailand, and ball bearings made of raw materials from "various" sources. In all, sixteen foreign-produced parts were identified.[107] That investigation concluded that if shipments of these import-dependent parts were stopped, it would be impossible to continue making the missile. When and if American-made substitutes for the foreign parts became available, production could be resumed in about 18 months (if the missile did not have to be redesigned—an issue not even considered). These revelations brought further investigations. It was found that the two principal reasons for the increasing use of foreign sources for components of weapons were higher performance and lower cost.[108] Indeed, in many cases the foreign parts are the *only ones available* that deliver the required performance.

The U.S. defense industry is now heavily, if not totally, dependent on foreign sources for computer memory chips, silicon for high-powered electronic switching, gallium arsenide-based semiconductors for high-speed data processing, precision glass for reconnaissance satellites and other military equipment, liquid crystal and luminous displays, and advanced fiber optics.[109] In some cases, the cause of the shift is that American firms have moved their facilities abroad in order to reduce their labor costs and gain access to foreign markets; in other cases, it is simply that American suppliers have chosen to leave the defense market for the far more attractive commercial market, whereas foreign suppliers have found the advanced-technology, high-cost aspect of the defense market attractive enough. In still other cases, the shift to offshore procurement has resulted from a foreign government's sponsorship of advanced technology for both commercial and military markets—a sponsorship which, at the component level, has not been as prevalent in the United States. Regardless of the cause, it is a fact that most U.S. weapon systems and subsystems today are dependent on offshore producers for numerous critical components. This trend is likely to get worse. In any case, the DoD's procurement policies require buying the best and the cheapest systems, which often turn out to be those produced abroad. Furthermore, various laws and executive-branch policies intended to encourage greater industrial cooperation with our allies have resulted in more joint production of weapon systems and more technology-sharing. In many of these joint activities, the components are produced abroad and shipped to the United States to be assembled into weapon systems by the U.S. prime contractors. This exacerbates the dependency at the component level. In the few cases in which Congress or the DoD has addressed foreign dependency directly, only prime contractors and entire weapon systems have usually been involved; for example, the "Buy American Act" applies only to procurement from prime contractors.

The increased awareness of this issue has raised many valid concerns about possible events in source countries, such as strikes, political unrest, political reactions to a U.S. action, or even terrorist attacks against plants. Unless the parts are stockpiled in the United States, such actions could cause serious disruption to U.S. production, especially in times of international crisis. However, the real issue regarding dependency on foreign production should be the long-term implications for the United States. Many feel that, once manufacturing has gone offshore, engineering capability will also be lost.[110] Thus, U.S. companies will no longer be capable of designing state-of-the-art components for advanced weapon systems. This is a valid concern, and one that the United States needs to address with appropriate long-term measures.

Unfortunately, now that there is a heightened awareness of foreign dependency, there is a serious danger of overreaction, especially by a Congress with protectionist tendencies. Requiring domestic production of all components of weapons would be prohibitively expensive, and might also jeopardize relations with our allies.[111] Yet this "quick fix" approach is the one usually taken by Congress when it addresses problems of this nature, or when the question of U.S. jobs and foreign competition has to be considered.

As with most difficult policy decisions, the right answer may be to regard each situation as a special case involving unique political factors and cost/benefit assessments. In some instances, the DoD's best policy may be to develop strategies to deal with future supply interruptions, such as stockpiling critical items or preparing designs that would replace foreign components with domestic components. In other cases, the U.S. government may have to fund domestic research and development for the next generation of components, in order to lessen future dependence on foreign sources and to make the United States a net exporter of the next-generation systems. In some extreme cases, the United States may have to subsidize domestic production of certain critical components to keep the production and, most importantly, the engineering capabilities in the United States. In general, the United States needs to look into the issue, to assign responsibility to someone to deal with it, to develop a long-term strategy, and to begin now to take actions to improve America's position in the future.

Civilian-Military Integration

Clearly, many of the broad problems faced by the U.S. defense industrial base, such as the disappearance of the lower tiers, the growing foreign dependency, the peacetime inefficiency, and the incapacity for production surges in periods of crisis could be solved by reversing the current trends toward increasing separation of the defense industry from its civilian counterpart[112] and turning toward far more integration of defense and civilian technologies and industries. The Department of Defense is not only experiencing a relatively flat budget or perhaps even a shrinking one (in real dollars), but is also being required to develop a new generation of weapon systems ("ceramic" tanks, "plastic" aircraft, space weaponry, etc.) and to simultaneously reduce the extremely high costs of individual weapon systems. At the same time, the national economy is seeing an equally dramatic need to do something about the national deficit, the lopsided trade balance, the deteriorating transportation infrastructure, and the overall decline in U.S. industrial competitiveness. Perhaps it is time to question the historical tendency to see the nation's security and its economy as in conflict and to think that money spent on defense hurts the economy. Shouldn't it be possible to simultaneously strengthen America's posture in both the military sphere and the economic sphere through far greater integration between defense and civilian technologies at both the engineering level and the production level?[113]

Traditionally, defense work has been so different from commercial operations (even where the products are similar) that the two sectors have been driven apart. How, it is asked, can industry combine its civilian and military operations when the government places special, military-unique requirements on everything from cost-accounting standards, through security, to design and production specifications? Yet integration, from the DoD's side, would offer the potential for lower costs, higher volume, greater factory automation, higher quality, increased competition, and greater surge capacity. From the commercial firms' perspective, it would offer greater availability of billions of dollars of government R&D funds, state-of-the-art engineering talent, high-technology management skills, and significant government investments in advanced manufacturing technologies and equipment. Why, then, has this integration not been achieved?

Historically, in the United States there have been few incentives to integrate civilian and military engineering and production. From the industrial side, even those firms working in both fields have felt it in their interest to specialize and have argued that the differences in marketing, engineering, pricing, and so on were so extreme that it was better to maintain the separation. The firms working exclusively in the commercial sector believed that doing business with the DoD was just too difficult. From the military perspective, the DoD buyers stressed maximum performance for each system and felt that the commercial emphasis on cost would result in unacceptably low performance for their weapon systems. The DoD argued that its "unique" military requirements and its specialized procurement and accounting requirements were dictated by the fact that public funds were being utilized. These are, of course, valid arguments, and they have to be addressed when developing new procedures to encourage integration.

Other public-policy matters have also been said to argue against integration. One commonly heard argument is that integration could have a very negative effect on the commercial economy since, historically, the DoD has not been very cost-conscious and has emphasized maximum performance. If this philosophy were allowed to permeate the commercial sector, it would drive costs up and make American firms even less competitive on an international basis.[114] However, if the DoD were to shift its way of doing business toward greater cost consciousness, this concern would be addressed. Another argument raised against integration is that firms with both defense contracts and a viable commercial business base have an unfair advantage over commercial firms that do not have defense contracts, since the existence of defense contracts provides "free" R&D and capital equipment that permit these firms to "unfairly" compete with others who do not have these advantages. Shifting defense more into the civilian "market economy" would address this concern.

Another frequently heard argument against encouraging integration is the fact that it has usually failed to work—that when defense firms have tried it, they have been largely unsuccessful.[115] Undoubtedly, integration cannot take place easily or rapidly. It requires a "cultural reorientation"—greater cost emphasis in engineering and manufacturing, as well as learning to "market" products in a totally different customer environment, are almost mandatory. Unfortunately, since most of the attempts at integration took place during periods of dramatic defense cutbacks, the opportunities for long-term planning were eliminated and the gradual transition necessary for a successful integration effort was not possible.

Ironically, the special-interest groups that have continually argued in favor of integration (which they call "conversion") are the ones that favor dramatic cutbacks in defense expenditures and worldwide disarmament.[116] They argue, primarily, that without arms production there will be no war. These groups view the arms industries, on both sides of the Iron Curtain, as the principal advocates of defense production, and believe that their conversion to civilian production will eliminate the demand for defense budgets. Whether these arguments are valid or not, they have a very vocal following and, for obvious reasons, receive much resistance from the military-industrial complex, from many policymakers, and even from many union members concerned about loss of jobs.

The relative decline in the United States' international industrial competitiveness has forced people to look more closely at the integration experiences of other developed countries. Almost every nation except the United States has a government-organized and government-funded program for the "linkage" of military and civilian industry. Also, other nations spend a significant share of their government sponsorship of R&D on "industrial development" (for "dual-use" technologies). In 1986, the United States spent only 0.2 percent of the government's R&D money on industrial development, whereas France spent 11.7 percent, West Germany 11.6 percent, Japan 6.1 percent, and the United Kingdom 8.5 percent.[117]

Consider the actions some countries have recently taken to increase the "linkage" between the military and civilian sectors.[118] The government of the United Kingdom used private venture capital to establish a firm called The Defense Technology Enterprises, Ltd., for the explicit purpose of transferring military technology to the civilian sector. Some of its 45 employees are located inside the Ministry of Defense's laboratories, and their job is to identify ideas that can be declassified and used in the private sector. (Australia has set up a similar organization.) The United Kingdom's Department of Trade and Industry also funds some civilian projects that are performed in the Ministry of Defense's laboratories; these laboratories are set up as "centers," and their function is to link funding from the government, the universities, and industry for the explicit purpose of using military technology to develop products for use in the civilian sector—particularly products, such as software and electronics, that are of mutual interest to the two sectors.

France has formed a council, at the ministerial level, to address the subject of dual-purpose advanced research, the budget for which research has tripled in recent years. Additionally, in 1987 France established a "working group to stimulate defense-civilian innovation" and set up a "special fund" for such activities.

Italy has established an Interministerial Coordinating Body for Defense and Civilian R&D. Also, a Ministry for Coordination of Initiatives in Scientific and Technical Research was set up and entrusted with providing funding for joint military-civilian R&D. The budget for this effort has more than tripled in the last few years.

Japan is explicitly trying to integrate its growing defense production capability into its civilian industries (see chapter 10). The Ministry of International Trade and Industry is charged with this responsibility; interestingly, the orientation of this body is primarily civilian.

Now may be the right time for the United States to shift toward an integrated commercial and military industrial environment. The two most persuasive reasons are (1) the existing problems (and the growing awareness of these problems) in the defense industrial base and (2) the decline in the country's international industrial competitiveness, and the resulting trade imbalances. The latter has had a serious impact on the economy and has become such a high-visibility political issue that many, particularly in Congress, are searching for ways to encourage a reversal of the downward trend.

In looking for ways to solve the problems of America's defense industrial base and to reduce the cost growth of weapon systems, people have been turning more and more to recommendations for greater use of "commercial practices" and "commercial equipment." By using commercial parts, the DoD would have the advantage of buying equipment that has met the market test for quality and price. This approach has the added benefit of a potential for rapid surges in production in the "bottleneck" areas (the lower tiers) during periods of international crisis. Idle production capacity would not have to be maintained, nor would special parts have to be built rapidly; there would simply be a diversion, under crisis conditions, from commercial products to military ones.[119]

Today, the most frequently heard issue on Capitol Hill is that of declining U.S. international competitiveness. Thus far, under the guise of national-security considerations, Congress has been shifting more and more toward a protectionist response to the decline. Certainly, such a short-term perspective will not yield any dramatic increases in U.S. economic strength; in fact, it will have the reverse effect. An alternative longer-range, more structuralist perspective—recognizing that, in the long run, the government must play a more stimulative role in order to strengthen U.S. international competitiveness—is gradually gaining a foothold.[120] Leaders of this school argue that since the United States' principle economic competitors (the Western European countries and Japan) all utilize "industrial strategy" to stimulate their market economies, the United States is at a distinct disadvantage in not doing so. Clearly, any such strategy adopted by the United States must recognize the gross differences among various industrial segments and must acknowledge that universal actions by the government are inapplicable. The proponents of "industrial strategy" also note that actions in some segments of industry will have much bigger "payoffs" than actions in other segments because of the strong linkages between the civilian and military sectors and/or because these industries provide the basic infrastructure on which the overall U.S. economy will build in the future. Examples of the crucial segments might include electronics, lightweight structural materials, advanced manufacturing equipment, and information systems.

Finally, it is important, especially in trying to get commercial firms interested in various kinds of defense work, to have very strong industry involvement not only in the selection of the various projects but also in the detailed implementation. Here are some of the recent joint industry-government "dual-use" efforts:

- The DoD spent around $650 million (over seven years) sponsoring the research and development of very-high-speed integrated circuits (VHSIC)—funding both the product technology and the manufacturing capability—with the clear intent that this investment be dual-purpose (i.e., both defense and civilian).[121]
- A 1987 study by the National Academy of Sciences[122] strongly recommended that the DoD spend between $200 million and $300 million a year on advanced manufacturing technologies (e.g., "flexible" and computer-integrated manufacturing) to benefit both defense and the economy. The DoD responded with increased funding.
- As a result of the growing concern[123] about foreign dependency in areas critical to defense, the DoD received congressional approval for a $600 million investment (over six years) for a prototype semiconductor-manufacturing plant (known as Sematech).
- In 1987 the president announced[124] that to help advance America's commercial position in the new field of superconductivity, as well as to "ensure use of superconductivity technologies in military systems as soon as possible," the DoD will invest $150 million (over the following three years) to "develop the required processing and manufacturing capabilities."
- In 1988 the DoD initiated Phase I (3 years, $250 million) of the Microwave and Millimeter Wave Monolithic Integrated Circuits (MIMIC) program. The clear objective of this dual-use program is to stimulate work with gallium arsenide.[125]

These steps indicate a growing willingness on the part of Congress to fund broad industrial-development projects that have dual-use applicability.[126] They are financed with defense dollars, and they are all at the lower tiers and/or at the manufacturing-technology level of the defense industry—the areas of significant overlap ("linkage") between the military and civilian sectors. This move toward simultaneous consideration of both military and civilian advantages should receive wider support within the U.S. government. However, it is very unlikely—at least with any sense of urgency—without a significant effort by the DoD and the Congress.

In other developed countries, as described above, there are organizations that look at both the military and the commercial sector of industry and recommend actions that would be in the national interest and steps (e.g., taxes or legislation) to be taken to encourage such actions. In the United States there is no organization charged with this responsibility or with that of taking actions to achieve the desirable dual industrial structure. A number of people have proposed non-defense agencies as the "natural" home for such U.S. activity and have suggested the Department of Commerce, or a new "combination" organization (based on the Department of Commerce and the U.S. Trade Representative), or a new organization created from elements of various government organizations. However, there is a widespread belief that such an initiative would have difficulty gaining acceptance within the United States, as it would appear to represent too much government interference with the free market. In fact, when the Assistant Secretary of Commerce under the Carter administration attempted to initiate a non-defense R&D investment program, he couldn't get it approved by the White House Domestic Council.[127] Thus, it is up to the Department of Defense—which has the need, the resources, the responsibility, and the political support—to take the leadership role. Obviously, the DoD would need to work closely with other government organizations (e.g., the Department of Commerce, the U.S. Trade Representative, and the Departments of Labor and the Treasury) to obtain not only their suggestions but their support. Because it will take years for any significant integration to take place, efforts must be initiated now to ensure that the next generation of weapon systems will have significantly lower costs and higher quality.

The specific steps necessary for the DoD to initiate such integration are the following:

- *Issue an explicit policy statement* to draw support from others that currently do not want to move in this direction.
- *Assign specific organizational responsibilities.* The primary responsibility would be within the Office of the Secretary of Defense, but the organizational and procedural infrastructure involving the military services as well as other government agencies must be built.
- *Identify and reduce, or remove, the current barriers to integration.* In some cases these will simply be government practices, but in others

they may be regulations. In a few cases, legislation will have to be changed.

- *Develop long-range strategies.* This includes the identification of high-priority areas, weapon-system programs, and industries; the creation of incentives for integration; the establishment of the necessary industry data bases (particularly at the lower tiers) that would provide the required visibility to assist with the corrective actions; and the identification and initiation of training activities to educate DoD participants in this initiative. Specific examples are required to demonstrate the intent of the program, as well as to work out the likely obstacles. It is critical that these not be done on a *ad hoc* basis; rather, they need to be well integrated into the overall DoD organization, procedures, and strategy.

For this DoD-led initiative to successfully improve the nation's security posture along with its international industrial competitiveness, the program must be implemented in two steps. First, the DoD must make its buying practices more like those of the civilian world; then, the second step would almost follow automatically. Commercial firms would see the added incentives of coming into defense business (for example, government-funded R&D and countercyclical business patterns), and full integration would occur; however, for this to be achieved, the DoD has to move well away from the current position of being so "different."

The above five actions primarily address the first and most crucial step of the integration effort; and clearly, there will be early fallout from this effort into the civilian world. Nonetheless, during the transition, defense-oriented and civilian-oriented industries must take full advantage of the lessons learned from prior attempts at "conversion" and/or "integration." The following list highlights some of these lessons.[128]

- Effective technology transfer occurs primarily through people working together.
- Maximum civilian-sector advantage is gained from military funding of "infant industries," due to the creation of new physical and human resources.
- In establishing a program for integration, "institutional structure" and "policy emphasis" are far more important than the specific types of technologies selected.

- Large defense prime contractors are not "defense" firms; they are "large systems producers." Their management expertise (with complex, state-of-the-art, advanced-mission systems) is their greatest advantage in the non-defense world.
- Many existing structures retard the operation of market mechanisms. Thus, a shakeup is needed in existing structures in order to achieve the changes that will allow and encourage integration. Specifically, for technology transfer to be achieved, either the recipient structure has to change to accept the new technology ("absorption") or the technology itself has to change to fit the recipient ("adaptation").
- It very much matters whether R&D investment is made in the "user" or the "supplier" plants. For a single application (e.g. defense), it probably makes more sense to fund the end user of the R&D (the defense prime contractor); but in stressing dual use of the R&D investment, it may make more sense to fund the suppliers (the parts manufacturers or the material manufacturers).
- Accepting the concept of "induced innovation" results in R&D *objectives* having a distinct influence on the evolution of technology. Thus, specifying dual use for the research program (vs. defense only) is likely to influence which technology gets emphasized and how the technology evolves (e.g., stressing maximum performance, or cost and performance).
- R&D for advanced military systems can be focused on either performance or quantity of the next-generation systems (where the latter is driven by cost considerations). Obviously, the R&D to increase the quantity of weapon systems will be much closer to that required for the civilian sector (to become much more competitive internationally).
- In the past, military R&D has far too often not recognized the dependence it has on a strong civilian technology base.
- Historically, the DoD has stimulated industry by being the guaranteed "first buyer" in new fields of technology. It would buy the initial production quantities of new items; then the proven equipment would be purchased by the civilian sector.
- Capital equipment, engineering innovation, production labor forces, and skilled management should be maximized in any integration efforts. Yet it must be recognized that these may be difficult to convert (especially the management).

• Two years is a reasonable "planning time" for all the work that must be done to blueprint the changeover of a product selected for integration. Absence of careful planning and reliance on "crash" operations usually lead to a high probability of failure.

In summary, it seems highly desirable for the Department of Defense to take the lead in achieving greater integration of military and civilian technology, both in engineering and in manufacturing. It also seems that there is likely to be little movement without a concerted government effort; such an effort should be part of a broad attempt to strengthen the overall defense industrial base of the United States.

Industrial Strategy

The defense industrial base is a valuable resource for a nation's security and for its economic competitiveness. All nations except the United States recognize this fact. As Senator Alan Dixon (D-Illinois) observed in 1988, "A series of studies conducted over a ten year period by Congress, the General Accounting Office, the Department of Defense, and others have consistently shown a steady, unchecked erosion of the defense industrial base in the United States; despite the uniformly adverse findings contained in the reports on such studies, the United States still lacks a coherent industrial base policy that is directly linked to national security strategy."[129]

America's policymakers fail to recognize that an effective market does not exist at any level of the defense industry. However, "there is almost universal agreement that when markets go astray the government must intervene."[130] Such a role for the government is also becoming more widely accepted in selected areas of the civilian economy.[131] But the DoD has its own unique needs and therefore must develop its own unique strategy (which must be, of course, fully consistent with any national economic strategies). It must also be recognized that in many segments of the U.S. economy the DoD is a relatively minor player and, thus, cannot be expected to carry the nation's economy. Rather, the DoD must focus its strategy on a few crucial segments (most of which will also have a significant positive impact on other portions of the economy)—for example, machine tools, super-materials, software, and electronics.

The issue is not whether the government should be involved in the defense industrial base; it is already intimately involved and cannot become disengaged. Thus, the proper role of the government becomes the issue. When free markets do not exist, it is not a choice between government involvement and good company management; both are required.[132] Additionally, the government should not usurp decision-making by individual firms; instead, it should shape the firms' decisions through carefully chosen tax, credit, procurement, and other policies and actions.[133]

There are three broad public-policy options for the U.S. defense industry.[134] The first is the nationalization of the major defense contractors. Long ago, the economist John Stuart Mill proposed this solution for England because he felt that economies of scale would predominate in the defense sector and lead to monopoly. Nationalization has been frequently proposed since Mill's time.[135] More recently, John Kenneth Galbraith argued that nationalization would bring American defense firms under public control.[136] The question, however, is whether this would result in public control or just provide political shelter.[137] In fact, nationalization is neither the "second-best" solution nor the will of Congress and the American people. Additionally, this approach would remove any vestige of competition from the field, and, as numerous studies have shown, publicly owned defense facilities are approximately 30 percent less efficient than their private counterparts. Nonetheless, nationalization is often proposed for the U.S. defense industry, perhaps more out of frustration than out of logic.

The second broad alternative that has been proposed is to essentially regulate the defense contractors as a kind of public utility, with a commission that is independent of the DoD.[138] Today all actions of defense contractors are controlled by the Federal Acquisition Regulations; however, the defense industry is never listed as a "regulated industry" because there is no external regulatory commission and because the DoD does its regulation at the micro level (welding specifications, inspection details, etc.) whereas normal regulation of an industry is done at the macro level (structure, profit, pricing, etc.). Experience with airlines, trucking, and nuclear power teaches that regulated industries are quite prone to capture by their regulatees, and that regulation tends to bring even greater inertia than currently exists in the defense industry. Changes in world conditions and rapid technological evolution require a defense industry that can move quickly, and regulation undoubtedly would hamper it. Furthermore, utilities are not known for cost consciousness; they simply pass on their cost increases to their customers. The only beneficiary of such a regulatory approach might be the defense industry itself, since profits in regulated industries tend to be significantly higher than those in the defense industry today. Yet this unattractive alternative appears to be the solution pushed most frequently by Congress and by many in the executive branch whenever the question of what to do about the defense industry comes up.

The third broad alternative, and the preferred one, is to create "effective" competition in the defense industry.[139] The government, as the sole buyer of defense equipment, must exercise its monopsony power and structure the defense industry in a way that would promote, not supplant, the natural market forces present in order to achieve efficiency, innovativeness, and responsiveness. Essentially, the role of the government would shift from one of issuing detailed regulations to one of influencing the structure and the competitive nature of the industry. Traditional market theory says that, as changes occur, markets adjust to "equilibrium." However, with the rapid technological evolution and the unique market conditions in the world of defense, there is enormous institutional resistance to change. This proposed approach represents a fundamental shift from the current adversarial, legalistic structure to an administrative one.[140] The government's role would change from one of an enforcer of a code of law (such as with antitrust actions) to one of an encourager of effective competition. The aim is to reduce overcapacity and obsolescence, wherever they are present—but through the creation of market forces rather than through directives and subsidies.

What is being proposed is *not* "national planning," in which bureaucrats who are ignorant of or indifferent to market forces shift capital from industry to industry to nurture their favorite "winners."[141]

The desired structure for the defense industry is one with neither a large number of firms nor a monopoly in each sector. Rather, from the government's viewpoint, there should be perhaps two or three strong competitors in each major segment of the industry. On some programs, it may not be necessary to actually have two firms producing the same items; there may only need to be an alternative—either having a different way to do the mission or a firm in a related market that can be brought in at any time. Additionally, it is critical, at the beginning of each program, to have alternative sources for new ideas, and to have them focused not just on improved performance but also on lower cost.

There are a wide variety of market-adjustment tools available to the government; many of them are used today, but not in any coordinated fashion. Once the stated objectives of an industrial strategy are clear, then these tools can be brought into focus. Examples include the use of industrial consortia (perhaps partially funded by the government); the sponsorship of multiple firms, each working on related component and subsystem research projects; subsidized capital investments; financing incentives (targeted tax policies, cash payments, differentiated profit policies, etc.); direct government procurement (particularly to get a new industry started, or to create a second source); protectionism (for an infant industry, and to create initial domestic competition); and trade policies. However, the major contract awards made on each weapon system are the best means of achieving the desired industrial structures. Each award dramatically alters the structure of the defense industry; therefore, in its decisions on individual weapon systems, the DoD must consider not just the proposal by the individual firm but also the impact of the award on the future of the defense industry. Again, this does not mean picking Firm A over Firm B; it means saying (e.g.) "the DoD needs to have three firms in this sector" and influencing the results of the competition to yield, over time, this desired characteristic. It also means applying the same techniques to the lower tiers of the defense industry in order to achieve similar characteristics at that level. For example, the same attention the DoD has paid to tanks, aircraft, and strategic missiles should be given to machine tools, super-materials, software, and certain electronic components.

To implement such a defense industrial strategy, the DoD must establish an organization with responsibility for it and then give that organization authority for direct inputs into the major resource and weapon-system decisions. The selected group will have to have adequate insight into the health, innovativeness, and responsiveness of the defense industry in order to determine the actions needed to support or enhance market forces (especially during periods of change). Again, it must be emphasized that the approach suggested here is not a highly activist industrial strategy, nor one that looks like a "U.S. MITI,"[142] nor a single organization that looks at overall U.S. industrial strategy. Rather, the idea is to have a defense-oriented organization geared to those segments of the economy that serve defense—either exclusively or in a dual-purpose role—and on whom the nation's defense is dependent. The focus would not be on individual firms but on the structure of crucial segments of the industry.

9 Personnel

The United States has over 2 million men and women on active duty in the military, another million in the active (selected) reserves, and another million civilian Department of Defense employees.[1] In spite of the automation of modern warfare, more than half of the annual defense budget still goes to pay for personnel. Thus, any analysis of the potential for cost reduction must address this subject.

Some major issues relative to personnel are the growing importance of the reserve forces; the choice between an all-volunteer military and the draft or "universal national service"; the role of women; the disproportionate representation of racial and ethnic minorities; and the possibility of alternatives to the high and rapidly rising costs of military retirement benefits.

Four Million People

Table 9.1 shows the distribution of current defense personnel.[2] From these figures it can be seen that the Army is more "labor-intensive" than the other services. (The Navy and the Air Force count very heavily on capital equipment, such as ships and planes.) It can also be seen that the Army counts extensively (and, to a lesser extent, so does the Air Force) on the reserves (a combination of National Guard units and the selected reserves).

Table 9.2 shows the distribution, from a military-usage viewpoint, of these 4 million people.[3] Clearly, the largest share of both the active-duty personnel and the selected reserves are associated with conventional warfare. The overwhelming percentage of the civilians are in support activities. One of the issues frequently raised within the Department of Defense is the large number of military personnel involved in "non-combat" activities, rather than directly in the strategic or tactical forces. The largest portion (almost half of those in the support category) are associated with operating the military bases. An additional significant number are involved in conducting either individual training or force-support training. Finally, about 5 percent of military personnel are involved in auxiliary activities, such as research and development, central communications, intelligence, and geophysical activities. It is argued that many of these support jobs could be done by government civilian employees or "contracted out" to the private sector.

Table 9.1
Total personnel and distribution by service, based on FY 1982 budget.

	Active duty	Selected reserve[a]	Civilians
Army	37%	69%	37%
Navy	26%	9%	29%
Marine Corps	9%	4%	2%
Air Force	28%	18%	24%
Defense agencies			8%
	100%	100%	100%
Total personnel	2,119,000	928,900	1,024,900

a. Includes National Guard (Army and Air Force).

In peacetime, over 10 percent of defense personnel are in training at any given time—a significantly larger percentage than that found in the private sector. This figure excludes the force training that units go through, and is considered to be more job or skill-related training. Frequently, as will be discussed below, one of the societal benefits of a large peacetime military force is to provide a great deal of basic education and skill development to people who might not otherwise have received it, and which they can fully utilize when they end their military service.

The growing importance of the selected reserve is based on the concept formally known as the "total force policy," which was implemented shortly after the adaptation of the all-volunteer service. As stated by the Department of Defense, "In structuring our forces, units are placed in the selected reserve whenever feasible to maintain a small and active component of the peacetime force, as national security policy and our military strategy permit."[4] This is, of course, not a new principle. It actually goes back to America's long history of the "citizen soldier." Obviously, it has both an economic and a political basis in our nation's history. The difference today is the large, worldwide dependence on the reserve forces to be participants in the very first few days of any conflict. As the Assistant Secretary of Defense for Reserve Affairs has stated, "Few combat contingencies anywhere in the world, even those far short of general war, can any longer be met adequately for more than a few days or weeks, without an early reserve activation."[5]

Table 9.2
Total personnel and distribution by mission, based on FY 1982 budget.

	Active duty	Selected reserves[a]	Civilians
Strategic forces	5%	3%	1%
Tactical/mobility forces	45%	77%	6%
Auxiliary activities	5%	2%	9%
Support activities	30%	13%	84%
Individuals (e.g., training)	15%	4%	
	100%	100%	100%
Total personnel	2,119,000	928,900	1,024,900

a. Includes National Guard (Army and Air Force).

There are many who argue that this growing dependence on the reserves is a highly desirable feature of our national-security posture (and one utilized by many other countries). However, it undoubtedly requires a very significant change in the reserve-force structure[6]—one the United States has been reluctant to make. For example, the selected reserves' training requirements of one weekend per month and two weeks of summer training per year are essentially the same as they were in 1952. Yet in 1952, weapons and tactics were simpler, and the reserves were not expected to be deployed early in a war, were not considered to be a leading force, and were not depended on to provide a timely response to a crisis. Thus, while it might be desirable (or even necessary) for the United States to become even more dependent on the use of reserve forces (as will be discussed below), a significant restructuring of the reserves will undoubtedly be required in order to make them a fully effective complement to the standing armies.

Volunteers versus Conscripts

One of the most politically loaded issues in defense management is that of an all-volunteer force versus a military draft or "universal service" of some form. In 1973, as one of the many societal effects of the Vietnam war, the United States shifted from a draft to an all-volunteer force. At that time, and ever since, the issue has raised four critical questions: Could enough high-quality people be induced to enter the services on a voluntary basis, particularly with the skills necessary to

Table 9.3
Measures of quality for male army recruits without prior military service.

	Draft		All-volunteer force			
	1960–1964	1971–1972	1974	1980	1981	1984
Percent holding high school diplomas	64	64	46	49	78	89
Percent with lowest acceptable mental-test score	19	22	19	50	32	12
Percent with some college	17	21	4	3	5	9

operate the very sophisticated equipment being increasingly supplied? Would enough people, in the age groups desired, be available in the years ahead? Would the costs associated with recruiting high-quality people be affordable? Even if these obstacles could be overcome, would the resultant force be "representative" of America, or would it be a "mercenary force" from the "under classes"? These (particularly the last one) are tough questions that must be addressed. Table 9.3, which represents one way of looking at the "quality" issue,[7] shows that immediately after the all-volunteer force was introduced there was a dramatic reduction in the number of high school and college graduates who volunteered. Additionally, there was a very significant increase in the "lowest acceptable mental-test score" category, and by 1980 the percentage of these very marginal recruits had reached 50 (which was consistent with the fact that over half of the volunteers lacked high school diplomas). However, table 9.3 also shows a dramatic change in the quality of the all-volunteer force during the early years of the Reagan administration. By 1986 the percentage of high school graduates in the Army had reached 91.[8] There was almost universal agreement that the "recruiting and retention of able men and women in the armed forces [was] the single most notable achievement in the Reagan Administration's four-year military buildup."[9] In 1985 the Army Chief of Staff stated: "Today's soldiers are at the top of the scale. With high-quality men and women joining the service, the state of discipline is superb; the indicators of morale and discipline are at all-time highs."[10] The reasons given for this dramatic turnaround in the quality of personnel were these: unemployed youths wanting jobs, the educational benefits

Table 9.4
Projected U.S. population aged between 18 and 21 years (in thousands).

	1983	1987	1991	1995
Male	8,356	7,356	7,196	6,608
Female	8,143	7,165	6,983	6,387
Total	16,499	14,521	14,179	12,995

offered by the armed services, the significant increases in military pay under the Reagan administration, and the chance to get away from home and to travel.[11] Thus, if the pool of available personnel could be maintained and the dollars made available, it would appear that the all-volunteer force was achieving its objectives.

However, the demographic trends raise a growing concern. Table 9.4 shows a population shift toward fewer male and female 18–21-year-olds in the 1990s.[12] This trend, of course, does not mean that there won't be enough people available; it simply means that the inducements have to be much greater, especially if the economy is in good shape and there are employment opportunities elsewhere.

The high quality of recruits achieved in the first half of the 1980s did not come without costs. President Carter's last full budget included $69.4 billion for personnel costs. In 1985, Congress voted $80.3 billion for personnel costs.[13] (Both figures are in 1986 dollars.) This pay increase was relatively small compared to the high buildup of the defense budget, but it was extremely effective in improving the quality and the morale of the military forces. The salary increases of the early Reagan years were enough to correct the comparatively low salaries (especially for officers) such that by 1987 the General Accounting Office was in a position to conclude that military salaries now exceeded those of comparable civilian government employees, and even compared favorably with those in the private sector (when benefits were included).[14] The GAO study was careful to point out that there are a number of non-economic factors that are disadvantageous to the soldier (frequent relocation, irregular hours, lack of overtime pay, and the difficulty a spouse has in establishing a career).

The increased personnel budgets of the 1980s were used not only for salaries, but also to attract or retain recruits. For example, an $8 million TV and magazine ad blitz in the spring of 1985 was combined with fat signup bonuses ($20,000–$26,000) and college benefits ($5,000–$8,000) for recruits who entered critical-need areas. Additionally, a new program for recruiters on community college campuses offered $20,000 for college expenses after two years of service. Overall, costs per Army recruit went from $1,704 in 1980 to $4,136 in 1985.[15] However, the gains in the quality of recruits for the all-volunteer service were not due entirely to pay or the condition of the economy; they also had to do with the military's return to high public esteem since the Vietnam era. A 1987 Gallup poll on "institutions most inspiring confidence" had the military in the number one place for the first time (above religion, the Supreme court, banks, and schools).[16]

Even with these very positive trends, many believe there is still a strong reason for returning to the draft: the fact that there are growing, unmet social needs in America, which are in conflict with the high cost of defense. Many believe that education, health care, child care, conservation, environmental protection, and numerous other social services could be improved if the nation were to institute some form of a draft or universal national service. In either of these cases, people would be given the choice between military service and such options as the Peace Corps, VISTA, the American Conservation Corps, state and local conservation corps, or local community-service programs. Because of the declining demographics for eligible volunteers, the rising cost for the all-volunteer military forces, and the concerns about the development of a nonrepresentative, mercenary army, there has been a growing cry—from a wide variety of sources—for a return to a draft or the initiation of some form of required national service.

Many of these demands come from the national-security perspective alone. For example, the historian Barbara Tuchman states, "I believe a citizen's army with no preferential deferments is not only the only just system but ultimately the only sound defense, and reenactment of the draft the only way we will be taken seriously by the antagonists and— if we believe national defense is so urgent—by ourselves."[17] This position is widely held throughout the world. Almost all the Western European countries (Belgium, Denmark, France, West Germany, Holland, Italy, Norway, Portugal, Spain, Sweden, and Switzerland) have conscription (the only exceptions in NATO are Britain, Canada, Luxembourg, and the United States), and all the countries of the Warsaw Pact have it too. The principal arguments are (1) costs (most countries' conscripts get less than the going rate for a young person's labor or for voluntary military service); (2) the desirability of "scooping up" large numbers of people who would otherwise be unemployed and give them schooling (Turkey, in particular, uses this argument); (3) that it is unfair to draw primarily from the least-educated and worst-off people (Holland and Norway stress this argument); and (4) a deep-seated mistrust of a professional standing army (a view particularly prevalent in France). In any case, all these nations find that conscription helps a great deal in producing reservists, since most countries require their conscripts to remain on the reserve rolls for several years after discharge from their approximately one year of active duty. As a result, West Germany, for example, has around 850,000 good reservists that could be mobilized rapidly in a crisis.[18]

In the United States there is still a great deal of political resistance to a reintroduction of the draft. People are taking a "wait and see" attitude toward the issue of rising costs and decreasing demographics. Nonetheless, many are arguing for a return to the draft or for some form of compulsory national service. The military have been among the leading advocates of the draft, because of their concern that after a few days of fighting in Europe there would be inadequate reserve personnel available to rapidly bring to the front.[19] In Congress, Senator Sam Nunn and Representative Les Aspin (heads of the Senate and House Armed Services Committees, respectively) have argued for some form of a compulsory national service program. One proposal, that seemed to appeal to them was for young adults to receive help with college expenses in exchange for one or more years of national service at low pay.[20]

The advocates of compulsory universal service argue that it would have three principal advantages: It would diminish the inequality of obligating only a few to serve; because all youths would serve in some capacity, the market available to the military would change drastically by introducing middle-class and upper-class recruits, who could no longer choose between pursuing entirely private ends and enlisting in the military; and there would be a civilian parallel to military service, which would tend to defuse objections to conscription from those who might tolerate civilian but not military service, and which would simultaneously address many of the nation's social needs.[21]

The ultimate issue here is one of values. This is a political question rather than an economic one. It is highly likely, therefore, that a shift

from the current all-volunteer service to some form of a draft or universal service is likely to come about through a dramatic change in world
economic or geopolitical conditions rather than through a reasoned
cost-benefit analysis.

Women and Minorities

Before World War II the American military was basically a "white
man's army," even though there had been significant historical contributions by minority members and by women. The social changes taking
place in the United States in the post-World War II era, combined with
the demographics, made it very clear that dramatic shifts in this orientation would be required, and desired. Yet such changes were relatively
slow in coming.

Prior to the passage of Public Law 90-130, signed on November 8,
1967, the total number of military women was restricted to a maximum
of 2 percent of cach service.[22] Things began to change rapidly with this
action. Then, in 1973, the draft was abolished. The subsequent enactment of the Defense Officer Personnel Management Act repealed long-
standing provisions of law containing unwarranted restrictions on the
utilization of women in military service. Finally, the Secretary of Defense, in a memorandum to the Secretaries of the military departments
dated July 19, 1983, called for full utilization of women consistent with
existing combat exclusion laws and related policies. Clearly a shift had
taken place in the utilization of women in the military.[23] Between 1972
and 1987 the percentage of women in the active enlisted force grew
from 1.6 to 9.6,[24] and by 1986 fully 12.2 percent of military recruits were
women.[25]

The current laws restricting the assignment of women in the Navy,
Marine Corps, Air Force, and their reserve components from combat
duty were enacted in 1948 when the women's auxiliary components
were made part of the permanent military structure.[26] Under these
statutes women may not be assigned to ships or aircraft engaged in
combat missions, nor may they be assigned to other than temporary
duty on Navy vessels except hospital ships, transports, and vessels of
similar classification. There are no statutory restrictions on the utilization of women in combat in the Army, the Army National Guard, or the
Army Reserve. However, Army Department policy parallels the other

statutes and restricts women from assignment in those skills and positions that "through doctrine, mission or battlefield location, invite the highest probability of direct combat action."[27] These restrictions obviously reduce the number of positions for female officers and enlisted career personnel.

In the American armed services as a whole, only about 61 percent of all positions are open to women (ranging from a low of 20 percent in the Marines through 50 percent in the Navy, 56 percent in the Army, and 96 percent in the Air Force). As a result, women are most heavily concentrated in financial, support, and administrative positions (23.2 percent of the women) and medical and dental positions (24.3 percent).[28] These are also the areas in which women are heavily concentrated in the civilian sector, where in 1986 they constituted 80.4 percent of the administrative-support work force and 84.1 percent of the health technicians (although they made up only 44.4 percent of the employed civilian workers).[29] Clearly, if the United States is to make greater use of women to strengthen its economic structure, and give them equal opportunities for job placement, the same thing must be done in the military organizations. The combination of the demographic trends and the very positive results that have been achieved by women in the services will add pressure on legislators and senior military officers to change many of the current restrictions and practices. To date, there have been gradual shifts in the percentages of women within each of the services, both as officers and as enlisted personnel, but the increases have been slow. By 1986, the percentages of women officers and enlisted personnel ranged from a high in the Air Force of 11 and 12.5 percent, respectively, to a low in the Marines of 3.5 percent and 5.5 percent, respectively; the Army and the Navy were in the 10 percent range for each of these categories.[30]

The quality of the women in the service has been very high. Their educational attainments and their entrance-test scores have been at least as good as those of male recruits, and there is general agreement that their job performance has been at least comparable to that of their male counterparts.[31] Consistent with this, women were promoted earlier than men (this applies to all officer and enlisted ranks with the sole exception of promotion to captain or admiral in the Navy).[32] Thus, with time, and as more women move into senior positions within the services, the United States should be able to take far greater advantage of this outstanding pool of potential military personnel.

While women are underrepresented in the military, the opposite has been true of racial and ethnic minorities. In 1986 almost 27 percent of the recruits were members of minorities, although the minority com-position of the civilian youth population between the ages of 18 and 21 was 17.8 percent.[33] The distribution is even more skewed when one looks at the numbers for minority women; the new recruit female pop-ulation is 33.4 percent minority, while the overall population is only 18.1 percent minority.[34]

Part of the reason that military service has been so attractive to minorities in the United States has to do with economic conditions. By the mid-1980s, there was a growing racial gap in unemployment rates for those between the ages of 16 and 24. For example, in 1983 the unemployment rate was 15 percent for white males and 34 percent for black males.[35] Thus, by 1986 one of every 12 employed black men between 18 and 44 was in the military, versus one in 25 whites. The military had become one of the largest employers of black Americans, with more than 400,000 blacks on active duty. Blacks were clearly overrepresented; they constituted nearly 20 percent of all active-duty personnel and 28 percent of the Army's enlisted personnel.[36]

Surveys conducted by the National Opinion Research Center show that blacks respond very positively to the fact that they are heavily represented in the armed forces.[37] This clearly is due in part to the extensive training that people receive while in the military—from basic language skills through trade skills (as noted above, one in every ten individuals is receiving training at any given time). From the trainee's viewpoint as well as from the nation's social perspective, the increased skills developed during military service will be of considerable assis-tance when the individual leaves military life. However, from the De-fense Department's viewpoint, as the demographic trends begin to affect enlistment, there is growing concern that the military is shoul-dering much of the social responsibility that would normally be assumed by other government agencies.

Many argue, however, that until the civilian institutions begin to provide fairer and better opportunities for blacks and other minorities, they will continue to perceive military service as a very desirable career path, and that race and ethnicity are not, and should not be, a major concern of the armed services. The only exception would be if the proportionate participation of any particular group were to become so exaggerated that it would distance the military from the society that it is intended to protect, so that the armed services would be viewed as a non-representative element in American society. Since we are far from that situation today in terms of either minorities or women, these two groups will continue to represent excellent sources of recruits to balance the declining populations in other segments of the population.

Military Pensions

The military retirement program, though politically loaded, is likely to be forced to change because of cost considerations. In 1972 this program cost $3.9 billion; by 1982 its cost had risen to $14.9 billion (a 60 percent real increase), and by 1989 it will cost approximately $24 billion.[38] Obviously, the costs and liabilities of a military retirement program increase as a growing number of people earn and receive retirement benefits. At the end of fiscal year 1983, for example, there were more retired (319,000) than active (300,000) military officers on the Department of Defense's payroll. Thus, there is an unfunded military retirement cost building up, which by 1982 had exceeded 500 billion dollars.[39] Clearly, this has become a major budget consideration. After Medicaid (which serves nearly 23 million people), the military retirement program (which benefits 1.4 million) is the most expensive of all federal entitlement programs financed exclusively from general revenues. But this is not a new issue. Since 1935, twelve advisory panels or commissions, including several within the DoD, have recommended fundamental changes in the military pension system. During the Reagan administration, Budget Director David Stockman, in a much-publicized moment of candor, described the system as a "scandal."[40]

Unlike Social Security or Civil Service retirement, the military retirement program requires no financial contribution from beneficiaries while they are employed. The entire cost of these large pensions is borne by the taxpayer and, therefore, must be assessed on a cost-benefit basis, relative to the recruiting and retaining of top-flight people for the military by other incentives. In this evaluation it must be recognized that military "retirees" are usually young. The median age at which people begin collecting benefits is 41, and fewer than one-sixth of military pensioners are 65 or older. Perhaps the worst aspect of the military retirement program is that its incentives work against the armed services' manpower needs and military-readiness goals. They encourage the most skilled officers to retire just when they are reaching the peaks of their careers, rather than to continue serving the country. In contrast, Civil Service retirees cannot draw pensions until 55, and then only if they have served 30 years. Those with 20–30 years of service cannot draw their Civil Service benefits until they are 60. In the military, more and more people have been retiring at about 40 years of age, depriving the services of their expertise and collecting retirement pay for the rest of their lives. A lieutenant colonel who retires after 20 years (when retirement pay is 50 percent of base pay) will have an annual pension of $20,500 plus cost-of-living increases (built in by legislation).[41] Thus, these people have an incentive to take the money and get another job (often in the defense industry, where their experience is directly relevant), rather than to stay in the service where their skills could be applied. With the high-technology weapon systems of today, physical prowess is far less important than it once was; therefore, the age of military personnel is less important than their skill and experience.

Since military pay now exceeds the pay for comparable civilian work, and since surveys of recruits indicate that military retirement is low on the list of reasons cited for joining up, the only argument left for the current retirement program is the added incentive for retention of those with 10–19 years' experience. For these people, greater emphasis on professionalism and career advancements, along with adequate compensation, should be sufficient incentives to stay (as they appear to be in the Civil Service). Thus, it is hard to come up with strong arguments for maintaining the current military retirement program.

Revisions should have the objective of providing needed retirement benefits, but simultaneously restraining the costs and (particularly) reversing the incentives for skilled people to leave at the peaks of their careers. Analogies to both industrial and Civil Service programs are applicable here. Unfortunately, these changes will be politically difficult to achieve. The 27 million veterans and 80 million people eligible for veterans' benefits and services constitute a powerful lobby (and include many members of Congress itself). In 1987, a bill to create a cabinet position for veterans' affairs cleared the house by a vote of 399 to 17 even though it was widely recognized that such a bill was bound to significantly increase the cost of veterans' benefits.[42] This issue may well have to wait until it can be addressed as part of a far more encompassing piece of legislation in order to stand the political heat.

As with most defense issues, there are no easy answers to the growing economic, demographic, and political issues in the defense-personnel area. As discussed, the remedies involved such substitutions as women for men, civilians for military personnel, high-tech hardware for manpower, reservists for full-time forces, and a restructured retirement program. Each of these alternatives has significant military, economic, and social implications that are difficult to deal with. The solutions will depend largely on such broad considerations as the condition of the national economy, the mood of the nation, and the geopolitical state of the world. Nonetheless, these issues must be addressed, as they directly affect the nation's future security and economic well-being.

10 Other Countries' Approaches

Consider the approaches to national security of Western European countries (France, the United Kingdom, West Germany, and Sweden), other capitalist countries (Japan and Israel), and the Soviet Union.[1] Significant differences exist with the United States in the ways these countries approach force planning, weapon selection, and defense budgeting, in the ways they acquire weapons, and in their methods of maintaining a defense industrial base.

The objective of this chapter is not to determine whether a particular approach is "better" or "worse." Rather, we must search for strengths and weaknesses in the approaches of these different countries to see if there are some lessons that the United States may be able to adapt to its own unique and desirable form of government and economic system.

Many aspects of these other countries' practices are worthy of investigation, from the far greater efficiency and effectiveness they achieve with stable, long-term budgets to the benefits they gain by recognizing that the defense industrial base is a valued national resource for which the government (as the sole buyer) has explicit responsibility.

Western European Countries

Many similarities, ranging from strategy and weapon selection through manpower problems (with the declining demographics in the draft-age population[2]) exist between the United States and its European allies. They, too, are faced with rising costs of acquiring and maintaining weapons. Christopher Bertram has said of West Germany that "we need to have a 6-percent growth in the defense budget just to sustain what we have."[3] The Europeans are also concerned about the large quantities of conventional systems (of increasingly high quality) that the Soviet Union can deploy against the NATO forces. Thus, they recognize the value of a strategy of "technological superiority," and they spend significant amounts on research and development. (In most cases, the ratio of R&D to production is quite high.[4]) However, in the four crucial areas—weapon-system requirements, budget planning, acquisition organizations and processes, and the defense industry—the United States and the European allies take dramatically different paths. In fact, although there are significant differences among the European countries, it is possible to group them into a "European model" that can be easily contrasted with the "American model."

The growing frustration in the United States with the defense-resource problems described above has resulted in an increasing demand for the adoption of the European approach to the acquisition of weapons.[5] Those who clamor for this change, particularly on Capitol Hill, fail to recognize that a major difference between the American and European approaches lies in the relative roles played by the U.S. Congress and the European parliaments in the defense-resource process. It is not that the European parliaments are disinterested or uninvolved in the major resource decisions associated with national security; rather, the issue is the difference in the type of involvement. In contrast with the annual, detailed, line-by-line review by the U.S. Congress of the DoD's budget, the European parliaments focus on a long-range (usually a five-year) fiscal plan. The intent of this is to make the defense ministries live within the "top lines" of these long-term budgets, but to leave the distribution of the dollars up to the defense ministries. Major weapon-system decisions, in which the parliament again plays a significant role, are the exceptions to the rule. However, even here the role is not that of an annual review but, rather, that of a decision to commit to a program—a decision that, once made, will be supported by the parliament as well as by the defense ministry (unless there are extreme changes in geopolitical or economic conditions). The parliaments still have annual debates on the budgets, but in most cases they are debating the sixth year of a budget rather than (as in the United States) the first year. This shift to a multi-year defense fiscal plan that is adhered to (by both the executive and legislative branches) is one of the biggest changes required in the United States if efficiency and effectiveness is to be achieved. This change would clearly take away a good deal of the program and budget "flexibility" that executive-branch and legislative-branch officials now have, and it would add the requirement for far greater realism in estimating the costs of individual weapons program and in estimating the "out-years" defense budgets—all highly desirable changes. In most cases, the Europeans have fiscal plans that stretch out well beyond the five-year period and allow them to see the financial impact of a future production program when a new development decision is made. As a result, they achieve far greater stability in resource planning and weapons requirements, and therefore they are able to acquire more weapons for the funds available.

The greater stability of the Western European defense resource plan goes hand in hand with a second dramatic difference between the European and American models: a difference in the way the defense industry is viewed. In contrast with the DoD's professed "laissez faire" approach to the defense industry, the European approach is to recognize the value—both to the national security and to the national economy—of a healthy, innovative, and responsive industrial base.[6] The Europeans accept the fact that, owing to the characteristics of defense work (small quantities and high specialization), there can be only a few firms in each segment of the defense industry (perhaps only one or two in some small countries). Yet they recognize that labor stability, R&D funding, lower-tier support, effective profits, and even international competitiveness must be maintained for these firms. Thus, each West European country has a government organization responsible for ensuring the oversight of, and the competitiveness of, its defense industry. Essentially, they each have a "defense industrial strategy." When there is enough domestic volume, competition is maintained. For example, in West Germany two companies are designated as the military computer companies. The R&D and the production are done by them (often under license to a foreign source), and it is clearly recognized that all work in this area will be done by one of these two firms. The two are in continuous competition, and thus have the necessary incentive for pushing new technology to achieve higher quality and lower cost. Even in those countries where the domestic market for a particular product is too small to support multiple sources, the single supplier is still extremely cost-sensitive because of the need to be price-competitive on the export market.[7] Dassault, France's only aircraft firm, produces a low-cost, high-performance military aircraft that is one of the world's most successful (from both a military and an economic viewpoint).[8] Many of Dassault's desirable characteristics are not found in U.S. aircraft companies (e.g., very small design teams, emphasis on incremental improvement of existing designs, minimal paperwork, maximum subcontracting,[9] emphasis on low-cost design for domestic and international reasons, and a very close working relationship with the government). It must be emphasized that all these characteristics exist within a sole-source private-sector defense supplier—but with conscious government involvement largely limited to the macro level, and a hands-off policy at the micro level. (Essentially, the government trusts the firm to do a good job, but provides some oversight to see that things are being done properly and tests extensively to make sure they have been.)

Sweden insists on self-sufficiency, has a small defense market, and yet has developed one of the best defense industries in the world. This is accomplished through long-term budget stability, time-phasing of programs (for the sake of labor stability within the industry), and a conscious attempt to integrate civilian and military industries (to allow for labor absorption during slack periods, and also to make the companies more price-sensitive and even "business-sensitive").[10] If a small country like Sweden can have an efficient and effective defense industry (even without a large share of exports—as is their explicit policy), certainly the United States, with its huge market, should be able to accomplish the same.

This brings us to the third of the broad differences between the American and European models: the organization and the process of acquisition. The first and most obvious difference in this area is the European concept of a single buying agency that is relatively independent (organizationally) of the military services. This contrasts with the American approach of assigning responsibility for the overall acquisition process to the Office of the Secretary of Defense, while program execution (requirements, selection, development, and production of weapon systems) is totally decentralized to the military services. Most European countries moved toward the centralized approach in the 1960s because they believed it would remove duplication of effort, would improve long-range planning and budget control across services and missions, and would achieve more uniformity in the approach to acquisition (including the interface between the government and the defense industry). Additionally, they believed that this would provide the acquisition organization with greater independence from the military services, and thus a greater opportunity to develop a more "professional" acquisition corps. We will return to the question of the applicability of this "centralized agency" approach to the United States later on. However, at this point it is appropriate to note the relative sizes (as shown in table 10.1, in terms of both people and budgets) for

Table 10.1
Relative sizes of acquisition activities.

	France	Sweden	West Germany	U.K.	Single U.S. agency (hypothetical)
People	30,000	3,132	19,000	35,000	539,400
Acquisition budget	$7.0B	$1.6B	$5.5B	$11.8B	$148.2B

the four European countries and what an equivalent single agency in the United States would be composed of.[11]

The size of a single U.S. defense acquisition agency would be staggering—more than ten times the size of the largest European agency. In fact, each European country's entire acquisition agency is smaller than the acquisition activity of the U.S. Army, Navy or Air Force alone. Thus, the question often arises as to whether an organization so large could achieve the same benefits that the Europeans derive from centralization. Yet, at a minimum, the United States must strive for ways to achieve the advantages of the "European model."

One other major distinction between the European approach to acquisition and the American is in the area of testing and evaluation. Since the European model assumes that a program, once approved by the parliament, has the full commitment of the government, the primary objective of testing and evaluation is to satisfy the military needs and to get the system into production as soon as possible. The Europeans have extremely thorough testing programs, but the testing is a "team effort," with close cooperation among the government procurement organization, the military, and the contractor.[12] In the United States, testing and evaluation is viewed (particularly by Congress) as a decision-making resource—the decision being whether to go ahead with the system. This philosophical contrast makes a very significant difference in terms of the relative cooperative nature of the development program, as well as the stability of the effort. It does not mean, of course, that unsatisfactory systems would be put into the field.

In broader terms, an important shift is taking place in the European approach to national security. In spite of their nationalism, the Europeans are gradually drifting toward more jointness in defense planning and in the development of weapons. Often the first steps have been bilateral (e.g., between West Germany and France, or between France and the United Kingdom), but the trend toward jointness is clearly there. They include joint brigades, joint military maneuvers,[13] joint R&D,[14] joint space programs, and many examples of joint development of next-generation weapon systems (including aircraft and missiles). Initially, these steps have been taken more for political than for economic reasons, and nationalism has often canceled out potential economic advantages. However, in the long run, these joint efforts are likely to lead to more compromising of differing national military "requirements" and to a more effective distribution of the industrial work (and therefore to greater efficiency). In many ways, the need for multinational programs in Europe mirrors the need for multi-service programs in the United States.

In attempting to answer the question of how well the Europeans do in comparison with the United States, we must recognize that, although their approaches to weaponry differ, both the Europeans and the Americans achieve the objectives they set out to realize. Whereas the Americans emphasize the objective of maximum performance in each individual weapon (and, thus, one would measure success by comparing American systems with others on the criterion of performance), the Europeans set out to minimize cost and risk in order to achieve an acceptable defense posture within their limited resources and, simultaneously, to achieve an advanced technology capability and a stable labor force in their industrial sector. Thus, one would expect to see lower-cost, lower-performance systems coming out of the European model—and a detailed investigation comparing aircraft-system developments in the United States versus the four countries of Europe confirmed this expectation.[15] A large number of U.S. aircraft that became operational between 1950 and 1980 were compared with comparable aircraft developed both by single nations in Europe and by multinational European efforts. The results were analyzed and compared in terms of schedule, cost, and performance. The data showed the United States developed its aircraft in approximately two years' less time than the Europeans, but with higher investments in R&D.[16] They also showed that the multi-nation European programs took approximately one year longer than the single-nation European programs; however, this longer term was also found when U.S. single-service programs were compared with U.S. multi-service programs.[17]

Figure 10.1 shows a comparison of aircraft costs (using the method-

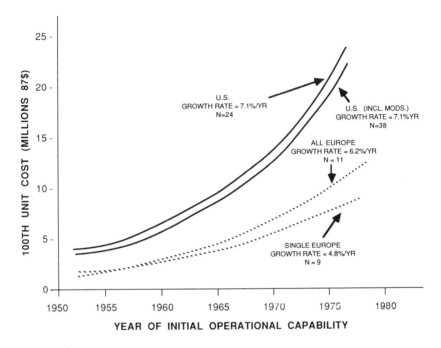

Figure 10.1
Cost comparison of U.S. and European fighter and attack aircraft for the years 1950–1980.

ology described in chapter 6). For the United States, cost growth is shown for both first-of-series aircraft and modification programs (e.g., the modification of the F-4A into the F-4D). For the European case, data are plotted for both single-nation and multi-nation ("all-Europe") developments. For consistency, R&D funds were excluded, and, owing to the smaller production quantities of the European programs, learning curves were used to normalize all data to the same quantity.[18]

Other studies have found that the actual cost growth rate for European aircraft is even higher than figure 10.1 shows, in some cases going to over 8 percent per year.[19] However, there is general agreement that, at any given time, European weapon systems have consistently cost less. This can be explained by the fact that the United States often strives for dramatic leaps forward in the "state of the art." As in the cases of the aircraft referred to as "high-mix" (i.e., state-of-the-art)

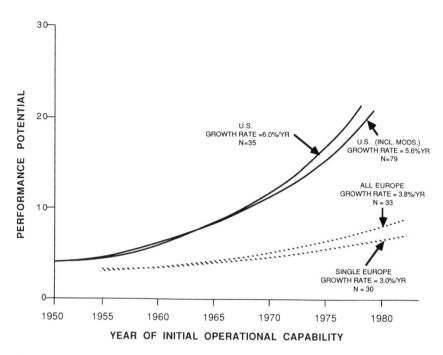

Figure 10.2
Performance comparisons of U.S. and European fighter and attack aircraft for the years
1950–1980.

systems in chapter 6, this significantly raises the cost of a weapon. The
cost of U.S. systems using proven technology ("low mix") are much
closer to those of the European systems—as would be expected, since
the Europeans have used proven technology in all their new systems.
The results of the U.S. emphasis on performance are clearly evident in
figure 10.2.

If one were to compare the data in figures 10.1 and 10.2 and plot them
as a function of performance achieved per unit of cost spent, the results
would show that the European and U.S. achievements are almost identical. The only significant difference is that the United States, because
of far larger production quantities, is able to achieve higher performance per unit cost with its modification programs. The fact that the
United States and the European countries achieve quite comparable
performance per unit cost while stressing very different things probably

means that each approach has some advantages and disadvantages. The European countries can more effectively utilize their advances in industrial technology to improve the performance of their weapons; the United States can learn to reduce costs. However, the fact that both have had costs rising faster than performance means that they both must make significant changes.

The United States might choose to emulate the following six characteristics of the European system:

· *Strong, centralized decision-making—on long-term budgets and programs as well as on procurement policy.* This comes from the European approach of a centralized, independent acquisition agency. It could be achieved in the United States by greatly strengthening the Office of the Secretary of Defense and the role of the Chairman of the Joint Chiefs of Staff. As was discussed above, this would be fully consistent with the intent of the Packard Commission and the Goldwater-Nichols Defense Reorganization Act. It means giving greater authority over all acquisition, resource, program, and policy decisions (such as weapons requirements, weapon-system selection, weapon-system cost, and development milestones) to the Under Secretary of Defense for Acquisition. It also means fully empowering the Vice-Chairman of the Joint Chiefs of Staff to assume a major role in integrating the services' budgets and weapons requirements, thereby ensuring that a "joint" military perspective would be realized. These changes would allow the United States to achieve a significantly greater degree of central control and integration of strategy, resources, and policy—something the Europeans achieve with a single buying agency. However, there should not be a centralization of day-to-day program management, nor is a centralized acquisition organization required. The European model of acquisition emphasizes decentralized execution and places the responsibility for a program with the program's manager. Such decentralization of execution can be accomplished via the services' acquisition organizations, but only if they are willing to delegate authority to the program managers.

· *Long-term (multi-year) stability in programs and budgets.* As was discussed above, program stability can dramatically improve efficiency of resource utilization. This objective is achieved in the European system by the close agreement and cooperation, on long-term budgeting and program decisions, between the parliament and the Minister of Defense. Thus, in order for the European model to be applied to the United States, a dramatic change is required in the way Congress and the executive branch deal with the multi-year U.S. defense program. Even a move to a two-year defense budget would be a significant step forward. Congress will be acting irresponsibly if it doesn't take such a step.

- *Specification by the services of "mission" (performance) require-ments rather than "weapon" (design) requirements.* The European central acquisition agencies have responsibilities that cover multiple-service efforts. Consequently, they are free to look at alternative approaches to solving military mission needs (thus avoiding service parochialism). The United States must change its "requirements pro-cess" from one that stresses "the next airplane" to one that discusses the military mission need (e.g., destroying an enemy airfield) and allows nontraditional solutions to evolve—all the way through the prototype-demonstration phase. This too has to be a major function of the Under Secretary of Defense for Acquisition. His major concern must be the early portion of a weapon system's evolution: require-ments, preliminary design, and weapon selection. His office is inde-pendent of the military services and, therefore, must ensure that all approaches have been appropriately explored and that broad consid-erations of national-security policy have been taken into account. From that point on, the services could then execute the program, within an agreed-to "baseline" of performance, cost, and schedule.

- *Early emphasis on cost as a design requirement and on long-term "affordability" of weapon systems.* A major difference in the "require-ments" process is that in Europe "program cost" is a greater factor in development decisions than in the United States. It is essential for the United States to make cost a similarly important consideration, since the quantity of weapons to be procured is directly related to their individual costs. Thus, instead of having military requirements solely based on a weapon's performance, the United States needs to specify the required number of weapons (and, therefore, the unit cost) as an equal requirement. By placing such early emphasis on "affordability," the European model forces the system to make the quantity-versus-quality, or cost-versus-performance, tradeoffs that are necessary in the preliminary design phase. It also introduces the fact that cost is a

technical-feasibility issue. Finally, the stability of the system requires
that costs be realistically estimated (including any necessary margins
for risk). Currently, the U.S. acquisition process provides incentives
to underestimate costs and to focus primarily on technical questions.
To have the United States shift to a strong emphasis on "affordability"
would again require that the Under Secretary of Defense for Acquisition provide the independent assessment of affordability that is offered by the centralized acquisition agency in the European model.

· *Professionalism throughout the acquisition community.* The European approach promotes professionalism through personnel continuity and stability. In a desirable U.S. model, the services' acquisition
executives should have the clear responsibility for promoting such
professionalism throughout all the services' acquisition communities
(military and civilian); the Secretary of Defense should be responsible
for seeing to it that political appointees have defense experience.

· *Explicit consideration of the industrial base in acquisition decisions
and budget planning.* The Europeans address the industrial base directly in their defense-planning and acquisition-management processes. Considerations such as the timing of new weapon programs,
the maintenance of competitive innovation among firms, the assurance of domestic sources for critical items, and the support of advanced manufacturing technology should explicitly be part of the U.S.
acquisition planning process. Furthermore, the Europeans recognize
that, as their countries' sole buyers of defense equipment, they have
a responsibility to worry about the health of their defense industries.
Thus, procurement policy, profit policy, cash flow, and risk are viewed
as tools to utilize in fulfilling their responsibility to maintain a healthy,
yet competitive, industrial base. For the United States to apply this
aspect of the European model would mean that the Department of
Defense would have to explicitly bring industrial-base considerations
into both its major acquisition decisions and its resource-allocation
decisions.

   In each of the above six areas there are *lessons* that the United States
can learn from the European model without *copying* the Europeans.
Rather, than copy, the United States should adopt some of the desired
characteristics in order to improve its overall "way of doing defense
business."

Japan and Israel

Two other important, though perhaps extreme, cases should be considered next. Japan is a nation whose economy is focused on the civilian sector and which had a long post-World War II history of trying to keep its defense expenditures under 1 percent of its gross national product. Israel has been forced by its neighbors to be defense-oriented, and has traditionally spent over 35 percent of its GNP on defense. Each of these countries has a strong capitalistic bias, a democratic political system, and extensive economic and military links to the United States. Perhaps surprisingly, each of them has an approach to defense that shares many characteristics with the "European model" but is tailored to the national interest and the culture.

Consider first Japan. With an increasingly powerful civilian economy, by the end of 1988 Japan was spending more on defense (measured in dollars) than any other nation in the world except the United States and the Soviet Union.[20] The Japanese plan to increase defense expenditures to well above 1 percent of their GNP.[21] As in all of their economy, they are taking a long-term perspective (with a continued emphasis on engineering education)[22] and are seeking long-term budget stability through a five-year plan that is relatively stable and is reviewed every three years.[23] They stress in their defense industrial sector the same characteristics found in their civilian sector: high volume (with a manufacturing-process orientation in engineering), low cost, and high quality.[24]

The Ministry of International Trade and Industry (MITI) will have a major role in steering Japan toward the desired industrial structure, striving for smooth transitions as technologies and products change.[25] One of the main reasons the MITI "works" is because the top people from the top universities are encouraged to take on the challenging role of "representing industry within the government and representing the government outside to industry."[26] Also, it is clear to the government people that they are doing "indicative" planning, rather than the highly restrictive "input-output" planning of the Soviet model. As in Europe and Israel, senior people from MITI will later go to work in industry and will, therefore, help improve government-industry relations— which is important in trying to "steer" major sectors of a nation's economy. In the United States such actions would run into the obstacles posed by laws intended to stop the "revolving door" between government and industry.

Perhaps one of the most important characteristics of the Japanese model is the fierce domestic competition that takes place before a Japanese industry goes international.[27] The few firms selected as the "likely candidates" receive initial government funding and full support from the Japanese banks, but they go at one another with a ferocity that hones their capabilities for the subsequent international competition. This "limited competition" (limited to only a few firms, but in no way limited in terms of its fierceness) stresses both quality and cost. The objective is not to make a profit but to get a significant market share in order to move down the learning curve. Failure in such competitions is taken very seriously; individuals have even been known to commit suicide as a result.[28] The availability of alternative sources makes it unnecessary to "bail out" failing firms. There is every reason to expect that the Japanese will apply these practices to their defense sector.

The Japanese are already ahead of the United States in many areas of electronics, and have been obtaining more and more U.S. patents.[29] Thus, one can expect that they will begin to export weapons as their defense industry builds up. In fact, a 1982 study conducted by a Japanese research center concluded that if Japan participated in the international arms trade it would control 40 percent of the market for military electronics, 46 percent of the military automotive market, 25–30 percent of the aerospace market, and 60 percent of the shipbuilding market.[30]

When former prime minister Nakasone was director general of Japan's defense agency, he published a defense industrial policy[31] (titled "Basic Policy for Development and Production of Defense Equipment") the five goals of which were these: to maintain Japan's industrial base as a key factor in national security, to acquire equipment from Japan's domestic R&D and production efforts, to use civilian industries, to have long-term plans for R&D and production, and to introduce "the principle of competition" into defense production. There are important lessons here for the United States: the desirability of industrial responsiveness as a part of basic military strategy, the stress on domestic R&D and production, the long-term perspective on resource commitments, and the introduction of continuous competition in the defense industry.

Perhaps the most striking difference between the Japanese model and the American one is Japan's emphasis on using civilian technology in military products and on adopting technology from military products in the civilian sector. As was discussed in chapter 8, this is best done by having the same people, in engineering and manufacturing operations, involved in both civilian and military activities. Mitsubishi clearly made good use of its experience producing the American F-15 fighter plane when it developed and produced the "Diamond" business jet. Similarly, the Japanese-developed protective paint (against electronic waves) used to improve TV reception in high-rise buildings can also be used in the development of stealth technology.

Essentially, the Japanese will select some technologies that have both military uses and significant commercial applications, and will focus on these when applying their five-point industrial strategy. Three such technologies they have already selected are computers, robotics, and aircraft.[32] Owing to their long-term orientation, the focus of their investments in defense will be on product and process R&D, particularly at the dual-use levels of the industry (i.e., materials, components, and manufacturing technology). One way of encouraging this dual-use approach, which the Japanese have found quite effective, is to have the industry pay for a significant share of the military R&D. This greatly encourages them to have the results of the R&D be applicable in both the civilian and military sectors. This technique will not work in the United States until the desired civilian-military integration has taken place at the factory level.

The United States does not have a MITI, nor should it. However, many of the characteristics of the Japanese model might prove highly advantageous if they were to be Americanized and applied to the U.S. defense acquisition system.

Turning to Israel, we find a country that is clearly defense-oriented. Most of the leaders of Israel's industry and government are former military leaders, and the whole nation is defense-conscious. Originally, Israel was largely dependent upon the French for its military equipment, but after the 1967 war the French stopped all arms shipments. The Israelis learned a bitter lesson about dependency and vowed that their defense sector would henceforth be self-sufficient. Since then, they have built up an impressive capability to develop and produce military equipment. They have a very modern tank plant producing a tank of their own design (and have even helped improve the U.S. M-60 tank by supplying lower-profile cupolas). They have a very modern aircraft plant producing advanced fighter planes of their own design. They are designing and producing missiles, ships, and guns that are equal to any in the world; and they are ahead of many advanced nations in electronic countermeasures and remotely piloted vehicles (as has been demonstrated in numerous Middle East conflicts). With such a small market, there is usually only one supplier of each type of critical equipment; but these firms are kept price-sensitive through continuous competition with alternative sources around the world. There are strong ties between the Ministry of Defense, the Ministry of Commerce, and the private sector. The government has clear responsibility for the health, the innovativeness, and the responsiveness of the defense industry. And Israel has the world's highest per-capita percentage of people with advanced degrees in the natural sciences and in engineering.[33]

The Israeli experience clearly demonstrates that, if properly scaled, managed, and planned, a viable and advanced defense R&D and production industry can be maintained with a very small market. The Israelis' problem is that they have allowed their defense sector to dominate their economy and have not integrated it with their civilian sector. Thus, they have not been able to achieve the economic growth that might otherwise accompany their advanced-technology capability. The lesson here for the United States is that, if we are to take full advantage of the $170 billion or more that we spend on weapons each year, we need to focus on using a significant part of those dollars to also help in the civilian sector.

The Soviet Union

The Soviet Union has consistently spent about 12 percent of its GNP on defense. Naturally, the Soviets' approach to defense is conditioned by their political system and their history. Many of the senior government leaders come from the military, and the country has historically had a security orientation. Thus, the defense industry receives priority in the allocation of manpower and materials,[34] and is the high-status area for scientists, engineers, and managers (in contrast with the U.S. case). Because of the longevity of the leaders in their positions, military planning has far greater stability—clearly an asset, from an economic-efficiency perspective.

The Ministry of Defense and the General Staff are institutions of great political power and have a monopoly on military expertise; there is no Central Committee Department to monitor the military activities of the Ministry or the General Staff,[35] and no continuous adjustment of defense programs by a counterpart of the U.S. Congress.

This stability of planning not only runs through the five-year fiscal plans and the military strategy; it also influences the weapons-acquisition program—even down to the R&D level. Stable budgets and constant manpower levels for the research institutions and design bureaus result in a regular progression of designs and prototypes, and also allow the Soviet research and design bureaus to maintain and develop a corps of experts (in contrast with the constant shifting of manpower with the cycles in the U.S. defense industry).[36]

Because of the emphasis on planning and on the meeting of targets, the Soviet design bureaus routinely *overestimate* (by about 30 percent or more) to cover unexpected future costs and potential schedule slippage.[37] Thus, their cost and schedule estimates become self-fulfilling prophecies. They rarely overrun and usually meet their schedules; however, the overconservative targets result in a significant cost penalty.

The high quantity and quality of the products the Soviets are producing are an indication that they have a relatively well-developed defense industry.[38] Perhaps one of its most distinguishing characteristics is the separation of research, development, and production. Weapon systems are developed in "development centers" under team leaders who have long periods of continuity. These development centers are technically controlled by the "research establishments," which publish "rules" defining what designs and equipment can be used. The new developments are then tested (independently) by the research centers, and the senior military and political figures then decide which of the various competitive developments should be put into production, and where.

This system has a number of important characteristics. The development laboratories develop a significant number of alternative systems (often more than in the United States). Thus, there is more "competition" for the production designs. However, it is a different form of competition—one between system designers. It might be better described as "professional rivalry" and/or "bureaucratic empire building." Essentially, the designers are competing for funds and for professional status rather than for specific contracts.[39]

Controlling the designs and products allowed in the development centers achieves far more standardization than is achieved in the United States, and the guaranteed employment in the Soviet system creates a great deal of pressure for follow-on systems. Thus, defense production is far less prone than in the United States to the "feast or famine" syndrome. In fact, the Soviet defense sector shows all the signs of strong bureaucratic "continuity"[40] (with the desirable features of stability and standardization, and the very undesirable feature of resistance to change).

Separating development and production makes it possible for a number of development projects (by different "R&D firms") to be carried on in the same production plant and increases the overall efficiency of the production plants. Also, this allows development to be a "business" unto itself, rather than just something with the short-term objective of getting a follow-on production program.

In reality, the Soviet system develops ties between the development community and the production community, with certain plants tending to take work from the same development centers—which facilitates the transitions between phases. They have also developed other techniques, such as personnel transfers, for smoothing these transitions. The American defense industry often argues that transitions from one firm to another are very difficult to achieve (even though American companies often do development in one part of the country and production in another); however, recently the United States has been solving the problem of firm-to-firm transition successfully in the case of competitive second-sourcing, as was discussed in chapter 6.

In spite of the separation of development and production, the Soviet system tends to develop designs that will be easy to produce. This is achieved partly by the Soviet incentive system, which awards the developer half of his total bonus the first year after the system is in production, thus encouraging him to both win the competition for production and design a system that is readily producible. Also, because of the lower technology in Soviet production plants, designs are made less demanding in terms of tolerances and materials. The net effect of all of this is that a Soviet design that is intended to achieve performance similar to that of a U.S. system might cost considerably less to build than the comparable U.S. system—if both were built in a U.S. plant.[41] An example of a high-performance, low-cost system is the Soviet Mig-25 aircraft. In 1977, Arthur Alexander wrote the following about this aircraft:

It does not require advanced electronics, exotic materials, precise manufacturing techniques, or complex structures. . . . It used stainless steel and aluminum as the primary air frame materials, instead of synthetic materials, as used by the U.S. Rivets were left unground (except in aerodynamically critical areas) and welding was said to be crude but adequate. Larger engines were used to overcome the drag penalties. The radar, though based on technology that was out of date by American standards, is one of the most powerful ever seen in an aircraft and therefore less vulnerable to jamming. The overall Mig-25 has been described by aerospace analysts as "unsurpassed in the ease of maintenance and servicing," "a masterpiece of standardization," and "one of the most cost-effective combat investments in history."[42]

Because of their historical experiences, as well as the planned nature of their economy, the Soviets place considerable emphasis on industrial-preparedness planning. One aspect of this planning is the fact that the Soviets often combine, in one plant, the manufacture of civilian and military products (for example, railroad cars and aircraft). This allows greater surge capability (in terms of available skilled workers) whenever an increase is required, and it also provides for the absorption of defense workers during slack periods of defense production.

The Soviet system does have some severe disadvantages. Though the defense industry is undoubtedly more effective than the civilian industry, it is still grossly inefficient. A good deal of this inefficiency must be attributed to both the industrial and political structures. The centrally administered Soviet economy tends to greatly discourage technological innovation.[43] By U.S. standards, it is rigid and constrained. The Soviets emphasize design continuity, they continue to use the same designers, they require that all designs conform to detailed plans and regulations, they have high barriers to entry for new organizations in established fields, they have large penalties for failure (thus tending toward conservatism), and they tend to manage R&D in an extremely risk-averse manner. Because their economy is planned on a detailed input-output basis (part by part, product by product, factory by factory, and so on), any small change (for example, a new part or a new material) causes significant revision to the overall plan, and thus is greatly discouraged. Simple changes in the budget are greatly resisted, because of their impact on the overall plan. Also, the unreliability of the suppliers greatly discourages the introduction of new parts or new suppliers once a reliable source has been found. Perhaps Gorbachev's introduction of more market forces into the Soviet system will help in this regard, but it is likely to take many, many years and may well face insurmountable obstacles.

One dramatic difference between the Soviet Union and the United States is the extreme, almost obsessive secrecy in connection with anything related to defense in the Soviet Union. This does help to prevent data from leaking to a potential adversary, and it does reduce "meddling" (not only by the press and people in other government agencies, but also by senior officials within the Ministry of Defense who do not have the specific "need to know"). However, it discourages technology transfer within the defense industry (and certainly between the defense sector and the civilian sector). Also, there is a very low level of "accountability" to management, government, and the public.

The "lessons" the United States might learn from observing the Soviet system might be these: Stress producibility in designs; don't ignore the civilian sector, particularly in terms of the dual-use demands that the military places on the civilian sector; appreciate the value of program and industrial stability, but develop institutional mechanisms to prevent retardation of innovation; integrate civilian and military production operations; and make industrial preparedness a key part of the nation's security posture. Finally, recognize that some of the inefficiencies in the U.S. system are "worth paying for." These include the advantages of democracy and freedom—both often inefficient, but worth any cost.

11 The Changes That Are Needed

Today's worldwide military situation is one of strategic nuclear parity between the superpowers and considerable imbalance in conventional forces. The conventional imbalance favors the Warsaw Pact over NATO in any European scenario. or in a conflict between the superpowers in an area such as Iran. Furthermore, the armed forces of the United States are not well prepared for regional conflicts; that type of warfare has traditionally received low priority from the Department of Defense.

Avoiding large-scale nuclear war must clearly be the highest U.S. priority. However, since the explosion of a single nuclear weapon (whether it came from the Soviet Union, the United States, or a Third World country) has a high potential to escalate to an all-out nuclear war, the United States must do everything in its power to prevent the use of even one nuclear weapon. To be able to prevent a regional conflict or a Central European war between the superpowers from escalating to a nuclear war, it is essential that the United States strengthen its capability for fighting and containing conventional conflicts. This is an enormous challenge, particularly in a period of level, or perhaps even shrinking, defense budgets. The record to date suggests that the DoD is not prepared to meet this challenge. Force structure and weapon selection have been driven primarily by the interests of the individual services rather than by the idea of an effective integrated force; resource planning and budgeting have been turbulent, and the instability has caused considerable waste; weapons cost are high and continue to rise; the time needed to develop and deploy systems is long and continues to grow; and the defense industrial base is getting more inefficient and ineffective, thus driving costs and quality still further in the adverse direction. Overall, the United States is getting fewer and fewer weapon systems, at high cost—and these are not the most militarily effective weapons, though their individual performance is very high. The data show that the United States would need at least a 5 percent per year real growth in the defense budget just to stay even. Since such continuous growth is not in the cards,[1] changes in "the way the DoD does its business" are clearly required if the United States is to maintain its national-security posture.

The objective of these changes must be the establishment of an affordable yet effective national-security posture. To be affordable, it must recognize that America's security position, as President Eisenhower stated, rests "not upon the military establishment alone but rather on two pillars—military strength . . . and economic strength based upon a flourishing economy."[2] Valid societal and economic demands on the nation's resources will require that the "affordability" of conventional military equipment be addressed by means other than continual increases in the defense budget. In addition, the need for a balanced national-security posture undoubtedly requires increases in military capability at the lower end of the conflict spectrum (i.e., in the realm of regional conflicts)—perhaps even at the expense of additional strategic capability, as long as deterrence can be maintained. Arms control can contribute much to advancing the objective of achieving a balanced force (at the strategic, conventional, and regional levels), not only by improving stability but also, simultaneously, by reducing the quantities required. However, here one must keep clearly in mind the third of the important considerations for an effective national-security posture: credibility. "Promises" in the arms-control arena are not enough.

Earlier Attempts and the Changing Environment

A more affordable, balanced, and credible national-security posture requires significant reforms of the system. But reforming this large and bureaucratic system has historically been very difficult. A look at the post-World War II era shows at least five major efforts at reforming various aspects of the system.[3] In the 1950s, President Eisenhower, supported by a large group of historians and political scientists (emphasizing military strategy), attempted to unify the military services. When he instituted the Joint Chiefs of Staff and the Operational Commanders, President Eisenhower intended that there would be an overall integration of strategy, operational plans, force structure, and weapons evolution. The separate services would remain the providers of the forces needed by the combat commands, but would not determine what to provide or how those forces would be employed. Eisenhower's objectives were not achieved. The individual services still control the budgets, the weapons requirements, the personnel assignments, and the promotions. Thus, the services control the system.

The second major reform was introduced by Defense Secretary Robert McNamara in the early 1960s. Supported by a group of systems analysts, a conscious effort was made to introduce cost-effectiveness considerations and overall long-term resource planning into the decisions on strategy, tactics, and weapons selection. The famous "Planning, Programming and Budget System" (PPBS) was the principal legacy of this era.

In the mid-1960s and the early 1970s, significant efforts were made in the direction of arms control. Now that the Soviets had a substantial nuclear capability and a mutual interest in limiting the arms race, the arms controllers were pushing to make arms control an equal partner with military preparedness in American defense policy. However, arms control was not integrated into the country's national-security posture; rather, it was thought of as an independent effort that was essentially in conflict with military considerations.

The fourth reform activity was initiated by Deputy Secretary of Defense David Packard, who attempted to get better control over the big weapon-system programs by instituting more centralized management and requiring the services to come to the Secretary of Defense to have these programs reviewed at each of their major milestones.[4] This was, at first, a strong management tool, but it deteriorated over time until it became largely a "rubber stamp" for the services' management of the programs.

Finally, in regard to the budget process itself, Congress became more and more frustrated over its inability to manage defense resources. By the late 1980s, there were four major stages in the review process (budget committees, authorization committees, appropriation committees, and the sequestration process). Congress was spending almost all its time addressing budget issues—and was not doing a good job of it.

The aggregate effect of these five changes has been dramatic, and each of them has had a very positive effect. Nonetheless, it cannot be stated that they succeeded. The cynic, of course, would say that change in government is never easy; and there is a long history to back up this view. Niccolo Machiavelli wrote in 1513, in *The Prince*, that

. . . there is nothing more difficult to take in hand, more perilous to conduct, or more uncertain in its success, than to take the lead in the introduction of a new order of things. Because the innovator has for enemies all those who have done well under the old conditions, and lukewarm defenders in those who may do well under the new. This coolness arises partly from fear of the opponents, who have the laws on their side, and partly from the incredulity of men, who do not readily believe in new things until they have had a long experience of them. Thus, it happens that whenever those who are hostile have the opportunity to attack they do it like partisans, whilst the others defend lukewarmly. . . .

The Department of Defense is perhaps one of the most resistant of organizations to change.[5] Any attempts to reform the DoD must recognize two important points: that it will take a significant time, because of the cultural resistance to change; and that a reform will not succeed until it can be incorporated into the military structure. Reform will have to come from the top down, and will require continued, aggressive leadership and an internal "selling" job over an extended period of time. A successful fundamental change must have three components: the *analytic* component (focusing on the deficiencies to be corrected), the *prescriptive* component (setting forth the objectives of the change and its general characteristics), and the *strategic* component (dealing with the strategy and tactics for the process of change.[6] These characteristics, combined with leadership in Congress, the executive branch, and the military, would result in the success, over an extended period of time, of the needed reforms in the efficiency and the effectiveness with which the nation utilizes its defense resources.

Fortunately, during the 1980s, significant steps were taken toward such needed reforms. There is considerable optimism that, if these efforts can be intensified, it may well be possible to realize the needed changes by the early years of the next century. The specific grounds for optimism are these: In 1981 certain members of Congress formed a widely accepted "military reform caucus." That same year, General David Jones (then Chairman of the Joint Chiefs of Staff) and General Edward Meyer (then Chief of Staff of the Army) both spoke out on the need for reform of the Joint Chiefs of Staff. In 1983, Archie Barrett's book *Reappraising Defense Organization* was published, and it was followed, in 1985, by a "staff report" on the same subject to the Senate Committee on Armed Services.[7] Unfortunately, while these broad structural reforms focusing on the military organization and the need for unification were being proposed, the newspapers were filled with stories of overpriced coffee pots, toilet seats, and hammers; as a result, the defense-reform bills that came out of Congress during the mid-1980s focused on "waste, fraud, and abuse" and frequently pulled both Congress' and executive branch's attention away from the needed basic changes.

To bring attention back to the broader issues, President Reagan established the Blue Ribbon Commission on Defense Management, headed by David Packard. This commission's first set of recommendations, presented on March 1, 1986, called for a major overhaul of the acquisition system, citing structural problems "far costlier" than the well-publicized coffee pots and toilet seats.[8] Packard stated at a White House ceremony that the implementation of the commission's recommendations could slash tens of billions of dollars from the annual defense budget. In response, President Reagan pledged to quickly adopt the panel's recommendations, "even if they run counter to the will of the entrenched bureaucracies and special interests," and issued a directive to the DoD to implement the commission's findings. The commission then followed up this initial acquisition report with similar reports calling for a new Planning, Programming, Budgeting System, a major reorganization of the Joint Chiefs of Staff and the unified commands, and significant changes in the government-industry relationship. Perhaps most important, at the end of the Packard Commission's deliberations, President Reagan asked David Packard to come back to him in one year and report on the progress in implementation by the DoD.

At the same time, Congress happened to be working on a bill to implement the earlier recommendations of the above-mentioned staff report. The Packard Commission's findings were incorporated into this bill.[9] Thus, unlike the recommendations of many other commissions and studies, these had a chance to "catch on" because of their support in Congress and the White House and because of the widespread recognition of the need for these changes.

In 1986 the Goldwater-Nichols Bill was passed, which incorporated many of the changes proposed in the congressional staff report and in the Packard Commission report. At the time, Senator Goldwater commented that this was the most significant thing he had done in all his years in the senate.[10] (In fact, it was the first major reorganization of the DoD since Eisenhower's in 1958.) This bill was followed in subsequent years by a series of amendments to the Defense Appropriations Bills that initiated dramatic changes on both the military side and the procurement side.

With the president's directive to follow the Packard Commission's recommendations and the legislation, the DoD had no choice but to react. The implementation was further reinforced when Frank Carlucci, a former member of the Packard Commission, was made Secretary of Defense. Surprisingly, the reforms were further helped along by the dramatic change in the defense budget that took place near the end of the Reagan administration. The fact that the five-year plan needed to be totally revised as a result of the leveling off of the budget forced Secretary Carlucci to decide whether to take the traditional approach of stretching out every program whenever the dollars required it (and thus raising their prices significantly) or to cancel some programs and try to keep the rest of them stable and efficient. Beginning with the budget for fiscal year 1989, Secretary Carlucci properly took the latter approach.[11] Carlucci, and the new Under Secretary for Acquisition, Robert Costello, also began to fight off the attacks on the defense industry that had been taking place during the "waste, fraud, and abuse" era, and moved toward a more natural, more businesslike buyer-seller relationship between government and industry.[12]

While these changes were being initiated, a significant study of national-security strategy for the 21st century was completed by a commission that was headed by then Assistant Secretary of Defense Fred Iklé and included many former defense officials and strategists as well as such luminaries as Henry Kissinger and Zbigniew Brzezinski. This commission concluded[13] that a major shift in the national-security strategy of the United States was required. They called for a far greater emphasis on meeting the threats of regional conflicts, including limited, non-nuclear attacks by the Soviet Union in the Persian Gulf or in other areas far from NATO's Central European front. They stated that a massive Soviet-bloc attack on Central Europe or an all-out Soviet nuclear attack on the United States was "much less probable than other forms of conflict." They went on to note that in a constrained-budget environment the United States may have to accept a greater risk of the unlikely large-scale attacks in order to reduce the risk of the more probable conflicts.[14] Finally, they recommended that about $12 billion per year be spent on preparing for low-intensity conflicts (about 4 percent of the defense budget), and that equipment be especially designed for such conflicts.[15]

Thus, efforts have been underway to build a consensus, and in some cases to take actual initial steps, for the implementation of many of the recommendations made in this book.

Congress is the one major institution that has escaped attention and pressure for reform. As Senator Goldwater stated upon his retirement, "If Congress can fix the Pentagon, it can clean up its own mess."[16] The issues to be addressed here include the multi-year defense budget; the need for Congress to address the broad policy issues, not the detailed "line items" of the defense budget; and the need to force Congress to reform its procedures so that senators and representatives will be encouraged to address defense issues on their merits rather than entirely on the basis of their constituents' local interests. Some members of Congress have argued for these reforms, but to date the changes have been slow in coming. An affordable yet effective defense posture requires "gutsy" political actions by the Congress as well as by the executive branch.

Strategy, Selection of Weapons, and Budget Reforms

Not only does a significant mismatch exist between the stated national-security strategy of the United States and the forces needed to implement that strategy; there is also a significant mismatch between the resources required to bring these two areas closer and the resources that are likely to be available in the future. Historically, the basic approach has been to assume a "linear" relationship between a strategy statement and the resultant force structure. The idea was to state a national-security strategy, assess the current forces, and then request the funds and new weapons to bring the two together. Unfortunately, since there are never enough funds to fill the gap, the assumption is to simply accept the mismatch and "buy the needed systems in the future." The reality, however, is that we will never get there. And, thus, we go on, year after year, with the existing mismatches and the frustrations, with neither an established intellectual framework for force planning nor the recognition that other issues besides pure "strategy" drive national-security considerations (e.g., domestic politics[17] and the budget levels set annually by the president and the Congress). Additionally, the long time period between the initial decision to develop and deploy a new weapon system and the actual full fielding (often more than 15 years) means that, even if we did a perfect job of matching strategy, forces, and resources, the world would undoubtedly have changed enough during that time that our strategy would be obsolete.

Addressing this critical issue requires numerous significant procedural and organizational changes, as well as basic "cultural" changes in the way in which the overall force planning process takes place. First, it must be recognized that the United States, like all nations, will be resource-limited in the future, and that a realistic estimate of the dollars that will be available, over a relatively long period, is required to place an "affordability" constraint on the strategy, as well as on the selection of weapons. It must be recognized that a resource-constrained strategy yields different forces than one gets by starting from an unconstrained strategy and stepping down to force planning, as we have traditionally done. Similarly, to acknowledge that today there is a wide distance between our desired strategy and our available forces and resources means that we are not in a position to do incremental analysis (the basic budget approach that defense goes through in its annual budget exercise); rather, we must step back and develop a new strategic consensus that would result in an affordable, balanced, and yet credible national-security posture.[18] Such a reevaluation is bound to recognize the need for increased conventional forces in Europe (or control of conventional arms) and increased emphasis on readiness for regional conflicts. It is also likely to result in significantly different emphases on the types of weapon systems and the force mixes that can be achieved within a nominal annual defense budget of $300 billion.

The second broad "cultural" change that needs to be made is this: If the military services are going to be fighting together, it only makes sense to do far more integrated planning, budgeting, and weapons selection. The United States basically operates under a dual command structure. Responsibility for fighting or planning to fight rests with the commanders-in-chief in the various military regions (Europe, the Pacific, etc.), but these people have almost no authority over the officers assigned to them or the decisions on what weapons to acquire and the relative budgets. The latter decisions all rest with the military services, which tend to put their traditional roles, missions, and equipment ahead of the "common good." The Goldwater-Nichols Bill specifically addresses this problem; however, much more is required.

The third (and equally difficult to achieve) broad cultural change is the recognition that in many possible conflicts the United States would be fighting with its allies. Again, greater "jointness" in planning force structure and equipment is required. (It is amazing that for decades the NATO forces have not had equipment to tell "friend" from "foe.") The "burden sharing" arguments tend to take the position that America's allies are not carrying their "share" of the costs of NATO's defense (and similar arguments are made in the case of Japan, South Korea, and other allies). However, this is a secondary issue; the primary one is how to effectively utilize the dollars being spent by the United States and the NATO allies. Greater integration in the planning process should make it possible to get either equal effectiveness for fewer dollars or greater effectiveness for the same dollars.

The fourth significant "cultural change" to be addressed is the relationship between arms control and the national-security posture. Traditionally, these have been independent variables, and in many years even contradictory ones. Acceptable arms-control agreements, especially in the conventional area, may be difficult to achieve; however, they have a higher probability of success if they are integrated into the overall national-security posture and, thus, have a great deal more credibility.

Approximately half of the dollars spent by the DoD are spent on manpower. Marginal adjustments in this area, such as reduced rotation rates or delayed retirement pay, though perhaps necessary, are not going to make up the large difference between strategy and force structure. Three basic changes immediately come to mind. The first is a greater reliance on reserves rather than standing forces. The European "neutral" countries (e.g., Austria, Sweden, Switzerland, and Finland) can mobilize a far larger percentage of their population (in many cases five to ten times more) than the NATO countries—and these countries (with the exception of Sweden) spend less than half as great a percentage of GNP as the NATO countries on defense.[19] Second, the United States must restructure its forces and equipment to be able to get more combat power and less support structure from the present total number of people. Britain, France, and West Germany have recently gone through restructurings aimed at this objective, but they still have a long way to go in changing the ratio of fighting forces to support forces (the so-called "tooth-to-tail ratio"). Since the United States has the largest ratio of support to fighting forces,[20] it needs to make the biggest effort in this direction. The third broad change—a numerical reduction in full-

time military personnel—will require some of the shifts in strategy
discussed above (for example, counting more heavily on the NATO
forces to defend their portions of the Central European front, and/or
counting on Japan to do a bigger share of its defense, and/or replacing
people with "smart weapons" in Central Europe). In any case, to
achieve significant cost savings (to free money for use in other areas
where it is badly needed) will require reductions in manpower and
greater dependence on reserves.

Changes in the United States' approaches to national-security strategy and budgeting require significant revisions of both procedures and
organization. At the procedural level, perhaps the best place to start
would be by moving from a one-year to a multi-year defense-budget
process. Even a two-year budget[21] would force decisionmakers to consider the longer-term implications of their decisions and would undoubtedly alter many of those decisions (although two years is not long
enough to see the implications of weapons developments and deployments, and the real objective should be to get the DoD and the Congress
to look five or even fifteen years ahead[22]). The most difficult institution
to move in this direction will be Congress, and it may be that only a
portion of the defense budget can be done on a biennial basis. However,
if this portion includes the major programs (with milestone funding for
extended time periods) and major chunks of the rest of the dollars (e.g.,
operating and maintenance costs, which do not change annually), then
significant steps will have been made toward a longer-term perspective.
Additionally, Congress must start reviewing defense budgets in terms
of missions rather than procurement items—for example, the B-1 must
be considered a part of the overall "strategic systems" investment area
rather than as part of "aircraft procurement."

Once this longer-term perspective has been introduced, the next
procedural change should be a stronger linkage between strategy and
the multi-year budget. All the proposed approaches[23] recommend
greater involvement by the president and place emphasis on the direct
involvement of the Chairman of the Joint Chiefs of Staff in putting
together an integrated-military-force plan and budget. They also emphasize the primary role of the Secretary of Defense and his Under
Secretaries for Policy and Acquisition in developing a coherent strategy
and resource policy. Stability in the program budgets and in the overall
requirements process is essential here. "Baselining" (e.g., establishing

a $20.6 billion level for 100 B-1Bs) and "milestone funding" (at the beginning of full-scale development and at the beginning of production, with a commitment not to change during that phase of the acquisition cycle) are two specific ways to achieve greater stability. Finally, each of the proposed new approaches places greater emphasis on specifying "needs" for new weapon systems in terms of their military missions rather than their design characteristics. The hope here is that more "nontraditional" approaches—in other words, techniques that take advantage of new technology, at lower costs—will be pursued.

Next, the DoD must add a phase to the programming, planning, and budgeting system: an *evaluation* phase. The current budget system—with its annual exercises, which overlap so much that at any given point people are working on three different budgets—never leaves time for evaluation of the plans. It is inconceivable that a corporation would operate in this fashion, spending all its time on planning and none on evaluating the implementation against the plans. Adding this phase to the PPBS system would mean updating the DoD's accounting system to permit programming, budgeting, and execution to be done on a unified basis. Such a step would allow decisionmakers to assess the outputs realized and the accomplishments achieved against the dollars expended.

From an organizational viewpoint, the crucial need is to strengthen the Secretary of Defense in his ongoing battles with the service bureaucracies. This can be partially achieved by giving stronger roles to the Under Secretary of Defense for Policy and the Under Secretary of Defense for Acquisition, who work closely together on force planning and affordability. However, the most significant change would be to strengthen the role of the Chairman of the Joint Chiefs of Staff, to provide an integrated *military* viewpoint to balance the more parochial inputs of the services. This latter step (the essence of the Goldwater-Nichols Bill) and the subsequent reorganization of the Joint Chiefs of Staff should make it possible for the Chairman of the Joint Chiefs to provide a strong yet more objective military perspective to the Secretary of Defense, thus strengthening the Secretary's hand.[24]

Essential to this strengthened role of the Chairman of the Joint Chiefs of Staff is an increase in the quality and independence of the Joint Staff reporting to the Chairman. Additionally, the Joint Staff should be supplemented with personnel who focus on force structure, planning, and resource planning, in order to provide the Chairman with independent recommendations in these areas (again to balance those received from the military services). As a result of the 1987 reorganization of the Joint Chiefs of Staff, such organizations were established and steps were taken to improve the quality and independence of the Joint Staff.[25] This shift toward more independence of the Chairman and the Joint Staff is a dramatic "cultural change," and there will have to be a number of rotations of personnel through the organization and continued pressure from the Secretary of Defense and the Chairman of the Joint Chiefs in order for the desired objectives to be achieved. In fact, some people feel that these objectives will never be accomplished, because both the Chairman and the Joint Staff still wear their respective services' uniforms. These reformers recommend more radical shifts toward a truly independent "unified general staff" whose officers would not be answerable to the Army, the Navy, or the Air Force.[26] Perhaps the threat of such extreme solutions (and others even more extreme—e.g., going to a single service, or a totally restructured military service structure oriented around strategic forces, European forces, and regional forces[27]), combined with a clear recognition by the military of the need for change, will be enough to bring about the dramatic reorientation that is required. Close scrutiny and continuous pressure will be necessary if the needed reforms are to be fully implemented.

Weapons-Acquisition Reforms

It is clear that there are basic problems in the current approach to the acquisition of weapons, and that deeply entrenched practices that have been developed over several decades must be changed. The objectives of the changes must be these: higher-quality weapon systems that fail less often and are easier to maintain, far less expensive weapon systems that will still have the high performance needed to maintain the technological leadership that is the essence of America's defense strategy, and more rapid fielding of new weapon systems (so that advanced technology can be brought to bear in sufficient quantity to make a difference in the outcome of a conflict).

These objectives should be achieved through natural (i.e., market-type) incentives rather than through increased government regulation. It is important to gear these incentives toward improved quality and lower cost, as well as toward the traditional goal of improved performance. It must be emphasized that regulation and incentives do *not* tend to go together; rather, they are antithetical, since regulation removes most natural incentives. The government, therefore, must create an environment in which both government employees and contractors have self-evident reasons for improving quality and lowering costs. Such incentives include promotions, profits, increased sales, and professional pride.

The need to be able to identify clear responsibilities is consistent with this broad approach of using incentives as the principle means of motivation. For this reason the United States should move toward far greater centralization of the process of making acquisition decisions. A strengthened Under Secretary of Defense for Acquisition and a strong role for the Vice-Chairman of the Joint Chiefs of Staff in the acquisition process will result in the desired centralization of decisionmaking on major acquisition activities. The inverse of this is that, once a major acquisition decision has been made, the full responsibility for the implementation must be delegated to the program manager.

Finally, Congress must play a cooperative role if any of these reforms are to improve the overall acquisition process. Most of the changes recommended can be implemented within existing legislation; however, Congress' full support and, in a few cases, new legislation will be needed to "allow" the changes to take place. Therefore, the members of Congress must recognize that they are key players in the acquisition process, and must learn to act responsibly in this process.

Shifting to the question of what are the most important specific changes required in "the way the DoD does its business," we find that no "right answers" exist. Certainly there is no single change that would dramatically transform the overall acquisition process. Thus, we are forced to establish a short list of interrelated changes that could, collectively, result in the necessary cultural change.

First,[28] and clearly of highest priority, is *enhancing the quality of acquisition personnel*. Without high-quality, experienced personnel running the acquisition system—from the political appointees on down—all the changes in the world are unlikely to result in success. There must be clear career paths, so that outstanding government people can get extensive acquisition experience and then continue to apply it as they move up through the acquisition world; and we must make every effort to retain these people, not only within the government but within the field of acquisition. Increased promotion potential is clearly a major incentive in this area (particularly for the military), as are increased salary opportunities (particularly for the civilians). Because of the emphasis on weapons' costs, it is critical that these people have not only a technical background buy also a production orientation. Additionally, at least some of the key acquisition personnel must have a clear understanding of the military mission, in order to be able to make cost/performance tradeoffs in an effective manner. In the long run, perhaps the most important thing is an improvement of the United States' overall educational system, which must equip people with the necessary technical and management skills. This is obviously well beyond the domain of the Department of Defense; however, it is an area where the DoD can make a major contribution toward the greater interest of the nation as well as toward its own interest.

After the shift to higher-quality personnel in the acquisition world has been made, the second step—*streamlining the acquisition organization and procedures*—will become far more effective. The objective is for a few qualified people to have the authority to make the key acquisition decisions. At the top level these are the senior acquisition executives; at the program level they are the program managers. Having very few others in the direct line eliminates those who now constantly "change" or "veto" the program manager's decisions. There will still be more than enough "checks and balances" left in the system, but it is recommended that there be no more than two levels of such "oversight" within the DoD (between the Under Secretary for Acquisition and the program manager). Consistent with this would be a rather dramatic reduction in the number of "staff" and "line" government personnel involved in the acquisition system. This reduction will be compensated for by the higher quality of the people who remain and by the fact that the government will need fewer regulations and less oversight of the contractors once there is a shift toward greater use of market incentives to control the contractors' behavior. An additional way of streamlining the acquisition system would be to develop a set of relatively simple government procurement regulations that would give the experienced procurement personnel far greater freedom to exercise their "management judgments."[29] This is the direction in which the DoD needs to

move. Legislation to remove Congress' detailed regulation of the procurement process will be needed.

Achieving program stability is the third of the needed specific
changes in the acquisition process. Far greater cost realism in the
planning of programs will be necessary. If costs were realistically estimated, so as to include the dollars associated with the risks of high-
technology development, there would be far less cost growth. Not only
would this help in achieving program stability; it would also help to
convince Congress and the public of the DoD's management skills.
Unfortunately, this cost realism has a price: If programs are estimated
realistically (i.e., at higher, "most-likely" costs), then other programs
will not fit into the budget. Therefore, the key to stability lies in selecting
those programs that are essential, and adequately funding them, rather
than in attempting to underfund a larger number of programs. Other
actions that might contribute to the needed program stability include
proving out the technology before starting the full-scale development
of a weapon system, minimizing the changes to a program as it evolves
and saving inevitable changes for future modifications to the system (in
a "block" fashion, so that program stability can be maintained to the
"baseline" for a significant period of time), and combining multi-year
budgeting and multi-year contracting (they go together, since you cannot make a contractual commitment without the longer-term budgetary
commitment[30]).

Achieving a far better *balance of cost and performance* in the initial
"requirements" process for a new weapon system, and maintaining this
balance as the program evolves, is the fourth required change. Here,
the military mission "need" must be well understood and represented
during the requirements process—but on a functional basis, not as a
detailed design requirement (e.g., "destroy an enemy runway" versus
"build a new bomber"). And the acquisition community must be heard
from in the tradeoffs between various performance characteristics of a
weapon system and their costs. This constant iteration between the
users and the developers should result in the most cost-effective
weapon system that can be obtained for the overall resources available
for the system (not simply for the up-front development money). Thus,
there must be high "visibility" into the production and support costs
when these design tradeoffs are being made. There must also be very
strong military involvement in the early operational testing of prototype

systems, in order to find where incremental increases in performance will be of the most value.

The fifth of the specific recommendations for change is *the use of advanced technology to reduce costs*. The idea is to use technology to simultaneously improve the performance, lower the total cost,[31] and improve the reliability of weapon systems. This means that much engineering effort should be devoted to the technology of manufacturing, as well as to the weapon system itself. Consistent with this, there should be an emphasis on the attainment of high quality through improvements in the production process. Furthermore, when the prototype of a next-generation system is under development, there should be an effort to determine not only whether the concept and the new technology will work but also whether the system will be affordable when it goes into production and into the field. Thus, cost should become a *design* parameter throughout a product's evolution. (This concept is known in the commercial world as "design to cost.") Finally, to take full advantage of the military potential of new technologies, organizational changes within the military services are necessary to ensure that nontraditional uses of advanced technology are encouraged, particularly when they offer the potential to fulfill a military mission in a new and different way at a much lower cost. This may well be the most difficult of the changes, since it runs directly against military "tradition;" however, it is one of the changes with the greatest potential payoff—in terms of both greater military effectiveness and lower cost.

Expanding the use of commercial products by the Department of Defense is the sixth required change. It involves taking advantage of the far higher volume in which commercial products are produced, the associated lower cost, and the higher quality of these products wherever their performance and environmental capability satisfies the military need. Traditionally, the assumption has always been that the armed forces need special equipment. In fact, however, low-cost, high-quality commercial equipment can be used for the vast majority of applications at the component level, the subsystem level, and even the system level. For the DoD to begin applying this concept widely would mean far less reliance on excessively rigid military specifications, far greater reliance on comparable commercial specifications, and significant changes in procurement practices. In some cases, changes in congressional legislation would also be necessary.

This leads to the seventh of the major changes required in acquisition practices: *increasing competition, which emphasizes quality and demonstrated performance*. Greater use should be made of market incentives, rather than regulation, to achieve higher quality and lower cost. In some cases there may be competition between different products to do the same mission; in others, the competition may be between the acquisition of a new weapon system and the modification of an older one; and in still other cases, it may be between two industrial suppliers of the same product. In any case, the government can increase its buying power by having a viable alternative at all times. The emphasis here should be on the commercial style of competition, where prior performance and quality are major considerations and price is a secondary one. This is particularly true in the case of high-technology weapon systems, where quality is crucial and where demonstrated performance on prior programs should matter much more than the technical details promised in a proposal. As was discussed above, the principal hindrances to the implementation of this recommendation are the fact that it takes money up front (for the second source) to achieve significant savings in the future and the fact that within the bureaucratic and regulatory structure it is much more difficult to make an award to a high-quality producer whose apparent cost may be slightly higher than it is to simply pick the "low bidder" regardless of prior performance or quality. These hindrances must be overcome if the Department of Defense is to effectively utilize natural market incentives to obtain high-quality, low-cost goods and services.

Industrial Revitalization

The U.S. defense industry suffers from many of the same problems that afflict significant sectors of the nation's civilian economy (e.g., steel, autos, electronics): overcapacity, a short-term perspective, and a lack of international competitiveness. In the case of the defense industry, the federal government must play a major role in correcting these problems, since—as the only buyer of these goods and as the banker, regulator, and specifier—the government is already deeply involved in this industry. Therefore, while the required structural changes will have to be based on inputs, understanding, and even self-generated actions from the defense industry, the government has no choice but to assume the responsibility for "creating" a healthy, responsive, and innovative defense industrial base, rather than simply making a few changes in regulations or tax policy.[32]

First, sufficient data must be gathered on the problems and the necessary actions in each of the tiers of the defense industry (particularly the lower tiers).[33] Second, organizational responsibility must be assigned at a sufficiently high level so that it can have a significant impact on major program and resource decisions.[34]

The next step should be to establish, with significant input and participation from the defense industry, the desired broad structural characteristics of each segment of the industry and then to propose specific corrective actions appropriate to the various segments. (For example, the munitions industry can frequently be "mothballed" but must have a tremendous surge capability in wartime, whereas the shipbuilding industry must build ships continually in order to maintain the technology but has minimal surge requirements in the early phases of any conflict.) Two political problems undoubtedly will arise during this process. First, there is a danger that, because the older industries have the most political power, there will be a tendency to try to help them, when in reality newer industries may need to be supported and some of the older ones should be allowed to disappear. Second, it must be recognized that many of the "traditional" segments of the defense industry (aircraft, ships, tanks, etc.) may not be the ones requiring the most critical support from the government; rather, it may be some of the lower-tier industries (e.g., advanced materials, special sectors of the electronics industry, or next-generation manufacturing equipment). These are basically dual-use industries, and with the Defense Department's support they may be able to help revitalize the U.S. defense industry and even to have a significant effect on U.S. industrial competitiveness and productivity in the civilian sector. To achieve the desired results, analysts must be free to make recommendations independent of political considerations, and yet be able to take advantage of the knowledge and experience on the industrial side. In other countries, such independence is often achieved by separating those who gather and analyze the data from those who make the management decisions.

This does *not* mean identifying which firms should remain in which sectors of the defense industry. Rather, it means estimating, segment by segment, such characteristics as approximately how many firms the demand can efficiently support, whether there is sufficient competition in the industry, whether there is sufficient innovation in the industry, whether the firms are sufficiently profitable to be able to reinvest, and whether there is a need for government investment. Once these characteristics are clearly identified, then both Congress and the DoD can evaluate the effects of their actions. For example, if it is clear that there already are too many firms in a given segment, then the next award should not set up an additional new firm; if there are too few firms in a segment, the next award should be geared toward trying to induce another firm to come into that sector. At present, there is no such evaluation made by either Congress or the DoD, and thus it is very likely that many of the actions taken by both of these branches of the government are highly counterproductive to the health, the responsiveness, and the innovativeness of the defense industry. In fact, it is clear that many of the efforts taken in recent years, such as the attacks by both Congress and the DoD on industrial cash flow and profits and the numerous proposed bills to set up trade barriers and require all defense equipment to be produced domestically, have been extremely short-term in orientation. Many of these efforts have had the effect of harming the defense industry or raising the cost of defense goods without at all moving toward the desirable long-term structural characteristics in the various segments of the industry.

The broad strategy for the defense industry discussed in chapter 8 can be summarized in five points:

- Develop a research-and-development strategy geared toward advanced materials, components, and manufacturing technology.
- Integrate, at the plant level, the defense economy and the civilian economy (with the Department of Defense taking the necessary steps to remove the existing barriers to this integration).
- Increase greatly the use of continuous competition, stressing quality and performance as the criteria for awards, along with price.
- Consider explicitly the impacts of all the DoD's major policy, resource, and program decisions on industrial strategy, and vice versa.
- Make the defense industrial base a critical part of the nation's overall national-security posture, approaching the strategic and tactical forces in importance.[35]

The implementation of such a strategy would have a dramatic effect on the "supply side" of the overall military-industrial base, and could do much to improve the overall efficiency and effectiveness with which the United States seeks to achieve its desired national-security objectives with the money provided by the defense budget.

Potential Savings

This book has focused on the need and the capability of the United States to develop a more affordable, balanced, and credible national-security posture. A very significant part of the realization of this objective, without dramatic increases in defense expenditures, must come through the increased effectiveness with which the dollars that are allocated are utilized. The challenge is to achieve significant savings in some areas through implementation of the required changes, so that these dollars could then be expended in other areas that are crucial to the nation's future security (e.g., conventional weapons and/or special equipment for potential regional conflicts).

To show the savings potential, under the assumption of an approximately $300 billion annual defense budget, the analysis discussed below has been conducted. Before going through the numbers, it is important to recognize that an institution as large as the U.S. Department of Defense cannot be changed rapidly, and that many of the recommended investments will require both organizational and procedural changes that go deeply into the "culture" of the institution. Thus, if any degree of realism is to be applied, it is clear that the projected impact of these changes will not be fully realized for 5 or 10 years. Similarly, because many of the changes actually require small initial increases in expenditures in order to save significant dollars later on, it must be recognized that in the first few years there will be little in the way of savings, but that the potential savings should begin to build up significantly after 3–5 years. Clearly, there are no "instant cures." Additionally, without sustained leadership it is highly unlikely that the proposed changes will be effectively and fully implemented; however, because of the growing awareness of the need for change and because of the evidence of initial efforts being made, there is considerable reason for optimism.

In generating the numbers given in the tables below, care was taken in two regards. First, there was an insistence that all the estimates be reasonable—that in every case some other analysis has yielded similar

Table 11.1

	Potential annual savings
Changes in industry	$16 billion
Improved weapons-acquisition practices	$23 billion
Improved budget practices	$17 billion
Changes in military personnel and facilities	$9 billion
Improved selection of weapons	$20 billion
Changes in strategy and force planning	$31 billion
Total (root-sum-square)	$50 billion

or higher potential savings, and that these independent sources are qualified to make such judgments. Second, one of the more common fallacies of similar studies is to list a large number of potential areas for savings and then to simply add them all up to arrive at a total value. Such an approach ignores the statistical nature of the analysis and the fact that many of these areas of potential savings overlap significantly. Therefore, the methodology utilized for the analysis contained below is the statistical approach of combining the root-sum-squares of the various areas of potential impact. This approach was used in arriving at the combination of the impacts at the "top level," as well as for combining the impacts within each area. Thus, the analysis represents a relatively conservative approach.

Table 11.1 breaks down the overall recommendations contained in this book into six major areas for potential savings. As can be seen from this table, billions of dollars can be realized in the areas of the defense industry, military personnel and facilities, government procurement practices, and budget practices. However, it is very important to recognize that the largest share of the potential dollar savings comes out of the combination of "improved weapons selections" and "strategy and force planning changes" (items 5 and 6). Also, the approximately $50 billion total potential savings that might be realized (from a $300 billion defense budget) is only about 17 percent. This is quite attainable if the changes can be implemented; in fact, other independent analyses have indicated greater savings—up to $100 billion—without a significant loss of military effectiveness.[36]

Consider each of the six specific areas of potential savings as amplified in table 11.2. In the area of *industrial savings,* the potential for reduction of overhead costs was demonstrated in the late 1980s when the DoD began to significantly increase the number of programs that were "continuously competed." In those cases, it was found that defense overhead could be reduced significantly without negative impacts on performance (in fact, often with positive impacts). A similar result was achieved by the overall U.S. industry as it started to compete more with the Japanese in the commercial sector. The estimate of 10 percent reductions in acquisition costs is believed to be quite realistic and is consistent with an independent analysis by J. Ronald Fox of the Harvard Business School.[37] Additionally, greater use of computer-aided design and manufacturing (a direction in which both the defense sector and the civilian sector are moving, but slowly) could result in savings significantly higher than the 3 percent projected here. However, these numbers are consistent with a study by the General Accounting Office, and with an independent study by the Defense Science Board.[38] A 1987 analysis by the Honeywell Corporation's Aerospace and Defense organization projected at least $5 billion in potential savings from industrial changes[39] while an independent estimate by Under Secretary of Defense Robert Costello indicated potential savings of approximately $25 billion.[40] Since the defense industry is likely to project relatively low savings in its own area, and the government might be expected to project unusually high savings from the industrial side, the estimate in table 11.2 (which is approximately the average of these two estimates) is probably "in the ballpark."

Let us now turn to the second major area, *improved government acquisition practices.* Eight of the exemplary subitems identified in table 11.2 show potential multi-billion-dollar savings. The totals for this overall area are very similar to those found by the Honeywell analyst (from the industrial perspective) and by the Grace Commission on Government Management (from the government perspective). It is important to recognize that these three analyses vary widely in terms of the details of the specific categories; however, since all three arrived at similar levels of potential savings, the numbers are probably in the right range. Additionally, each of those eight subitems shown in table 11.2

Table 11.2

Problem area	Rationale for efficiency	Potential annual savings (in billions)
Industry		
High overhead costs in factories	Based on civilian business, 10% of acquisition costs	$15
Inefficient use of computer-aided design and manufacturing	Savings of 3% in design and production	$ 5
	Subtotal (root-sum-square)	$16
Weapons-acquisition practices		
Little use of commercial systems, subsystems, and components	Individual items at least 50% cheaper (applicable to at least 5% of acquisition costs)	$15
Lack of continuous competition	Net savings on applicable programs ($\approx$20%)—appliable to $\approx$50% of production programs	$10
Inefficient government procurement regulations and laws	Will be hard to remove, but estimates of savings range from 5% to 30% of acquisition costs (so low end reasonable)	$ 8
Excessive specifications (product and process)	Overspecification raises acquisition costs by 5%	$ 8
Excessive prime-contractor facilities and labor	More than required, e.g., in aircraft industry, for effective competition (5% of related production)	$ 3
Excessive data and reporting requirements	Estimated at 5% of development costs	$ 3
Long development cycles	Shorter cycle could reduce full-scale developments by $\approx$5%	$ 2
Lack of independent development of "standard" subsystems	Higher volume and reduced design costs should save 25% (on perhaps 5% of acquisition dollars)	$ 2
	Subtotal (root-sum-square)	$23

(Table continued on next page.)

Table 11.2 (Continued)

Problem area	Rationale for efficiency	Potential annual savings (in billions)
Budget practices		
Lack of budget stability	Instability, stretchouts, etc. have 10%–15% impact on acquisition (some will still continue; therefore use 10%)	$15
Lack of multi-year funding (budgets and contracts)	Efficient ordering and capital invest-ments (5% of production)	$ 5
Inefficiently low production rates	Learning-curve theory (5% of production)	$ 5
Congressional budget add-ons	Will always have some, but can save at least $500 million per year	$ 0.5
	Subtotal (root-sum-square)	$17
Military personnel and facilities		
Military retirement system	Delay retirement pay (similar to gov-ernment civilian employees)	$ 8
Many unneeded military bases	Numerous studies have shown po-tential savings of up to $5 billion per year	$ 3
Frequent military job rotations	Inefficiencies and moving costs	$ 1
	Subtotal (root-sum-square)	$ 9
Selection of weapons		
Designs primarily for maximum per-formance (with "gold plating)	"Design to cost" and producibility should save a net of 10% of produc-tion costs	$15
Designs based on traditional equip-ment types	Use of advanced technology in non-traditional equipment has big poten-tial, but hard to overcome service resistance (10% of production realistic)	$10
Overlap in roles and missions of services	Redundant R&D and production; po-tential large, but realistic savings are 5% of acquisition dollars	$ 8
	Subtotal (root-sum-square)	$20
Strategy and force planning		
High cost of troops in Europe	Bringing back 100,000 soldiers would still leave 4 div. in Central Europe	$30
Overly rapid strategic-force modernization	Already have "overkill," redun-dancy, and relative invulnerability (15% of strategic-force acquisition dollars)	$ 8
	Subtotal (root-sum-square)	$31

has independent analyses that justify the details of the subcategories[41]; for example, the Defense Science Board (made up of defense-industry executives, who might tend to be somewhat critical of the use of the commercial components) projected much *greater* potential savings from use of commercial systems, subsystems, and components.[42]

The potential savings from *improved government budget practices* receive relatively little public attention. Nonetheless, savings here, especially from increased budget stability, could be quite significant. In fact, savings of between 10 and 40 percent have been projected.[43] Nonetheless, most analyses acknowledge that budget instabilities (such as stretchouts) are likely to continue in the future,[44] and thus the level of around 10 percent shown here might be considered realistic. The other examples shown in this category are also believed to be conservative estimates. Even the small projection of savings on congressional add-ons[45] (which undoubtedly will continue at some level).

The root-sum-square of these first three categories (industrial, procurement, and budget practices) yields potential savings of about $33 billion a year. An independent 1988 assessment of the effects of these three categories by Under Secretary Costello stated that the federal government could potentially save $30 billion to $45 billion a year in these three areas.[46]

In the area of *military personnel and facilities,* encouraging experienced military officers and enlisted men and women to stay in the services beyond the 20-year retirement point (essentially by creating a retirement program similar to the one used in the civilian portions of the government and in the private sector) could save at least $8 billion annually.[47] Additionally, numerous analyses have shown that closing hundreds of unneeded facilities among the nation's 3,800 military installations[48] has the potential of saving at least $5 billion a year. In 1988, Congress passed legislation to set up a nonpartisan commission to address base closures. The $3 billion shown in the table is believed to be realistically achievable through such a bipartisan effort. Finally, keeping personnel in their assignments for only a few extra months would not only have a positive effect on efficiency; it would also result in very significant annual savings.[49] Thus, the overall savings in the personnel area should be at least $9 billion per year,[50] excluding the impact of personnel reductions and/or a shift to greater dependence on the reserves—which are covered under "changes in strategy and force planning."

In the crucial area of *improved weapon selections,* the first, and perhaps most obvious, savings will come from declining to push for the last 5 percent of performance (which may well raise the cost of a program by 30 percent or more) and by eliminating the desirable but unnecessary features of a weapon system (the "gold plating"). Estimates of potential savings in this category alone range from 20 percent to 40 percent of the cost of acquisition efforts.[51] This basic "cultural change" will run into considerable institutional resistance and will take time to implement; thus, a 15 percent reduction in the production costs of systems after a number of years seems realistic.[52] A second possibility here is the far greater use of nontraditional weaponry. Not only does this have the potential of replacing expensive equipment with far less costly equipment; in addition, a change such as replacing aircraft with remotely piloted vehicles and cruise missiles would also bring significant savings in terms of personnel and operations. The fact that this change will encounter extreme resistance leads to the relatively low estimate (10 percent of production costs) shown in the table. Finally, the current overlap in the services' roles and missions results in expensive equipment being developed and produced independently by multiple services. Sorting this out could yield increased production volume of the same system for multiple-service use, or the elimination of some of the redundant systems,[53] and achieve significant savings.

The last and largest area of potential savings is that of changes in strategy and force planning. Maintaining our commitments but relying more on reserve forces is one of the more obvious ways to realize significant savings. For example, we could keep up our commitment to NATO with far fewer people deployed full-time in Europe. Since "people costs" constitute over half of the defense budget, any attack on costs must consider changing strategies in this area. A variety of ways have been proposed to achieve this: increasing our dependence on reserve forces for all worldwide missions (recognizing both the higher risk and the shift in equipment mix that this entails); conventional-force arms-control agreements; having the allies pick up a larger share of the "burden"; and shifting from a labor-intensive to an equipment-intensive force (with larger numbers of inexpensive "smart" weapons deployed along the East-West frontier to stop any initial Warsaw Pact thrust). A move by the United States to a four-division force in Europe (covering the part of the central front for which the United States has direct responsibility) would allow a demobilization of about 100,000 soldiers and savings of around $30 billion.[54] Obviously, this should be done slowly, over a number of years, and with a clearly stated military rationale to prevent giving the appearance of weakening NATO's posture or intent.

A second example: Slowing the modernization of the strategic force (which has an overkill capability, built-in redundancy, and relative invulnerability) could yield significant savings.[55] The desired approach should be a long-term plan to modernize each leg of the strategic triad periodically, and in a countercyclical fashion, in order to achieve both economic efficiency and continued force modernization. The actual savings potential with such an approach is significantly higher than the number shown in table 11.2; however, because of the strong symbolism (military and politically) of the strategic forces, the $8 billion is perhaps a realistic level to achieve within a few years.

The "strategy and force planning" area offers many more opportunities for multi-billion-dollar savings, and should receive the highest priority over the coming years. It is clearly the area that demands the most attention from Congress, the executive branch, and the senior leaders in the defense community (particularly the Secretary of Defense and his staff).

Conclusion

Annual savings of $50 billion can be realized within five or ten years. The dollars saved must be used to strengthen the United States' capability to contain regional conflicts and to give the United States a more balanced conventional-warfare capability in Central Europe (so that we would not have to use nuclear weapons in a conflict there). The savings and the increased military capability are urgently needed, but both will take a number of years to be realized. Therefore, the time to act is now. The nation's security requires it, and the taxpayers not only deserve it but should demand it.

Notes

Chapter 1

1. *U.S. News & World Report,* November 16, 1987, page 17.

2. *Washington Post,* November 1, 1986.

3. The issue of "waste, fraud, and abuse" will be put into perspective, in considerable detail, in chapter 6.

4. Comptroller General, "Acquisition of Major Weapon Systems," Department of Defense Report B163058, July 1972.

5. "Inaccuracy of Department of Defense Weapons Acquisition Cost Estimates," House Committee on Government Operations, November 16, 1979.

6. No doubt some performance-related improvements in the tanks were made during this period; however, the 50 percent cost increase is unaffordable. For a far longer list of such items (and for the data on the tanks), see chapter 6.

7. This issue will be discussed extensively in chapter 7. For an excellent historical perspective, see Elting Morrison's *Man, Machines, and Modern Times* (MIT Press, 1966). For a more recent discussion, see J. Gansler, "The U.S. Technology Base: Problems and Prospects," in *Technology, Strategy, and National Security,* ed. F. Margiotta and R. Sanders (National Defense University Press, 1985).

8. *New York Times,* October 3, 1984.

9 Defense Systems Acquisition Review Council Working Group, Final Report, December 19, 1972. See also J. Gansler, *The Defense Industry* (MIT Press, 1980), page 16; see chapter 6 of the present volume for a more recent update.

10. *Washington Post,* October 26, 1986.

11. Based on the Air Force's commitment of $20.6 billion for 100 aircraft. This was in 1981 dollars; later problems with the B-1B raised the cost still further.

12. Congressional Budget Office, Analysis of Defense Budget Justification Data, 1986. (This number is in 1985 dollars.)

13. Ibid.

14. From a presentation by Rep. Newt Gingrich at West Point in 1983. Both figures are in 1982 dollars.

15. Norman Augustine, president of Martin Marietta and former Undersecretary of the Army, is the author of *Augustine's Laws* (American Institute of Aeronautics and Astronautics, 1982).

16. A study done in 1981 by the Air Force Systems Command indicated an average cost growth of nearly 100 percent ("Affordable Acquisition Approach," February 9, 1983). The difference between this and the previously quoted GAO studies represents the difference in programs selected as well as the differences in how the effects of inflation have been treated.

17. D. Lockwood, "Cost Overruns in Major Weapon Systems: Current Dimensions of Long-Standing Problems," Congressional Research Service Report 83-194F, Library of Congress, October 15, 1983.

18. From 1969 to 1975 the annual procurement account dropped from $44 billion to $17 billion (with the effects of inflation removed).

19. For a discussion of foreign dependency, see J. Gansler, "U.S. Dependence on Foreign

Military Parts: Should We Be Concerned?," *Issues in Science and Technology* 2, no. 4, 1986. See also chapter 8 of the present volume.

20. House Armed Services Committee, Industrial Base Panel, "The Ailing Defense Industrial Base: Unready for Crisis," *Congressional Record,* December 31, 1980; Defense Science Board Task Force, report on industrial responsiveness, November 21, 1980; Air Force Systems Command statement on defense industrial base issues, November 13, 1980; Gansler, *The Defense Industry.*

21. This analysis was done on the F-16 fighter plane, then in production by General Dynamics Corporation in Air Force Plant 4 (Fort Worth, Texas).

22. For a fuller discussion of this strategy shift, see J. S. Gansler, "Industrial Preparedness: National Security in the Nuclear Age," *Military Engineer,* November–December 1983, pages 483–490. See also chapter 8 below.

23. For example, almost every year during the mid-1980s the Congress processed more than 150 "procurement reform" bills, many of which were counterproductive, some of which were self-contradictory, and a few of which were absurd (S.R. 1957 specified that the price of a toilet seat could not exceed $125). The DoD's approach to correcting the perceived problem of the high cost of spare parts was to add thousands of employees (the Air Force alone added over 3,000 people just to check the prices of spare parts). As a result of this "fix," the time to obtain spare parts doubled. Clearly, primary attention needs to be given to the large-dollar items (weapon systems) rather than to the small-dollar items (spare parts) if procurement costs are to be reduced significantly. The small, commercial-like items, unfortunately, are the ones that have appeal to the press, and thus they have received a disproportionate amount of the Department of Defense's attention. In fact, the DoD now has 30–40 percent of the government's in-plant representatives (auditors, et al.) looking at spare parts, which actually represent only 3–4 percent of DoD's acquisition dollars.

24. These are discussed in summary fashion in J. Gansler, "Improving Weapons Acquisition," *Yale Law and Policy Review,* fall/winter 1986.

25. This number (from table 11.1 below) is believed to be conservative, since it is the "root-sum-square" of the values in the table rather than the arithmetic sum of $116 billion. See chapter 11 for a discussion of the methodology and the basis for the numbers.

26. CSIS Defense Organization Project, "Towards a More Effective Defense," Georgetown University, February 1985.

27. Senate Committee on Armed Services, "Defense Organization: The Need for Change," October 16, 1985.

28. Upon his retirement in September 1986, Senator Goldwater called this bill (known formally as the Goldwater-Nichols Department of Defense Reorganization Act of 1986) "the most significant thing I have done in all my years in Washington."

Chapter 2

1. Sun Tzu, *The Art of War* (Oxford University Press, 1963), page 39.

2. M. Howard, *The Causes of War and Other Essays* (Harvard University Press, 1983), page 207.

3. B. Tuchman, "The American People and Military Power in an Historical Perspective," *International Institute of Strategic Studies,* spring 1982, page 5.

4. T. Schelling, *Arms and Influence* (Greenwood, 1966), page 16.

5. G. Herken, *Counsels of War* (Knopf, 1985), page 9.

6. B. Brody, *Strategy in the Missile Age* (Princeton University Press, 1959).

7. U. Nerlich, "Change in Europe: Secular Trends?" *Daedalus,* winter 1981, page 85.

8. These five possibilities are from S. Gray, "Strategic Forces, General Purpose Forces, and Crisis Management," *Annals of the American Academy of Political and Social Science* 457 (September 1981), page 76.

9. P. Williams, *Crisis Management: Confrontation and Diplomacy in the Nuclear Age* (Wiley), page 138.

10. Schelling, *Arms and Influence,* page 206.

11. For an excellent discussion on terminating nuclear wars, see C. Abt, *A Strategy for Terminating Nuclear Wars* (Westview, 1985).

12. Holloway, "Military Power and Political Purpose in Soviet Policy," *Daedalus,* winter 1981, page 19.

13. For a full discussion of this issue, see B. Rockman, "Mobilizing Political Support for U.S. National Security," *Armed Forces in Society,* fall 1987, pages 17–43.

14. H. Kissinger, *Nuclear Weapons and Foreign Policy* (Norton, 1957), page 128.

15. S. Huntington, *The Common Defense* (Columbia University Press, 1961), page 127.

16. B. Lidell Hart, *The Sword and the Pen: Selections from the World's Greatest Military Writings* (Cassell, 1978), page 51.

17. M. Howard, *Clausewitz* (Oxford University Press, 1983), page 20.

18. A. de Tocqueville, *Democracy in America.*

19. S. Hoffman, *Dead Ends: American Foreign Policy in the New Cold War* (Ballinger, 1983), page 82.

20. For example, see J. Gaddis, *The Long Peace: Inquiries into the History of the Cold War* (Oxford University Press, 1987), or C. Evans, *The Micro Millennium* (Viking, 1979).

21. H. York and J. Wiesner, "National Security and the Nuclear Test Ban," *Scientific American,* October 1964, pages 27–37.

22. Reinhold Niebuhr, quoted in *Time,* June 20, 1986, page 71.

23. Herken, *Counsels of War,* page 263.

24. D. Ford, "A Reporter at Large: The Button," *New Yorker,* April 1 and 8, 1985.

25. Herken, *Counsels of War,* page 138.

26. Ibid., page 300.

27. Ibid., page 128.

28. Ibid., page 263.

29. Ibid., page 301

30. *New York Times,* November 29, 1987.

31. Hoffman, *Dead Ends,* page 102.

32. Herken, *Counsels of War,* page 305.

33. Ibid., page 110.

34. For a discussion of these two issues, see T. Brown, "U.S. and Soviet Strategic Force Levels: Problems of Assessment and Measurement," *Annals of the American Academy of Political and Social Sciences,* September 1981, pages 19–20.

35. N. Gayler, "The Way Out: A General Nuclear Settlement," *Yale Law and Policy Review* 5, no. 134 (1986), page 136. Consistent with this argument, from 1967 to 1987 the United States reduced the number of nuclear warheads in its arsenal by 8,000 while actually increasing the arsenal's destructiveness (N. Podhoretz, "Do We Have Greater Numbers Than We had 20 Years Ago?" *Washington Post,* June 22, 1988).

36. C. Grey, "Soviet-American Strategic Competition: Instruments, Doctrines, and Purposes." In *Long-Range U.S.-USSR Competition: National Security Implications* (National Defense University, 1976).

37. Soviet Premier Nikita Khrushchev stated that, for this reason, the Soviet Union would never make a surprise attack on the United States. See Huntington, *Common Defense,* page 120.

38. *New York Times Magazine,* November 1, 1981, page 99.

39. For a good discussion of the "survivability problem," see the article with this title by B. Scrowcroft, J. Deutch, and R. Woolsey in the *The Washington Post* of December 3, 1987.

40. Herken, *Counsels of War,* page 259.

41. Ibid., page 260.

42. Ibid., page 125.

43. Ford, "A Reporter At Large," *New Yorker,* April 8, 1985, page 90.

44. Herken, *Counsels of War,* page 144.

45. Ford, "A Reporter At Large," *New Yorker,* April 8, 1985, page 84.

46. Herken, *Counsels of War,* page 314.

47. H. Kahn, *On Thermonuclear War* (Princeton University Press, 1960).

48. Herken, *Counsels of War,* page 304.

49. D. Callio, review of *Europe: A Tapestry of Nations,* by Flora Lewis, Book World section, *Washington Post,* November 15, 1987, page 4.

50. J. Dean, "MBFR: From Apathy to Accord," *International Security,* spring 1983, page 117.

51. *The Economist,* August 30, 1986, page 3 of the survey article.

52. Dean, "MBFR," page 117.

53. *Washington Post,* December 5, 1987.

54. M. Taylor, "Deterrence: The Trouble with 'No First Use,'" *Washington Post,* April 18, 1982.

55. W. Drozdiak, "A Reflective General Rogers Ponders the Future Course of NATO's Forces," *Washington Post,* December 7, 1983.

56. Schelling, *Arms and Influence,* page 47.

57. Herken, *Counsels of War,* page 103.

58. Callio, review of *Europe: A Tapestry of Nations* (see note 49 above).

59. *U.S. News and World Report,* November 19, 1984, page 54.

60. See, for example, J. Chace, "Ike was Right," *Atlantic Monthly,* August 1987, pages 39–41.

61. *New York Times,* November 29, 1987.

62. For an excellent discussion of the implications of the INF agreement for Europe, see Edward Luttwak, "Why the INF Pact Means the Nuclear Era is Over," *Washington Post,* November 29, 1987.

63. E. Luttwak, *Coup d'Etat: A Practical Handbook* (Harvard University Press, 1979), page 65.

64. J. Lodal, "U.S. Strategic Nuclear Forces," *Adelphi Papers* (International Institute of Strategic Studies, London), spring 1982, page 36.

65. *The Economist,* October 3, 1982, page 19.

66. For a good discussion of some of the options for strengthening NATO, see R. Komer, "Costs and Benefits of a Credible Conventional Component," *Armed Forces Journal,* May 1984, page 112.

67. R. Halloran, *To Arm a Nation: Why America Isn't Ready to Defend Herself* (Macmillan, 1986).

68. For an analysis of the Soviet example of restraint see P. Jabber, "U.S. Interests in Regional Security in the Middle East," *Daedalus,* winter 1981, page 77.

69. For example, each of the superpowers considers the Persian Gulf critical.

70. Hoffman, *Dead Ends,* page 260.

71. Ibid., page 102.

72. *U.S. News and World Report,* November 23, 1987, page 17.

73. Report of the Secretary of Defense, Casper W. Weinberger, to the Congress, February 5, 1986, page 70.

74. International Institute of Strategic Studies, Strategic Survey 1985–1986, page 20.

75. Ibid., page 21. (In 1985 alone, 950 people were killed by terrorism.)

76. Ibid., page 22.

77. Huntington, *The Common Defense,* page 344.

78. One author who makes this same point, and who argues for different equipment for Europe as well, is Leonard Sullivan, Jr. ("From Psychosis to Armored Sunroofs," *Armed Forces Journal International,* March 1988, page 46).

79. S. Chubin, "U.S. Security Interests in the Persian Gulf in the 1980s," *Daedalus,* winter 1981, page 55. As another example, consider the inability of the U.S. to dislodge General Manuel Noriega from Panama in 1988—even though the Panamanian military forces were grossly overmatched.

80. For an excellent discussion of what can be done in terms of "listening in on other people's conversations," see James Bamford, *The Puzzle Palace: A Report on America's Most Secret Agency,* (Houghton Mifflin, 1982).

81. By 1982 there was evidence of the use of biological weapons in some Third World conflicts. There were also charges that the Soviet Union had supplied poisonous biolog-

ical weapons for use by the governments of Laos, Kampuchea, and Afghanistan (as reported in *Washington Post,* January 30, 1982).

82. By the end of the 1980s, India, Israel, South Africa, and other countries had the capability to make nuclear weapons, and India, Israel, and Brazil were developing ballistic missiles (*Business Week,* January 11, 1988, page 59).

83. Ballistic missiles were used in the Iran-Iraq war, and in 1988 the Chinese sold Saudi Arabia the East Wind, a surface-to-surface missile with a range of 1,860 miles (*U.S. News and World Report,* March 28, 1988, page 11).

Chapter 3

1. A. Schlesinger, Jr., "Foreign Policy and the American Character," *Foreign Affairs,* fall 1983, page 14.

2. R. Forsberg, "The Freeze and Beyond: Confining the Military to Defense as a Route to Disarmament," *World Policy Journal* 1, no. 2 (1984), page 288.

3. Ibid., page 310.

4. B. Brody, *The Absolute Weapon* (Harcourt Brace, 1946), page 76.

5. R. McNamara, "The Military Role of Nuclear Weapons: Perceptions and Misperceptions," *Foreign Affairs,* fall 1983, page 79.

6. Adm. N. Gayler (USN, ret.), in *Congressional Record,* 97th Congress, First Session, July 17, 1981, page S7835.

7. S. Hoffman, "A Case of Dr. Kissinger," *New York Review of Books,* December 1979.

8. M. Bundy, G. Kennan, R. McNamara, and G. Smith, "Nuclear Weapons and the Atlantic Alliance," *Foreign Affairs,* spring 1982, page 759.

9. H. Kahn, *Thinking About the Unthinkable in the 1980s* (Simon and Schuster, 1984), page 76.

10. S. Weiss, "Why We Must Think About Protracted Nuclear War," *Wall Street Journal,* August 30, 1982.

11. Ibid.

12. H. Smith, "How Many Billions for Defense?" *New York Times Magazine,* November 1, 1981, page 79.

13. J. Amos and W. Taylor, *American National Security: Policy and Process* (Johns Hopkins University Press, 1984), page 227.

14. R. Herman, "One Country Digs In," *Washington Post,* December 8, 1987.

15. M. Howard, *The Causes of War* (Harvard University Press, 1983), page 2.

16. G. Wilson, "U.S. Troop Pullout in Europe Would Provoke Allies, Study Says," *Washington Post,* April 18, 1982.

17. C. Builder, "The Prospects and Implications of Non-Nuclear Means for Strategic Conflict," *Adelphi Papers,* no. 200 (1985), page 3.

18. Sun Tzu, *The Art of War.*

19. *The Economist,* April 19, 1986, page 58.

20. Ibid.

21. E. Zumwalt, "Admiral Holloway Has It All Wrong," *Washington Post,* September 26, 1981.

22. M. Howard, *Clausewitz* (Oxford University Press, 1983), page 34.

23. L. Gelb, "A Practical Way to Arms Control," *New York Times Magazine,* June 15, 1983, page 33.

24. C. Bertran, "This Is No Way To Choose Our Weapons," *Washington Post,* August 19, 1983.

25. J. Newhouse, "Why Reagan Needs SALT," *Washington Post,* September 8, 1981.

26. For example, see J. Vinocure, "West Europeans Are Enthusiastic," *New York Times,* November 19, 1981.

27. H. Kissinger, *Nuclear Weapons and Foreign Policy* (Norton, 1957), page 61.

28. J. Schell, "Why INF Won't Change the Fate of the Earth," *Washington Post,* December 1987.

29. Kahn, *Thinking About the Unthinkable in the 1980s,* page 25. (Between 1967 and 1983 the number of weapons was reduced by 30 percent and the aggregate megatonnage declined by 75 percent.)

30. *New York Times,* November 29, 1987.

31. This comes from an analysis by John Steinbrenner of the Brookings Institution, and was quoted in the *New York Times* on November 29, 1987.

32. D. Oberdorfer, "Soviets Hint At Major Shift in Military Posture," *Washington Post,* November 30, 1987.

33. Sen. S. Nunn, "Renegotiate the ABM Treaty?" *U.S. News and World Report,* December 14, 1987.

34. Even by the "peace" advocates. For example, see Forsberg, "The Freeze and Beyond," page 289.

35. S. Schmemann, "West Rebuffs East on Pact on Europe Troop Cuts," *New York Times,* December 6, 1987.

36. J. Hoagland and J. Diehl, "Pole Proposes Cuts in Bloc's Tanks, Planes," *Washington Post,* November 12, 1987.

37. For a full discussion of this in a historical context, see A. Ulam, *The Rivals: America and Russia Since World War II* (Penguin, 1971).

38. D. Holloway, "Military Power and Political Purpose in Soviet Policy," *Daedalus,* winter 1981, page 13.

39. D. Simes, "The Military and Militarism in Soviet Society," *International Security,* winter 1981–82, page 123.

40. Ibid., page 127.

41. O. Penkofskiy, *The Penkofskiy Papers* (Doubleday, 1965), page 252.

42. J. Erickson, "The Soviet View of Deterrence: A General Survey," *Survival,* November/December 1982, page 249.

43. J. Baylis and G. Segal, *Soviet Strategy* (Croom Helm, 1981), Quoted in *Survival,* May-June 1982, page 141.

44. Kahn, *Thinking About the Unthinkable in the 1980s,* page 76.

45. S. Myer, "Soviet Theater Nuclear Forces," *Adelphi Papers*, No. 187 (1983), page 32.

46. D. Hart, "Soviet Approaches to Crisis Management: The Military Dimension," *Survival*, September-October 1984, page 221.

47. Federal Emergency Management Agency, *A Comparison of Soviet and U.S. Civil Defense Programs* (1987), page 3.

48. Simes, "The Military and Militarism in Soviet Society," page 140.

49. Marshal A. Grechko, *The Armed Forces of the Soviet State* (Voennoe Izdated'stvo, 1975), page 90. Quoted in *Soviet Military Thought*, no. 12, page 802.

50. W. Lee, "The Shift in Soviet National Priorities to Military Forces 1958–85," *Annals of the American Academy of Political and Social Science*, September 1981, page 58.

51. Department of Defense, *Your Defense Budget*, fiscal year 1985, page 4. (Investment includes procurement, military construction, and research and development. The total for the USSR is an estimate of what it would cost the U.S. to duplicate the USSR's investment activities.)

52. Report of the Secretary of Defense, Casper Weinberger, to the Congress on the FY 87 Budget and FY 87 Authorization Requests, February 5, 1986, page 15.

53. Air Marshall Sir Frederick Sowrey (ret.), "An Unconventional Approach to Defense Resources," *Survival*, November-December 1982, page 252.

54. M. Moore, "INF Treaty Raises Apprehensions within NATO," *Washington Post*, December 5, 1987. See also *U. S. News and World Report*, December 14, 1987, page 31.

55. Moore, "INF Treaty Raises Apprehensions Within NATO."

56. Some of the material presented here was first published in J. Gansler, "We Can Afford Security," *Foreign Policy*, no. 51 (1983), pages 64–84.

57. This three-part approach was presented by Leonard Sullivan, a former Assistant Secretary of Defense, in a variety of "informal briefings" (one of them at a Rand-sponsored symposium in 1981 and one of them at an American Defense Preparedness Association-sponsored symposium in the same year).

58. Report of the Secretary of Defense to the Congress on FY 87 Budget, February 5, 1987.

59. Congressional Budget Office, "Defense Spending: What Has Been Accomplished?" (staff working paper, April 1985), page 5.

60. *Washington Post*, November 24, 1987.

61. Ibid.

62. *Washington Post*, March 18, 1985.

63. Department of Defense Long-Range Logistics Plan, prepared by the Deputy Assistant Secretary of Defense for Logistics and Materiel Management, October 1983.

64. D. Evans, "The B1: A Flying Edsel for America's Defense?" *Washington Post*, January 4, 1986.

65. G. Adams, "Defense Choices and Resource Constraints: The Dilemma of the Investment Driven Defense Budget," *Yale Law and Policy Review*, 5, no. 1 (1986), page 30.

66. The overwhelming share of the $120 billion spent between 1965 and 1973 went for equipment used or left in Vietnam, not for modernization of the forces. See S. Karnow, *Vietnam: A History* (Viking, 1983).

67. J. Mullins, *The Defense Matrix: National Preparedness in the Military Industrial Complex* (Avant, 1986).

68. Col. O. Collins, "Combat Sustainability and Reconstruction Warfare: The Missing Link in Air Force Basic Doctrine," *Air Force Journal of Logistics,* Summer 1987, page 34.

69. *Time,* August 6, 1984, page 19.

70. Ibid.

71. F. Hyatt, "U.S. Found to Lack Supplies for War," *Washington Post,* August 3, 1984.

72. Ibid.

73. Rep. J. Courter, "The Gathering Storm," page 8.

74. R. Barnard, "A Short War: Navy and Air Force Face Severe Missile Shortage," *Defense Week.*

75. G. Wilson, *"Missiles Too Costly for Practice by Pilots," Washington Post,* June 23, 1980.

76. *Time,* March 7, 1983, pages 14 and 15.

77. F. Iklé, statement to the Senate Arms Service Committee, reported in article by J. Record ("A Three War Strategy?"), *Washington Post,* March 22, 1982.

78. C. Mohr, "Air Force Studies Says Budgets, Uncut, Still Won't Buy Arms in Five Year Plan," *New York Times,* February 4, 1983.

79. W. Kaufmann, "The Defense Budget," in *Setting National Priorities: The 1982 Budget,* ed. J. Pechman (Brookings Institution, 1982).

80. Adm. N. Gayler, "The Way Out: A General Nuclear Settlement," *Yale Law and Policy Review,* fall-winter 1986, page 145.

81. A. Tonelson, "The Trillion Dollar Paper Tiger" (review of R. Halloran's *To Arm a Nation*), *New York Times Book Review,* November 30, 1986, page 7.

82. M. Getler, "Splurging on Arms Doesn't Make Us Safe," *Washington Post,* June 24, 1984.

83. This was discussed in detail by UN Ambassador Jeane J. Kirkpatrick in an address to the American Defense Preparedness Association in Washington, D.C., on March 28, 1984.

84. G. Rathjens and J. Ruina, "Nuclear Doctrine and Rationality," *Daedalus,* winter 1981, page 187.

85. R. Smith, "Army Begins Producing Chemical Weapons, Ending Eighteen Year Moritorium," *Washington Post,* December 17, 1987.

86. For a discussion of this subject, see R. Blackwell, "The Outlook is Grim for Conventional Arms Control," *Washington Post,* December 20, 1987.

87. European Security Study, *Strengthening Conventional Deterrence in Europe: Proposals for the 1980s* (Saint Martin's, 1983), page 34.

88. Most analysts recognize that comparing a country's defense expenditures against its GNP is a very unsatisfactory way to measure a country's defense burden (see G. Kennedy, *Defense Economics,* [Saint Martin's, 1983])—for one thing, it does not capture the

relative costs of conscripted and volunteer troops. Nonetheless, it may be a useful initial surrogate for the defense commitments of a country.

89. P. Williams, "The Nunn Amendment: Burden Sharing and U.S. Troops in Europe," *Survival*, January-February 1985.

90. For a discussion of this issue see M. Nacht, "Towards an American Conception of Regional Security," *Daedalus*, winter 1981, page 20.

91. A. Pierre, ed., *The Conventional Defense of Europe: New Technologies and New Strategies* (Council on Foreign Relations, 1986), page 5.

92. *U.S. News and World Report*, November 23, 1987, page 31.

93. W. Kaufmann, in *Setting National Priorities: The 1982 Budget*, ed. J. Pechman *(Brookings Institution), 1982), page 154.*

94. *Ibid., page 172.*

95. *Secretary of Defense, National Security Strategy Report of the President (to the Congress), February 1988, page 21.*

96. *G. Wilson, "Pentagon Draft's Plans for War 'Surge' Output: Throw-Away Design Ordered for Munitions," Washington Post, January 4, 1986.*

97. F. Hyatt, "Hard Choices Confront Pentagon, Panel Says: Future Force Seen as 'Hollow' or Smaller," *Washington Post*, November 26, 1985.

98. Sen. S. Nunn, "Renegotiate the ABM Treaty?" *U.S. News and World Report*, December 14, 1987, page 30.

99. Y. Lubkin, "NATO Can Win with the Offensive Defense," *Strategic Policy*.

100. R. Komer, "The High Cost of Ruling the Seas," Washington Post, February 7, 1982.

101. J. Gaddis, "Containment: Past and Future," *International Security*, spring 1981, page 98.

102. R. Burt, "U.S. Defense Policy in the 1980s," *Daedalus*, winter 1981, page 172.

103. One who made this point was Andreas von Bulow, head of the Social Democratic Party's Commission on Security Policy in the Bundestag (see A. Pierre, ed., *The Conventional Defense of Europe: New Technologies and New Strategies* [Council on Foreign Relations, 1986], page 7). Also see "The Security of the Federal Republic of Germany and the Development of the Federal Armed Forces," White paper, Federal Minister of Defense, Bonn, September 4, 1979, page 126.

104. Gen. B. Palmer, Jr., *The Twenty-Five Year War: America's Military Role in Vietnam,* (Simon and Schuster, 1984), page 1.

105. For example, in 1984, Army Chief of Staff General John Wickham, Jr., and Air Force Chief of Staff General Charles Gabriel held a press conference to announce a program to consider 31 joint Air Force/Army "initiatives." However, a large part of this agreement failed to reach fruition. This was more a set of individual initiatives by the two men than a set of real joint initiatives by their respective institutions. See *Aerospace Daily,* May 28, 1984, page 129.

106. "U.S. Defense Policy in the 1980s," *Daedalus*, winter 1980, page ix.

107. Lubkin, "NATO Can Win with the Offensive Defense."

108. M. Rich, E. Dews, and C. Batten, Improving the Military Acquisition Process: Lessons from Rand Research, Rand Corporation report R3373-AF/RC, 1986, page 24.

109. Palmer, *The Twenty-Five Year War,* page 207.

110. M. Handle, "Numbers Do Count: The Question of Quality Versus Quantity," *Journal of Strategic Studies,* September 1981, page 226.

111. E. Joffe and G. Segal, in *International Institute for Strategic Studies,* July-August 1985, page 146.

Chapter 4

1. Some of the material in this section comes from my paper "We Can Afford Security," *Foreign Policy,* summer 1983, pages 64–84.

2. Report of the Secretary of Defense to the Congress, February 5, 1986, page 19.

3. *U.S. News and World Report,* November 9, 1987, page 25.

4. The lower figure comes from the Congressional Budget Office study Defense Spending and the Economy (February 1983; page 43); the higher figure comes from an earlier estimate by P. Lewis ("Defense Costs and the Economy," *New York Times,* December 19, 1976). The data from both sources have been scaled up to correspond to the budget levels of the late 1980s.

5. See R. Edwards, M. Reich, and T. Weisskoff, *The Capitalist System* (Prentice-Hall, 1972), page 372; P. Baran and P. Sweezy, *Monopoly Capital* (Monthly Review Press, 1966), page 176.

6. B. Blechman and V. Utgoff, "The Macroeconomics of Strategic Defenses," *International Security,* winter 1986–87, page 59.

7. *Washington Post,* March 31, 1985.

8. M. R. Smith, *Military Enterprise and Technological Change: Perspective on the American Experience* (MIT Press, 1985), page 4.

9. L. Dumas, "Innovation Under Seige," in *The Political Economy of Arms Reduction* (Selected Symposium 80, American Association for the Advancement of Science, 1982, ed. L. Dumas).

10. B. Blechman, E. Gramlich, and R. Hartman, "Setting National Priorities: The 1975 Budget" (Brookings Institution, 1974).

11. Congressional Budget Office, "Defense Spending and the Economy" February 1983, page 68.

12. W. Leontief and M. Hoffenberg, "The Economic Impact of Disarmament," *Scientific American,* April 1961, page 9.

13. J. F. Lawrence, "Spending for Defense: Boom or Bust?" *Los Angeles Times,* January 10, 1978.

14. J. K. Galbraith, *The New Industrial State* (Houghton Mifflin, 1967).

15. C. Schultz, "Do More Dollars Mean Better Defense?" *Challenge,* January-February 1983, pages 30–31.

16. G. Adams, "Defense Spending and the Economy: Does the Defense Dollar Make a Difference?" (Center on Budget and Policy Priorities, July 1987), page 3.

17. Ibid.

18. Source: study by Coopers & Lybrand comparing defense inflation rates with equivalent rates for consumer goods for the period 1976–1979, done for the DoD in 1980 (unpublished).

19. For example, see L. Thurow, "Beware of Reagan's Military Spending," *New York Times,* May 31, 1981.

20. D. P. Moynihan, "Reagan's Doctrine and the Iran Issue," *New York Times,* December 21, 1986.

21. *U.S. News and World Report,* July 11, 1983, pages 34–35.

22. For a full discussion of the B-1 lobbying, see N. Kotz, *Wild Blue Yonder: Money, Politics, and the B-1 Bomber* (Pantheon, 1988).

23. *Washington Post,* December 1, 1985.

24. B. Frye, *Modern Political Economy* (Martin Robertson, 1978).

25. B. Keller, "Billions for Defense: The Spending Debate," *New York Times,* May 14, 1985.

26. The data on which this figure is based (which were provided by the Stockholm International Peace Research Institute) appeared in the *Washington Post* on December 1, 1985, and in "Global Competition: The New Reality" (the final report of the Presidents Commission on Industrial Competitiveness, 1985).

27. J. Schumpeter, *Capitalism, Socialism, and Democracy* (Harper, 1942).

28. R. Nelson, "High Technology Policies: A Five-Nation Comparison," American Enterprise Institute, 1984, page 28.

29. S. Melman, "Twelve Propositions on Productivity and the War Economy," *Challenge,* March-April 1975, pages 6–11.

30. D. Noble, "Social Choice in Machine Design," in *Studies in the Labor Process,* ed. A. Zimbalist (Monthly Review Press, 1979), pages 25–26.

31. Ibid.

32. Nelson, "High Technology Policies," page 19.

33. Office of Management and Budget data, given in *Newsweek,* March 10, 1986, page 5.

34. Nelson, "High Technology Policies," page 21.

35. Melman, "Twelve Propositions."

36. T. Misa, "Military Needs, Commercial Realities, and the Development of the Transistor, 1948–1958," in *Military Enterprise and Technological Change: Perspectives on the American Experience,* ed. M. R. Smith (MIT Press, 1985), pages 276–287.

37. "Pentagon Infiltrating U.S. Economy," *Washington Post,* April 1, 1985.

38. *Washington Post,* December 1, 1985.

39. G. Kennedy, *Defense Economics,* (St. Martin's 1983), page 21.

40. H. Sapolsky, *The Polaris System Development: Bureaucratic and Programmatic Success in Government* (Harvard University Press, 1972), pages 112, 129.

41. For an interesting historical discussion of this issue, see P. Kennedy, *The Rise and Fall of the Great Powers* (Random House, 1988).

42. For a detailed discussion of the second alternative, and R. Rosecrance, *The Rise of the Trading State* (Basic Books, 1986).

43. *Washington Post,* September 3, 1981.

44. The well-known economist Herb Stein is one who frequently states this position.

Chapter 5

1. Some of the material in this chapter comes from my paper "Reforming the Defense Budget Process," *The Public Interest,* spring 1984, pages 62–75.

2. J. Colvard, "Technological Transformation of Defense," *Bureaucrat,* spring 1985, page 17.

3. D. Rice, "Defense Resource Management Study: Final Report," February 1979.

4. Ibid., page 4.

5. W. Kaufmann, "The Defense Budget" (Brookings Institution, 1982), page 135.

6. P. Tyler, "How the U.S. Cloaks a $24 Billion Budget," *Washington Post,* March 26, 1986.

7. D. Morrison, "Pentagon's Top Secret 'Black' Budget Has Skyrocketed during Reagan Years," *National Journal* 18 (1986), page 492.

8. For example, see the April 1986 report of the President's Blue Ribbon Commission on Defense Management.

9. "Budgeting for Defense Inflation," (Congressional Budget Office, January 1986).

10. G. Wilson, "Congressional Freeze on 1986 Budget Won't Halt the Rise in Defense Outlays," *Washington Post,* May 12, 1985.

11. However, Congress must "fully fund" the complete weapon system. This law came about because the Navy used to budget for only the first year of a ship's construction, but Congress was actually committed—after that—to the rest of the ship (in future budgets).

12. The source of this table is the Annual Summary of the Secretary of Defense's Annual Report, entitled "Defense '84, Meeting the Challenges," published in March 1984. Note that the difference between these numbers and the 1985 budget (figure 5.2) represents the difference between budget submittals and congressional authorizations for the year 1985.

13. A common congressional "trick" to help reduce the budget is simply to defer salary increases—for either civilian or military employees—until a subsequent year. This works only because of the one-year budget process.

14. Strong support for each program exists within the military, the defense industry, the national unions, and the communities involved, so Congress receives a lot of pressure against any proposed cancellation (and little support for it).

15. L. Korb, "A Blueprint for Defense Spending," *Wall Street Journal,* May 20, 1987.

16. See, for example, Comptroller General of the United States, "Managing the Cost of Government; Building an Effective Financial Management Structure," Report GAO/AFMD-84-43, General Accounting Office, March 1984.

17. M. Marder, "Hill Fights Reagan for Soul of Foreign Policy," *Washington Post,* September 2, 1984.

18. L. Hamilton, in *Foreign Affairs,* 1978, and quoted in "Hill Fights Reagan" (note 17).

19. Quoted in Marder, "Hill Fights Reagan."

20. T. Powers, "What's Worse than the MX?" *Washington Post,* March 31, 1985.

21. I. Destler, Institute for International Economics, quoted in M. Marder, "External Issues: Schism Over Security Interests Is Broad and Deep," *Washington Post,* September 3, 1984.

22. Draft report of CSIS Study on Defense Acquisition in the United States, April 9, 1986, page 26.

23. See S. Gilman, "Philosophical Challenge and Historical Ironies," *Bureaucrat,* spring 1985, page 10.

24. See M. Marder, "Deliberate Discord: Government Founded on Jealousy and Not Confidence," *Washington Post,* September 2, 1984.

25. G. Fossedal, "The Military-Congressional Complex," *Wall Street Journal,* August 8, 1985.

26. Report by the Office of the Secretary of Defense Study Team on "Management of the Office of the Secretary of Defense," October 1987, page IV-10.

27. Not every one of these congressional staffers is directly on the staff of a representative or a senator. (A representative is allowed 22 staffers; a senator, depending on the population of his state, 70 to 80.) A large number of these—and often the senior ones—are staff members of committees or subcommittees, and under the control of the committee chairman.

28. E. Planin, "Big Turnover and Low Pay on the Hill: Inexperience is Mark of Many Key Aides," *Washington Post,* November 9, 1987.

29. U.S. Senate Committee on Armed Services Staff Report to the Senate Committee on Armed Services, October 16, 1985, page 592.

30. In 1985, after the Armed Services and Appropriations committees got through with the process, 200 amendments were added in the House and the Senate during the 18 days of debate over the defense bill.

31. J. Courter, "Micromanaging Defense to Death." *Insight,* February 3, 1986, page 78.

32. One suggestion is to require a two-thirds majority vote to reopen the budget issue, either in the current year or for the next fiscal year.

33. This, and a number of the other budget recommendations offered herein, can also be found in "Strengthening the Federal Budget Process: A Requirement for Effective Fiscal Control" (Committee for Economic Development, June 1983).

34. For one proposed plan, see "National Security Planning and Budgeting" (Report to the President by the President's Blue Ribbon Commission on Defense Management, June 1986), page 19. Also, it should be noted that the timing of a two-year budget would be important (in the first year of Congress' two-year term—to minimize the tendency for "electioneering"), and it would have to be redone for the next two years well in advance, since the DoD's internal budget-preparation cycle is 18 months. (Hence the desirability of binding of the Congress for the third year—at least at the "top line.")

35. President's Private-Sector Survey on Cost Control, Task Force Report on The Office of the Secretary of Defense, July 13, 1983.

36. A two-year ("biennial") budget was put into the 1986 Defense Authorization Act, and the DoD did submit a two-year budget for fiscal years 1988 and 1989. Unfortunately, Congress, by and large, did not treat it very seriously. This area is going to require far

greater internal reform in Congress if Congress is to move in the direction of a multi-year budget process.

37. "The Budget Process in DoD," oral presentation by Vincent Puritano, Assistant Secretary of Defense (Comptroller), University of Kentucky, December 2, 1983.

38. A. Jordan and W. Taylor, Jr., *American National Security: Policy and Process* (Johns Hopkins University Press, 1984), page 121.

39. Ibid.

40. G. Fossedal, "Bureau-Capsizing Ideas Which Rattle Weinberger Would Improve Defense," *New York City Tribune,* March 7, 1986.

41. M. Bisnow, "Memo to Congress: Fire Half Your Staff," *Washington Post,* January 17, 1988.

42. "National Security Planning and Budgeting (Report to the President by the President's Blue Ribbon Commission on Defense Management, June 1986), page 17.

43. R. Parry, "Defense PAC Money Skyrockets," *Washington Post,* April 1, 1985.

44. At the time, Senator McIntire was the powerful chairman of the Senate Subcommittee on Defense Research and Development.

45. S. Roberts, "Political Aims of Lawmakers Bring Military Budget Rises," *New York Times,* May 17, 1985.

46. Ibid.

47. H. Dewar, "Lawmakers Are Up on Arms: MX Votes Reflect Invulnerability of Big Weapon Systems," *Washington Post,* March 24, 1985.

48. Ibid.

49. "Waste in the Pentagon," *New York Times,* September 13, 1981.

50. C. McCarthy, "Pork With a Ph.D.," *Washington Post,* July 19, 1986.

51. Ibid.

52. Fossedal, "Bureau-Capsizing Ideas" (note 40 above).

53. J. Courter, "Micromanaging Defense to Death," *Insight,* February 3, 1986, page 78.

54. J. Kester, "Under Seige," *Military Logistics Forum,* September-October 1984, page 27. (Kester was Special Assistant to Defense Secretary Harold Brown in the Carter administration).

55. Courter, "Micromanaging Defense to Death," page 78.

56. Senator John Tower, speech at the National Defense University to a symposium on the defense industrial base, December 10, 1987.

57. *Washington Post,* November 14, 1987.

58. A major part of this section comes from a paper by the present author that appeared as "Program Instability: Causes, Costs and Cures" in *Defense Management Journal,* (second quarter, 1986), pages 3–11.

59. "Affordable Acquisition Approach," Air Force Systems Command.

60. "Army Affordable Acquisition Approach," Army Materiel Command, September 1985.

61. "Affordable Acquisition Approach," Air Force Systems Command.

62. "Army Affordable Acquisition Approach," Army Materiel Command.

63. "Fiscal 1987 and 1988 Budget Request," *Washington Post,* February 9, 1987.

64. "The Weinberger Legacy," *International Herald Tribune,* December 24, 1987.

65. Ibid.

66. Six percent of the cuts in procurement and 9 percent of the cuts in R&D were attributed to Congress; the rest came from the Army.

67. Vince Puritano (former DoD Comptroller), statement to Procurement Round Table, Washington, April 16, 1986.

68. Rand Corporation report R3373-AF/RC, Santa Monica, January 1986, page 28.

69. D. Rice, Defense Resource Management Study, Final Report, February 1979, page 4.

70. President's Blue Ribbon Commission on Defense Management, "An Interim Report to the President," February 28, 1986, page 5.

71. David Holloway, "Military Power and Political Purpose in Soviet Policy," *Daedulus,* winter 1981, page 18.

72. F. Iklé, A. Wohlstetter, et al., "Discriminate Deterrence" (Report of the Commission on Integrated, Long-Term Strategy), January 1988.

73. "National Security Planning and Budgeting" (Report to the President by the President's Blue Ribbon Commission on Defense Management, June 1986), page 3.

74. See A. Barrett, *Reappraising Defense Organization* (National Defense University Press, 1983).

75. For an outstanding discussion of this issue, see S. Huntington, *The Soldier and the State: The Theory and Politics of Civil-Military Relations* (Belknap Press of Harvard University Press, 1957).

76. S. Huntington, *The Common Defense* (Columbia University Press, 1961), page 161.

77. M. Rovner, "Defense Dollars and Sense: A Common Cause Guide to the Defense Budget Process" (Common Cause, 1983), page 2.

Chapter 6

1. "A Formula for Action, A Report to the President on Defense Acquisition," page 5.

2. Opening statement by Sen. Dan Quayle, Chairman, Task Force on Selected Defense Procurement Matters, Senate Armed Services Commission, September 13, 1984.

3. *Aviation Week and Space Technology,* July 7, 1986, page 11.

4. The majority of these numbers come from repeated references. See, for example, page 3 of "A Formula for Action" (the Packard Commission report).

5. "A 7-Ton Clerical Fluke: Anchor Arrives Instead of Lamp," *Washington Post,* April 13, 1985.

6. Source: "Procurement Awards by Size" (published annually by the DoD) for the year 1976. (Specifically, for that year there were 10,000,163 action items, of which 9,946,000 were under $10,000 and only 216 were over that amount.

7. "Affordable Acquisition Approach," Air Force Systems Command.

8. As reported by Brigadier General Richard Smith at an Air Force Association meeting, January 14, 1985.

9. This description, and particularly the problems noted, draws heavily upon—in some cases I have quoted directly from it—"A Formula for Action." The original draft of this material was prepared by William Perry (the chairman of the Packard Commission's task force on Acquisition, and a former Under Secretary of Defense for acquisition).

10. J. Stolarow, "Inaccuracy of Department of Defense Weapons Acquisition Cost Estimates" (House Committee on Government Operations, November 16, 1979).

11. A major share of the discussion of this specific case comes from an article by J. Kushman, Jr.: "Northrop's Struggle with the MX," *New York Times,* November 22, 1987.

12. In the Federalist Papers, as quoted on page i of Thomas B. Delaney's paper "The Federal Acquisition Regulation System: A Review and Analysis" (Office of Management and Budget, November 1986).

13. "Defense, Inc.," *Washington Post,* March 31, 1985.

14. *Washington Post,* September 17, 1986.

15. Stanford Research Institute, 1963, quoted on page i of Delaney, "Federal Acquisition Regulation System" (note 12 above).

16. Commission on Government Procurement, December 1972, quoted in Delaney, "Federal Acquisition Regulations System."

17. "A Formula for Action."

18. "Proposal for a Uniform Federal Procurement System" (Office of Management and Budget, Office of Federal Procurement Policy, February 26, 1982), page 23.

19. M. Weidenbaum, *The Modern Public Sector: New Ways of Doing the Government's Business* (Basic Books, 1969), page 48.

20. Oral presentation by Air Force procurement expert Major General Bernard Weiss at Defense Science Board 1986 Summer Study on Commercial Components, Colorado Springs.

21. Raytheon Vice-President Joseph Shea, in connection with a Defense Science Board Task Force, compared in detail the government's requirements and those being passed on to various levels of the supplier base in his firm. After his analysis—which showed the significant amplification of the requirements as they went down into the lower tiers—he went back (in 1974) and attempted to revise Raytheon's procedures so that they would be less restrictive. This was not an easy task, since there was concern that the prime contractor would then be assuming a larger share of the risk than might make good business sense.

22. The times given in this section for "typical" programs in each phase of the acquisition cycle are representative of a wide variety of weapon systems developed during the 1970s and the 1980s. The time spans considered are those of seven specific programs: Phalanx, Sea-Launch Cruise Missile, Captor, Patriot, Stinger, A-10, and EF-111A. See J. R. Fox and J. L. Field, *The Defense Management Challenge: Weapons Acquisition* (Harvard Business School Press, 1988) for details of these programs and others.

23. W. Adams, "The Military-Industrial Complex and the New Industrial State," *American Economic Review* 58, no. 2 (1968), pages 655–661.

24. J. McKee, Concentration in Military Procurement Markets: A Classification and Analysis of Contract Data, Rand Corporation report RM-6307-PR, 1970, page 16.

25. M. J. Green, ed., *The Monopoly Makers: Ralph Nader's Study Report on Regulation and Competition* (Grossman, 1973), page 8.

26. An earlier version of this list appeared on pages 30 and 31 of my book *The Defense Industry* (MIT Press, 1980). A shorter list making the same point appears on page 164 of Gavin Kennedy's book *Defense Economics* (St. Martin's, 1983).

27. G. C. Lodge, review of *The Ethical Basis of Economic Freedom* (ed. I. Hill), *New York Times,* October 24, 1976.

28. R. Lipsey and K. Lancaster, "The General Theory of the Second Best," *Review of Economic Studies* 24 (1956, 1957), pages 11–32. For a simple mathematical treatment of this theory, see J. Henderson and R. Quante, *Macroeconomics Theory: A Mathematical Approach* (McGraw-Hill, 1971), pages 286–288.

29. Sen. George Mahan, speech to National Securities Industries Association, Washington, January 1976.

30. Barry Bosworth, at meeting on Defense Industrial Strategy, National Defense University, November 10, 1987 (unpublished remarks).

31. E. Corey, *Procurement Management: Strategy, Organization, and Decision Making* (Van Nostrand Reinhold, 1978).

32. The idea for this table and much of the material in it comes from an unpublished paper by Sherri L. Wasserman Goodman, "Legal Dilemmas and the Weapons Acquisition Process: The Role of Contract in the Procurement of the SSN-688 Attack Submarine" (Harvard University, September, 1987).

33. For a good discussion of the bargaining environment, see B. Frey, *Modern Political Economy* (Martin Robertson, 1978).

34. The trend has been toward less government ownership. In the 1950s it was about 70%, by 1963 it was 55%, and by 1976 it was 35%. The remaining amount is still very significant.

35. For an example of a typical distribution, in FY 1975, between government and contractor facilities for aircraft modifications, see Gansler, *The Defense Industry,* page 35.

36. The Army, using the Army Arsenal Act of 1853 (which clearly has a public-sector bias), tends to do more of its work "in house"; the Air Force, using the Air Force Arsenal Act of 1951 (which leaves the choice up to the Secretary of the Air Force), tends to favor the private sector for manufacturing but still uses its own laboratories and repair depots extensively. The Defense Industrial Reserve Act of 1973 maintains the ambiguity over the guidance of Congress in this area.

37. The four basic principles underlying the contracting process are that a contract shall be awarded on a competitive basis, that it shall be awarded to a contractor who is deemed responsible (financially and otherwise), that the type of contract shall be appropriate for the particular procurement, and that defense procurement programs shall be used to implement national social and economic policies (minimum wages, working conditions, small business set-asides, etc.). These were discussed in detail in *Aviation Week,* February 27, 1985.

38. *Fortune,* April 14, 1978, page 15.

39. This number was supplied to me in 1986 by the contract manager of the program.

40. *Washington Post,* March 31, 1985. Almost identical numbers are given in the *New York Times* of May 15.

41. F. Elliott, "F-14 Costs: Up, Up and Away," *Navy News and Underseas Technology,* February 13, 1987, page 1.

42. J. Gerth, "Pentagon Buying: Need for Businesslike Business," *New York Times,* May 15, 1985.

43. "GAO Finds Navy Repairs Invariably Top Estimates," *Journal of Commerce,* January 16, 1986, page 24b.

44. Statement by Joseph Bower of Harvard Business School, January 31, 1985.

45. R. Atkinson and F. Hyatt, "Defense Inc.," *Washington Post,* March 31, 1985.

46. Ibid.

47. These problems include an extremely high false-alarm rate for the diagnostic kit intended to help with maintenance, fuel leaks from the aircraft, the fact that the offensive avionics system jams the defense electronics system, the fact that the terrain-following radar shows mountains that don't exist, and stalling with normal payloads. See F. Kaplan, "B1 Problems Could Cost $3 Billion, Aspin Says," *Boston Globe,* February 13, 1987.

48. "GAO Finds Navy Repairs Invariably Top Estimates," *Journal of Commerce,* January 16, 1986, page 24b.

49. H. Sapolsky, *The Polaris System Development: Bureaucratic and Programmatic Success in Government* (Harvard University Press, 1972).

50. T. Hayes, "Arms Suppliers Pushed on Cost and Quality," *New York Times,* June 11, 1984.

51. For example, see H. L. Gilmore, "Consumer Product Cost Revisited," *Quality Progress,* April 1983, pages 30–31.

52. *U.S. News and World Report,* June 4, 1984, page 73.

53. For a good discussion of this see R. Waterman, Jr., *The Renewal Factor: How the Best Get and Keep the Competitive Edge* (Bantam, 1987), page 110.

54. Augustine, president of Martin Marietta and former Under Secretary of the Army, is the author of *Augustine's Laws,* first published by the American Institute of Aeronautics and Astronautics in 1982. An expanded version was published in 1986 by Penguin Books.

55. See figure 1.1.

56. *Washington Post,* May 19, 1985; *New York Times,* May 14, 1985. Both of these reports were based on a Congressional Budget Office analysis.

57. Rockefeller Brothers' Fund, *International Security—The Military Aspect* (Doubleday, 1958), page 34.

58. M. Peck and F. Scherer, *The Weapons Acquisition Process: An Economic Analysis.* (Harvard University Press, 1962).

59. The systems cited in figure 6.2 are all Air Force systems. The data are from "Affordable Acquisition Approach (A^3)" (Air Force Systems Command, Andrews Air Force Base).

60. Source: J. Gansler and C. Henning, "European Weapons Acquisition Practices: Implications for the U.S." (forthcoming).

61. Ibid., page 11.

62. R. Atkinson and F. Hyatt, "To Prepare for War We Need a Revolution," *Washington Post,* December 15, 1985.

63. L. Shearer, in *Parade,* December 22, 1985, page 18.

64. C. Morris, "Our Muscle-Bound Navy," *New York Times Magazine,* April 24, 1988.

65. Presentation by Andy McMahan, Vice-President for Manufacturing at General Dynamics, at meeting of American Defense Preparedness Association, Washington, December 11, 1986.

66. *U.S. News and World Report,* February 25, 1985, page 62.

67. Ibid.

68. This conclusion comes from an unpublished study done for the Air Force Electronics Systems Division, Hanscom Air Force Base, Bedford, Mass., in 1987.

69. House Committee on Government Operations, "Inaccuracy of Department of Defense Weapons Acquisition Cost Estimates" (November 16, 1979).

70. Comptroller General of the United States, "Acquisition of Major Weapon Systems."

71. "Affordable Acquisition Approach," Air Force Systems Command.

72. E. Gibbon, *The Decline and Fall of the Roman Empire* (Penguin edition, 1981, page 69).

73. N. Augustine, *Augustine's Laws,* page 67.

74. D. Griffiths, "Costs Overruns: Fading Fast," *Military Logistics Forum,* November-December 1986, page 45.

75. U.S. General Accounting Office, "Status of Major Acquisitions as of September 30, 1981: Better Reporting Essential to Controlling Cost Growth," Report no. MASAD-82-94, April 22, 1982, page 8.

76. N. Augustine, *Augustine's Laws.* In a detailed comparison of major milestones for weapon systems, Augustine found a "fantasy factor" (slippage) of about 33 percent on milestones that covered periods of up to 8 years.

77. Congressional Budget Office, "Effects of Weapons Procurement Stretchouts on Costs and Schedules," November 1987.

78. Senator Jeff Bingaman, "Sludge in the Defense Pipeline: Slow Procurement Rates Build Towards a Cost Explosion," *Los Angeles Times,* January 5, 1986.

79. F. Scherer, *The Weapons Acquisition Process: Economic Incentives* (Harvard Business School Press, 1967), page 289.

80. Occasionally a program is canceled by Congress (as was the DIVAD in 1985) or by the services (the Low-Level, Laser Guided Bomb was canceled by the Air Force Secretary in 1985). In these cases, the headlines always point out how much money was "wasted" on the program before it was canceled.

81. With regard to the negative effects of increased regulation, see E. Gerloff, The Management of Government R&D Projects: The Effects of the Contractual Requirement to Use Specific Management Techniques, doctoral disertation, University of Texas, Austin, 1971, page 118.

82. F. Scherer, *Industrial Market Structure and Economic Performance* (Rand-McNally, 1970), page 199.

83. On a typical weapon-system proposal (one by the LTV Corporation to the Navy for a new airplane), each copy of the final document consisted of 194 books, having 82,000 pages, stacking 25 feet high, and weighing 7,500 lbs. (LTV newspaper, *Profile*, February 6, 1975). This particular proposal did not win a contract.

84. In a proposal for selling the Air Force an improved version of the F-15 (known as the Strike Eagle), McDonnell Douglas and six of its subcontractors (Hughes Aircraft, IBM, GE, Sperry, Ford, and Litton) developed a prototype on their own. Hughes had to invest $15 million and McDonnell $25 million (*Fortune*, November 2, 1981, page 16).

85. The total cost of the industry's proposal efforts on the TFX aircraft (later called the F-111) was estimated to be $45 million.

86. A contrary theory is that the government simply picks the firm whose "turn" it is. See J. Kurth, hearings of Joint Committee on Defense Production, 95th Congress, September 29–30, 1977.

87. Scherer, *Industrial Market Structure*, page 9. For details on two specific examples, see G. C. Wilson, "The Condor Missile and Its Friends," *Washington Post*, November 9, 1976, and R. J. Art, *The TFX Decision: MacNamara and the Military* (Little, Brown, 1968).

88. For a discussion of these two points, see Scherer, "The Weapons Acquisition Process," page 27.

89. From a report in which Lieutenant General James W. Stansberry (U.S. Air Force, retired) analyzed the procurement process for the Packard Commission (February 28, 1986).

90. In order to meet the minimum standard of responsibility, a contractor must have adequate financial resources, be able to comply with the required or proposed performance schedule, have a satisfactory record of performance, have a satisfactory record of integrity, and be otherwise qualified under applicable laws and regulations. While this may be somewhat difficult to demonstrate in the case of an aircraft supplier, it rarely is in the case of a parts supplier, and thus essentially everyone is allowed to bid on contracts for most products. Even prior questionable legal behavior is often not considered a basis for excluding a bidder.

91. Report of the Commission on Government Procurement, December 1972.

92. Scherer, *The Weapons Acquisition Process*, page 48.

93. In the 1984 Competition in Contracting Act, Congress specifically changed the requirement from "effective competition" to "full and open competition."

94. Another example: The Army's Rock Island Arsenal held a competition for an $11,000 item and, after putting an announcement in the *Commerce Business Daily*, got over 100 responses. The cost of reproducing and sending out the invitation to bid was over $5,000. This is not a cost-effective way to do business. (This case was reported at the National Contract Management Association Meeting of October 30, 1985.)

95. This argument is presented extremely well in a paper by Colleen A. Preston (a staff member of the House Arms Services Committee): "Improving the Acquisition Process— The Role of Congress," written for a Center for Strategic and International Studies Program in 1987. See especially pages 8 and 26.

96. U.S. Postal Service Procurement Manual, September 30, 1987.

97. See, for example, Adams, "The Military Industrial Complex," page 10; Peck and Scherer, *The Weapons Acquisition Process,* page 46.

98. See Scherer, *Industrial Market Structure,* page 266.

99. Such as the Herfindahl-Hischman Index.

100. Assistant Attorney General Douglas Ginsberg, head of the Department of Justice Anti-Trust Division; stated on January 9, 1986 and reported in the Bureau of National Affairs' Anti-Trust and Trade Regulation Report, volume 50 (1986), page 57.

101. For example, Boeing had 100 percent of the bomber market when it made the B-52 but after that had 0. Rockwell had 0 until it made the B-1, then it had 100 percent, and when the B-1 was completed it went back to 0. Northrop had 0 percent until it produced the B-2; it then had 100 percent. Yet these three firms are clearly all in the "bomber business."

102. L. Ellsworth and M. J. Green, eds., *The Monopoly Makers: Ralph Nader's Study Report on Regulation and Competition* (Grossman, 1973), page 8.

103. Adams, "The Military Industrial Complex," page 10.

104. In the case of the Advanced Tactical Fighter, teams of two or three of the aircraft prime contractors were encouraged to bid together against other comparable teams for the prototype phase. In this way, the government is able to keep multiple suppliers when there is only a single program planned for a decade or more, and the contractors are able to divide up the risk and the high costs associated with such proposal activities. However, such teams do not necessarily represent increased efficiency (unless they result in greater specialization), and two firms on the same team certainly do not represent competition for each other. Thus, there is considerable controversy over whether teaming is good or bad from the government's viewpoint.

105. For examples of the benefits of competition on each of the above parameters, related to particular weapon systems, see L. Kratz and J. Gansler, "Effective Competition During Weapon System Acquisition," National Contract Management Association, McLean, Virginia, December 31, 1985, pages 1–3.

106. On June 28, 1985, in a case involving a professional service contract, the GAO overturned the government's award to the low bidder because the government had stated in the Request for Proposal that cost was a secondary consideration. (See Comptroller General's Decision on Protest by DLI Engineering Corporation.)

107. Public Law 98-369, Section 2753.

108. This concept is applicable even to competitions for simple items such as spare parts. In 1987, Major General Smith of the Air Force Logistics Command set up a concept called "Blue Ribbon Suppliers" according to which he was willing to give contracts to suppliers who had performed well in the past even if their bids were up to 20 percent higher than a new bidder's. Such recognition of the importance of past performance is crucial to the development of a strong defense industrial base, as well as to the acquisition of high-quality goods. For a discussion of this concept as it began to be applied in the Navy, see S. Zimmerman, "Low Bids No Longer Enough at Naval Avionics Center," *Navy News and Undersea Technology,* January 25, 1988, page 8.

109. For a full discussion of each of these cases, see Kratz and Gansler, "Effective Competition During Weapon System Acquisition" (note 105 above).

110. Kratz, "Competition During Weapon System Acquisition," Federal Acquisition Research Symposium, Richmond, Virginia, November 1985.

111. The Multiple Launch Rocket System was designed competitively for the Army, and per-unit production cost was stressed in the development phase. See MLRS Case Study (Cambridge Case Clearinghouse, Cambridge, Mass.).

112. A classic example: The Army had a program for a new helicopter (the LHX) that was to cost tens of billions of dollars. In March of 1987 the Army was quoted in the *New York Times* as saying that "competition, which is to continue through the research phase and into the helicopter's production, is crucial to restraining the program's cost." However, as the defense budget started to tighten up, the Army was quoted as saying, "You'll see us down-select by the end of Fiscal Year 1988 and go to just one design team. . . . It's too expensive to keep two working for any length of time." (*New York Times*, January 17, 1988)

113. Joe Bain concludes that, in defense contracting, the main effect of economies of scale is to help in sales-promotion activities—which are not necessarily in the government's interest. He finds that the data call into question the very large economic efficiencies that might be normally expected from scale economies. See J. S. Bain, *Barriers to New Competition: Their Character and Consequences in Manufacturing Industries* (Harvard University Press, 1956), pages 57 and 211.

114. For detailed examples and historical data, see Kratz and Gansler, "Effective Competition During Weapon System Acquisition."

115. *Washington Post,* May 19, 1985.

116. Ibid.

117. R. Ropelewski, "Negotiating Contracts for F-100, F-110 Improvements," *Aviation Week and Space Technology,* May 20, 1985, page 18. See also "Great Engine War" (Cambridge Case Clearinghouse).

118. Sometimes even Congress has resisted the introduction of a second course. See J. S. Gansler, "Defense Spending: How About Some Real Competition?" *Washington Post,* April 4, 1982.

119. Scherer, *The Weapons Acquisition Process.*

120. Public Law 98-92.

121. The Navy had set up a Rear Admiral as the Competition Advocate the year before. *Navy News and Underseas Technology* of March 1, 1985, describes the role of Rear Admiral Stewart Platt in this capacity.

122. One of the undesirable characteristics of the CICA is that it encourages protests through a new procedure. However, this provision could be removed through subsequent legislation without hampering the intent of the law.

123. Electronics Industries Association, "Trends in Competition" (Defense Market Analysis, 1988), page 25.

124. E. White, "Defense Industry Slims Down to Survive," *Wall Street Journal,* September 30, 1987.

125. When Navy Secretary Lehman said that he might buy F-14s instead of F-18s, the price of the F-18 dropped dramatically (*Defense Management Journal,* fourth quarter 1985, page 43).

126. For an example of the impact of picking the low bidder and getting a low-quality product, see F. Hyatt and R. Atkinson, "Pentagon Seemed Lax on Defects," *Washington Post,* March 15, 1985.

127. Scherer, *The Weapons Acquisition Process,* page 49.

128. D. Morrison, "Defense Focus," *National Journal,* November 7, 1987, page 2827.

129. This case has received considerable press—almost annually. For example, see M. Weisskopf, "Fine Print for U.S. Fruitcakes," *Washington Post,* December 24, 1985.

130. One company, with only 10 employees, submitted 50 protests in the three years following the passage of the law. See S. Sugawara and E. Tucker, "Companies' Contract Appeals Clog Government Purchasing," *Washington Post,* July 16, 1988.

131. J. Gansler, "But Check the Price of That Fruitcake!" *Washington Post,* January 4, 1986.

132. C. Sugarman, "Uncle Sam Goes Shopping," *Washington Post,* December 2, 1987.

133. C. Sugarman, "Life in the Checkout Lane at Fort Belvoir Commissary," *Washington Post,* December 2, 1987.

134. R. Stimson and M. Barnett, "Buying Commercial: What Works and What Doesn't," *Defense Systems Management Review,* spring 1980.

135. W. Suss, "How to Sell to Uncle Sam," *Harvard Business Review,* November-December 1984.

136. G. Fossedal, "The Military-Congressional Complex," *Wall Street Journal,* August 8, 1985.

137. Senate Resolution S.1958, "To Prohibit the Department of Defense from Obligating or Expending any Funds for the Procurement of Certain Toilet Seat Shrouds in Excess of $125," 99th Congress First Session, December 17, 1985.

138. General Accounting Office B-200233, September 26, 1980.

139. W. Kirby, Expanding the Use of the Commercial Products and "Commercial-Type" Acquisition Techniques in Defense Procurement: A Proposed Legal Framework, report prepared for President's Blue Ribbon Commission on Defense Management, June 1986.

140. Use of Commercial Components in Military Equipment, briefing report, Defense Science Board 1986 Summary Study.

141. *New York Times,* November 8, 1987; *Washington Post,* March 22, 1985; *U. S. News and World Report,* November 16, 1987; *Washington Post,* May 12, 1985, June 2, 1984, November 27, 1985.

142. Packard Commission Survey of Public Opinion on Defense Procurement, 1986.

143. For some early examples, see *Aerospace Daily,* June 20, 1988, page 443, and the cover story of *Business Week,* July 4, 1988.

144. See R. Kaufman, *The War Profiteers* (Anchor Books, 1972); C. Pursell, Jr., *The Military Industrial Complex* (Harper and Row, 1972); W. Cole, *Roosevelt and the Isolationists, 1932–1945* (University of Nebraska Press, 1983).

145. E. Luttwak, *The Art of War* (Simon & Schuster, 1984), page 265.

146. At the AFCEA national conference, Washington, June 22, 1988.

147. R. Atkinson, and F. Hyatt, "The Arms Makers' Ethics," *Washington Post,* February 1, 1985.

148. Final report of the President's Private-Sector Commission on Government Management (the Grace Commission), March 1985, book II, page ES-9.

149. For an example of significant quality problems with a weapon system, see Richard Halloran, "The Trouble With Defense Contractors," *New York Times Magazine*, December 8, 1985, pages 142ff.

150. F. Hyatt and R. Atkinson, "Air Force Found Inefficiency at Six Weapons Contractors," *Washington Post*, April 21, 1985.

151. For an extensive discussion of some of the effects of congressional regulation on defense costs, see F. Hyatt and R. Atkinson, "To Pentagon, Oversight Has Become Overkill," *Washington Post*, July 4, 1985.

152. D. Morrison, "Overstocked," *National Journal*, November 7, 1987, page 2827.

153. Ibid. Another example: A large number of Army helmets were scrapped erroneously. "It was just a mistake," a senior DoD official stated. "They simply miscoded the helmets." (*Washington Post*, February 28, 1985)

154. G. Wilson, "Lack of Spare Parts," *Washington Post*, February 28, 1985. See also "Army's Lack of Spare Parts Found Costly," *Washington Post*, February 22, 1988.

155. Steven Ryan, Senate Government Affairs Committee Counsel, stated that "the way the people are maintaining [spare-parts stocks] is by buying too much of everything." (*National Journal*, November 7, 1987, page 2827)

156. See "Navy Cancels GE Job Totaling 79.6 Million for Aircraft Engines," *Wall Street Journal*, December 28, 1984.

157. S. Auerbach, "Reagan Imposes Restraints on Machine Tool Imports: Five Year Curb Granted on Security Grounds," *Washington Post*, December 1, 1986.

158. In the name of national security, more than 6,000 bailouts have occurred since 1958. See "Contracting Conducted Over Golden Safety Net," *Washington Post*, March 31, 1985.

159. The following list is based on a summary by T. Reinkober, M. Nugent, and K. Krieg for the Packard Commission in a draft dated January 24, 1986.

160. In 1984, Air Force buyers ordered 83 bolts of a type that had not been made for 20 years at a price of $17.59 each. Had they ordered these bolts when the production line was still in existence, they could have gotten 1,200 for the same price; however, there would have been headlines saying that the Air Force had bought over 1,000 unneeded bolts.

161. At an Air Force Association meeting on January 14, 1985, Major General Dewey Low stated that the Air Force often buys the same item five or ten times a year.

162. One extreme example: The Defense Contract Audit Agency looked at 310 items of support equipment which were passed through the prime contractor from two tiers of subcontractors. The auditor estimated that if the government had bought the equipment directly from the vendors the price would have been $531,000. Purchased through the prime contractor, the items cost $1,438,000. (Office of Federal Procurement Policy, Report to the Congress, "Review of the Spare Parts Procurement Practices of the Department of Defense," June 1984, page 6)

163. Major General Dewey Low, at an Air Force Association meeting on January 14,

1985. (This meeting was videotaped and used to educate Air Force personnel on the spare-parts issue.)

164. Brigadier General Richard Smith, of the Air Force Logistics Command, at an Air Force Association presentation on this topic, January 14, 1985.

165. M. Moore, "Pentagon 'Savings' May Shock the Taxpayer," *Washington Post,* April 8, 1987.

166. *Time,* April 8, 1985, page 24. For an additional listing of such examples, see *USA Today,* April 29, 1985.

167. This came about as a result of the requirement that 5 percent of the DoD's business be given to small and disadvantaged firms, which had been receiving less than 3 percent of the DoD's contract dollars (*Washington Post,* editorial, January 11, 1988).

168. Ibid.

169. Those indicted in this case included a member of Congress, a former White House aide, a California attorney who was a close friend of the Attorney General, and the Attorney General's former investment advisor. The Attorney General himself was under investigation. (Ibid.)

170. Senator Lowell Weicker. (Ibid.)

171. P. Earley, "Sherick Seeks to Plug Pentagon Dike," *Washington Post,* November 26, 1984.

172. Report of the Secretary of Defense Frank C. Carlucci to the Congress on the Amended FY 1988/FY 1989 Biennial, Budget, February 18, 1988, page 143.

173. J. Kitfield, "Best of Times, Worst of Times," *Military Logistics Forum,* July–August, 1986, page 7. See also R. Reich, "On the Brink of an Anti-Business Era," *New York Times,* April 12, 1987.

174. "Pentagon Fraud Unit Marches Slowly," *Washington Post,* February 10, 1987.

175. Ibid.

176. For an example of this, see R. Atkinson and F. Hyatt, "The Arms Makers' Ethics," *Washington Post,* September 15, 1985.

177. For examples of falsified statements, see N. Black, "B-1 Firm Suspended From New Contracts," *Washington Post,* November 10, 1987, and P. Tyler, "Contractors Sought to Withhold Cost Overrun Data," *Washington Post,* September 26, 1984.

178. This is a particularly serious offense because it affects the potential performance of the weapon systems, as well as being a financial issue. See R. Halloran, "Pentagon Calls Product Substitution a Key Fraud Problem," *New York Times,* October 18, 1987; see also "Military Supplier To Plead Guilty in Parts Scheme," *New York Times,* November 29, 1987.

179. One specific case of kickbacks connected with a direct sale to the government involved several clothing companies and a few DoD employees (see "Nation's Armed Forces Running Short of Uniforms," *New York Times,* February 21, 1988).

180. For some examples, see E. Pound, "Investigators Detect Pattern of Kickbacks for Defense Business," *Wall Street Journal,* November 11, 1985, and E. White, "U.S. Charges 19 in Kickback Schemes Involving Defense Firms in California," *Wall Street Journal,* July 25, 1986.

181. H. Kurtz, "Meese Unveils Plan to Fight Defense Fraud," *Washington Post,* September 17, 1985.

182. R. Marcus, "The Case Against General Dynamics Tripped Over Two Little Words," *Washington Post,* July 30, 1987.

183. "Government Procurement Reforms: The Need to Consider Long-Term Effects," *Program Manager,* November-December, 1987, page 14.

184. G. Anthes, "Audit Agency Staff Grows, So Does Backlog," *Washington Business Journal,* January 19, 1987.

185. M. Mintz, "GAO Auditing Defense Firms," *Washington Post,* October 6, 1985.

186. J. Barry, "In Bureaucratic Splendor," *Business Month,* January 1988, page 59.

187. "U.S. Defense Acquisition: A Process in Trouble" (Center for Strategic and International Studies, Georgetown University, 1987), appendix A, page 57.

188. Forty percent of those on the Defense Contract Audit Agency's auditing staff had two years or less on the job (G. Anthes, "Audit Agency Staff Grows, So Does Backlog," *Washington Business Journal,* January 19, 1987).

189. V. Guidry, Jr., "Fifty Percent of Defense Buyers Don't Trust Firms," *Baltimore Sun,* July 12, 1986.

190. It was not at all uncommon for the length of time to make an award to more than double during this period. In the Defense Advance Resource Projects Agency, the award time went from 90 days to over 270 days.

191. J. Colvard, Deputy Chief of Navy Materiel, "Procurement: What Price Mistrust?" *Government Executive,* March 1985, page 20.

192. "Government Procurement Reforms: The Needs to Consider Long-Term Effects," *Program Manager,* November-December, 1987, page 15.

193. President's Blue Ribbon Commission on Defense Management, A Quest for Excellence: Final Report to the President, June 1986.

194. "Business Are Signing Up For Ethics 101," *Business Week,* February 15, 1988, page 54.

195. For a complete discussion of this program, see J. Artabane, W. Spriggs, and C. Kirwin, "Government Contractors, Self Governance Obligations and Employee Relations" (Washington Legal Foundation, 1988).

196. Packard Commission, "A Formula For Action," page 27.

197. E. Staats, "Public Service and the Public Interest," Webb Lecture, National Academy of Public Administration, Washington November 20, 1987, page 7.

198. J. Havemann, "Volcker Sees Crisis For Public Service," *Washington Post,* December 4, 1987.

199. J. Dickenson, *Appointee Aggravations,"* *Washington Post,* December 10, 1985.

200. Eighty percent of the presidential appointees surveyed said that they were thrown into their jobs without being told what the president wanted them to accomplish, what their relationship was to his overall program, how the federal government works, or how to deal with Congress and the press.

201. From an interview in Studs Turkel's *The Good War* (Pantheon, 1984), page 327.

202. "A Conversation with Joseph Bower: Run the Federal Government Like a Business? Forget It," *U.S. News and World Report,* April 23, 1984, page 77.

203. Federal regulations require that senior defense appointees divest themselves of all stocks, bonds, and interest in profit-sharing plans of any firm with defense contracts of more than $25,000 per year.

204. National Association of Public Administration, "Leadership in Jeopardy: The Fraying of the Presidential Appointment System" (Final Report of the Presidential Appointee Project), November 1985.

205. Quoted by Elmer Staats in his Webb Lecture (note 197 above).

206. Packard Commission, "A Formula for Action," page 28.

207. J. R. Fox, "Revamping the Business of National Defense," *Harvard Business Review,* September-October, 1984, page 69.

208. General Accounting Office, "DoD Acquisition: Capabilities of Key DoD Personnel in Systems Acquisition," report no. GAO/NSIAD-86-45, May 1986.

209. J. R. Fox and J. L. Field, *The Defense Management Challenge: Weapons Acquisition* (Harvard Business School Press, 1988).

210. "Joint Program Management Study" (Air Force Systems Command, Andrews Air Force Base, Washington 1984), page 6.

211. M. Weisskopf, "Navy Pushes Business Skills," *Washington Post,* March 15, 1985.

212. In the mid-1980s each of the services established a well-defined acquisition career program. The Army set up a Materiel Acquisition Management Program, and the Navy a Materiel Professional Program. The Air Force issued Detailed Career Planning Regulations for technical personnel and program managers.

213. Based on an interview (conducted by the author) of Dag Törnblom, System Development Director of Sweden's Defense Materiel Administration, in 1987.

214. An initiative to "streamline" the acquisition organizations was a major recommendation of the Packard Commission. Such streamlining has been attempted—with varying degrees of success—by the services.

215. Fox and Field, *The Defense Management Challenge,* page 247.

216. Packard Commission, "A Formula for Action," page 29. The commission went on to specifically recommend that recruitment and retention of key civilians be correlated with pay incentives, and that advancement be based on performance.

217. These jobs are defined under Civil Service Title VIII as GS-1102 positions.

218. Office of Federal Procurement Policy, "Report on the Acquisition Work Force through FY1982," October 1983. The percentage of the contracts and procurements specialists between grades GS-9 and GS-12 having college degrees ranged from 20 to 46; above grade GS-13, between 18 and 66 percent of the specialists had degrees.

219. The Packard Commission drew an analogy to the requirement that now exists for accounting personnel, and recommended an entry-level criterion of 24 semester hours in business-related courses or equivalent experience. The Office of Personnel Management didn't agree with these recommendations; the GAO offered the suggestion that perhaps only contracting personnel assigned to work on major weapon systems might be required to have a particularly high level of skill, and thus perhaps a separate Civil Service job classification system might be established for the contracting officers in this area. For a

detailed discussion of the DoD's civilian workforce, see Fox and Field, *The Defense Management Challenge*.

220. To avoid any conflict of interest, it would be necessary to specify that these industry people would not work on programs directly involving the companies from which they had come, and that after leaving the government they could not work for a company with which they had been directly involved while managing a program. Such constraints would not prevent employees from going back to the firms from which they had come, yet they would preclude even the appearance of a conflict of interests.

221. For a detailed discussion of this idea and the prior experiences, see the 1987 Procurement Round Table report titled "Strengthening Government Acquisition Management Through Selected Use of Experienced Industrial Managers."

222. Packard Commission, "A Formula for Action," page 28.

Chapter 7

1. These four points were raised by Under Secretary of Defense William J. Perry in his FY 1982 R&D presentation to Congress (January 20, 1981), yet they remain challenges even after the doubling of the acquisition budget during the Reagan administration.

2. C. Danhof, "Government Contracting and Technological Change," Brookings Institution, 1968.

3. In 1984 total federal R&D expenditures were $44.2 billion, of which $29.3 billion went for national defense (66%). The next largest item was $4.8 billion for health, followed by $2.6 billion for energy and $2.3 billion for space. (Source: National Science Foundation, as reported by James Schwartz, *Washington Post,* December 10, 1985.) This represented a dramatic buildup in defense R&D, from $13.6 billion in FY 1980 to $31.3 billion in FY 1985. (S. A. Cain, "The Fiscal Year 1989 Defense Budget," Center on Budget and Policy Priorities, Washington, February 22, 1988.)

4. J. S. Gansler, *The Defense Industry* (MIT Press, 1980), pages 101 and 102.

5. As quoted in Walter McDougall's book *The Heavens and The Earth: A Political History of the Space Age* (Basic Books, 1986), page 229.

6. Ibid., page 319.

7. An interesting example of technology following strategy might well be the Strategic Defense Initiative of President Reagan. The technologists, largely caught off guard, began a crash program to try to come up with technologies that could implement the stated strategy.

8. J. Canan, *The Super Warriors: The Fantastic World of Pentagon Super Weapons* (Weybright and Tulley, 1975), page 14.

9. This group had a "congressional caucus" led by members of both the house and the senate, and had quite an academic following. For an example of their arguments, see M. Handel, "Numbers Do Count: The Question of Quality Versus Quantity," *Journal of Strategic Studies,* September 1981, pages 225–260.

10. Such an orientation to the requirements process has been reinforced by legislation and implemented through Office of Federal Procurement Policy Directive A-109, which requires clear "mission area need statements" before a new weapon system can be initiated.

11. The author has written about this subject previously, and some of the material in this

section is derived from those works. See "Managing Defense Technology: Problems and Needed Changes," in *Defense Technology*, ed. A. Clark (Praeger, 1988); "The U.S. Technology Base: Problems and Prospects," in *Technology, Strategy, and National Security*, ed. F. Marjiotta and R. Sanders, (National Defense University Press, 1985); "The Defense Industry's Role in Military R&D Decision Making," in *Genesis of New Weapons: Decisionmaking and Military R&D*, ed. F. Long and J. Reppy (Pergamon, 1980).

12. It took the Navy over 20 years to field the Harpoon anti-ship missile.

13. The Israeli Scout vehicle and the U.S. Aquilla are both reconnaissance drones that were initiated in 1973. The Israelis had the Scout in their force structure by 1978 and used it effectively in the 1982 battles in Lebanon against Syria. The U.S. is still trying to decide if the Acquilla should be developed and deployed. For a more detailed discussion of the history of these unmanned vehicles, see S. Shaker and A. Wise, *War Without Men: Robots on the Future Battlefield* (Pergamon Brassey, 1988).

14. The Army has been the service most resistant to such changes; it even maintained a cavalry until the beginning of World War II. In 1987 the Army's R&D expenditures were only $4.7 billion—only 30% of the Air Force's $15.2 billion. For an excellent historical perspective on the military's resistance to nontraditional technology, see E. Morrison, *Men, Machines, and Modern Times* (MIT Press, 1966).

15. T. Kuhn, *The Structure of Scientific Revolutions* (University of Chicago Press, 1970).

16. Canan, *Super Warriors*, page 106.

17. Norman Augustine estimates that the last 10% of performance costs one-third of the total cost and causes two-thirds of the total problems (speech, "A Viewpoint of Industry," 1987). In many advanced systems, the ratios come out even higher.

18. The number of soldered joints in just the guidance and control system of four missiles investigated varied between 21,000 and 35,000. These soldered joints were a major reason for the report's conclusion that some of the weapons could fail. (R. Smith, "Navy Management Blamed for Faulty Missiles," *Washington Post*, September 25, 1987.)

19. For a quantitative comparison of the maintenance and downtime rates of a number of Air Force and Navy aircraft with respect to their increasing complexity, see Handel, "Numbers Do Count" (note 9 above). See also F. Spinney, "Defense Facts of Life," *Armed Forces Journal*, May 1980, page 30. Norman Augustine has correlated the failure rate of airborne electronics equipment versus its unit cost and found that the equipment has many more failures as it becomes more expensive and complex. (Augustine's Laws, page 56).

20. Norman Augustine has correlated the number of development flights versus the complexity (or unit cost) of surface-launched missiles and has shown an extremely high correlation in the negative (perverse) direction—i.e., the very complex systems receive a minimal number of R&D flight tests, whereas the very simple systems receive a very large number of flight tests (*Augustine's Laws*, pages 380–381).

21. *Defense Daily*, December 3, 1987, page 203.

22. This was a major point of the Packard Commission's defense-acquisition investigations. The commission concluded that the development of such complex systems as the IBM 360 computer, the Boeing 767 transport, the AT&T telephone switch, and the Hughes communication satellite each compared in complexity and size to the development of a major weapon system—yet each of these systems took only about half as long

to develop and cost considerably less (Packard Commission, "A Formula for Action," 1986, page 11).

23. From 1964 to 1977, the amount of money in the technology base was cut in half in real dollars (see statement by William J. Perry, Under Secretary of Defense for Research and Engineering, to 97th Congress, 1st session, 1981, page 13). Even during the enormous buildup in R&D funds during the Reagan administration, the science and technology program was actually reduced; from 1983 to 1985 it went from $3.5 billion to $3.1 billion (in constant FY85 dollars). (Technical Marketing Society of America, "Aerospace Market Outlook," 1984, page 3).

24. G. Eads and R. Nelson, "Governmental Support of Advanced Civilian Technology: Power Reactors and the Supersonic Transport," *Public Policy,* summer 1971, pages 406–407.

25. For an extensive discussion of the benefits of smaller size in achieved innovation and growth, see F. M. Scherer, *Innovation and Growth: Schumpeterian Perspectives* (MIT Press, 1984), especially pages 224 and 237. In addition, see J. M. Blair, *Economic Concentration: Structure, Behavior, and Public Policy* (Harcourt Brace Jovanovich, 1975); J. Jewkes et al., *The Sources of Innovation* (Norton, 1971), pages 71–85; D. Mueller, *The Rate and Direction of Inventive Activity* (Princeton University Press, 1962), pages 323–346.

26. The Small Business Innovative Research Program was created by the Small Business Innovation Development Act of 1982 (Public Law 97-219).

27. Office of Technology Assessment, U.S. Congress, Draft Technical Memorandum, "The Defense Technology Base: Introduction and Overview," December 3, 1987, page 34.

28. *New York Times,* October 5, 1986.

29. Versus a little over 20% in 1964. (See E. Bloch, "Managing for Changing Times," *Issues in Science and Technology,* winter 1986, page 25.)

30. Source: "University Responsiveness to National Security Requirements," Report of the Defense Science Board Task Force, January 1982, pages 2–3 and 2–4.

31. GAO report, "Acquisition of Major Weapon Systems," 1972.

32. P. Drucker, "Best R&D Is Business Driven," *Wall Street Journal,* February 10, 1988.

33. For example, by the Defense Science Board in its 1985 Summer Study entitled "Practical Functional Performance Requirements."

34. For a specific quantitative demonstration of this, see J. Gansler, "Time and Cost Reductions in Flight Vehicle Acquisitions," Advisory Group for Aerospace Research and Development, NATO, Toulouse, France, May 11, 1987, pages 25–27. For a discussion of some specific examples of the modification route, see "Fresh Wine in Old Battlers: Upgrading Vintage Hardware Can Boost Business Along with Defenses," *U.S. News and World Report,* February 15, 1988, pages 53–55.

35. Eads and Nelson, "Governmental Support of Advanced Civilian Technology," page 426.

36. This concept was pushed by a number of people—most notably by Assistant Secretary of Defense Leonard Sullivan during the 1970s.

37. The measure of performance used here (and in chapter 6) is based on the TASCFORM

methodology, which provides a first-order indication of a plane's performance potential by calculating a numerical score based on its inherent physical capabilities. Some of the parameters included in the model are range, speed, maneuverability, payload, basing mode, target acquisition, and fire-control capability. These factors are either normalized against a consistent standard or assigned a graduated evaluation score. The relative weights for performance factors are based on the consensus judgments of experienced operational pilots as well as military analysts. The final performance are scores based on a weighted calculation. This methodology was developed by The Analytic Sciences Corporation for the Office of the Secretary of Defense over a number of years in the late 1970s and the early 1980s. For some applications of it, see "Tactical Combat Forces of the United States Air Force, Issues and Alternatives," Congressional Budget Office, April 1985, and G. Hildebrandt et al., "Accounting for the Cost of Tactical Aircraft," Rand Corporation, July 1986.

38. The data used to generate the "Soviet growth rate" line were taken from classified DoD sources. However, this aggregate curve, as presented, is unclassified. The data for this high/low analysis are contained also in J. Gansler and C. Henning, "European Weapons Acquisition Practices" (forthcoming).

39. As told to the author by Secretary of Defense James Schlesinger in 1987.

40. Lanchester's Law states that overall military force effectiveness is proportional to unit equipment effectiveness times the square of the number of units. Thus, as equipment becomes more comparable, numbers become more significant. If the American equipment is twice as good as the comparable Soviet equipment but the Soviets have twice as much of it, then Lanchester's Law says that the forces are not equivalent; rather, the Soviet forces are twice as effective.

41. See "Joint Logistics Commanders, "Joint Program Management Study" (Department of Defense, 1984).

42. Gansler and Henning, "European Weapons Acquisition Practices" (forthcoming).

43. An example of increased costs due to additional demands is the multiservice requirements process for the evolution for the joint Air Force-Navy F-111 program. This is described in detail in Robert Ark's book *The TFX Decision: McNamara and the Military* (Little, Brown, 1968).

44. Joint Logistics Commanders, "Joint Program Management Study." The data are based on systems-acquisition reports to Congress for 36 single-service programs and 16 joint programs.

45. For an example, see Gansler, *The Defense Industry,* page 18.

46. This is based on the average price of a new car in 1972 dollars. (Source: National Automobile Dealers' Association.)

47. The example being considered here is quite typical of the exercise that the Air Force went through in the consideration of the advanced tactical fighter for the early 21st century. The first designs done by a number of aircraft manufacturers came out with a unit cost of about $110 million (as reported to the author by the Air Force Program Manager).

48. Motorola, Inc., Tempe, Arizona, December 1985 (data presented to the Packard Commission).

49. Defense Science Board Summer Study Task Force, Department of Defense, "Report on Use of Commercial Components and Military Equipment," 1986.

50. Such numbers have actually been demonstrated with specific examples. One (noted in the report cited in note 49) involves a secure telephone built with commercial components by the National Security Agency.

51. This approach—emulating successful programs—was utilized in the Packard Commission's report "A Formula For Action," and was recommended by William Perry, a former Under Secretary of Defense for Research, Development, and Acquisition. Six of the twelve characteristics listed here were noted in the Packard Commission's report.

52. One example of a DoD program in which cost realism has always been emphasized is the Navy's Submarine Launched Ballistic Missile program. Cost overruns have been minimized, and performance, schedule, and other targets have been realized. (See Sapolsky, *The Polaris System Development,* and a 1988 report on the SLBM program by the House Armed Services Committee.)

53. The United States is only beginning to discover the "cost of quality." For typical commercial systems, it is believed that the cost of poor quality is more than 25% of the cost of an item. For defense-related systems, it is believed to be significantly higher; this warranted the attack on the cost of poor quality that was initiated by Under Secretary Robert Costello in 1988.

54. R. Nelson, *High Technology Policies: A Five Nation Comparison* (National Academy Press, 1985), page 13.

55. A 1980 Summer Study by the Defense Science Board specified the following areas for major long-term R&D investment by the DoD: very-high-speed integrated circuits; active and passive stealth; advanced software/algorithm development; microprocessor-based personal learning aids; fail-soft/fault-tolerant ("self-policing") electronics; rapid solidification; machine intelligence; supercomputers; advanced composites; high-density, monolithic, focal-plane arrays; radiation-hardened, advanced electronics; space nuclear power; high-power microwave generators; large space structures; optoelectronics; space-based radar; and short-wavelength lasers.

56. To give an idea of the magnitude of the investments required on the industrial side, note that in 1984 McDonnell Douglas committed to a $1 billion investment in automation (*Aviation Week and Space Technology,* April 9, 1984, page 24).

57. In 1987 a Defense Science Board task force, chaired by MIT Provost John Deutch, found the DoD's technology base to be "increasingly short-sighted, underfunded, and poorly managed" (*Aerospace Daily,* March 24, 1988).

58. For a full discussion of joint sponsorship by industry and government of "dual-use" R&D, see Eads and Nelson, "Government Support of Advanced Civilian Technology," pages 105–427.

59. E. Bloch, "Managing for Challenging Times: A National Research Strategy," *Issues in Science and Technology,* winter 1986, page 24.

60. E. Douglas, "VHSIC Is the Key to Tomorrow's Weapons," *Barron's,* October 3, 1983.

61. The National Academy of Sciences recommended that this be increased to over $300 million per year. See "Manufacturing Technology: Cornerstone of a Renewed Defense Industrial Base," Committee on The Role of the Manufacturing Technology Program in

the Defense Industrial Base, Manufacturing Studies Board, Commission on Engineering and Technical Systems, National Academy of Sciences, Washington, 1987.

62. Congressional Budget Office, "The Benefits and Risks of Federal Funding for Sematech," September 1987.

63. "The President's Superconductivity Initiative: Fact Sheet," White House press release, July 28, 1987.

64. The extreme, perhaps, was reached in 1988 when one company was proposing (to the Navy) that engineers be paid $7.29 per hour—less than unskilled clerical workers were receiving. See "Navy Competition Advocate Vows to 'Ferret Out' Abuse," *Washington Technology,* March 10–23, 1988, page 1.

65. Two examples of industrial collaborative efforts in the U.S. are the Semiconductor Manufacturing Technology Institute and the Microelectronic and Computer Technology Corporation. Such collaborative research efforts have been more common in Japan than in the U.S., and the DoD's involvement in such efforts has been a relatively recent thing. Whether industry will fully take part in these activities and support them, as is required, remains to be seen. See D. Sanger, "Trying to Regain the Market in Chips," *New York Times,* March 8, 1987.

66. A. Toffler, Future Shock, (Bantam Books, 1970).

67. Public Law 85-325, February 1958.

68. This statement was made by Hugh Witt of United Technologies Corporation in testimony before the Committee on Defense Procurement of the Senate Armed Services Committee on February 20, 1987. It appeared in the *Wall Street Journal* on February 13, 1987.

Chapter 8

1. For a general discussion of America's industrial problems, see *Business Week's* special issue on "The Reindustrialization of America," (June 30, 1980).

2. For a detailed discussion of the history of the U.S. defense industrial base, with numerous references, see chapter 2 of J. S. Gansler, "The Diminishing Economic and Strategic Viability of the U.S. Defense Industrial Base," Ph.D. dissertation, American University, 1978 (Ann Arbor: University Microfilm).

3. During the Revolution, ships and artillery pieces came from the private sector, while guns and munitions came mostly from government arsenals.

4. During World War II, $26 billion was invested in new plants and equipment (about two-thirds provided by the government)—usually near, or at, existing private facilities. The lion's share went to the large firms. Thus, when the war ended and these facilities were sold (at attractive prices), it was not surprising that 250 of the nation's largest firms acquired more than 70% of the plants sold. See J. M. Blair, *Economic Concentration,* page 380.

5. House Armed Services Committee Defense Industrial Base Panel, "The Ailing Defense Industrial Base: Unready for Crisis" (H.R. Doc. No. 29, 1980); Defense Science Board Task Force, "Report on Industrial Responsiveness" (Department of Defense, November 21, 1980); U.S. Air Force, "Statement on Defense Industrial Base Issues," November 12, 1980; Gansler, *The Defense Industry.*

6. One Wall Street analyst (Gary Reich of Shearson, Lehman, and Hutton) stated, "The

government is doing its damndest to put the defense industry out of business" (quoted in an editorial by George Melloan, "How to Lose the U.S. Military Technology Edge," *Wall Street Journal,* March 1, 1988).

7. Grumman signed a fixed-price, zero-profit, billion-dollar contract to design an electronic upgrade for its F-14 and A-6 aircraft. (D. Morrison, "Defense and Industry," *Government Executive,* September 1987, page 40.)

8. One of the more extreme of these programs was the Advanced Tactical Fighter. The initial development contracts were awarded for $691 million each, and the prototype programs were expected to cost over $1 billion each. Only the winning firm—if there is a program at all—will be able to recover its losses. (R. Stevenson, "Military Contractors Squeezed," *New York Times,* November 16, 1987.)

9. *Washington Technology,* March 10–23, 1988, page 1.

10. For an excellent discussion of the role of governments in encouraging necessary structural changes in selected industries, see J. L. Bower, *When Markets Quake: The Management Challenge of Restructuring Industry* (Harvard Business School Press, 1986).

11. This list comes from *Military Logistics Forum,* July–August, 1986, page 13.

12. For example, IBM has traditionally constrained its defense work—even during periods when the economy had gone quite sour and IBM's commercial business was in trouble—so that DoD business would not come to dominate the corporation.

13. This is from a memorandum Eisenhower signed in 1946 while Chief of Staff of the Army (as reported in an article by H. Subkoff and S. Aubin: "Government and Defense Industry: Partners or Adversaries?" *The Retired Officer,* 1988, page 40).

14. Gansler, *The Defense Industry,* page 37.

15. Galbraith, *The New Industrial State.*

16. M. L. Weidenbaum, "The Military/Space Market: The Intersection of the Public and Private Sectors," U.S. Senate Hearings, Subcommittee on Anti-trust and Monopoly of the Committee on the Judiciary, 90th Congress, 2nd session. Pursuant to SR233, June 17 and 21 and September 10, 1968.

17. For a more detailed discussion of these concentration ratios relative to traditional measures, see Gansler, *The Defense Industry,* page 43. See also Blair, *Economic Concentration,* pages 11 and 12; Scherer, *Industrial Market Structure,* page 123; Kaysen and Turner, *Anti-trust Policy,* page 30; Bain, *Industrial Organization,* page 424; McKie, "Concentration and Military Procurement Markets," page 12 and appendix.

18. For a full discussion of this subject, see Gansler, *The Defense Industry,* pages 46–50.

19. In one case, Congress passed legislation that "no new munitions plants can be built in areas that are not adjacent to current munitions plants."

20. LTV is an example of a firm that has shifted from being predominantly a defense prime contractor to being largely a defense subcontractor.

21. This cyclical behavior also has a dramatic impact on communities. For example, in Palmdale, California, the site of Air Force Plant 42, employment dropped by 60 percent in one year. In another year, enrollment in the school district jumped by 25 percent. "In several periods Palmdale was a virtual ghost town with houses boarded up and streets

overrun by tumbleweeds; but by 1985 [with the B-1B] they were high on the hog" (*U.S. News and World Report,* February 25, 1985, page 63).

22. Another example of high turnover: In 1966 Boeing hired 37,000 people while 25,000 quit. Boeing representatives said they had to "hire three to get one" (*Aerospace Daily,* September 1, 1978). However, this short-term instability is not characteristic of all segments of the defense industry; aerospace and munitions tend to have less short-term turnover than many other segments of the U.S. manufacturing industry.

23. *Washington Post,* April 1, 1985. (Based on a Congressional Budget Office study.)

24. J. Mathews, "With the B-1 Reborn, California Starts Flying High Once Again", *Washington Post,* October 6, 1981.

25. S. Sherman, "Keeping the B-1 Alive," *Fortune,* November 2, 1981, page 112.

26. Between 1967 and 1980 there was only a 16% increase in scientists and engineers in the United States, versus 62% in the United Kingdom, 82% in West Germany, 56% in France, and 132% in Japan. (Halprin, Berman, and Teubal, "The Trade-off between Economic Growth and Military Industries," SAPIR Conference, March 1988.)

27. In the early 1970s there were around 125 employees per aircraft; by the mid-1980s this had more than doubled. The number of production workers per aircraft was around 75 in the early 1970s and approximately 140 by 1985. (Based on an unpublished 1987 study of the aircraft industry done for the Office of the Secretary of Defense.)

28. C. Mitchell and T. Carrington, "Many Defense Firms Make High Tech Gear in Low Tech Factories," *Wall Street Journal,* October 8, 1987.

29. These particular facilities have since been modernized—with the help of funds from the Navy.

30. These disincentives include awards primarily based upon R&D proposals, with production as the logical follow-on (thus, production costs are not driving the contract awards); an extremely large uncertainty with regard to future business, which greatly discourages capital investments (the uncertainty is driven by the one-year budget and the all-or-nothing nature of the competitions); the existence of considerable excess capacity (which discourages additional investments); the fact that the total market is not expected to grow (and is more likely to shrink); the fact that the cost-accounting standards, which control how defense contractors do their bookkeeping, depreciates equipment on the basis of "estimated service life" rather than the shorter time allowable for tax purposes; the fact that the acquisition costs of new plants and equipment far exceed the depreciation allowances, thus requiring even higher investments in order to "stay even"; environmental and safety regulations that impose severe capital-investment requirements (not just for defense but for all of U.S. industry; however, for defense they are also built into all of the contract clauses); the fact that the low profit-on-sales realized by defense contractors limits the dollars available for investment; and the investment community's poor view of defense as a business area, which makes it difficult and expensive for the defense companies to raise either equity or debt money.

31. One such study, done by the National Academy of Sciences, was quoted on page 1 of the *Wall Street Journal* of October 8, 1987. Another, the Department of Defense's "Defense Financial and Investment Review," (June 1985), found that "DoD contractors employed 42 percent as much facilities capital per dollar of sales as did durable goods manufacturers." For a lengthy discussion of additional studies reaching the same conclusions, see Gansler, *The Defense Industry,* page 293, note 60.

32. *Washington Post,* April 1, 1985.

33. "Defense Financial and Investment Review," June 1985, page E-2.

34. For an explanation of why one would expect to find higher profits here, see Bain, *Industrial Organization,* page 423.

35. These negotiated contract levels are presented in "Defense Financial and Investment Review" (June 1985), page V-45.

36. Based on the average of 35 defense contractors sampled in 1965–1967 and published in "Industry Advisory Council Report to Secretary of Defense," June 11, 1971.

37. Based on DoD "Profit 76" data obtained by Coopers & Lybrand from 61 companies having annual DoD sales of approximately $15 billion (1977).

38. J. R. Fox, *Arming America,* page 331.

39. This is based upon the DoD report "Defense Financial and Investment Review" (June 1985). But the data for defense exclude shipbuilding, which would actually lower defense profits somewhat. Additionally, it should be noted that defense profits during the early part of the 1980s rose dramatically, as a result of the Reagan buildup, while the U.S. economy was in a recession. For this period, profits on durable goods fell below those in defense. However, this period is believed to be an anomaly, and the long-term trends indicated above are probably more typical.

40. W. J. Baumol, *Economic Theory and Operations Analysis,* (Prentice-Hall, 1972), page 347.

41. This survey was undertaken by the Office of the Secretary of Defense as part of the "Profit 76" study. See Profit 76 summary report, December 1976.

42. For a detailed comparison of a wide variety of studies, see Gansler, *The Defense Industry,* pages 86 and 87.

43. For example, in the DoD's "Defense Financial and Investment Review" of June 1985, it was reported that in the early 1970s durable goods exceeded defense, that in the early 1980s defense exceeded durable goods, and that in between they were quite comparable.

44. A comparison of ten large military contractors found that their average return on equity was about 25%, versus about 12.8% for overall manufacturing, mining, and trade corporations. (Senate Congressional Record, April 17, 1985, page S4326.)

45. "Defense Financial and Investment Review," pages V-43 and V-44.

46. Ibid., page III-6.

47. Manufacturing Studies Board, National Research Council, "Towards a New Era in U.S. Manufacturing: The Need For a National Vision" (National Academy Press, 1986), page 127.

48. The latter trend has already begun. The Grumman Corporation has stated that, as a corporate policy, it plans on moving more into electronics (*New York Times,* March 8, 1987). The acquisition of Sanders by Lockheed for $1.2 billion, in the mid-1980s, is an example of the acquisition of an electronics firm by an aerospace company. See also D. Morrison, "Up In Arms," *National Journal,* July 11, 1987, page 1785.

49. W. Adams and J. Brock, "The Hidden Costs of Failed Mergers," *New York Times,* June 21, 1987.

50. Some programs in which such "teaming" was being encouraged by the DoD in the mid-1980s were the Air Force's Advanced Tactical Fighter, the Navy's Advanced Tacti-

cal Aircraft, the Army's LHX light helicopter, the Navy's V-22 tilt-rotor aircraft, and the Integrated Electronic Warfare System.

51. The quote is from Wolfgang H. Demisch of First Boston Corporation. (D. Morrison, "Defense and Industry," *Government Executive,* September 1987, page 40.)

52. W. Adams and J. Brock, *The Bigness Complex: Industry, Labor, and Government in the American Economy* (Pantheon, 1987).

53. J. Robertson, "IBM's FSD Sees Growth in Systems Integration Business," *Electronic News,* January 1988.

54. F. M. Scherer, *The Weapons Acquisition Process,* page 351.

55. Between 1985 and 1987 the Department of Justice recorded the registration of 66 cooperative R&D consortia. A number of these involved major defense contractors. For example, a Software Productivity Consortium was established by eleven major defense contractors (M. Schrage, "Software Research Groups Set," *Washington Post,* October 10, 1984).

56. General J. P. Mullins, *The Defense Matrix: National Preparedness and the Military Industrial Complex* (Avant Books, 1986).

57. For the purposes of this presentation, the case of subcontracting between large firms that were simply sharing the prime-contractor business is excluded; it was covered in the preceding chapter.

58. Senate Hearings on Competitive Defense Procurements, 1968, page 18.

59. See chapter 6 of *The Defense Industry* for a detailed discussion of this particular problem.

60. Robertson, "IBM's FSD Sees Growth in Systems Integration Business."

61. See G. Fossedal, "More Audits Won't Curb Defense Waste," *Wall Street Journal,* June 30, 1986.

62. The increase in defense expenditures in 1979 caused the lead times seen by defense firms to reach 100 weeks for aluminum extrusions, 115 weeks for large aluminum and steel forgings, 115 weeks for large titanium forgings, and 80 weeks for titanium sheet and plate. (Source: Joint Logistics Commanders Subpanel on Lengthening Lead Times, Letter 173, July 25, 1979.) For a list of 15 parts whose cost more than doubled, in many cases in a single year, see pages 134 and 135 of *The Defense Industry.* The original source for this was a Defense Logistics Agency Study dated January 10, 1975.

63. Brigadier General James Stansberry, Air Force Study of Subcontractor Management, spring 1972. A gross example of this involved the AWACS aircraft. The prime contractor (Boeing) was supplying a modified commercial aircraft on a cost-plus basis, while Westinghouse and its suppliers were developing a new state-of-the-art radar system on a fixed-price basis as subcontractors.

64. In the mid-1970s, when inflation rose rapidly, many small defense firms went bankrupt. Others took the prime contractors and the DoD to court over the differences in clauses—at great expense, but often to no avail.

65. For a discussion of the increased costs associated with these paperwork items, see Defense Supply Agency, "A Study of Increased Procurement Costs in the Industrial Production Base" (June 1985).

66. Gansler, *The Defense Industry,* pages 138–141. The DoD's "Defense Financial and Investment Review" (June 1985) reached the same conclusion.

67. For example, the government rescued Lockheed, which had 24,000 employees, $2.5 billion in outstanding contracts, and $250 million advanced by the airlines and the banks. It was understandable why the government had to step in, but Lockheed's subcontractors would not have been as fortunate if they had been in a similar but reduced-scale situation.

68. Conference Board, "Report on Investment in the Defense Industry," January 1976.

69. For a more extensive discussion of these barriers to entry, see *The Defense Industry,* pages 148–151.

70. Refer to the Small Business Act of 1958 for details. The Small Business Administration implements this legislation. For this purpose, a small business is generally defined as one with fewer than 500 people (in the case of R&D) and fewer than 1,000 (in the case of computers).

71. In the case of "minority firms" the law goes even farther: The Small Business Administration will actually be the "contractor," will take the job at the market price, and will underwrite the difference (up to 40 percent, per a 1975 ruling) between this price and the cost to the firm.

72. Adams and Brock, *The Bigness Complex,* page 61.

73. "Defense Financial and Investment Review" (June 1985), page E-2.

74. An Air Force study reached a similar conclusion and recommended that a separate pool of money be set aside for such activities. (1984 Air Force Production Base Analysis, "Blueprint for Tomorrow", Air Force Systems Command, Andrews Air Force Base.)

75. The closest civilian-sector analogy to this requirement would be the rapid buildup of inventories that a firm would require for items in which there is sudden buying interest. This analogy was suggested to the author by the economist William Baumol in 1975.

76. Bernard Baruch, as quoted in G. Lincoln, *Economics of National Security: Managing America's Resources for Defense* (Prentice-Hall, 1954), page 4.

77. Statement by Under Secretary of Defense Fred Iklé, Detroit, November 9, 1987; Leslie Bray, testimony before Joint Committee on Defense Production, November 24, 1976. The buying and selling of the raw materials in the stockpile is a politically sensitive subject, since such sales or purchases could significantly influence the market prices of these commodities.

78. Lincoln, *Economics of National Security* (note 76 above), page 291.

79. Ibid., page 304.

80. The most significant investigations in this area were done in the late 1970s. The first of these was in the 1975 annual report of Congress' Joint Committee on Defense Production. A 1976 study by the Defense Science Board concluded that defense planning at that time was "worthless" and should be "drastically revised" ("Industrial Readiness Plan and Programs," August 1976, published in April 1977). A classified 1980 study done for the National Security Council compared U.S. and Soviet mobilization capabilities and concluded not only that the U.S. was unprepared but that the Soviet Union had taken significant industrial-preparedness actions.

81. These are known as "plant equipment packages" (PEPs). There were almost 35,000 pieces of equipment assigned to approved PEPs in 1980. The average age of this equip-

ment was over 20 years, and much of it was related to the munitions industry (where a rapid buildup is clearly required and where more modern equipment will be needed—a fact recognized by the Army in 1976 when it slowly began a munitions-modernization program).

82. Fred Iklé, speech in Detroit, November 8, 1987.

83. For a detailed discussion of these options, see Col. O. M. Collins, "Combat Sustainability and Reconstitution Warfare," *Air Force Journal of Logistics,* summer 1987, pages 33–38, and Gansler, *The Defense Industry,* pages 115–125.

84. National Security Strategy Report of the President (to the Congress), February 1988, page 21.

85. Fred Iklé, speech in Detroit, November 9, 1987.

86. *Aerospace Daily,* December 26, 1984.

87. This is the criterion under which export licenses are reviewed. However, this rule has not been updated to take into consideration today's world. It was instituted in the 1960s, when there were only two major powers, and when the principal technology-transfer mechanism was the sale of equipment rather than technology transfer itself.

88. This is in spite of the fact that Congress has passed a law requiring specific congressional approval of all foreign sales of military equipment. (The law is written so that inaction amounts to approval.)

89. R. E. Harkavy, *The Arms Trade and International Systems* (Ballinger, 1974), page xiv.

90. L. M. Simons, "Grumman Set to Refund Iran $28 Million," *Washington Post,* February 10, 1976.

91. In 1976 the Shah of Iran was quoted as saying that, because he did not want to bankrupt the Grumman Corporation (the sole producer of the Navy's premier fighter aircraft, the F-14), he would provide $28 million of "advanced payments" against a future military equipment purchase. (Ibid.)

92. For a listing of the annual sales level of these ten countries in 1986, see *U.S. News and World Report,* February 3, 1986, page 37.

93. R. House, "Brazilians Find Arms Buyers in Conflict Zones," in *The Military Balance, 1985–86* (International Institute for Strategic Studies), page 197.

94. *Washington Post,* June 19, 1984.

95. In 1980 U.S. sales were $14.8 billion; by 1986 they were down to $7.1 billion (*Washington Post,* November 16, 1987).

96. "Too Much Barter is Bad for You," *The Economist,* May 9, 1987, page 61.

97. In 1985, a survey of 154 military contractors by the International Trade Commission found that foreign military contracts associated with offsets totaled $22.5 billion between 1980 and 1984—nearly half of the $47.8 billion in total foreign military sales (C. Farnsworth, "The U.S. Giveaway," *New York Times,* December 7, 1986).

98. Even the U.S. took part in this form of enticement when it sold the AWACS airplane to the NATO countries at $69 million each, while the U.S. was paying $104 million each (J. Finney, "Pentagon Accused of Selling a Plane at Too Low a Price," *New York Times,* March 3, 1976). See also Office of Management and Budget, "Third Annual Report on

the Impact of Offsets in Defense-Related Exports," December 1987, page 6, for a discussion of the attractive offset provisions.

99. For example, the U.S. F-16 aircraft cost more for the U.S. because it was produced in Europe as well as in the U.S. (M. Rich et al., "Multinational Co-Production of Military Aerospace Systems," Rand Corporation Report R2861-AF, October 1981, page 105).

100. For an example of this in the civilian sector see R. Reich, "A Faustian Bargain with the Japanese: Boeing's Joint Venture," *New York Times,* April 6, 1986).

101. H. Rowan, "U.S. Risks A Bundle Selling High Tech to Japan," *Washington Post,* November 28, 1982.

102. Rich et al., "Multinational Co-production."

103. Even U.S. firms appear to be significantly involved in bribery. See Anthony Sampson, *The Arms Bazaar* (Viking, 1977).

104. For some examples of this dependence, see "The Case of Jet Engines," *U.S. News and World Report,* February 8, 1982, page 59, and "Assessing Production Capabilities and Constraints in the Defense Industrial Base," GAO Report PEMD-85-3, (1985), page 32.

105. *U.S. News and World Report,* March 18, 1985.

106. For a discussion of this subject, see National Research Council, "Foreign Production of Electronic Components and Army Systems Vulnerabilities" (National Academy Press, 1985).

107. E. Marshall, *Science,* October 10, 1986, page 141.

108. "A Study of the Effect of Foreign Dependency," briefing to the Joint Oversight Committee on Foreign Dependency, October 25, 1985 (from a study done for the Joint Logistics Commanders). See also Defense Science Board, "Report on Semiconductor Dependency," February 1987.

109. National Research Council, "Foreign Production of Electronic Components and Army Systems Vulnerabilities," 1985.

110. See, e.g., S. Cohen and J. Zysman, *Manufacturing Matters: The Myth of the Post-Industrial Economy* (Basic Books, 1987).

111. For a more extensive discussion of this whole issue, see J. S. Gansler, "U.S. Dependence on Foreign Military Parts: Should We Be Concerned?" *Issues in Science and Technology,* volume 2, number 4 (1986), pages 17 and 18.

112. *The Economist,* August 8, 1987, pages 15 and 16.

113. Some of the material in this chapter comes from J. Gansler, "The Need—and Opportunity—for Greater Integration of Defense and Civil Technologies in the United States," in *The Relations between Civil and Defense Technologies* (Martinus Nijhoff, 1989). A shortened version appeared in the fall 1988 issue of *Issues in Science and Technology.*

114. For a full presentation of this case against integration, see the works of Seymour Melman—e.g., *The Permanent War Economy* (Simon and Schuster, 1974).

115. For example, Grumman went into the "flexible bus" business in the early 1970s, and lost $134 million. (P. Gates, *New York Times,* March 8, 1987).

116. For a good presentation making this same point, see Gordon Adams' speech to the

Woman's Leadership Conference of the Committee for National Security, Washington, June 1985.

117. "International Science and Technology Data Update, 1986" (report prepared by Directorate for Scientific, Technological, and International Affairs, Division of Science Resource Studies, National Science Foundation). A somewhat similar set of numbers is given in R. Nelson, "High-Technology Policies: A Five Nation Companion," page 24.

118. Much of the following information came from the NATO Advanced Research Workshop on the Relationship Between Defense and Civil Technologies, Wiston House, Sussex, England, September 1987.

119. The Russians build railroad trains and tanks in the same plant, so they can rapidly shift back and forth.

120. For example, see B. Scott and G. Lodge, *U.S. Competitiveness in the World Economy* (Harvard Business School Press, 1985), and Cohen and Zysman, *Manufacturing Matters*.

121. E. Douglas, "VHSIC Is the Key to Tomorrow's Weapon's," *Barron's,* October 3, 1983.

122. Manufacturing Studies Board, "Manufacturing Technology: Cornerstone of a Renewed Defense Industrial Base" (National Academy Press, 1987).

123. Congressional Budget Office, "The Benefits and Risks of Federal Funding for Sematech," September 1987. See also H. Rowen, "Chip Makers Lose Ground," *Washington Post,* February 22, 1987.

124. White House press release, July 28, 1987, "The President's Superconductivity Initiative: Fact Sheet."

125. R. Wehner, "Defense Teams Await MIMIC Contract Awards," *Washington Technology,* February 4–17, 1988, page 6.

126. In 1988 a subcommittee of the Senate Armed Services Committee on "Industrial Base and Technology" was set up under Senator Bingaman to explore this issue; and it was made one of the major "initiatives" of the new Under Secretary of Defense (for Acquisition), Robert Costello. (He was a former Director of Purchasing for General Motors, so he had the necessary commercial experience.)

127. Toward the end of the Carter administration, Jordan Baruch (Assistant Secretary for Technology) held an extensive series of national meetings and proposed specific R&D initiatives.

128. See B. Udis, *From Guns to Butter: Technology Organization and Reduced Military Spending in Western Europe* (Ballinger, 1978); N. Ball, "Converting the Work Force: Defense Industry Conversion in the Industrialized Countries," *International Labor Review,* volume 125, number 4 (1986).

129. "Defense Industrial Base Preservation Act of 1988," draft of March 19, 1988, submitted to the Senate as S1892, (page 2).

130. Scherer, *Industrial Market Structure,* page 412.

131. "The Reindustrialization of America," special issue of *Business Week,* June 30, 1980.

132. Bower, *When Markets Quake,* page 2.

133. R. Reich, *The Next American Frontier* (Times Books, 1983), page 109.

134. For a discussion of these three options, see Adams and Brock, *The Bigness Complex*, pages 345ff.

135. For example, Rep. Clyde Tavenner proposed it in 1914 to "prevent profiteering, fraud, and false patriotism," and Bernard Beruch in 1931 to "tak[e] the profits out of war." For a more extensive discussion of some of these proposals, see E. Molander, "Historical Antecedents of Military Industrial Criticism," *Military Affairs,* April 1976, pages 60 and 61.

136. J. K. Galbraith, "The Big Defense Firms Are Really Public Firms And Should Be Nationalized," *New York Times Magazine,* November 16, 1979.

137. Experience has shown that publicly owned facilities (depots, munitions plants, etc.) are even harder to close or control than those in the private sector.

138. For a discussion of this approach, see G. Hall, "Defense Procurement and Public Utility Regulation," Rand Corporation report, 1968.

139. There are a wide variety of suboptions within this category. For a discussion of a number of them, see *The Defense Industry,* pages 236–243.

140. Bower, *When Markets Quake,* page 90.

141. Reich, *The Next American Frontier,* page 234.

142. Nelson, "High Technology Policies," pages 85–86.

Chapter 9

1. *Washington Post,* November 19, 1987.

2. Manpower Requirement Report for FY 1982, Department of Defense, April 1981.

3. Ibid.

4. Manpower Requirement Report for FY 1987, page II-1.

5. Statement of Assistant Secretary of Defense for Reserve Affairs James Webb at hearing before Subcommittee on Manpower and Personnel of Senate Armed Services Committee, 99th Congress, First Session, 1986.

6. For an extended discussion of this issue see J. Lacey, "Whither the All Volunteer Force?" *Yale Law and Policy Review,* Fall-Winter 1986, pages 38–73.

7. R. Danzig and P. Szanton, *National Service: What Would it Mean?* (Lexington Books, 1986), page 76. (The majority of the data in this table come from the Department of Defense Manpower Data Center Report 0584.)

8. R. Halloran, "Better Educated Recruit Revives Volunteer Force," *New York Times,* October 11, 1987.

9. R. Halloran, "Pentagon Taking Renewed Pride in its Personnel," *New York Times,* May 16, 1985.

10. Ibid.

11. Based on a survey of noncommissioned officers throughout the services (*New York Times,* May 16, 1985).

12. Lacey, "Whither the All Volunteer Force?" (page 70). The original source for these data is M. Binkin, *America's Volunteer Military: Progress and Prospects* (Brookings Institution, 1984).

13. *New York Times,* May 16, 1985. Both figures include pay for retired military person-nel, and both are in 1986 dollars.

14. *Washington Post,* November 14, 1987. The data for this conclusion come from a GAO study and from R. Stubbings and R. Mendel, *The Defense Game* (Harper and Row, 1986).

15. M. Adams, "Army Mounts a Recruiting Blitz," *U.S.A. Today,* January 10, 1985. The source of data presented here is the DoD's U.S. Army Recruiting Center.

16. *U.S. News & World Report,* January 12, 1987, page 13.

17. B. Tuchman, "American People and Military Power in an Historical Perspective," *Adelphi Papers,* No. 173 (spring 1982), page 13.

18. "Conscription: Not Entirely Fair, But Not Entirely Foul," *The Economist,* May 9, 1987.

19. General Bernard Rogers, the former NATO Commander, has made this case and has argued for a draft lottery. He suggests that each draftee be trained in a crucially needed combat skill for 4 months and then released to pursue a civilian career unless war breaks out. See G. Wilson, "General Urges Reviving of Draft," *Washington Post,* March 2, 1985.

20. P. Taylor, "Military Buildup Faulted by Democratic Centrists," *Washington Post,* September 17, 1986.

21. Danzig and Szanton, *National Service,* page 82.

22. "Military Women in the Department of Defense," Office of the Secretary of Defense, July 1987, page 3.

23. Ibid., page v.

24. Military Manpower Task Force, "A Report to the President on the Status and Pros-pects of the All-Volunteer Force," November 1982, page ii-18.

25. "Population Representation in the Military Services, FY1986," Office of the Assistant Secretary of Defense (Force Management and Personnel), August 1987, page ii-22.

26. "Military Women in the Department of Defense," page v.

27. Ibid.

28. "Population Representation in the Military Services, FY1986," page ii-12.

29. U.S. Bureau of Labor Statistics, "Employment and Unemployment, A Report on 1986," tables 3 and 22.

30. "Military Women in the Department of Defense," pages 3 and 45.

31. Military Manpower Task Force, November 1982, page ii-18. Nearly all the women (98.9 percent) who enlisted in FY1986 were high school graduates, versus 90.8 percent of the men ("Population Representation in the Military Services for FY1986," page ii-22).

32. "Military Women in the Department of Defense," pages 29 and 72.

33. "Population Representation in the Military Services, FY 1986," page ii-24.

34. Ibid., page ii-25.

35. Danzig and Szanton, *National Service,* page 51.

36. E. Dorn, "Blacks Need A Defense Policy," *Washington Post,* October 5, 1986.

37. Ibid.

38. E. Luttwak, *The Art of War*, page 209.

39. Comptroller General of the United States, "Managing the Cost of Government," GAO/AFMD-84-43, March 1984.

40. J. Bickerman, "Our Military Pensions Are A Scandal," *Washington Post*, March 10, 1985.

41. Halloran, "Pentagon Taking Renewed Pride In Its Personnel."

42. *Washington Post*, November 19, 1987.

Chapter 10

1. For additional details on these countries, see "Weapons Acquisition Processes of Selected Foreign Governments," General Accounting Office, February 1986; Art, V. Davis, and S. Huntington, *Reorganizing America's Defense Leadership in War and Peace* (Pergamon Brassey, 1985); A. Mayer, "Military Procurement Procedures of Foreign Governments: Centralization of the Procurement Function," Congressional Research Service Report, December 11, 1984; R. Magnan, "In Search of the End Game—A Comparison of U.S. and Foreign Weapons Acquisition Systems" (unpublished study, 1984); M. Edmonds, *Central Organizations of Defense* (Westview, 1985); "Budgeting Issue—Budgeting Practices in West Germany, France, Sweden, and Great Britain," General Accounting Office Report, November 1986; A. Alexander, "Weapons Acquisition in the Soviet Union, United States, and France," Rand Corp. paper, March 1973; R. Perry, "European and U.S. Aircraft Development Strategies," Rand Corp. paper, December 1971; M. Lorell, "Multinational Development of Large Aircraft—The European Experience," Rand Corp. report, July 1980; R. Perry, "A Dassault Dossier: Aircraft Acquisition in France," Rand Corp. report, September 1973; A. Alexander, "Design to Price from the Perspective of the United States, France, and the Soviet Union," Rand Corp. paper, February 1973.

2. West Germany will have a sharp decline in draft-age youths by the 1990s, leaving a shortage of some 100,000 soldiers a year. (Gerald Seib, "NATO Hopes to Curb Nuclear Peril by Using High-Tech Devices," *Wall Street Journal*, June 5, 1984.)

3. Christopher Bertram is the former director of the International Institute for Strategic Studies in London and an editor of the Hamburg-based *Die Zeit*. (M. Gordon, "ET Weapons to Beef Up NATO Forces Raise Technical and Political Doubts," *National Journal*, February 19, 1983, page 369)

4. In the 1975–78 time period, the British Royal Air Force spent 16% of its budget on R&D and only 16% on procurement of production hardware. (J. Harrison, U.K. Ministry of Defense, at American Institute of Aeronautics and Astronautics Seminar, Amsterdam, June 19, 1978.) Also, in 1984 both Britain and the U.S. spent about $3.20 on procurement for every dollar they spent on R&D. (B. Schemmer, "Does the U.S. Now Have the World's Worst Weapon System Acquisition Process?" *Armed Forces Journal International*, September 1984, page 93.)

5. Senator Alan Dixon (D-Illinois) sponsored S2035, which called for consolidation of all procurement in the Office of the Secretary of Defense. Senator William Roth (R-Delaware) and Representative John Dingell (R-Michigan) are also on record as favoring a centralized agency. Also, see W. Tremayne, "Consolidated DoD Procurement: The Time Is Still Right," *Defense Management Journal*, third quarter, 1986, and "U.S. President's Private Sector Survey on Cost Control Report," September 15, 1983, page 134.

6. For example, in the United Kingdom—where a contractor's profit is measured as a function of capital employed—the government raised the percent profit from 14% to 20% since it felt that the industry wasn't making a reasonable profit. (E. Kurth, "Profit on Capital Employed in Government Contracting, British Style," *Public Contract Law Journal,* volume 9, number 1, June 1977, pages 55–71.)

7. As much as half of French and Italian arms production and a third of British and West German production go to overseas sales (*Washington Post,* April 19, 1987).

8. E. Ulsamer, "The Designers of Dassault: Men Who Take One Step at a Time," *Air Force,* August 1970, page 32.

9. This achieves flexibility and minimizes overhead during slack periods. Matra, the French missile and space firm, subcontracts almost all its manual work (*The Economist,* October 6, 1979, page 83).

10. Further proof that Sweden values its defense industry as a national resource that must be protected is its extensive civil defense program, which involves not only shelters and population evacuation but the building of underground plants and depots. For a discussion of how Switzerland approaches civilian and industrial protection, see R. Herman, "One Country Digs In: Living With a Nuclear Threat," *Washington Post,* December 8, 1987.

11. These are U.S. equivalent FY86 dollars, and the U.S. information assumes that the acquisition activities of the Air Force, the Army, the Navy, Strategic Defense, and the other defense agencies would be combined into a single organization. The European data were supplied by individual countries through personal correspondence or taken from the GAO report "Weapons Acquisition—Processes of Selected Foreign Governments." The U.S. data were taken from an internal U.S. Air Force briefing: "An Assessment of European Defense Systems Acquisition" (September 15, 1987).

12. Magnan, "In Search of the End Game," page 84. For a description of this study see B. Knickerbocker, "Study Says Pentagon Could Benefit from Allies' Example in Buying New Weapons," *Christian Science Monitor,* April 2, 1984.

13. For example, see S. Schemann, "West Germans Are Moving to Center Stage, Reluctantly," *New York Times,* January 3, 1988.

14. For example, "Esprit" (a $10 billion program involving electronics R&D).

15. J. Gansler and C. Henning, "European Weapons Acquisition Practices" (forthcoming).

16. The data for this schedule comparison came from Rand Corp. Report R-2861-AF and from *Jane's All the World Aircraft.* These sources used different starting points for their data bases, but the results were consistent, in terms of the average delivery-time differences.

17. This increased time is due primarily to negotiations over relative priorities, requirements, budgets, etc. among the multiple players.

18. The cost data for U.S. aircraft were taken from the "U.S. Military Aircraft Cost Handbook" (Management Consulting and Research, Inc., March 1, 1983). The European cost data were taken from the following sources: R. Facer, "The Alliance and Europe: Part II Weapons Procurement in Europe—Capabilities and Choices," *Adelphi Papers* No. 108 (1975), page 8; M. Lorell, *Multinational Development of Large Aircraft,* page 45; Defense Marketing Service technical reports.

19. For additional discussions of European aircraft costs, see Keith and Hartley, *NATO Arms Cooperation* (Allen & Unwin, 1983); Keith, Hartley, and Cubitt, "Cost Escalation in the UK" (The Civil Service Expenditure Committee, Appendix 44, HECP 535-III, Session 1976/1977); Green, "Cost Forecasting and Control in the 1980s, From the Perspective of a Defense Contractor," *Journal of Cost Analysis,* Vol. 1, No. 1, spring 1984; D. Kirkpatrick and P. Pugh, "Towards the Starship Enterprise—Are the Current Trends in Defense Unit Cost Inexorable?" *Journal of Cost Analysis,* Vol. 2, spring 1985; M. Kaldor, "Technical Change in the Defense Industry," in *Technical Innovation and British Economic Performance* (Macmillan, 1980).

20. On the basis of current exchange rates and the NATO definition of defense spending, Japan should spend about $40 billion (*The Economist,* February 13, 1988, page 63).

21. H. Rowan, "U.S. Has Japan Up In Arms," *Washington Post,* September 6, 1981.

22. D. Halberstam, *The Reckoning* (William Morrow, 1986), page 276.

23. Magnan, "The Search of the End Game," page 34.

24. Halberstam, *The Reckoning,* page 716.

25. One technique that MITI uses is to form "recession cartels" in industries with excess capacity, temporarily restricting output and therefore driving up prices. The key to the success of the program lies in the explicit subsidies given to firms that agree to scrap excess capacity and in the firms' use of these subsidies to retrain and relocate their workers for more profitable endeavors. (R. Reich, *The Next American Frontier,* Times Books, 1983, page 199.)

26. For an excellent discussion of MITI, its role, and its people, see C. Johnson, *MITI and the Japanese Miracle* (Stanford University Press, 1982).

27. Halberstam, *The Reckoning,* page 305; Adams and Brock, *The Bigness Complex,* page 357.

28. Magnan, "In Search of the End Game," page 81.

29. In 1986 three of the top five firms in terms of number of U.S. patents received were Japanese (*The Economist,* May 9, 1987, page 82).

30. G. Giorgerini, "Economy and Defense: The Japanese Dilemma," *Military Technology,* volume 7, number 2 (1983), page 34.

31. Originally published in July 1970. See *Defense and Foreign Affairs,* July 1983, page 25.

32. When the Japanese couldn't get the electronic countermeasure system for the F-15 from the United States, they developed their own. Undoubtedly, it will be a future export product—perhaps to the U.S.

33. Per 10,000 participants in the labor force in 1982, Israel had 5.5 with advanced degrees in the natural sciences and engineering, versus 4.6 for the U.S., 3.5 for the U.K., 1.7 for Japan, 1.3 for Germany, and 0.8 for Sweden. (UNESCO and Israel National Council for Research and Development data, published in "Export Led Growth Strategy for Israel" [Jerusalem Institute of Management, 1987], p. 177.)

34. R. Amann, J. Cooper, and R. Davies, *The Technological Level of Soviet Industry,* (Yale University Press, 1977), page 407.

35. D. Holloway, "Military Power and Political Purpose in Soviet Policy," page 26.

36. To overcome the institutional inertia that often comes with stability—which is detri-

mental to R&D—the Soviets encourage inventions through monetary awards (often as much as $10,000 per year, for three years) based on savings realized. This encourages invention for the sake of cost reduction. (Scherer, *Industrial Market Structure*, page 398.)

37. Magnan, "In Search of the End Game," page 31.

38. Much of the information in this section comes from the investigations of Arthur J. Alexander of the Rand Corporation, who spent a number of years studying the Soviet defense industry. For example, see "The Process of Soviet Weapons Acquisition," presented to the European Study Commission, Paris, 1977; "Weapons Acquisition in the Soviet Union, U.S., and France"; "R&D and Soviet Aviation," Rand Corp. Report R589-PR, 1970.

39. Magnan, "In Search of the End Game," page 49.

40. Holloway, "Military Power and Political Purpose in Soviet Policy," page 25.

41. A 1976 study of comparably performing U.S. and Soviet jet engines found that the Soviet engines, if built in the U.S., would cost between one-third and one-half as much (internal DoD memorandum, "Unclassified Summary of a Classified Study on Aircraft Engine Costs and Design," enclosure to S-5463-DE-4, January 14, 1977).

42. Alexander, "The Process of Soviet Weapons Acquisition," page 4.

43. I. Selin, "Why the Soviets Can't Compute: Gorbachev's Managers Have No Incentive to Build High-Tech Products." *Washington Post*, January 2, 1988.

Chapter 11

1. A study by a group of senior defense experts recommended a long-term real growth rate of 3% per year, but even this would not be enough without changes in the weapons-acquisition-cost area. See Iklé et al., "Discriminate Deterrence."

2. Huntington, *The Common Defense*, page 66. Also see P. Kennedy, *The Rise and Fall of the Great Powers*.

3. See S. Huntington's foreword to *The Defense Reform Debate: Issues and Analysis*, ed. A Clark et al. (Johns Hopkins University Press, 1984).

4. Deputy Secretary Packard established the Defense Systems Acquisition Review Council (DSARC) for the purpose of getting this control over the acquisition process.

5. D. Jones, "What's Wrong With the Defense Establishment?" in *The Defense Reform Debate*, pages 272–273.

6. S. Huntington, "Reform and Stability in South Africa," *International Security*, spring 1982, page 11.

7. "Defense Organization: The Need for Change," Staff Report to the Committee on Armed Services, United States Senate, October 16, 1985.

8. M. Weisskopf, "Pentagon Overhaul Proposed," *Washington Post*, March 1, 1986.

9. In fact, after the April report appeared, David Packard, William Perry (who had headed the acquisition task force), and the author appeared before both the House Armed Services Committee and the Senate Armed Services Committee and received overwhelming and enthusiastic support for the Packard Commission's recommendations. An offer was made to incorporate them into the bill that was then making its way through Congress.

10. His actual words were "It's the only . . . damned thing I've done in the Senate that's

worth a damn." (George Wilson, "Pentagon Reform Bill Sweeps Through Senate," *The Washington Post,* May 8, 1986).

11. For some examples of programs canceled, see D. Morrison, "And Now, the Guillotine," *National Journal,* February 27, 1988, page 523.

12. E. Lachica, "Pentagon Backs Off From Two Cost Policies, Saying Suppliers Deserve Fairer Shake," *Wall Street Journal,* April 14, 1988.

13. Iklé et al., "Discriminate Deterrence."

14. D. Oberdorfer, "Report Urges Major Changes in National Security Strategy," *Washington Post,* January 11, 1988.

15. Some examples that they noted were robotic reconnaissance vehicles, low-cost space systems, long-endurance unmanned aircraft, motion-sensor monitors, explosive detectors, digital graphics, and operations that don't rely on overseas bases.

16. B. Goldwater, "If Congress Can Fix the Pentagon, It Can Clean Up Its Own Mess," *Washington Post,* October 12, 1986.

17. R. Betts, "Dubious Reform: Strategism Versus Managerialism," in *The Defense Reform Debate,* page 73.

18. See R. McFarlane, "Time Out on Defense: Without a New Strategic Consensus, Budget Cuts Will Only Bring Chaos," *Washington Post,* January 3, 1988.

19. J. Clarke, "NATO, Neutrals in National Defence," *Survival,* November-December 1982, page 262.

20. S. Canby, "Military Reform and the Art of War," in *The Defense Reform Debate,* page 133.

21. This has been the recommendation of numerous commissions and investigations, including the Packard Commission (see page 22 of its National Security Planning and Budgeting Report of June 1986).

22. The DoD traditionally generates both 5-year and 15-year fiscal plans. (The latter is known as the "extended planning annex.") However, the 5-year plan tends to be focused largely on the first year, because the "out years" are not "believable" and the extended planning annex is largely ignored. Realistic use of these longer-range fiscal plans is required for any coherent force planning.

23. For example, see the eight-step approach to a new planning, programming, and budgeting system recommended by Rep. Les Aspin, Chairman of the House Armed Services Committee ("Searching for a Defense Strategy," September 1987). Also, see the Packard Commission's report on "National Security Planning and Budgeting."

24. For other writings supporting this view, see T. Dupuy, "Military Reform: The Case for a Centralized Command," *Washington Post,* June 9, 1984, and P. Gorman, "Towards a Stronger Defense Establishment," in *The Defense Reform Debate,* page 289.

25. Through changes in the personnel system brought about by the Goldwater-Nichols Bill as well as the establishment of the "J7" operational plans and interoperability organization and the "J8" force structure, resource, and assessment organization, the Joint Staff has begun to evolve in the direction desired.

26. See J. Kester, "War and Money," *The Washingtonian,* January 1983, page 84.

27. As recommended by Morton Halpern, a former member of the National Security Council, in numerous papers and presentations.

28. The Packard Commission's report has these items in a different order, but they are similar to the seven items shown here.

29. The U.S. Postal System made such a shift in 1988. See J. Mackley, "New Procurements Overhauls $4 Billion Process," *Federal Times,* October 12, 1988.

30. However, this does not mean that you need to budget for the termination liability associated with multi-year contracting (a position that the DoD comptroller has historically taken). Rather, the budgeting for this "insurance policy" should be treated as normal insurance policies are: on a statistical basis.

31. Including the cost of support.

32. No one from the DoD now sits on the federal Economic Policy Council. Perhaps the inclusion of a DoD representative on this council would be desirable in that it would give recognition to the importance of defense's role in the U.S. economy.

33. One suggestion for a way to define what are the critical defense sectors was to use a combination of three criteria: Is it essential to national defense? Can the products be obtained only from a limited number of sources? Are the lead times to produce products in the U.S. long (i.e., years versus months)? (Letter to Don Carson of The Analytic Sciences Corporation, in connection with a DoD study of the defense industry, from Vaughn L. Beals, Jr., chairman of Harley-Davidson, September 16, 1987.)

34. In 1988 the then Under Secretary of Defense, Robert Costello, began such an initiative at a high level within the DoD. It remains to be seen whether such an individual effort can be institutionalized in the future.

35. For an amplification of this last point, see J. Gansler, "Needed: A Three-Element National Security Posture," *Sea Power,* December 1984, pages 52–62.

36. R. Halloran, *To Arm A Nation: Rebuilding America's Endangered Defenses* (Macmillan, 1987).

37. Fox, *Arming America.*

38. These analyses were both done in 1984 dollars and are summarized on page i-5 of the Grace Commission's report (March 1985).

39. Honeywell Aerospace and Defense, "The Cost Impact of Recent Defense Acquisition Financial Policy Changes," position paper, May 1987, page 1.

40. G. Wilson, "Army Faces Deep Personnel Cuts to Pay for Arms," *Washington Post,* February 11, 1988.

41. Taking each of the other items in this broad category, the relevant independent studies are the following: A GAO study found a potential savings from continuous competition of about $3.5 billion in equipment and $4 billion in spares; the Grace Commission found about $5 billion in equipment and $3 billion in spares. Since these are in 1984 dollars they are close to the numbers in the table, although the assumption for the analysis contained herein is that far more of the savings will come in the equipment area (see chapter 6). The outside references for the effects of government procurement regulations are an analysis by General B. Weiss (USAF), who stated that he thought 15–30% of the costs of equipment were attributable to this, and a study by the Center for Strategic and International Studies at Georgetown University ("U.S. Defense Acquisition: A Process in Trouble," March 1987), which indicated savings of 5–10% (page 51). In terms of the impact of excessive specifications for products and processes, the same CSIS study indicated

impacts in the range of 5–15% and the Grace Commission indicated about $2 billion from military specifications for parts alone. In the area of labor instability, the few studies available indicate that "dramatic" improvements in labor productivity could be realized if stability were achieved in defense plans, so that the projected 5% saving is quite conservative. The analysis of excessive prime-contractor facility and labor cost is based on a detailed study of the aircraft industry by the Office of Management and Budget and the Department of Defense (referenced above) and was confirmed by the Grace Commission study, which estimated a saving of $2–3 billion in 1984 dollars. The impact of excessive data and reporting requirements had a comparable level of about $3 billion in the Grace Commission report; while the impact of long development cycles was analyzed in considerable detail by the Defense Science Board in a 1985 study and again by the Packard Commission in 1986. The estimate shown for the "lack of independent development of standard subsystems" is the same as that shown in the President's Private Sector Survey on Cost Control.

42. The Defense Science Board's 1986 Components Study indicated that on electronic systems in which commercial components were utilized the savings could be in the range of 8:1 (700%).

43. CSIS study of March 1987, "U.S. Defense Acquisition," page 51.

44. For example, the Defense Science Board study indicated 10–15%, a Congressional Budget Office study indicated 5–10%, and the data of chapter 5 clearly indicate that the numbers shown here are quite realistic.

45. In FY84 these add-ons cost $4.6 billion (*U.S. News and World Report,* June 4, 1984, page 76). In FY89 they cost $4.3 billion (Washington Post, July 25, 1988).

46. P. Almond, "Changes Can Save Billions in Defense," *Washington Times,* February 11, 1988.

47. *U.S. News and World Report,* July 11, 1983, page 6.

48. M. Thompson, "Closing Bases: Pentagon-Capital Hill Detente?" *Washington Post,* April 19, 1988.

49. The Grace Commission estimated savings of up to $700 million (in 1984 dollars) in travel costs alone.

50. The Grace Commission estimated over $10 billion of potential savings (in 1984 dollars) in this area.

51. Under the category of "excessive requirements," a 1987 Center for Strategic and International Studies estimate showed a potential of 20–40%. However, the CSIS went on to say that much of this problem may well continue and thus it is perhaps realistic to expect savings only in the range of up to 15% (the number used here). See "U.S Defense Acquisition: A Process in Trouble," page 51.

52. Iklé, et al., "Discriminate Deterrence."

53. Some of the systems that are frequently cited as examples are the Air Force's A-10, the Army's attack helicopters, and the Marines' Harrier jets. All three of these systems used for close air support are extremely expensive and are produced in relatively low quantities. The Grace Commission found over $3 billion worth of potential savings in this

area. However, their investigation was quite limited. It is believed that far more could be done in this area, through greater use of joint (multi-service) planning.

54. These numbers (the specific recommendations of David Calleo of the Johns Hopkins School of Advanced International Studies) are contained in an article by James Chance: "Ike Was Right," *Atlantic Monthly,* August 1987, pages 39–41.

55. Iklé et al., "Discriminate Deterrence."

Selected Bibliography

Abt, C. *Strategy for Terminating a Nuclear War*. Westview, 1985.

Adams, G. "Defense Spending and the Economy: Does the Defense Dollar Make a Difference?" Center on Budget and Policy Priorities, Washington, D.C., July 1987.

Adams, G. "The Iron Triangle: The Politics of Defense Contracting." Council on Economic Priorities, New York, 1981.

Adams, W., and Brock, J. *The Bigness Complex: Industry, Labor, and Government in the American Economy*. New York: Pantheon, 1987.

Adams, W. "The Military-Industrial Complex and the New Industrial State." *American Economic Review* 58, No. 2, May 1968.

Air Force Systems Command. "Affordable Acquisition Approach (A_3)." Andrews Air Force Base, February 1983.

Air Force Systems Command. Statement on Defense Industrial Base Issues (General Alton Slay). Andrews Air Force Base, November 1980.

Alexander, A. J. "Weapons Acquisition in the Soviet Union, U.S. and France." Rand Corp. Report P-4989, Santa Monica, 1973.

Alexander, A. J. "R&D in Soviet Aviation." Rand Corp. Report R-589-PR, Santa Monica, November 1970.

Alexander, A. J. "Design to Price from the Perspective of the U.S., France and Soviet Union." Rand Corp. Report P-4967, Santa Monica, 1978.

Amann, R., Cooper, J. M., and Davies, R. W. *The Technological Level of Soviet Industry*. New Haven: Yale University Press, 1977.

Amos, J., and Taylor, W. *American National Security: Policy and Process*. Baltimore: Johns Hopkins University Press, 1984.

Art, R. J. *The TFX Decision: McNamara and the Military*. Boston: Little, Brown, 1968.

Art R., Davis, V., and Huntington, S. *Reorganizing America's Defense Leadership in War and Peace*. Washington, D.C. Pergamon-Brassey, 1985.

Augustine, N. R. *Augustine's Laws*. American Institute of Aeronautics and Astronautics, Inc., 1982; Penguin 1986.

Averitt, R. T. *The Dual Economy: The Dynamics of American Industry Structure*. New York: Norton, 1968.

Bain, J. S. *Barriers to New Competition: Their Character and Consequences in Manufacturing Industries*. Cambridge: Harvard University Press, 1956.

Bain, J. S. *Industrial Organization*. New York: Wiley, 1959.

Bamford, J. *The Puzzle Palace: A Report on America's Most Secret Agency*. Boston: Houghton Mifflin, 1982.

Baran, P. M., and Sweezy, P. A. *Monopoly Capital*. New York: Monthly Review Press, 1966.

Barrett, A. D. *Reappraising Defense Organization*. Washington, D.C.: National Defense University Press, 1983.

Baylis, J., and Segal, G. *Soviet Strategy.* London: Croom Helm, 1981.

Blair, J. M. *Economic Concentration: Structure, Behavior, and Public Policy.* New York: Harcourt Brace Jovanovich, 1972.

Blechman, B., and Utgoff, V., "The Macroeconomics of Strategic Defenses." In *International Security.* Cambridge: MIT Press, 1966.

Bower, J. L. *When Markets Quake: The Management Challenge of Restructuring Industry.* Boston: Harvard Business School Press, 1986.

Brody, B. *Strategy in the Missile Age.* Princeton University Press, 1959.

Brody, B. *The Absolute Weapon.* New York: Harcourt Brace, 1946.

Bucy, F. J. "An Analysis of Export Control of U.S. Technology: A DoD Perspective." Defense Science Board report, February 1976.

Builder, C. H. "The Prospects and Implications of Non-Nuclear Means for Strategic Conflict." *Adelphi Papers,* No. 200, International Institute for Strategic Studies, London, 1985.

Cahn, A. H., Kruzel, J. J., and Dawkins, P. M. *Controlling Future Arms Trade. New York: McGraw-Hill, 1977.*

Canan, J. W. *The Super Warriors: The Fantastic World of Pentagon Super Weapons.* New York: Weybright and Talley, 1975.

Caves, R. E. *American Industry: Structure, Conduct, Performance,* Englewood Cliffs, N.J.: Prentice-Hall, 1964.

Chandler, A. D. Jr. *Strategy and Structure: Chapters in the History of the Industrial Enterprise.* Cambridge: MIT Press, 1962.

Chubin, S. "U.S. Security Interests in the Persian Gulf in the 1980s." *Daedalus,* Journal of the American Academy of Arts and Sciences, winter 1981.

Clark, A., ed. *Defense Technology.* New York: Praeger, 1988.

Clark, A., ed. *The Defense Reform Debate: Issues and Analysis.* Baltimore: Johns Hopkins University Press, 1984.

Cohen, S., and Zysman, J. *Manufacturing Matters: The Myth of the Post-Industrial Economy.* New York: Basic Books, 1987.

Cole, W. *Roosevelt and the Isolationists, 1932–1945.* Lincoln: University of Nebraska Press.

Colvard, J. E. "Technological Transformation of Defense." *Bureaucrat,* the Journal for Public Managers, spring 1985.

Commission on Government Procurement. "Final Report of the Commission on Government Procurement." Washington, D.C.: Government Printing Office, December 1972.

Comptroller General of the United States. "Managing the Cost of Government." GAO/AFMD-84-43, March 1984.

Comptroller General of the United States. "Acquisition of Major Weapon Systems." Department of Defense Report B163058, July 1972.

Conference Board. "Report on Investment in the Defense Industry." 1976.

Congressional Budget Office. "Effects of Weapon's Procurement Stretchouts on Costs and Schedules." Washington, D.C., November 1987.

Congressional Budget Office. "Budgeting for Defense Inflation." Washington, D.C., January, 1986.

Congressional Budget Office. "Defense Spending: What Has Been Accomplished?" Staff working paper. Washington, D.C., April 1985.

Congressional Budget Office. "Defense Spending and the Economy." Washington, D.C., February 1983.

Corey, E. R. *Procurement Management: Strategy, Organization and Decision Making.* Boston: CBI, 1978.

CSIS Defense Organization Project. "Towards a More Effective Defense." Final Report. Georgetown University, Washington, D.C., February 1985.

Danhof, C. G. "Government Contracting and Technological Change." Brookings Institution, Washington, D.C., 1968.

Danzig, R., and Szanton, P. *National Service: What Would it Mean?* Lexington, Mass.: Lexington Books, 1986.

Defense Science Board. "Task Force Report on Industrial Responsiveness" (Chairman, Robert Fuhrman). Department of Defense. Washington, D.C., November 1980.

Delaney, T. B. "The Federal Acquisition Regulation System: A Review and Analysis." Washington, D.C.: Office of Management and Budget, November 1986.

Department of Defense, Office of the Assistant Secretary of Defense for Installations and Logistics (Procurement). "Profit '76, Summary Report." December 1976.

de Tocqueville, A. *Democracy in America.* New York: Vintage Books, 1945.

Dumas, L. J., ed. "The Political Economy of Arms Reduction." American Association for the Advancement of Science Selected Symposium 80. Washington, D.C., 1982.

Edwards, R. C., Reich, M., and Weisskoff, T. E. *The Capitalist System.* Englewood Cliffs, N.J.: Prentice-Hall, 1972.

Erikson, J. "The Soviet View of Deterrence: A General Survey." *Survival,* The International Institute of Strategic Studies. London, November-December 1982.

European Security Study. *Strengthening Conventional Deterrence in Europe: Proposals for the 1980s.* New York: Saint Martin's Press, 1983.

Evans, C. *The Micro Millennium.* New York: Viking Press, 1979.

Federal Emergency Management Agency. "A Comparison of Soviet and U.S. Civil Defense Programs." Washington, D.C., 1987.

Fesler, J. W. *Industrial Mobilization for War.* Washington, D.C.: Government Printing Office, 1947.

Finney, B. *Arsenal of Democracy.* New York: Whittlessey House of McGraw-Hill, 1941.

Fisher, I. N., and Hall, G. R. "Risk and the Aerospace Rate of Return." Rand Corp. Report RM-5440-PR, Santa Monica, December 1967.

Fisher, I. N., and Hall, G. R. "Defense Profit Policy in the United States and the United Kingdom." Rand Corp. Report RM-5610-PR, Santa Monica, October 1968.

Ford, D. "A Reporter at Large: The Button." *The New Yorker,* April 1985.

Forsberg, R. "The Freeze and Beyond: Confining the Military to Defense as a Route to Disarmament." *World Policy Journal,* 1, Number 2, winter 1984.

Fox, J. R., and Field, J. L. "The Defense Management Challenge: Weapons Acquisition." Harvard Business School, 1988.

Fox, J. R. *Arming America: How the U.S. Buys Weapons.* Cambridge: Harvard University Press, 1974.

Friedman, N., and Gray, C. S. "U.S. and U.S.S.R. Mobilization Policies." Hudson Institute, Croton-on-Hudson, N.Y., May 1979.

Frye, B. S. *Modern Political Economy.* New York: Martin Robertson, 1978.

Gaddis, J. L. *The Long Peace: Inquiries into the History of the Cold War.* New York: Oxford University Press, 1987.

Galbraith, J. K. *Economics and the Public Purpose.* Boston: Houghton Mifflin, 1973.

Galbraith, J. K. *The New Industrial State.* Boston: Houghton Mifflin, 1967.

Gansler, J. S. The Defense Industry. Cambridge: MIT Press, 1980.

General Accounting Office. "Budgeting Issue—Budgeting Practices in West Germany, France, Sweden and Great Britain." Boulder: Westview Press, November 1986.

General Accounting Office. "Weapons Acquisition—Processes of Selected Foreign Governments." Washington, D.C., February 1986.

Gibbon, E. *The Decline and Fall of the Roman Empire.* New York: Penguin Books, 1941.

Goure, L. "War Survival in Soviet Strategy: U.S.S.R. Civil Defense." Center for Advanced International Studies, Washington, D.C., 1976.

Green, M. J., and Ellsworth, L., eds. *The Monopoly Makers: Ralph Nader's Study Report on Regulation and Competition.* New York: Grossman, 1973.

Gummett, P., and Reppy, J. *The Relations Between Civil and Defense Technologies.* Dordrecht: Martinus Nijhoff, 1988.

Hadley, A. T. *The Straw Giant: Triumph and Failure: America's Armed Forces, a Report from the Field.* New York: Random House, 1986.

Hall, G. R. "Defense Procurement and Public Utility Regulation." Rand Corp. report, Santa Monica, May 1968.

Halloran, R. *To Arm A Nation: Why America Isn't Ready to Defend Herself.* New York: Macmillan, 1986.

Harkavy, R. E. *The Arms Trade and International Systems.* Cambridge: Ballinger, 1975.

Hart, B. L. *The Sword and the Pen: Selections from the World's Greatest Military Writings*. London: Cassell, 1978.

Herken, G. *Councils of War*. New York: Alfred Knopf, 1985.

Hitch, C. J., and McKean, R. *The Economics of Defense in the Nuclear Age*. Cambridge: Harvard University Press, 1960.

Hoffman, S. *Dead-Ends: American Foreign Policy in the New Cold War*. Cambridge: Ballinger, 1983.

Holloway, D. "Military Power and Political Purpose in Soviet Policy." *Daedalus,* Journal of the American Academy of Arts and Sciences, winter 1981.

Howard, M. *Clausewitz*. Oxford University Press, 1983.

Howard, M. *The Causes of War and Other Essays*. Cambridge: Harvard University Press, 1983.

Huntington, S. *The Common Defense: Strategic Programs and National Politics*. New York: Columbia University Press, 1961.

Huntington, S. *The Soldier and the State: The Theory and Politics of Civil-Military Relations*. Cambridge: Belknap Press of Harvard University Press, 1957.

Iklé, F., Wohlstettler, A., et al. "Discriminate Deterrence." Report of the Commission on Integrated, Long-Term Strategy. Washington, D.C., January 1988.

Jacquemin, A. P., and DeJong, H. W., eds. *Markets, Corporate Behavior and the State*. The Hague: Martinus Nijhoff, 1976.

Johnson, C. *MITI and the Japanese Miracle*. Stanford University Press, 1982.

Kahn, H. *Thinking About the Unthinkable in the 1980s*. New York: Simon and Schuster, 1984.

Kahn, H. *On Thermonuclear War*. Princeton University Press, 1960.

Kahn, H. *On Escalation, Metaphors and Scenarios*. New York: Praeger, 1965.

Kahn, H. and Schneider, W., Jr. "The Technological Requirements of Mobilization Warfare." Hudson Institute, Croton-on-Hudson, N.Y., May 1975.

Kaldor, M. *The Baroque Arsenal*. New York: Hill & Wang, 1981.

Karnow, S. *Vietnam: A History*. New York: Viking, 1983.

Kaufman, R. F. *The War Profiteers*. New York: Bobbs-Merrill, 1970.

Kennedy, G. *Defense Economics*. New York: St. Martin's 1983.

Kennedy, P. *The Rise and Fall of the Great Powers: Economic Change and Military Conflict from 1500–2000*. New York: Random House, 1988.

Kissinger, H. *Nuclear Weapons and Foreign Policy*. New York: Norton, 1957.

Komer, R. "Costs and Benefits of a Credible Conventional Component." *Armed Forces Journal,* May 1984.

Kotz, N. *Wild Blue Yonder: Money, Politics, and the B-1 Bomber.* New York: Pantheon Books, 1988.

Knox, D. W. *A History of the United States Navy,* revised edition. New York: Putnam, 1948.

Kratz, L. A., and Gansler, J. S. "Effective Competition During Weapon System Acquisition." National Contract Management Association, McLean, Va., December 1985.

Kuhn, T. S. *The Structure of Scientific Revolutions.* University of Chicago Press, 1970.

Lee, W. T. "The Shift in Soviet National Priorities to Military Forces, 1958–85." *The Annuals,* The American Academy of Political and Social Science. Beverly Hills: Sage Publications, September 1981.

Lens, S. *The Military-Industrial Complex.* New York: Pilgrim, 1970.

Lewis, F. *Europe: A Tapestry of Nations.* New York: Simon & Schuster, 1987.

Lockwood, D. "Cost Overruns in Major Weapon Systems: Current Dimensions of Long-Standing Problems." Congressional Research Service Report No. 83-194F. Washington, D.C.: Library of Congress, October 1983.

Lincoln, G. A. *Economics of National Security: Managing America's Resources for Defense.* Englewood Cliffs, N.J.: Prentice-Hall, 1950.

Lodal, J. "U.S. Strategic Nuclear Forces." *Adelphi Papers,* The International Institute of Strategic Studies, London, spring, 1982.

Long, F. A., and Reppy, J. *Genesis of New Weapons: Decisionmaking and Military R&D.* New York: Pergamon, 1980.

Luttwak, E. N. *The Art of War.* New York: Simon and Schuster, 1984.

Luttwak, E. N. *Coup d'Etat: A Practical Handbook.* Cambridge: Harvard University Press, 1979.

Margiotta, and Sanders, eds. *Technology, Strategy and National Security.* Washington, D.C.: National Defense University Press, 1985.

Martinson, O. B., and Mayer, S. C. "An Annotated Bibliography of (DoD) Profits Studies, Developed for Profit '76." Logistics Management Institute, Washington, D.C., September 1975.

Mayer, A. "Military Procurement Procedures of Foreign Governments: Centralization of the Procurement Function." Congressional Research Service Report, December 1984.

McDougall, W. A. *Heavens and The Earth: A Political History of the Space Age.* New York: Basic Books, 1986.

McKee, J. W. "Concentration in Military Procurement Markets: A Classification and Analysis of Contract Data." Rand Corp. Report RM-6307-PR, Santa Monica, June 1970.

McNamara, R. S. "The Military Role of Nuclear Weapons: Perceptions and Misperceptions." *Foreign Affairs,* fall 1983.

Melman, S. "Twelve Propositions on Productivity and the War Economy." *Challenge,* March-April 1975.

Melman, S. *The Permanent War Economy*. New York: Simon and Schuster, 1974.

Melman, S. *Pentagon Capitalism: The Political Economy of War*. New York: McGraw-Hill, 1970.

Milward, A. S. *War, Economy and Society: 1939–45*. Berkeley: University of California Press, 1977.

Morrison, E. *Men, Machines and Modern Times*. Cambridge: MIT Press, 1966.

Mullins, J. P. *The Defense Matrix: National Preparedness in the Military-Industrial Complex*. Avant Books, 1986.

Nacht, M. "Towards an American Conception of Regional Security." *Daedalus,* Journal of the American Academy of Arts and Sciences, winter 1981.

National Association of Public Administration. "Leadership in Jeopardy: The Fraying of the Presidential Appointment System." Final Report of the Presidential Appointee Project, November 1985.

National Commission on Supplies and Shortages. "Government and the Nation's Resources." Washington, D.C.: Government Printing Office, December 1976.

National Research Council. *Towards a New Era in U.S. Manufacturing: The Need for a National Vision*. Washington, D.C.: National Academy Press, 1986.

National Research Council. *Foreign Production of Electronic Components and Army Systems Volnerabilities*. Washington, D.C.: National Academy Press, 1985.

Nelson, D. M. *Arsenal of Democracy: The Story of American War Production*. New York: Harcourt Brace, 1946.

Nelson, R. R. "High Technology Policies: A Five Nation Comparison." American Enterprise Institute, Washington, D.C., 1984.

Office of Federal Procurement Policy. "Proposed for a Uniform Federal Procurement Systems." Washington, D.C.: Office of Management and Budget, February 1982.

Palmer, B. *The Twenty-Five Year War: America's Military Role in Vietnam*. New York: Simon and Schuster, 1984.

Pavitt, K. *Technical Innovation and British Economic Performance*. London: Macmillan, 1980.

Peck, M. J., and Scherer, F. M. *The Weapons Acquisition Process: An Economic Analysis*. Cambridge: Harvard University Press, 1962.

Penkofskiy, O. *The Penkofskiy Papers*. New York: Doubleday, 1965.

Perry, R., et al. "System Acquisition Strategies." Rand Corp. Report R-733-PR/ARPA, Santa Monica, June 1971.

Pierre, A. J., ed. *Council on Foreign Relations*. New York, 1986.

President's Blue Ribbon Commission on Defense Management. "A Quest for Excellence." Final report to the President. Washington, D.C., June 1986.

President's Blue Ribbon Commission on Defense Management. "A Formula for Action." A report to the President on defense acquisition. Washington, D.C., April 1986.

Prestowitz, C. V. *Trading Places: How We Allowed Japan to Take the Lead.* New York: Basic Books, 1988.

Pursell, C. *The Military Industrial Complex.* New York: Harper and Row, 1972.

Rathjens, G., and Ruina, J. "Nuclear Doctrine and Rationality." *Daedalus,* Journal of the American Academy of Arts and Sciences, winter 1981.

Reich, R. B. *The Next American Frontier.* New York: Times Books, 1983.

Rice, D. B. "Defense Resource Management Study: Final Report." Washington, D.C.: Government Printing Office, February 1979.

Rich, M., Dews, E., and Batten, C. L. "Improving the Military Acquisition Process: Lessons from Rand Research." Rand Corp. Report R333-AF/RC, Santa Monica, January 1986.

Rockman, B. A. "Mobilizing Political Support for U.S. National Security." *Armed Forces in Society,* fall 1987.

Rosecrance, R. *The Rise of the Trading State: Commerce and Conquests in the Modern World.* New York: Basic Books, 1986.

Rovner, M. *Defense Dollars and Sense: A Common Cause Guide to the Defense Budget Process.* Washington, D.C., 1983.

Sampson, A. *The Arms Bazaar.* New York: Viking, 1977.

Sapolsky, H. M. *The Polaris System Development: Bureaucratic and Programmatic Success in Government.* Cambridge: Harvard University Press, 1972.

Schelling, T. *Arms and Influence.* Westport, Conn.: Greenwood, 1966.

Scherer, F. M. *Innovation and Growth: Schumpeterian Perspectives.* Cambridge: MIT Press, 1984.

Scherer, F. M. *Industrial Market Structure and Economic Performance.* Chicago: Rand-McNally, 1970.

Scherer, F. M. *The Weapons Acquisition Process: Economic Incentives.* Cambridge: Harvard University Press, 1964.

Schlesinger, J. R. *The Political Economy of National Security: A Study of the Economics Aspect of the Contemporary Power Struggle.* New York: Praeger, 1960.

Schultz, C. "Do More Dollars Mean Better Defense?" *Challenge,* January-February 1983.

Schumpeter, J. *Capitalism, Socialism, and Democracy.* New York: Harper and Brothers, 1942.

Scott, B. R., and Lodge, G. C. *U.S. Competitiveness in the World Economy.* Boston: Harvard Business School Press, 1985.

Shaker, S., and Wise, A. *War Without Men: Robots on the Future Battlefield.* Washington, D.C.: Pergamon-Brassey, 1988.

Simes, D. K. "The Military and Militarism in Soviet Society." *International Security,* winter 1981–82.

Smith, H. *The Russians*. New York: Times Books, 1983.

Smith, M. R., ed. *Military Enterprise and Technological Change: Perspective on the American Experience*. Cambridge: MIT Press, 1985.

Spinney, F. C. "Defense Facts of Life." *Armed Forces Journal,* May 1980.

Staats, E. B. "Public Service and the Public Interest." Webb Lecture, National Academy of Public Administration, Washington, D.C., November 1987.

Stolarow, J. "Inaccuracy of Department of Defense Weapons Acquisition Cost Estimates." House Committee on Government Operations. Washington, D.C.: Government Printing Office, November 1979.

Stubbing, R. A., and Mendel. R. A. *The Defense Game*. New York: Harper & Row, 1986.

Sun Tzu. *The Art of War*. Oxford University Press, 1963.

Terkel, S. *The Good War*. New York: Pantheon Books, 1984.

Tuchman, B. "The American People and Military Power in an Historical Perspective." International Institute of Strategic Studies, spring 1982.

Ulam, A. B. *The Rivals: American and Russia Since World War II*. New York: Penguin, 1971.

Ullman, H., Taylor, W., and Blackwell, J. *U.S. Defense Acquisition: A Process in Trouble*. New York: Praeger, 1988.

U.S. Congress, Committee on Government Operations. "Inaccuracy of Department of Defense Weapons Acquisition Cost Estimates." Washington, D.C.: Government Printing Office, November 1979.

U.S. Congress, House Armed Services Committee. "The Ailing Defense Industrial Base: Unready for Crisis." Industrial Base Panel report (Chairman, Richard Ichord). Washington, D.C.: Congressional Record, December 1980.

U.S. General Accounting Office. "DoD Acquisition: Capabilities of Key DoD Personnel in Systems Acquisition." GAO/NSIAD-86-45, May 1986.

U.S. Senate. Goldwater-Nichols Department of Defense Reorganization Act of 1986. Washington, D.C., September 1986.

U.S. Senate. "Defense Organization: The Need for Change." Committee on Armed Services. Washington, D.C., October 1985.

Waterman, R. *The Renewal Factor: How the Best Get and Keep the Competitive Edge*. New York: Bantam, 1987.

Weidenbaum, M. L. *The Economics of Peace-Time Defense*. New York: Basic Books, 1974.

Weidenbaum, M. L. *The Modern Public Sector: New Ways of Doing the Government's Business*. New York: Basic Books, 1969.

Weidenbaum, M. L. "Arms and the American Economy: A Domestic Convergence Hypothesis." *American Economic Review,* July 1968.

Williams, P. *Crisis Management: Confrontation and Diplomacy in the Nuclear Age.* New York: Wiley, 1976.

Wyden, P. *Day One: Before Hiroshima and After.* New York: Simon and Schuster, 1984.

Yarmolinsky, A. *The Military Establishment: Its Impacts on American Society.* New York: Harper and Row, 1971.

Index